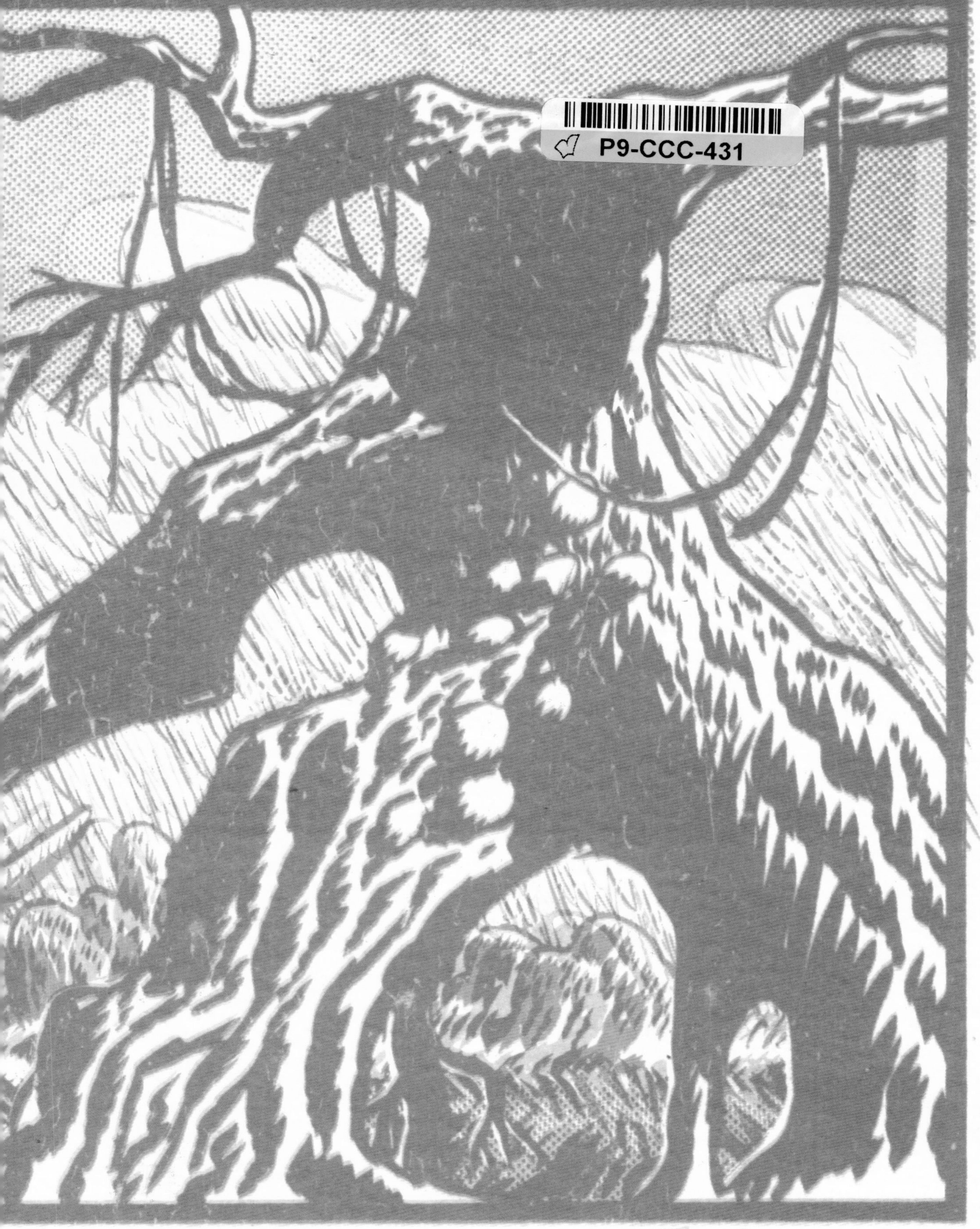

JOE KUBERT

◀FRONT ENDPAPERS An amazing historic artifact: the drawing of Tor that Joe Kubert showed to Archer St. John in the beginning of 1953. This rarity demonstrated to the publisher how 3-D comic illustration could work. Previously unpublished.

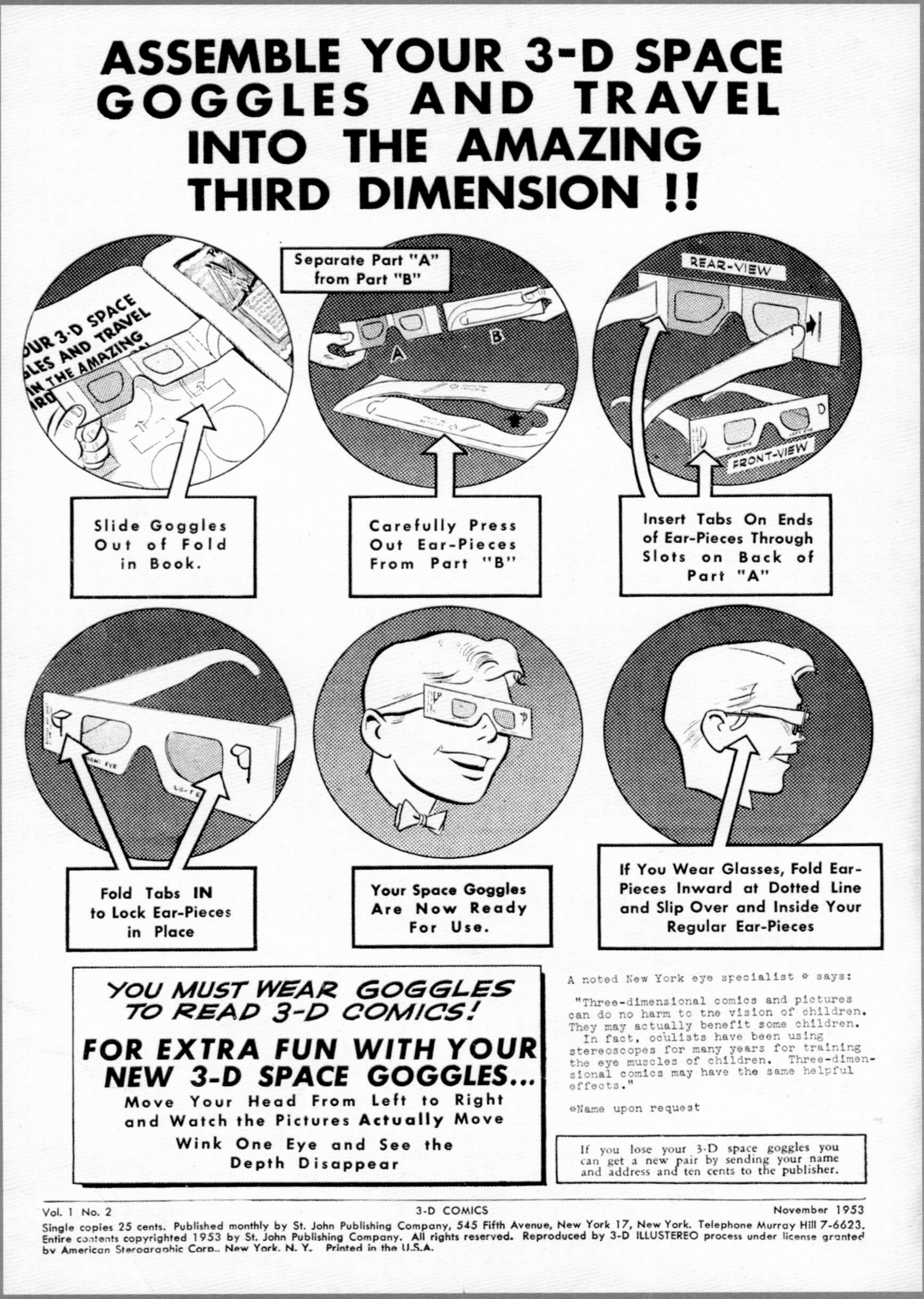

ASSEMBLE YOUR 3-D SPACE GOGGLES AND TRAVEL INTO THE AMAZING THIRD DIMENSION !!

Slide Goggles Out of Fold in Book.

Separate Part "A" from Part "B"

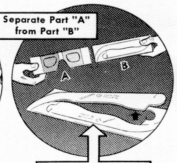

Carefully Press Out Ear-Pieces From Part "B"

REAR-VIEW / FRONT-VIEW

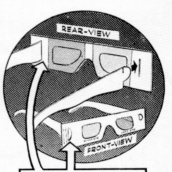

Insert Tabs On Ends of Ear-Pieces Through Slots on Back of Part "A"

Fold Tabs IN to Lock Ear-Pieces in Place

Your Space Goggles Are Now Ready For Use.

If You Wear Glasses, Fold Ear-Pieces Inward at Dotted Line and Slip Over and Inside Your Regular Ear-Pieces

---

YOU MUST WEAR GOGGLES TO READ 3-D COMICS!

FOR EXTRA FUN WITH YOUR NEW 3-D SPACE GOGGLES...

Move Your Head From Left to Right and Watch the Pictures **Actually Move**

Wink One Eye and See the Depth Disappear

A noted New York eye specialist ✶ says:

"Three-dimensional comics and pictures can do no harm to the vision of children. They may actually benefit some children.
In fact, oculists have been using stereoscopes for many years for training the eye muscles of children. Three-dimensional comics may have the same helpful effects."

✶Name upon request

If you lose your 3-D space goggles you can get a new pair by sending your name and address and ten cents to the publisher.

Vol. 1 No. 2   3-D COMICS   November 1953

Single copies 25 cents. Published monthly by St. John Publishing Company, 545 Fifth Avenue, New York 17, New York. Telephone Murray Hill 7-6623. Entire contents copyrighted 1953 by St. John Publishing Company. All rights reserved. Reproduced by 3-D ILLUSTEREO process under license granted by American Stereographic Corp., New York, N. Y. Printed in the U.S.A.

ABOVE This vintage page from a St. John comic shows how to use 3-D space goggles. It also reveals that noted doctors say that reading 3-D comics is good for you! *3-D Comics* #2, November 1953.

FELIX THE CAT'S 3-D Glasses

TOBY TOBY PRESS

INSERT EARPIECES THROUGH SLOTS FROM OTHER SIDE

RIGHT EYE

LEFT EYE

INSERT EARPIE SLOTS FROM

HARVEY FAMOUS NAME COMICS

GREEN —

YOUR BEST COMICS BUY

3-D

LEFT EYE

RIGHT EYE

AMAZING

yoe BOOKS

EDITED & DESIGNED BY
CRAIG YOE

KATY KEENE 3-D PIN-UP GLASSES

RIGHT EYE

LEFT EYE

SUPER-S

INSERT EARPIECES THROUGH SLOTS FROM OTHER SIDE

RIGHT EYE

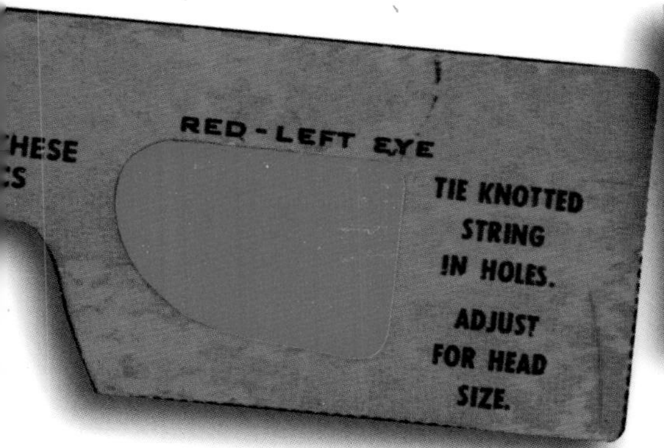
RED-LEFT EYE
TIE KNOTTED STRING IN HOLES.
ADJUST FOR HEAD SIZE.

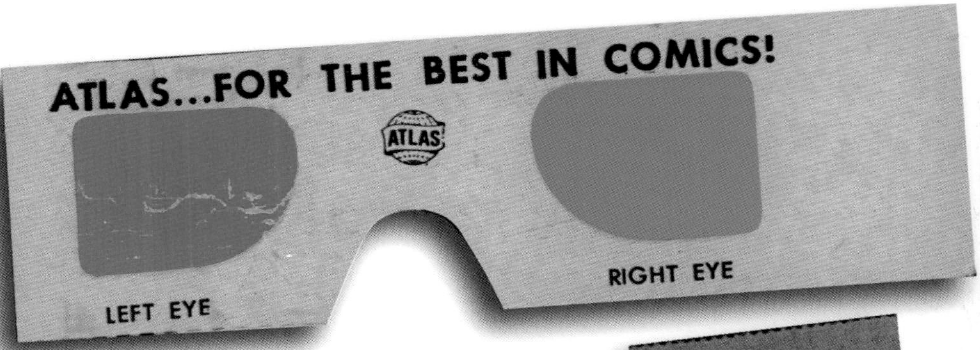
ATLAS...FOR THE BEST IN COMICS!
ATLAS
LEFT EYE
RIGHT EYE

3-D COMICS

IDW

PRODUCED BY
CLIZIA GUSSONI

INTRODUCTION AND COVER BY
JOE KUBERT

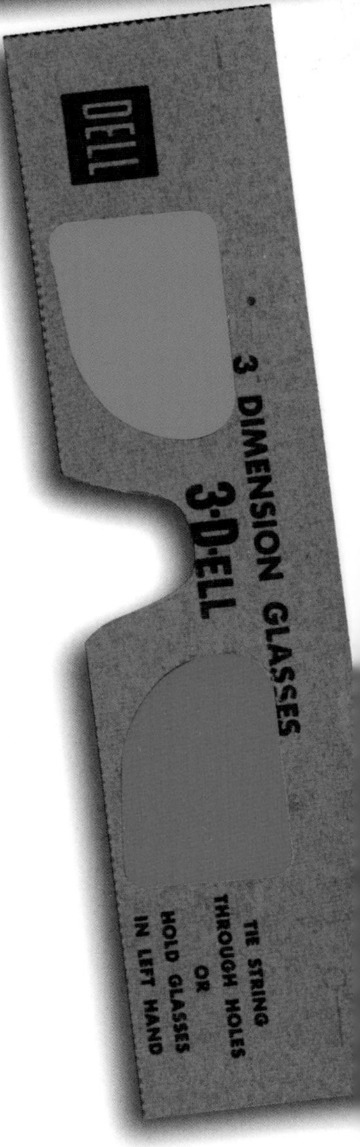
DELL
3 DIMENSION GLASSES
3-D-ELL
TIE STRING THROUGH HOLES OR HOLD GLASSES IN LEFT HAND

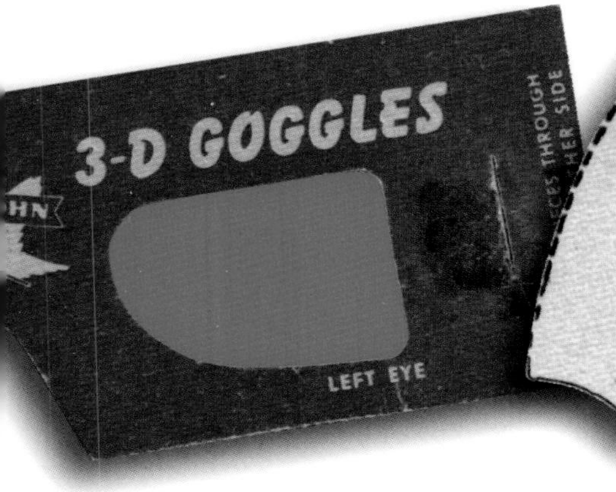
3-D GOGGLES
LEFT EYE

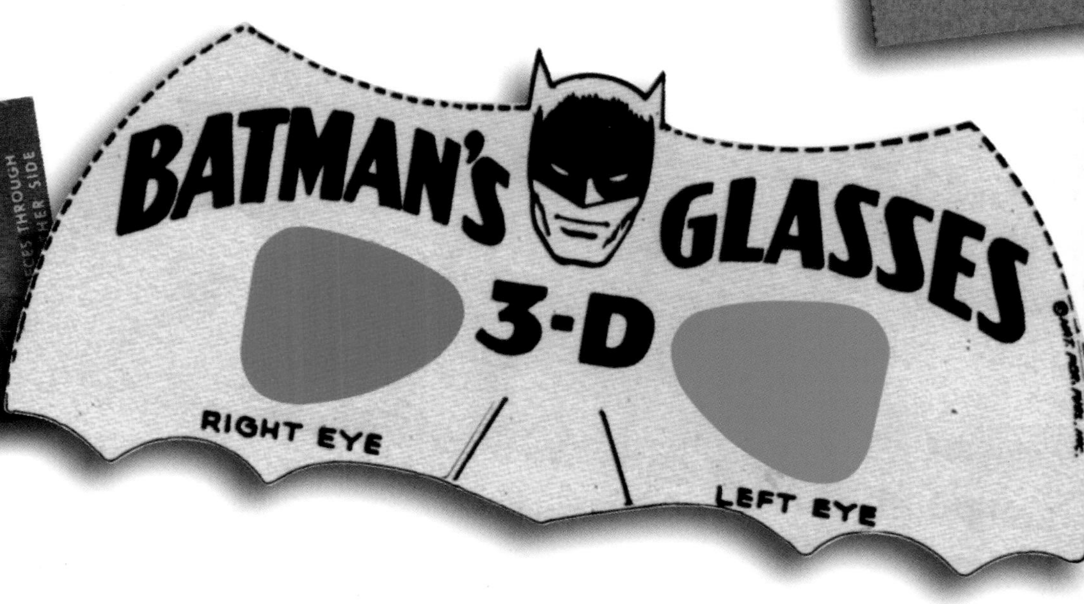
BATMAN'S GLASSES
3-D
RIGHT EYE
LEFT EYE

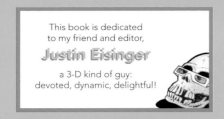

This book is dedicated
to my friend and editor,

Justin Eisinger

a 3-D kind of guy:
devoted, dynamic, delightful!

If you like this book, please blog, facebook, and tweet about it!
Visit the International Team of Comics Historians blog www.TheITCHblog.com.
Become a fan of YOE Books on Facebook! Friend Craig Yoe on Facebook!

3-D comics pioneer Leonard Maurer unsuccessfully tried to convince Archer St. John, publisher of the first 3-D comic, to print the original 3-D comic books on a high quality paper. The browned, aged paper of the 1950s printing makes seeing the 3-D effect nearly impossible on the surviving copies. We try to achieve the very finest reproduction in all Yoe Books to showcase the worthy, classic comics material. In this book, it was especially important to achieve the best reproduction possible for an optimum reading experience. That's why we chose to print it in six colors on carefully chosen paper. Enjoy!

ISBN-13: 978-1600108532
14 13 12 11 1 2 3 4

Joe Kubert has been a superhero of mine since I was a young kid. My deepest thanks for his immense contribution to this book.
For information about The Kubert School, which offers students a high quality and challenging education in Cartooning and Graphic Art, visit http://kubertschool.edu.

Many thanks to Joan Maurer, who consented to be interviewed for this book and provided rare artifacts.

The talented Luke McDonnell drew the characters on the left hand side of the cover.

A special thank you to Brian Pearce, who expertly helped with the production of this book..

A big 3-D thank you to:
Giovanna Anzaldi, Bob Beerbohm, Warren Bernard, Pete Carlson, Robert Carter, Paul Castiglia, Mike Chen, Grant Geissman, Victor Gorelick, Heritage Auction Galleries, Alan Kaplan, Robert Kass, John Sterling Lucas, Bill Major, Michelle Nolan, Don Oriolo, Jeff Rader, Aaron Repko, Steven Ringgenberg, Brent Seguine, Bhob Stewart, Chris Thompson, and Susan Allen Yonas. A big thank you to Rod Ollerenshaw for his help, encouragement, and for lending us his 3-D camera!

Recommended reading. Anyone interested in the history of 3-D will find the book *Amazing 3-D* (Little Brown and Company; 1982) by Hal Morgan and Dan Symmes indispensable. It also has a great section on comics. Covering much the same grounds, but with an emphasis on popular movies and excellent information on comics, is *Fantastic 3-D* (Starlog Press; 1982) edited by David Hutchison. Joe Kubert fans—and who reading this book isn't?—will love *Man of Rock: A Biography of Joe Kubert* by Bill Schelly (Fantagraphics Books; 2008). *Andru + Esposito Partners for Life* by Mike Esposito and Dan Best (Hermes Press; 2006) covers that artistic team and their foray into 3-D. *The Three Stooges Scrapbook* by Jeff Lenburg, Joan Howard Maurer, and Greg Lenburg (Citadel Press; 1982) has a terrific chapter on all Stooges comics, including the 3-D issues. *AH in 3-D* was a special issue of *Amazing Heroes* magazine on 3-D edited by Kim Thompson (Fantagraphics; No. 158, February 1989). In-depth research on Archer St. John is to be found in the excellent book *Confessions, Romances, Secrets and Temptations: Archer St. John and the St. John Romance Comics* by John Benson (Fantagraphics Books; 2007). Finally, students and fans of comics history should read and treasure each and every issue of Roy Thomas' *Alter Ego* magazine (TwoMorrows; #77, May 2008) with "Joe Kubert & The Gospel According to Archer St. John" by Ken Quattro. That and other sundry issues of *Alter Ego* were an invaluable help in the preparation of this book.

3-D comics of the '50s were all printed within a matter of months. *Amazing 3-D Comics* prints the story in esthetic, not chronological, order.

Identifying the creators of unsigned comics is an art and a science. A number of experts were consulted, but the final attributions are my own and any corrections are most welcome.

YoeBooks.com Operations: Craig Yoe & Clizia Gussoni, Chief Executive Officers and Creative Directors; Sandy Schechter, VP of Research; Design Associates: Nancy Bond, Mark Lerer; Media Associates: Steve Bennett, David Burd, Beth Davies, David Donihue, Steven Thompson, Doug Wheeler.

IDW Operations: Ted Adams, CEO & Publisher • Greg Goldstein, Chief Operating Officer • Matthew Ruzicka, CPA, Chief Financial Officer • Alan Payne, VP of Sales • AnnaMaria White, Dir., Marketing and Public Relations • Dirk Wood, Dir., Retail Marketing. Editorial: Chris Ryall, Chief Creative Officer, Editor-In-Chief • Scott Dunbier, Senior Editor, Special Projects • Andy Schmidt, Senior Editor • Justin Eisinger, Senior Editor, Books. Design: Robbie Robbins, EVP/Sr. Graphic Artist

To locate a comic shop near you, call 1-800-ComicShop or go to ComicShopLocator.com.

RIGHT **Coming atcha! *The Space Kat-ets* #1, December 1953.**

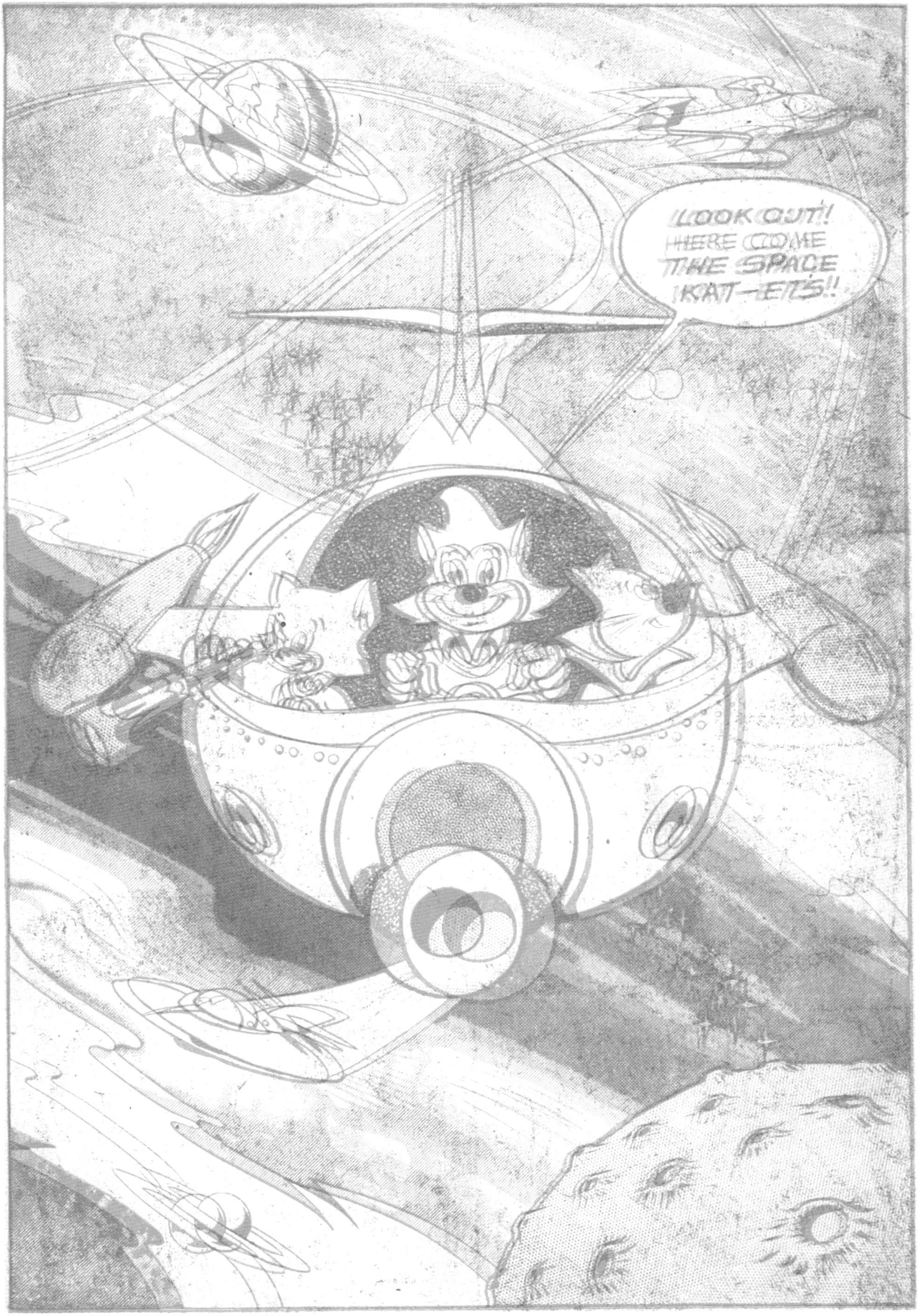
LOOK OUT!! HERE COME THE SPACE KAT-ETS!!

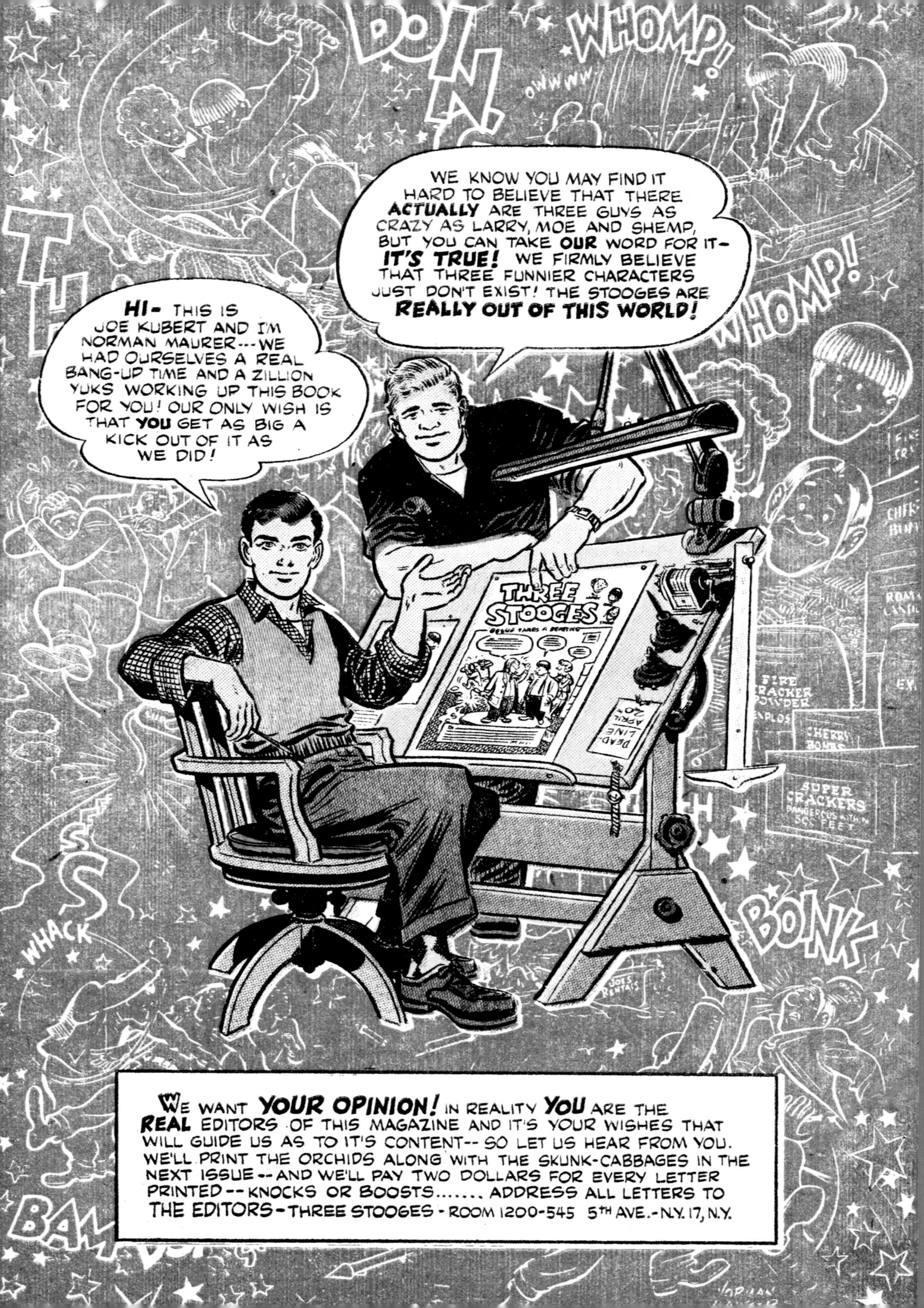
WHOMP!
OWWWW
HI- THIS IS JOE KUBERT AND I'M NORMAN MAURER--- WE HAD OURSELVES A REAL BANG-UP TIME AND A ZILLION YUKS WORKING UP THIS BOOK FOR YOU! OUR ONLY WISH IS THAT YOU GET AS BIG A KICK OUT OF IT AS WE DID!
WE KNOW YOU MAY FIND IT HARD TO BELIEVE THAT THERE ACTUALLY ARE THREE GUYS AS CRAZY AS LARRY, MOE AND SHEMP, BUT YOU CAN TAKE OUR WORD FOR IT- IT'S TRUE! WE FIRMLY BELIEVE THAT THREE FUNNIER CHARACTERS JUST DON'T EXIST! THE STOOGES ARE REALLY OUT OF THIS WORLD!
WHOMP!
WHOMP!
THREE STOOGES
DEAD-LINE APRIL 20th
FIRE CRACKER POWDER
CHERRY BOMBS
SUPER CRACKERS
BONK
WHACK
WE WANT YOUR OPINION! IN REALITY YOU ARE THE REAL EDITORS OF THIS MAGAZINE AND IT'S YOUR WISHES THAT WILL GUIDE US AS TO IT'S CONTENT-- SO LET US HEAR FROM YOU. WE'LL PRINT THE ORCHIDS ALONG WITH THE SKUNK-CABBAGES IN THE NEXT ISSUE--AND WE'LL PAY TWO DOLLARS FOR EVERY LETTER PRINTED-- KNOCKS OR BOOSTS....... ADDRESS ALL LETTERS TO THE EDITORS-THREE STOOGES-ROOM 1200-545 5TH AVE.-N.Y. 17, N.Y.

INTRODUCTION

by Joe Kubert

I was in the army from 1950 to 1952 and, for part of that time, I was stationed in Germany. While there, I came across a publication that featured photographs in 3-D and that included glasses—red and green. But I gave it no other thought.

When I came back to the U.S. after the service, I got together with Norman Maurer. We had gone to school together. Norman was a dear friend, and was a very successful cartoonist. Before I was drafted, I had been a cartoonist and was packaging and putting together comic books for St. John Publishing. Norman and I decided to pool our efforts, become partners, and put out books for St. John.

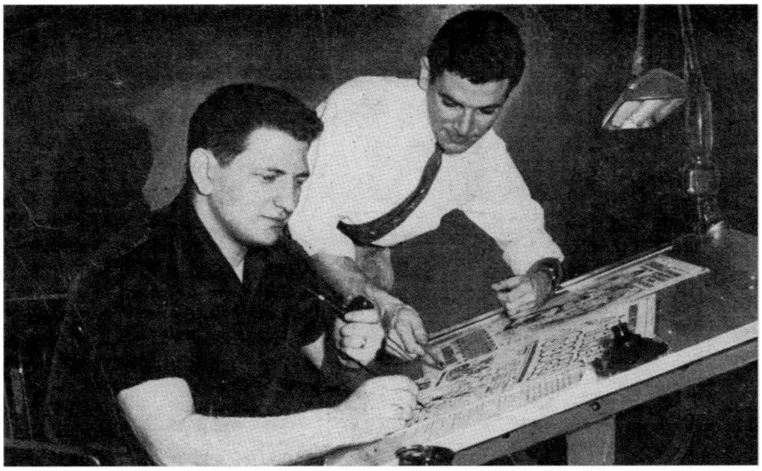

In 1952 there were a lot of titles. They were selling for ten cents and the competition was very keen. So, Norm and I sat down to try to figure out how we could do something a little bit different from what had been done before, so that it could stand out against the, perhaps, three or four hundred different titles that were on the stands at that time.

I kicked around the idea of doing a 3-D version of a comic book—just as a thought—and it brought back to mind what I had seen in Germany. We made the attempt and a lot of tests. Norman had called in his brother, Lenny, who had a background in printing and print media. The three of us sat down and worked at it. At first, we figured it could never be done.

LEFT & ABOVE **Joe Kubert and Norman Maurer as toons and in real life at the drawing board. The drawing and the photograph are from *The Three Stooges* #1, September 1953; artist, Norman Maurer.**

The actual making of 3-D comic book artwork was not a problem. We drew on multiple layers of acetate to get the variety of planes of depth. Depending on how many "buildings" of acetate we had, it resulted in the numbers of depth that we could achieve. In other words, if we wanted three planes of depth, we would do that with three acetates. We did the different drawings that we wanted to separate into different fields of depth. If we wanted six levels, we would do it on six acetates. Norm, Lenny, and I designed our stuff so that the composition would generate the best effect in 3-D.

The first red-and-green glasses we put together as samples were made from acetates we took off lollipop covers. The lollipops came wrapped in colored cellophane, we just took a red one and a green one. We made ourselves a pair of glasses out of a piece of cardboard, and that's what we viewed our material with. Figuring out the art and how it worked really wasn't that complicated. Stereopticons in 3-D had been around for decades. It wasn't a question of being able to do it in 3-D. The real difficulty was to try to get a

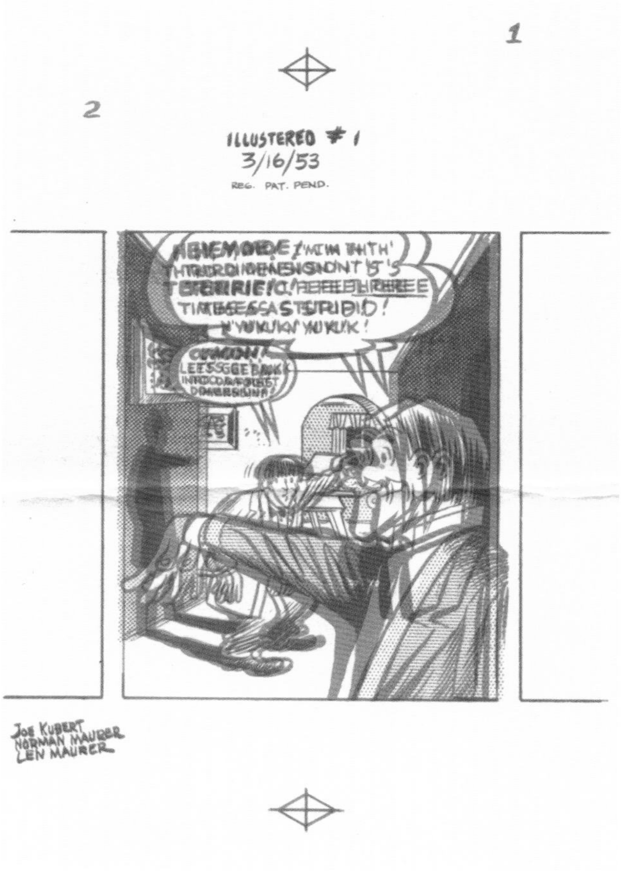
1
2
ILLUSTERED #1
3/16/53
REG. PAT. PEND.
JOE KUBERT
NORMAN MAURER
LEN MAURER

book out, with the 3-D effect and the glasses, that would sell for a price that the public could afford. We knew it couldn't be more than 25 cents.

Eventually, through trial and error, and working at it very hard, Norman, Lenny, and I finally came up with a workable way of producing a 3-D comic book that would include the glasses.

We brought the idea to Archer St. John who was the boss of the St. John Publishing company. He thought it was a terrific idea but, rather than doing a new book, he asked if we could convert to 3-D *Mighty Mouse*, a comic he had been licensing from Terrytoons. He had a whole book ready to go to press, all in black and white, and on boards. Archer asked if we could convert that into 3-D, which is what we did. *Mighty Mouse* was the first three-dimensional comic book.

St. John Publishing went to press with *Mighty Mouse* two or three times. It sold about a million and a quarter copies and that's what bought my first house!

Then, we did three-dimensional comics with The Three Stooges, my character Tor, and more. And, that was really the problem: not only did *we* do some more, *everybody* did some more! This has happened time and time again. When a competitive publisher sees that something the other guy is doing is selling, immediately he'll come out with four or five more of the same thing. Everybody's trying to grab hold of the goose that lays the golden egg, not figuring that, if they're grabbing it by the throat, it's not going to last very long. The gimmick, to put it shortly, just petered out. There were so many books! Everything was turned into 3-D. Everybody was publishing 3-D and not paying too much attention to the subject matter, figuring that the gimmick would continue to sell. Needless to say, it did not.

As a matter of fact, that pretty much drove St. John Publishing out of the business, as it did several others. At that time, you didn't know what the sales were until three or four months after the book was on the stands. Many of the publishers just kept publishing new 3-D books, so that, by the time the third or fourth publication came out, they were selling less than ten percent of their run and they just couldn't afford that.

What goes around comes around, and it comes around consistently. 3-D is being used today in some of the biggest movies. The movie houses are converting to enable them to show the features in 3-D. TV is also turning out 3-D programming. I have no doubt that, eventually, just as it petered out the last time, it will again, especially if they start flooding the market with these 3-D pictures, figuring that it's the gimmick that is going to sell. Story and storytelling is what is most interesting to an audience. After a while, the fascination of 3-D won't make any difference at all.

It was exciting creating the process of 3-D for comic books and I hope the work presented in *Amazing 3-D Comics* will be as interesting to you as it was to me when we made them!

In his 70-plus years of working in comics, Joe Kubert has produced countless stories for countless characters, including DC Comics' Hawkman, Tarzan, Enemy Ace, Sgt. Rock, The Flash, and Batman, as well as his own characters: the heroic caveman, Tor, and Abraham Stone. Kubert has been a penciler, inker, letterer, colorist, newspaper strip cartoonist, school founder and teacher, correspondence course developer, author, artist, and editor. Joe Kubert lives and works in New Jersey. Visit http://kubertschool.edu

ABOVE **Norman Maurer's original 3-D experiment with The Three Stooges shown to Archer St. John. Previously unpublished.**

RIGHT-HAND PAGE ***3-D Comics* #2, November 1953; artist, Joe Kubert. Tor in actual 3-D on the cover! Artist Neal Adams was an eleven-year-old army brat when he spied a Tor 3-D comic while traveling through Europe. He later said, "It blew my mind. I don't even remember the trip back; I just remember that book."**

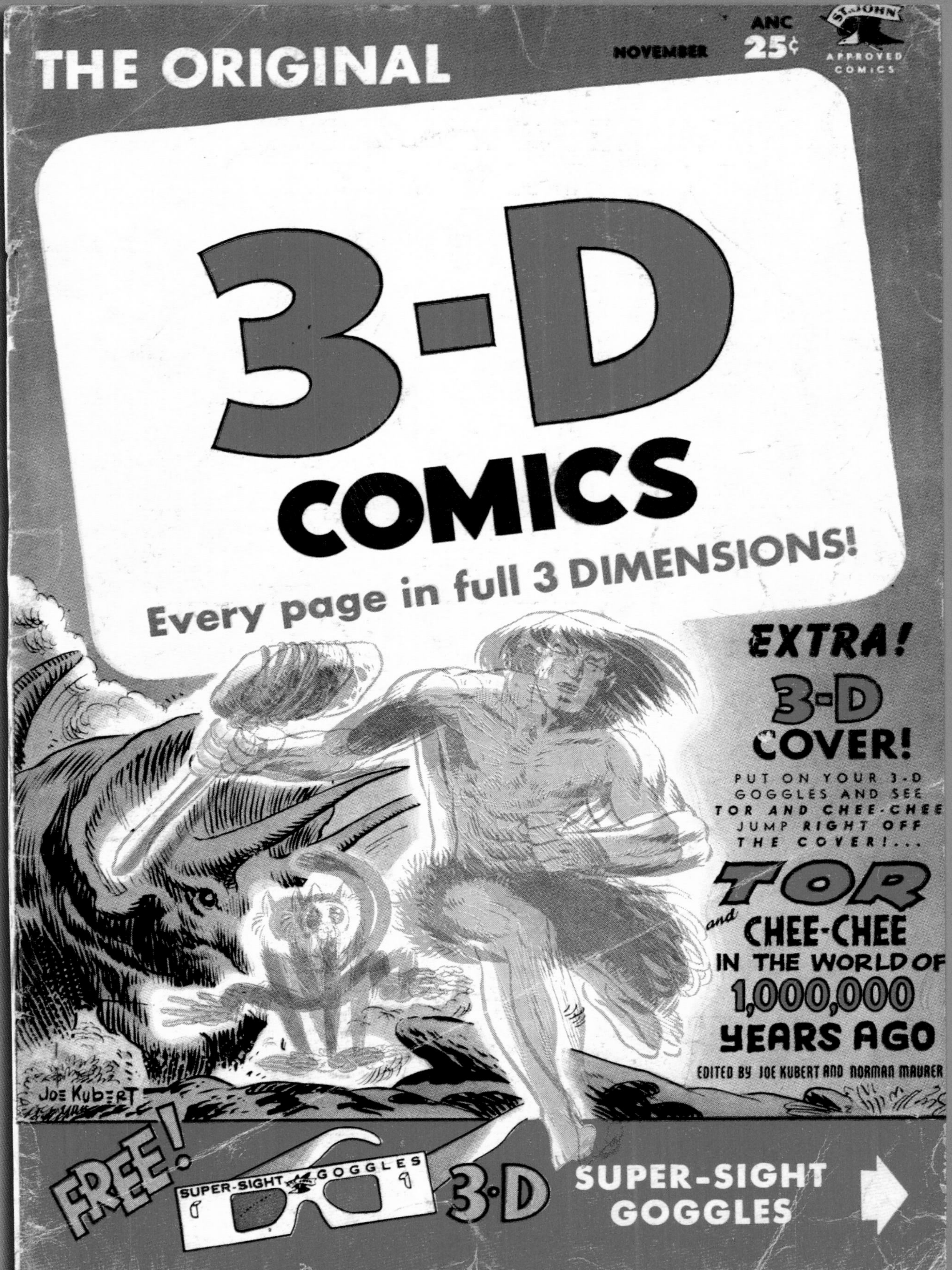
THE ORIGINAL
NOVEMBER
ANC
25¢
ST. JOHN
APPROVED COMICS
3-D
COMICS
Every page in full 3 DIMENSIONS!
EXTRA!
3-D
COVER!
PUT ON YOUR 3-D GOGGLES AND SEE TOR AND CHEE-CHEE JUMP RIGHT OFF THE COVER!...
TOR
and
CHEE-CHEE
IN THE WORLD OF
1,000,000
YEARS AGO
EDITED BY JOE KUBERT AND NORMAN MAURER
JOE KUBERT
FREE!
SUPER-SIGHT GOGGLES
3-D
SUPER-SIGHT
GOGGLES

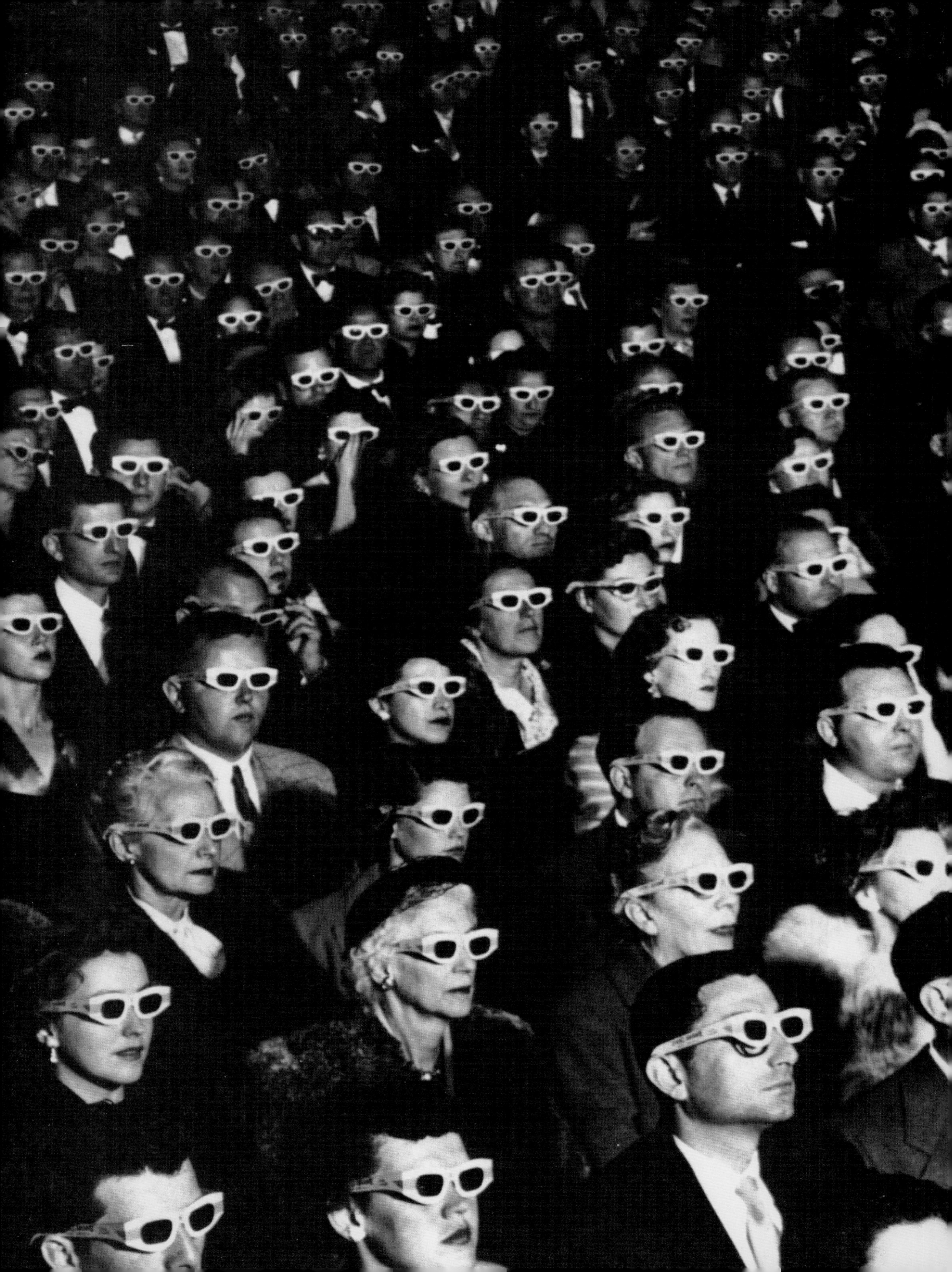

AMAZING 3-D COMICS

by Craig Yoe

3-D or not 3-D? There was no question about it in the mid 1950s, when, for a few months, nearly every comics publisher jumped onto the speeding 3-D wagon. The 3-D mania produced amazing comics with spectacular effects by some of the best artists in the medium. That's just before the wagon went over a cliff to crash and burn—which would be a great 3-D scene. This totaled vehicle even took a few comic book companies with it.

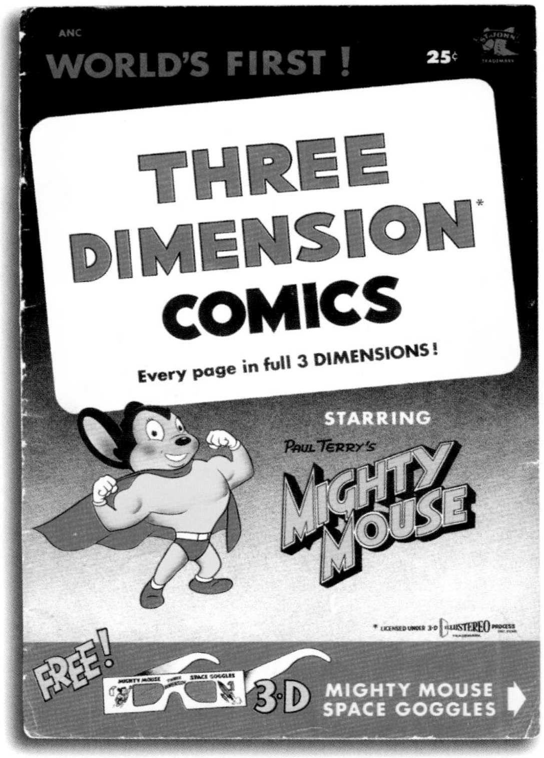
ANC
WORLD'S FIRST!
25¢
THREE DIMENSION* COMICS
Every page in full 3 DIMENSIONS!
STARRING
PAUL TERRY'S
MIGHTY MOUSE
FREE!
3-D
MIGHTY MOUSE SPACE GOGGLES

3-D was B.C. according to 3-D historians Hal Morgan and Dan Symmes. They tell us Euclid himself "laid out the principles of binocular vision... He demonstrated that the left and right eyes each see a different image of the same object or scene and that it is the merging of these images that creates the perception of depth." Early experimentation perfected stereoscopic photographs, viewed on a small device called a stereoscope. This device became a living room fixture in the 1870s, and was as common as a TV or computer in a home today.

The first documented 3-D movie experience premiered at the Astor Theater in New York, on June 10, 1915. Edwin S. Porter (director of the celebrated *Great Train Robbery*, 1903) along with William E. Waddell screened a trio of experimental short 3-D films. But it wasn't until the low-budget *Bwana Devil* drew record crowds in 1952 that Hollywood took a big interest in 3-D—and now, more than ever, 3-D is the darling of the film industry. As for the printed page, red and green "anaglyph"-type printing was pioneered in the 1920s by inventor Alfred Macy and his printing partner, American Colortype. A number of brochures and magazines followed through the decades.

As Joe Kubert relates in this book's introduction, it was a 3-D magazine he saw in the 1950s that was the catalyst for the 3-D comic craze. Thanks to Kubert, the brothers Norman and Leonard Maurer, and their publisher Archer St. John, comic books literally entered a new dimension. The day before July 4th, 1953, an innovative comic burst like fireworks on the newsstands. On the cover, the Mouse roared, "WORLD'S FIRST! THREE DIMENSION COMICS! Every page in full 3 DIMENSIONS!" This huge title dwarfed the Mighty Mouse logo and even the Mouse himself. The cover further proclaimed that the kid willing to plunk down a quarter—rather than the usual dime that was the price of admission for a standard comic—got "FREE 3-D MIGHTY MOUSE SPACE GOGGLES" (a nod to America's fascination at that time with all things space-related).

LEFT-HAND PAGE **A packed house for a screening of *Bwana Devil*, 1952.**

ABOVE **Here he comes to save the day! The world's first 3-D comic! *Three Dimension Comics* #1, September 1953.**

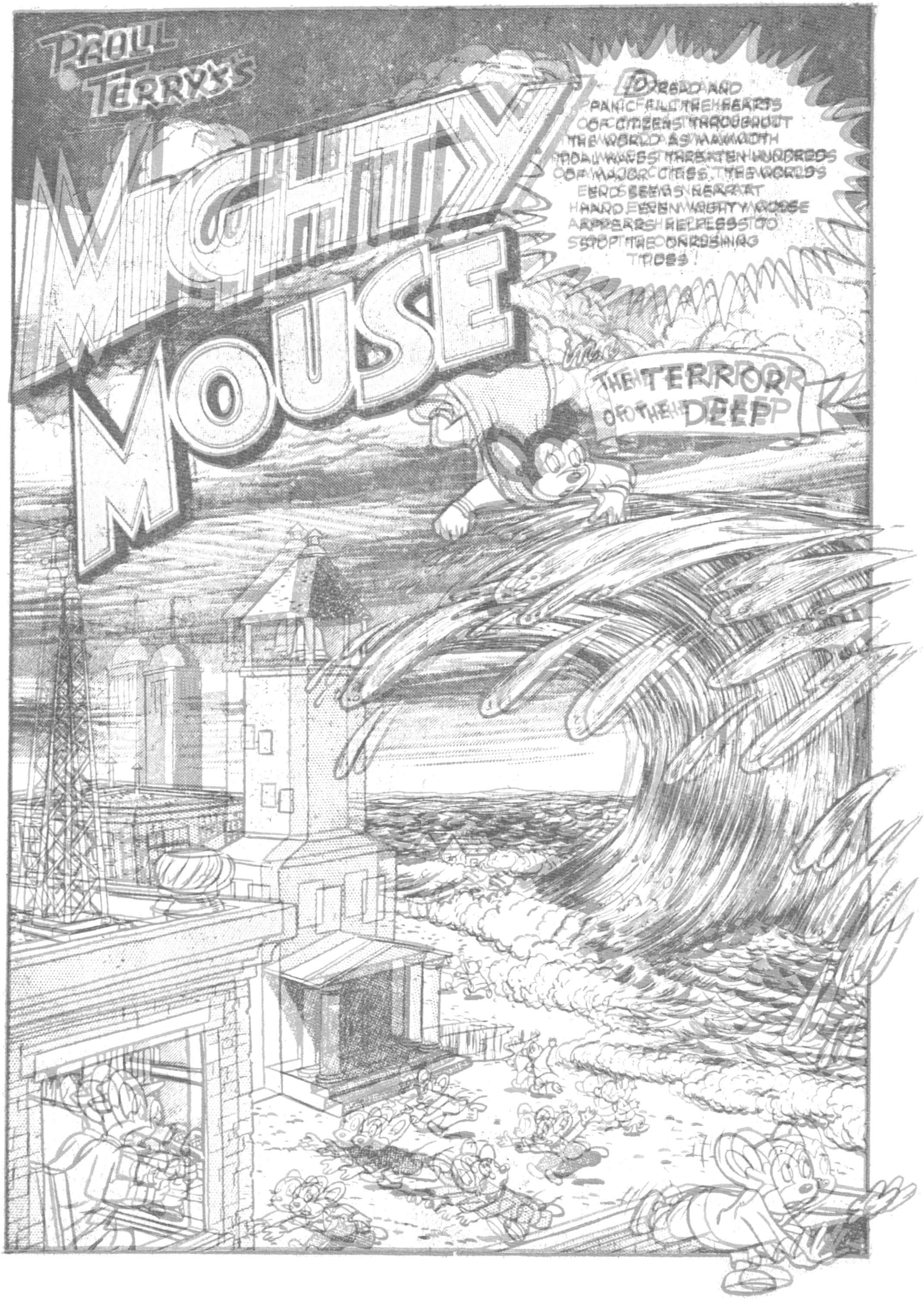
PAUL TERRY'S
MIGHTY MOUSE
in
THE TERROR OF THE DEEP
DREAD AND PANIC FILL THE HEARTS OF CITIZENS THROUGHOUT THE WORLD AS MAMMOTH TIDAL WAVES THREATEN HUNDREDS OF MAJOR CITIES. THE WORLD'S END SEEMS NEAR AT HAND. EVEN MIGHTY MOUSE APPEARS HELPLESS TO STOP THE ONRUSHING TIDES!

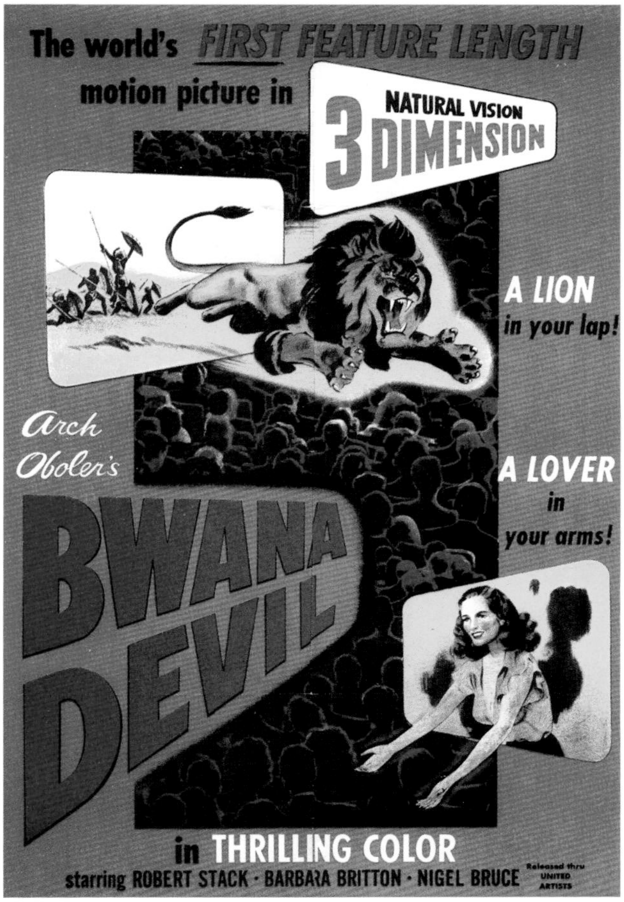
The world's FIRST FEATURE LENGTH
motion picture in
NATURAL VISION
3 DIMENSION
A LION
in your lap!
Arch Oboler's
BWANA DEVIL
A LOVER
in
your arms!
in THRILLING COLOR
starring ROBERT STACK · BARBARA BRITTON · NIGEL BRUCE
Released thru UNITED ARTISTS

LEFT-HAND PAGE **This *Mighty Mouse* splash page makes a big splash! *Three Dimension Comics* #2, November 1953.**

LEFT **A lion in your lap! A lover in your arms! Poster for the *Bwana Devil* movie, 1952.**

BELOW, LEFT **The first 3-D comics publisher Archer St. John in the early 1950s. In the early '20s, Archer ran a crusading, one-man newspaper in Berwyn, Illinois, a town which Al Capone was trying to infiltrate. The gangster's men kidnapped, handcuffed, and blindfolded Archer for a day, just before an election, thwarting his anti-mob publishing efforts.**

BELOW, RIGHT **[From left] Moe Howard of The Three Stooges with Norman and Leonard Maurer.**

The first printing sold out and the comic immediately went back to press, a rare occurrence for comic books. After nearly a million and a quarter copies sold, two more *Mighty Mouse* 3-D comics from St. John Publishing soon followed.

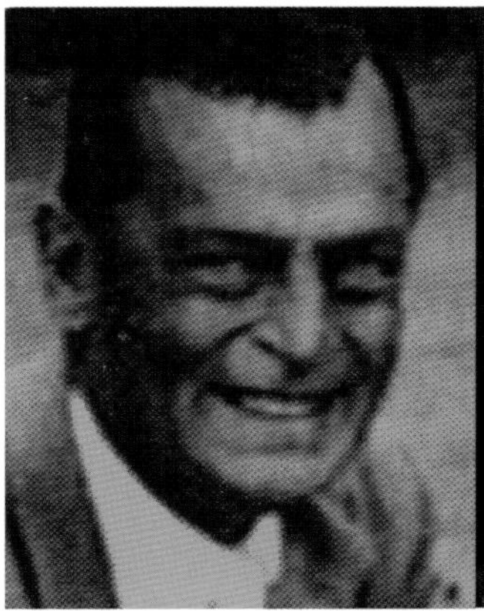

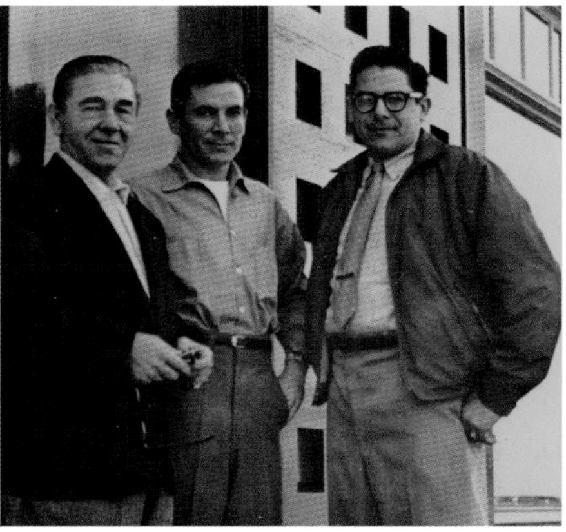

Comics historian Ken Quattro relates the beginnings of 3-D comics in Roy Thomas' *Alter Ego* magazine. Quattro explains what happened after Joe Kubert had seen 3-D photo magazines while stationed in Germany, "this spark of an idea was rekindled to full flame when he, Norman Maurer, and Norman's brother Leonard happened to be driving past the Paramount Theatre in New York City while it was showing the new film *Bwana Devil*. Written and directed by Arch Oboler, the cheaply made 3-D exploitation film, which promised 'A lion in your lap! A lover in you arms!' was an immediate success and sparked a flood of imitators.

"According to Leonard Maurer, Kubert's remark upon seeing the movie marquee, 'Gee, wouldn't it be great if we could make a 3-D comic book?' inspired Norman to return home and virtually overnight create the printing process that would result in 3-D comic books."

Quattro continues, "In one long night, Norman Maurer drew the first 3-D comic page, entitled 'The Three Dimensional Stooges in the Third Dimension,' to Leonard's specifications. Early the next day, the Maurers waited for the midtown Manhattan Woolworths to open in order to purchase lollipops. 'We figured we could get red and green cellophane from lollipop wrappers,' Norman was quoted in *The Three Stooges Scrapbook*. 'We bought two packages and made a funny pair of glasses which, believe it or not, worked perfectly.'"

Kubert and Maurer christened their innovation the '3-D Illustereo Process' and hired a lawyer to seek a patent. They gave Archer St. John the first crack at publishing 3-D comics. Joe drew up a sample of a 3-D Tor (see the front endpaper) and Norman brought his Three Stooges drawing (see page 8). St. John was greatly excited, but first wanted the cartoonists to turn a *Mighty Mouse* comic about to go to press into a 3-D product. The Terrytoon character starred in St. John's most popular comic and the Mouse's flying antics were perfect for 3-D.

Working feverishly and in secret, the artists completed the artwork for the first 3-D comic in three days and nights. They used an approach similar to creating an animation cel, with layers of acetate and much laborious hand-work. The duo flew to Washington, D.C. to have the book printed and covertly oversee the production outside of the incestuous New York City print shops, which might leak the news.

The comic book industry was fighting a losing battle with the new medium of TV and had distribution problems. Most damaging of all were the blows of criticism from anti-comics psychiatrist Dr. Fredric Wertham and Senate investigations linking comic books to juvenile delinquency. Joan Maurer

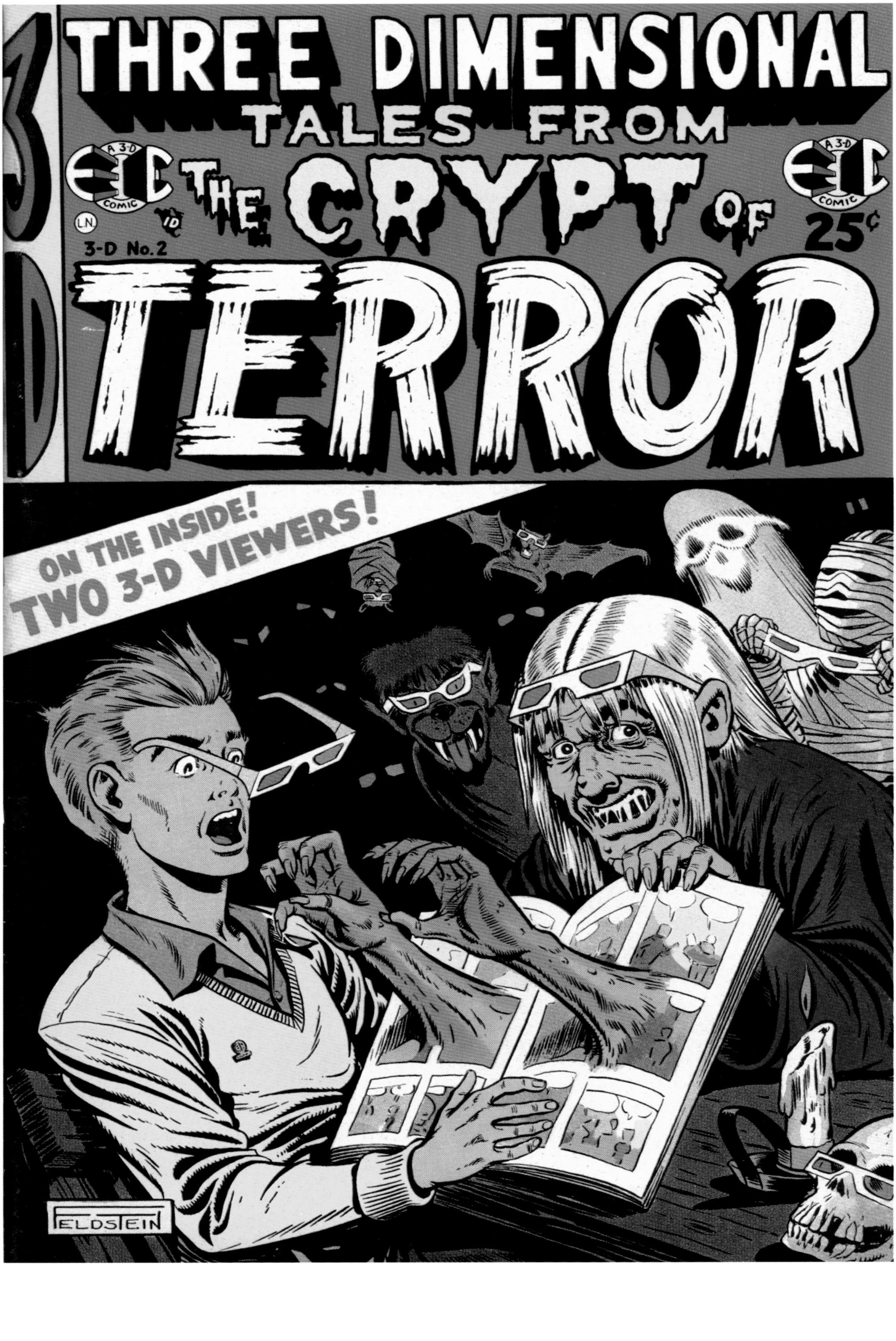

3-D
THREE DIMENSIONAL
TALES FROM
THE CRYPT OF
TERROR
A 3-D EC COMIC
L.N.
ID
3-D No.2
25¢
ON THE INSIDE!
TWO 3-D VIEWERS!
FELDSTEIN

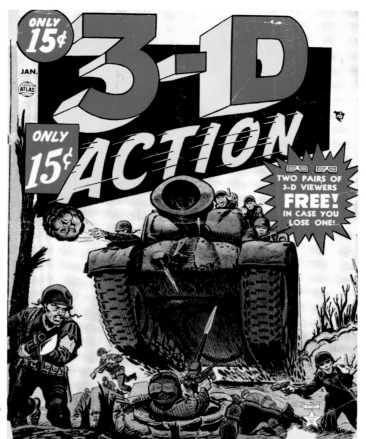

(wife of Norman Maurer and daughter of The Three Stooges' Moe Howard) recalls in an interview for this book, "Norman saw the comic book field and his connection to it going downhill and he thought, 'Gee, if we can do the books in 3-D, that might kind of give it a shot in the arm.' And Norman was looking for something to try to trigger his own career, too."

ONLY 15¢
3-D
JAN.
ATLAS
ONLY 15¢
ACTION
TWO PAIRS OF 3-D VIEWERS FREE! IN CASE YOU LOSE ONE!

A shot in the arm came in the form of a robust rodent. When *Three Dimension Comics* starring Mighty Mouse hit, the comic hit big!

"When there is a wrong to right,
Mighty Mouse will join the fight
'Here I come to save the day!'
That means that Mighty
Mouse is on the way!"

Joan Maurer exclaims, "Between the eyestrain you could get and the increased price for them, I'm surprised they were so successful."

Successful they were! A mouse led the way and the race was on between publishers to produce the red and green comics and glasses. They smelled green money—though many of them ended up in the red after the last kid bought his last 3-D comic, a few months later.

Another concurrent 1950s comic book phenomena was *Mad* and its many imitators. Joe and Norman produced one of the best of the look-alikes, *Whack*. *Whack* itself went 3-D—and even good-naturedly satirized the 3-D phenomenon when the fad's downfall started. Titled *3-D-T's*, the stories, one in 3-D and one not, are reprinted in this book.

Before the first wave of 3-D comics did a deep six, nearly every comics publisher of the time got into the act producing five score of red and green "REAL adventures that JUMP out of the page!" DC Comics came out with their heavy hitters, *Superman* and *Batman*. Even the famed EC published collections of their entertaining comics redrawn for 3-D.

Though they had licenses with Walt Disney and Warner Bros. and produced *Donald Duck* and *Looney Tunes* comics, Dell curiously did only minor books in 3-D, called *3-D-ell*, starring Rootie Kazootie and Flukey Luke. But soon 24 Disney pocket-size 3-D comics featuring Donald Duck and Mickey Mouse appeared as Cheerios cereal premiums. Maybe Disney's deal with Cheerios precluded Dell from producing regular 3-D comics featuring the Disney menagerie.

Marvel (Atlas) brought out three books for the 3-D fury: a western, a war comic, and a funny animal offering. None of those were drawn for 3-D, but were converted from inventory stories. Toby published a comic with that wonderful, wonderful cat, Felix. Artists Otto Messmer and Joe Oriolo, with their bouncy three-point perspectives, shine in this medium. Harvey Comics put out some of the very finest 3-D comics drawn especially for the effect. Editor Sid Jacobson proudly told comics historian and critic John Benson in *Alter Ego*, "They were terrific. Really, I think they were the best 3-D books that were out."

After years of publishing *Jungle Comics*, *Planet Comics*, and other bestselling titles, Fiction House's last hurrah was a 3-D comic that featured the final adventures of their lead character, jungle queen Sheena, and an uncharacteristic humor/funny animal comic, *3-D Circus*, with art by Jerry Iger.

LEFT-HAND PAGE **Coming atcha... to getcha! *Three Dimensional Tales From The Crypt of Terror* #2, Spring 1954; artist, Al Feldstein. This cover is reproduced from publisher William Gaines' file copy in the collection of Grant Geissman.**

ABOVE **Publishers like Atlas (Marvel) started including "two pairs of 3-D viewers... in case you lose one!" *3-D Action* #1, January 1954; artist, Sol Brodsky.**

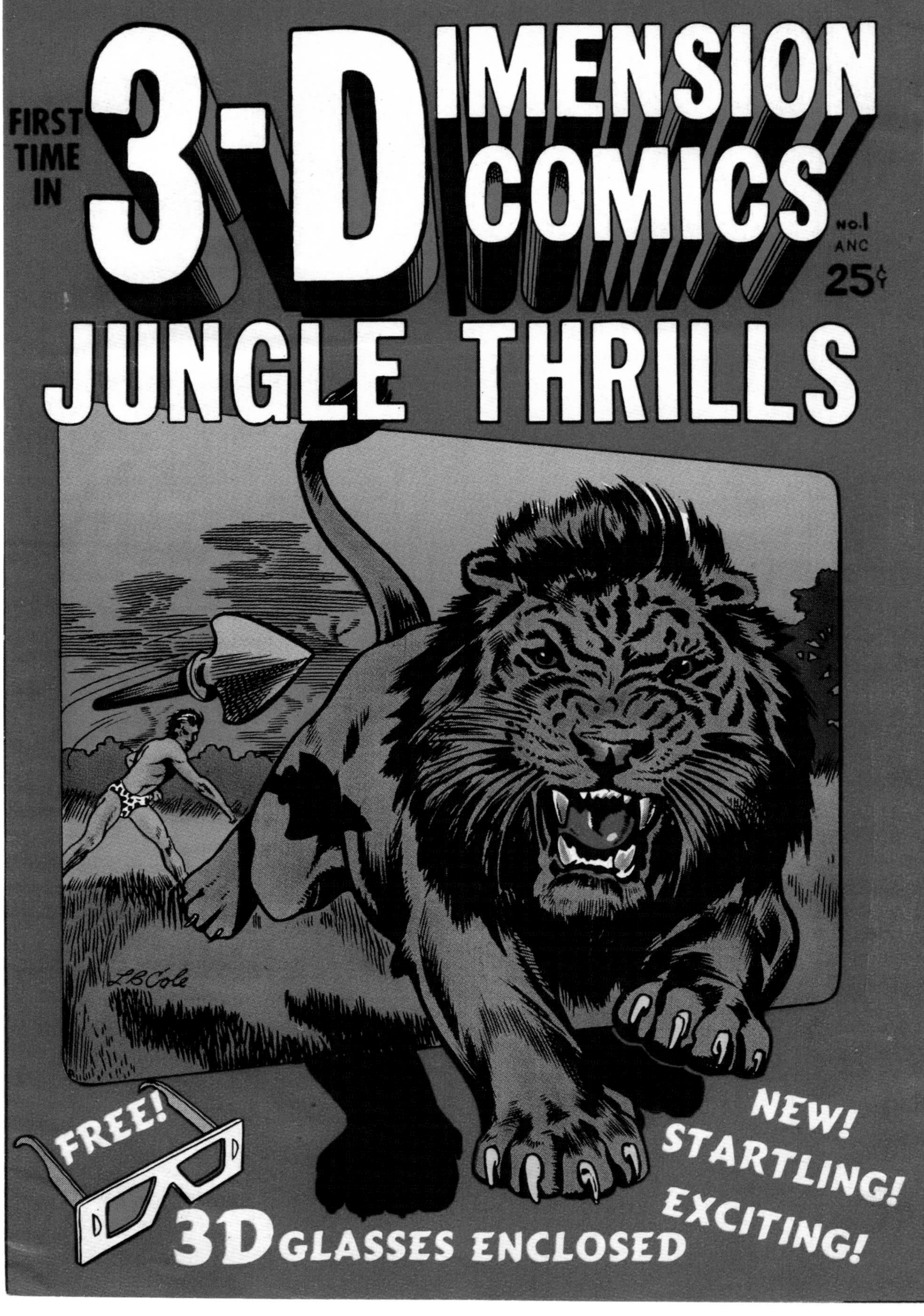

FIRST TIME IN
3-DIMENSION COMICS
No. 1
ANC
25¢
JUNGLE THRILLS
L.B. Cole
FREE!
3D GLASSES ENCLOSED
NEW! STARTLING! EXCITING!

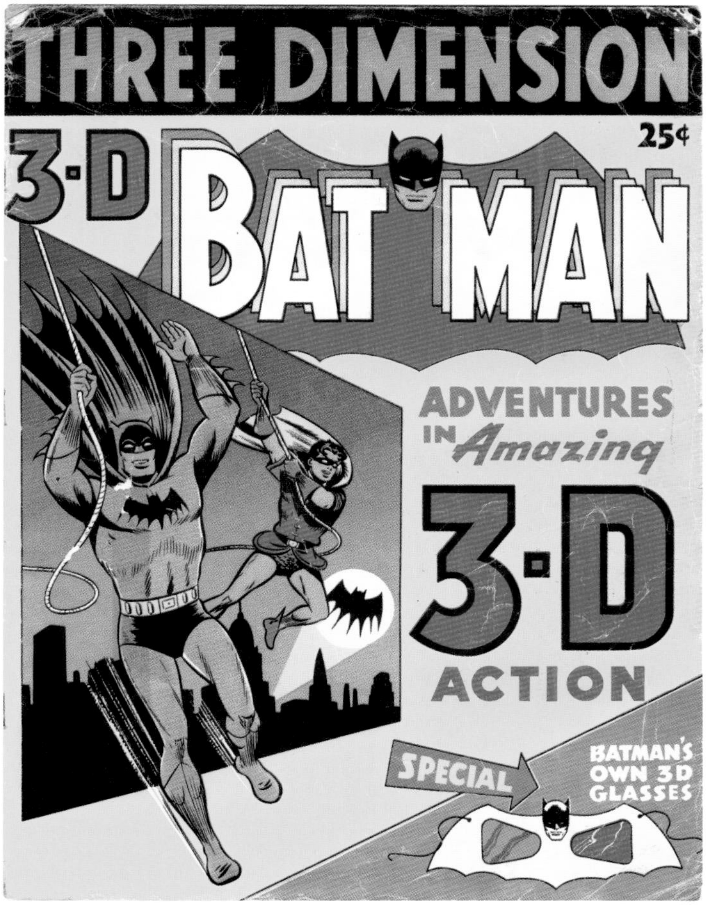
THREE DIMENSION
3-D
25¢
BATMAN
ADVENTURES IN Amazing 3-D ACTION
SPECIAL
BATMAN'S OWN 3D GLASSES

LEFT-HAND PAGE **A rare cover proof from the Heritage Auction Galleries. *Jungle Thrills* #1, December 1953; artist, L.B. Cole.**

ABOVE ***3-D Batman* #1, 1953. According to the cover, you actually get Batman's *own* 3-D glasses!**

BELOW **Joan Maurer and her son, Jeffrey Scott, reading the first 3-D comic book. Scott went on to be an Emmy-winning animation screenwriter and is the author of *How To Write for Animation*. Blame it on 3-D!**

Like many late adapters in a hurry to cash in, Fiction House published Sheena stories not drawn for 3-D. Stock stories were quickly converted to the process, but seeing the curvaceous leopard-clad lass in 3-D is still a treat!

Cartoonist Mike Esposito told an interesting story about himself and his art partner Ross Andru. In the 1950s, they had come up with their own *Mad*-style comic, *Get Lost,* and were set to do the publication for the Leader News periodical distribution company that advanced them a quite generous fee. "When we got the check in our hands for 10 grand, which was more money than we had ever seen, we went down the hall to the elevator, dancing and jumping up and down like two kids. We were like two idiots. We were going to do *Get Lost*. But (the Leader News representative Mike) Estrow said to us, 'Don't do *Get Lost* yet, but do a 3-D comic first.' We said, 'Why?' And he said, '*Mighty Mouse* came out in 3-D for a quarter and sold over a million copies. We gotta go 3-D.'"

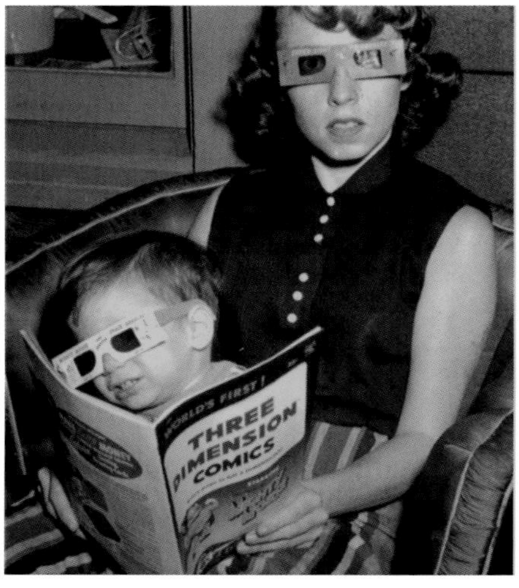
WORLD'S FIRST!
THREE DIMENSION COMICS

Esposito said, "It was the kiss of death."

The artist went on to explain, "3-D destroyed companies. The company that put out *Mighty Mouse* went bankrupt after that, because 3-D was a one-shot type thing. People read one and that was it. They didn't want to buy the next one because it was a gimmick. So we said, 'What are we gonna do? He wants a 3-D comic,' and our brains were so smart you know, 'Let's do something that no one's done—let's do romance.' *3-D Love* and *3-D Romance* were our two books with the glasses."

Cartoonist Mike Esposito continued, "We used a different business name for those books: Steriographic Publications. You don't use the same corporation for tax purposes. Once we knew it was going to be 3-D we created the name Steriographic, as opposed to MikeRoss Publications because the books were going to be in stereo. A lawyer told us to use a different name; people did it all the time. It wasn't my brilliance or Ross' brilliance. It was the lawyer's, and he was a sharp guy.

"However, it cost us a fortune. We lost $25,000 of our own money, which was a lot of money in those days. The books didn't sell at all, they sold 5,000 comic books out of a 500,000 [print run], and we took a bath. Because who wants to read about love in 3-D? They're not naked. The reason why nobody did 3-D love stories was because it wouldn't work. Usually they do 3-D action, things jumping at you, arms coming at you. They didn't last. They all went bankrupt."

There was a terrific opening panel (reproduced on page 19) in *3-D Love,* featuring an interesting see-through effect not seen before. We don't show a whole story from that book in *Amazing 3-D Comics* because love comics by their nature don't lend themselves to dynamic 3-D effects, as Esposito explained.

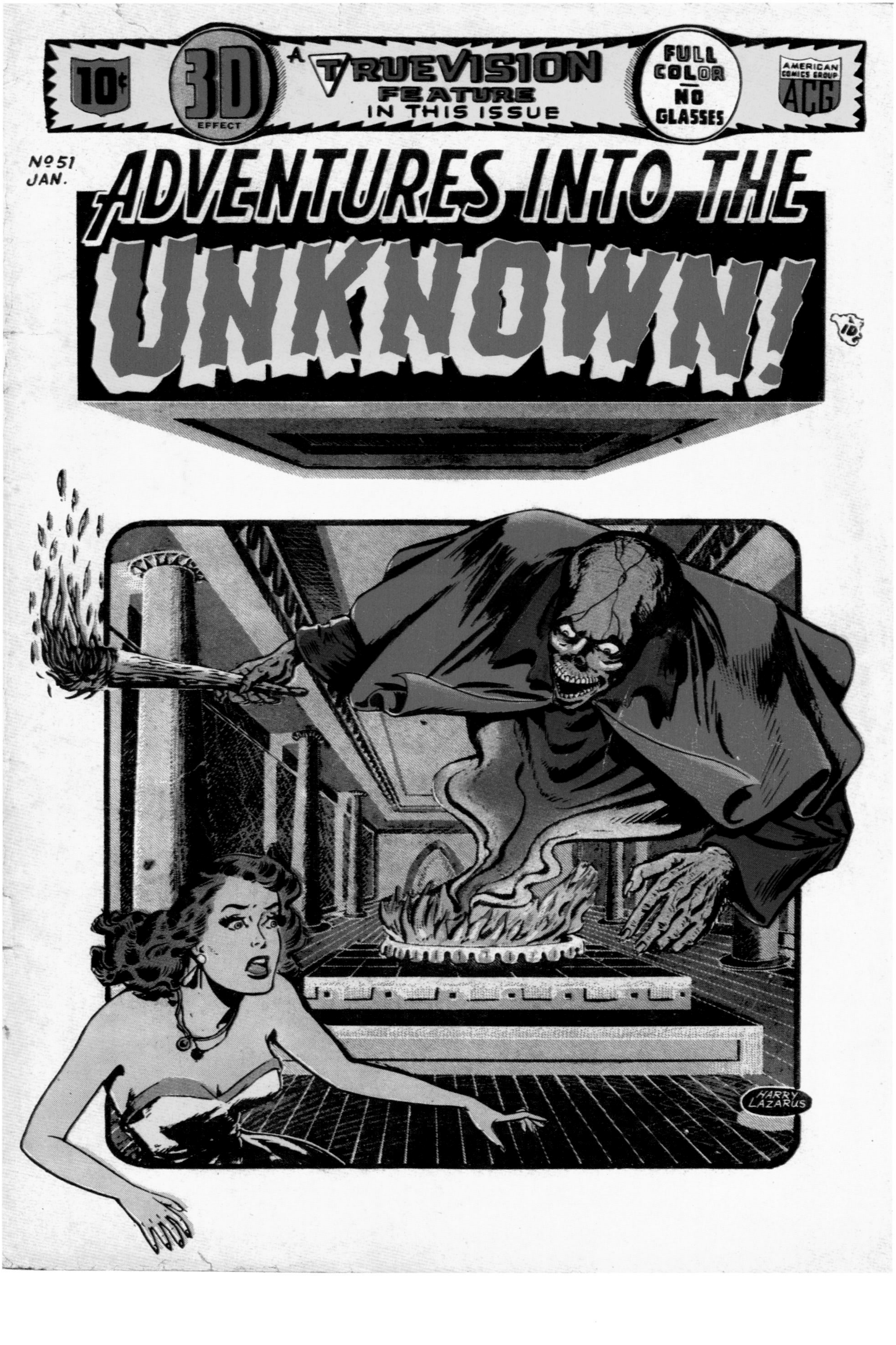

10¢
3D
EFFECT
A TRUEVISION FEATURE IN THIS ISSUE
FULL COLOR
NO GLASSES
AMERICAN COMICS GROUP
ACG
No 51
JAN.
ADVENTURES INTO THE UNKNOWN!
HARRY LAZARUS

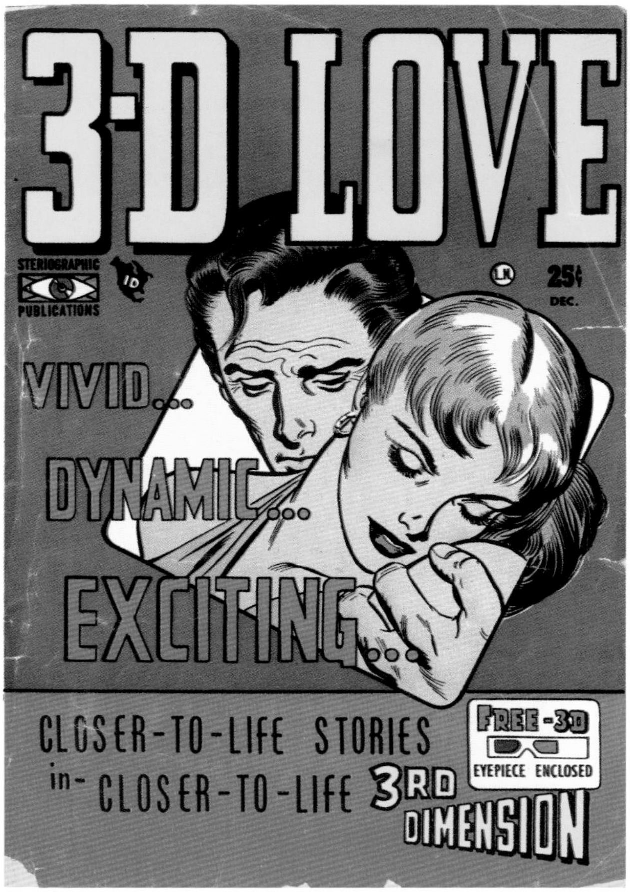
3-D LOVE
STERIOGRAPHIC
PUBLICATIONS
25¢
DEC.
VIVID...
DYNAMIC...
EXCITING...
CLOSER-TO-LIFE STORIES
in- CLOSER-TO-LIFE 3RD DIMENSION
FREE-3-D
EYEPIECE ENCLOSED

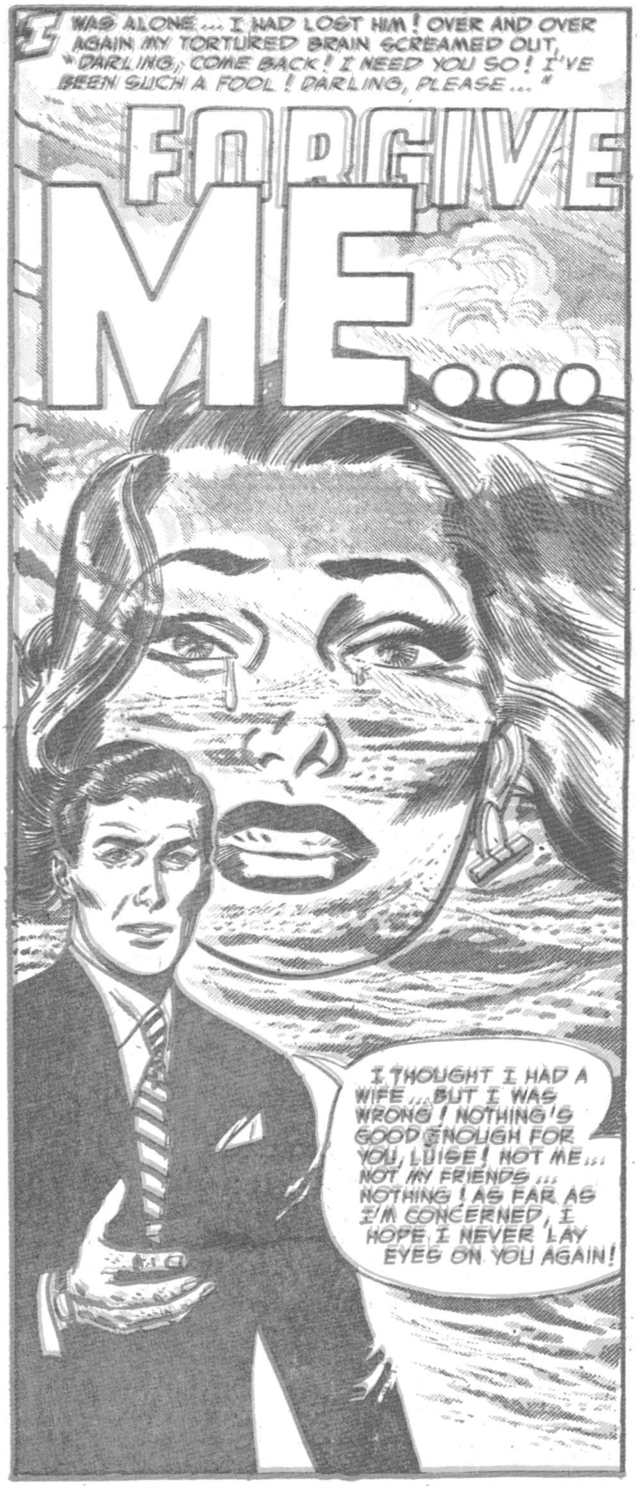
I WAS ALONE... I HAD LOST HIM! OVER AND OVER AGAIN MY TORTURED BRAIN SCREAMED OUT, "DARLING, COME BACK! I NEED YOU SO! I'VE BEEN SUCH A FOOL! DARLING, PLEASE..."
FORGIVE ME...
I THOUGHT I HAD A WIFE... BUT I WAS WRONG! NOTHING'S GOOD ENOUGH FOR YOU, LUISE! NOT ME... NOT MY FRIENDS... NOTHING! AS FAR AS I'M CONCERNED, I HOPE I NEVER LAY EYES ON YOU AGAIN!

Before the fad faded, every genre of comics got 3-D-ized. Lovers, funny animals, funny people, cavemen, cowboys, puppets, pin-up queens, monsters, and superheroes—all got three-dimensional adventures in deep space to the deep sea. The delightful diversity of the subject matter of 1950s comics is seen through the red and green specs.

3-D comics weren't always easy to read and were time consuming to produce. The glasses put them at a much higher price point, which could make for more profits, but also provided sales resistance if a kid already had one or two of the 3-D comics strewn on his bedroom floor. A number of publishers tried fascinating approaches to create easy-on-the-eyes, ten-cent three-dimensional comics. They were more traditional in their creation and in the full color printing. The American Comics Group (ACG) had "3-D effect TrueVision, Life & Color—Without Glasses!" They used this technique in the horror/fantasy title *Adventures Into The Unknown*, their romance comic *Lovelorn*, and their humor titles, *Cookie* and *The Kilroys*. Magazine Enterprises (ME) simply touted their *Tim Holt* comic, drawn by Frank Bolle, as "3-D Drawings in Full Color!"

Each publisher was excited about the innovation of 3-D and tried to differentiate themselves by adding new wrinkles to the process.

Harvey had *3-D Blinkey* where, by looking first through one lens and then the other, you got alternate versions of a

LEFT-HAND PAGE **ACG comics touted, "3-D Effect. A TrueVision Feature in this Issue. Full-Color, No Glasses." The cover is *Adventures Into The Unknown* #51, January 1954; artist, Harry Lazarus.**

ABOVE **All you need is 3-D Love! Cover and splash detail of *3-D Love* #1, December 1953; artists, Ross Andru and Mike Esposito.**

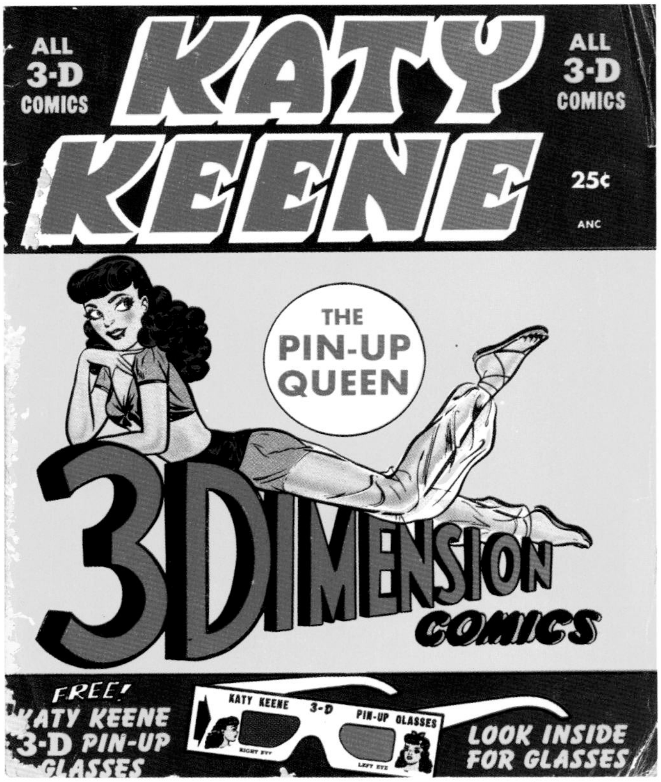
ALL 3-D COMICS
KATY KEENE
ALL 3-D COMICS
25¢
ANC
THE PIN-UP QUEEN
3 DIMENSION COMICS
FREE! KATY KEENE 3-D PIN-UP GLASSES
KATY KEENE 3-D PIN-UP GLASSES
LOOK INSIDE FOR GLASSES

ABOVE ***Katy Keene Three Dimension Comics* #1, 1953; artist, attributed to Bill Woggon. Inside, the pin-up queen in red and green!**

RIGHT-HAND PAGE **3-D cups! Even comic book ads got the 3-D treatment. This brassiere ad appeared in the children's comic book *Noodnik*, December 1953, published by Comic Media.**

story—*tres trois* cool! Harvey also, in their *Jiggs and Maggie* title, interestingly added yellow and black to the usual red and green used in 3-D to make their comics more colorful and in an attempt to improve readability. This comic appeared in January of 1954. The lone 3-D story in the book was probably a leftover inventory from an aborted *Jiggs and Maggie* 3-D comic. This issue didn't even come with glasses. It was hoped kids had leftover "goggles"—though it is said that Harvey had millions of glasses in their warehouse left over from the fad.

Surprisingly, Archie Comics did not use Archie for their 3-D outing, but instead did a 3-D *Katy Keene* comic. In an interview for this book, Victor Gorelick, Editor-in-Chief of Archie, says that cartoonist Bob White did the production on *Katy Keene*. He "colored" Bill Woggon's backgrounds with shades of the blue and red to provide a twist. Dell's *3-D-ell* used fumetti-style comics featuring photographs of miniature table top puppets.

In some comic books, there were panoramic two-page spreads called 3-Diorama (one of which serves as *Amazing 3-D Comics'* back endpaper). In others, readers were invited to compare covers printed traditionally with the 3-D versions inside (see pages 109/110, and 131/132). Everybody had an angle.

Alex Toth recalled his foray into "Deep Dimensions"—a version of 3-D comics—in an interview with *Graphic Story Magazine*, "[The publisher Lev] Gleason had called me in to talk over a special issue of *Crime and Punishment* he had in mind. He had just come back from seeing *The Robe*, the first wide-screen CinemaScope film. 'What we're going to do is try and get the wide screen effect in our pages,' he said. 'I want the artwork to look like it's really coming out at you!' I said 'Well, I'm going to need all the help I can get. Let me work with Duo-Tone Craftint; I can model the figures using the gray tints, and use exaggerated perspectives to bring things out the way you want.' He indicated he wanted lots of spectacular effects and the curved page borders to produce them. Despite my objections to this device of his, I agreed to try it."

Toth went on, "After he okayed my use of Duo-Tone, I went ahead with a sample page to show him and his new editor, Harold Straubing, the effect of it. Straubing was a former comics editor at the *New York Herald-Tribune*. I showed them the Duo-Tone page. Straubing put the kibosh on it, saying, 'The screen's much too fine to reduce and print well; we'll have a lot of trouble with it.' I reminded him I was working half-up from print size, and that it would reduce just fine. 'No,' he said, 'go to the next bigger screen.' I knew a bigger screen was going to look like chicken wire even after reduction, and I told him so. But I lost the fight."

Toth continued, "The book was 28 or 30 pages, plus a cover, and I had to do two finishes a day to make the too-close deadline. I cut a template, scooping the bottom, top, and sides, and used it to outline the pages. It was all very strange, but a lot of fun..."

There were a myriad of names publishers called the 3-D glasses: Super-Sight Goggles, Space Goggles, Magic Specs, Magic Viewers, 3-D Viewers. You got "Batman's Own 3-D Glasses" and Katy Keene's "3-D Pin-up Glasses." All these cardboard and acetate viewers—the covers emphasized—came "FREE!"—the buyers just had to pay two and a half times the price of a normal comic book. Some of the books even came with two pairs, though all of the original glasses are quite rare. If the comics survive, the glasses are usually long gone.

Top artists, a who's who of 1950s comics, took part in the 3-D revolution, including Matt Baker, Sy Barry, L.B. Cole, Johnny Craig, Jack Davis, Bill Elder, George Evans, Al Feldstein, Al Hartley, Russ Heath, Graham Ingels, Al Jaffee,

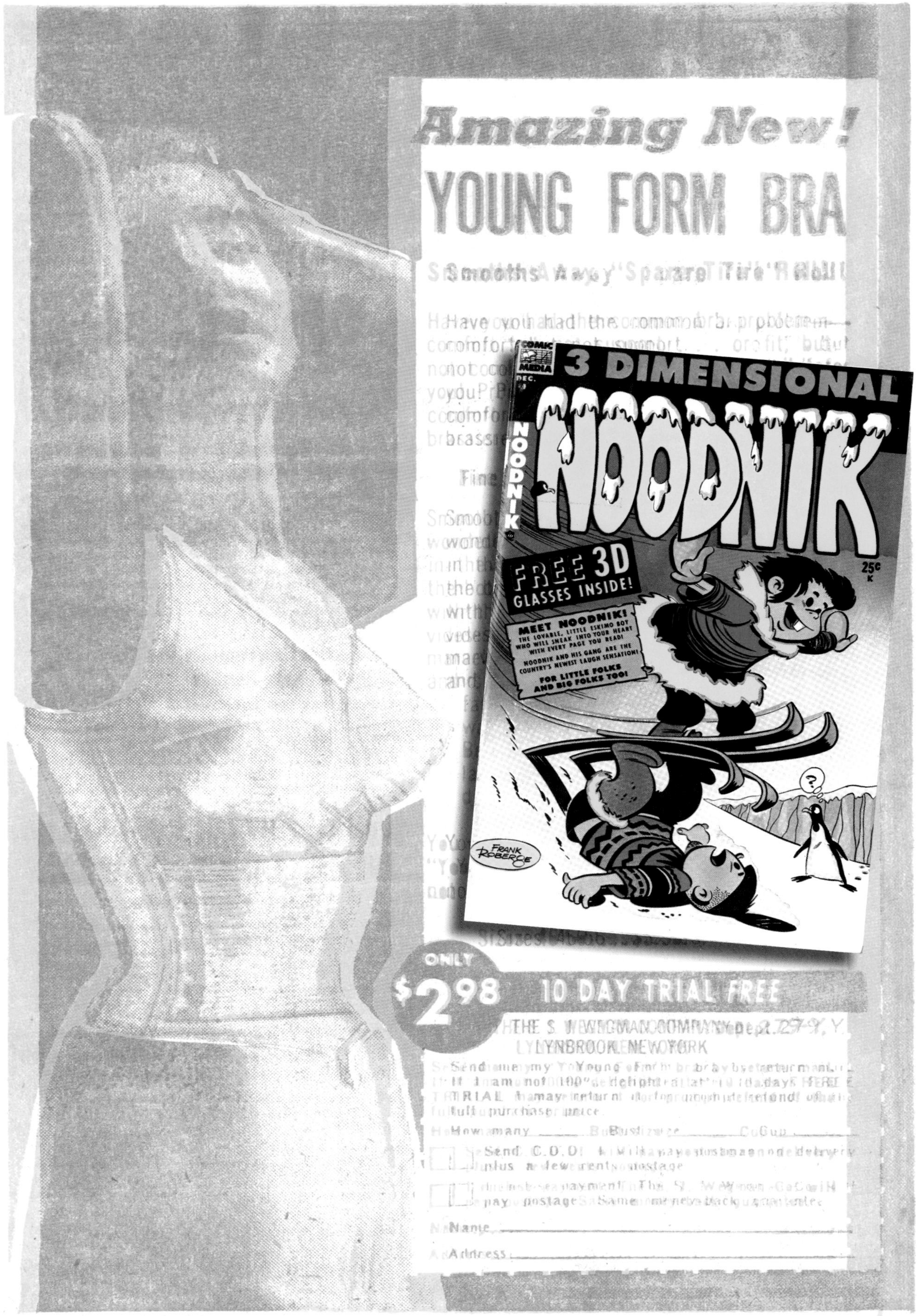
Amazing New!
YOUNG FORM BRA
COMIC MEDIA
DEC.
3 DIMENSIONAL
NOODNIK
FREE 3D GLASSES INSIDE!
25¢
MEET NOODNIK! THE LOVABLE, LITTLE ESKIMO BOY WHO WILL SNEAK INTO YOUR HEART WITH EVERY PAGE YOU READ! NOODNIK AND HIS GANG ARE THE COUNTRY'S NEWEST LAUGH SENSATION!
FOR LITTLE FOLKS AND BIG FOLKS TOO!
FRANK ROBERGE
ONLY $2.98
10 DAY TRIAL FREE
LYNBROOK, NEW YORK
Name
Address

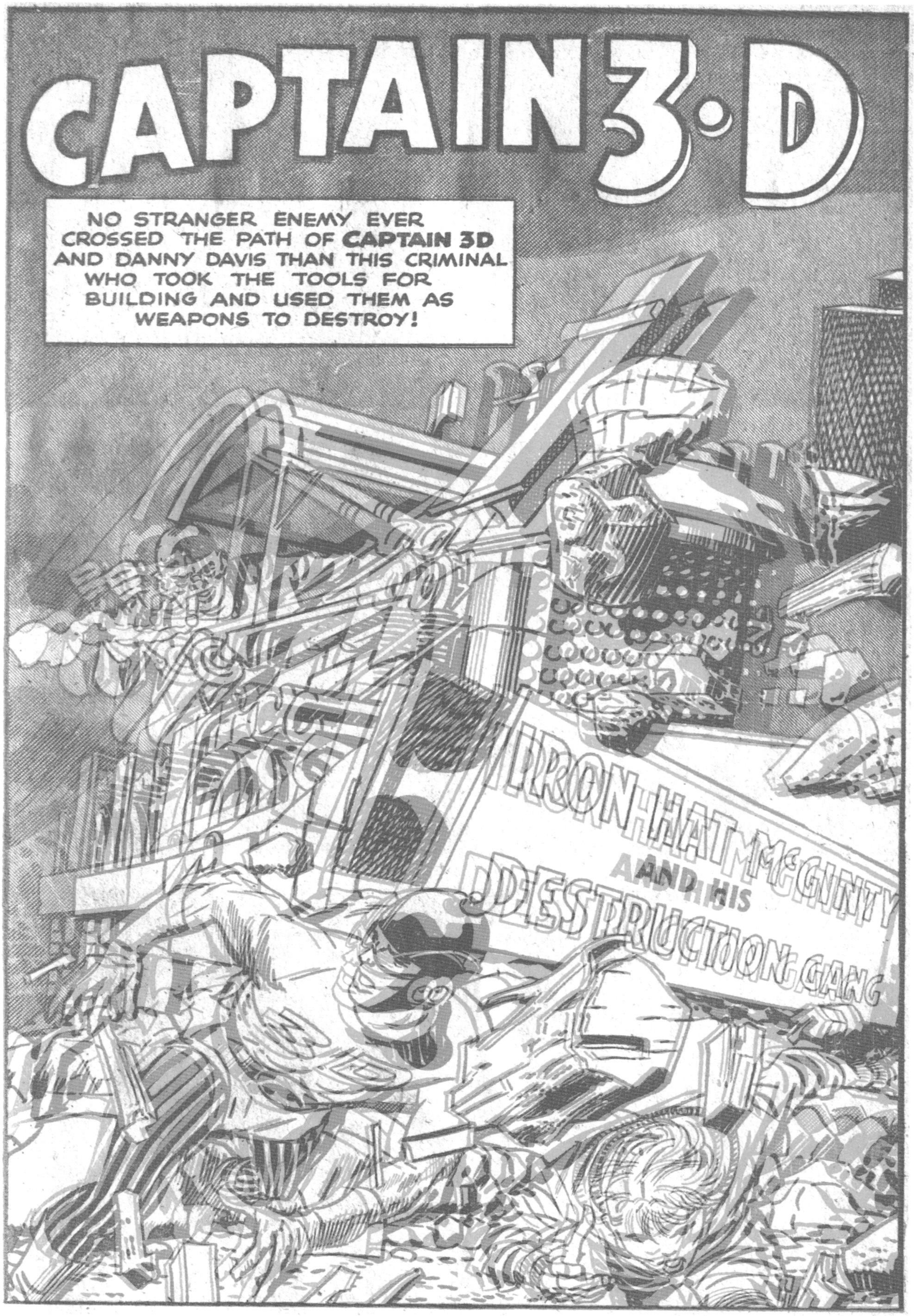
CAPTAIN 3-D
NO STRANGER ENEMY EVER CROSSED THE PATH OF CAPTAIN 3D AND DANNY DAVIS THAN THIS CRIMINAL WHO TOOK THE TOOLS FOR BUILDING AND USED THEM AS WEAPONS TO DESTROY!
IRON HAT McGINTY AND HIS DESTRUCTION GANG

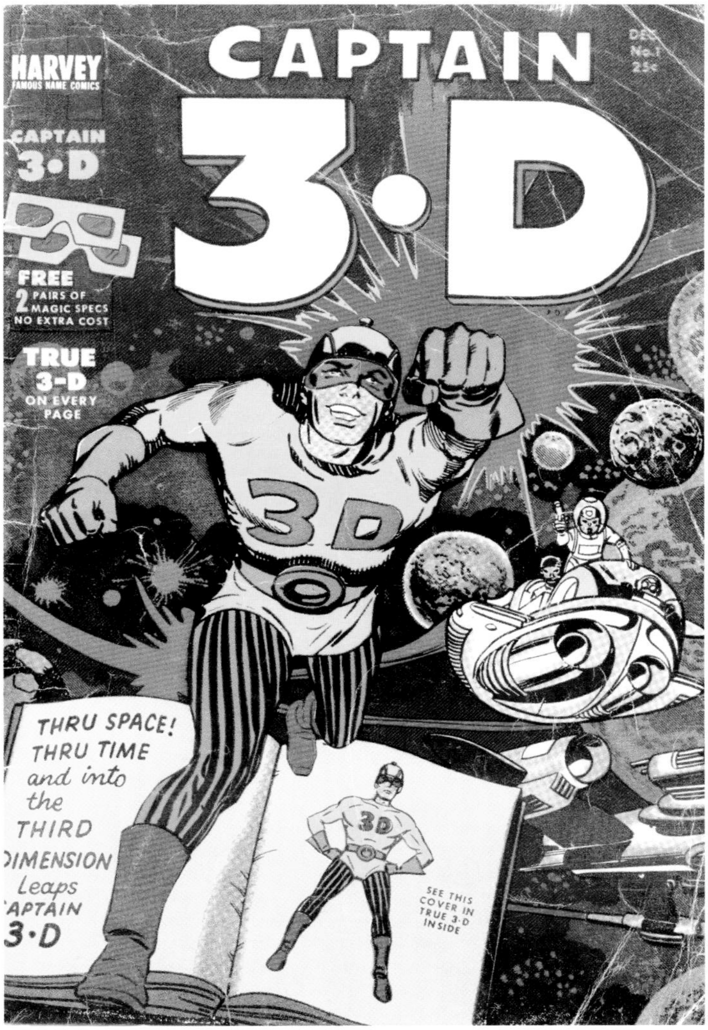
HARVEY
FAMOUS NAME COMICS
CAPTAIN
3-D
DEC
No.1
25¢
CAPTAIN
3-D
FREE
2 PAIRS OF MAGIC SPECS NO EXTRA COST
TRUE
3-D
ON EVERY PAGE
3D
THRU SPACE!
THRU TIME
and into
the
THIRD
DIMENSION
Leaps
CAPTAIN
3-D
3D
SEE THIS COVER IN TRUE 3-D INSIDE

LEFT-HAND PAGE AND ABOVE ***Captain 3-D* #1, December 1953. Artwork for Captain 3-D was by the Simon and Kirby shop, including Steve Ditko, doing some of his first work in comics, and the great Mort Meskin.**

Bob Kane (or more likely his ghosts), Bernie Krigstein, Harvey Kurtzman, Otto Messmer, Jim Mooney, Howard Nostrand, A.W. Nugent, Bob Powell, Milt Stein, Alex Toth, George Tuska, Maurice Whitman, Bill Woggon, Wally Wood, and, of course, Joe Kubert and Norman Maurer.

As the fad became feverish, even minor toons and unknowns got the 3-D comic book treatment: Little Eva, Jet Pup, The Hawk, Noodnik, Billy and Buggy Bear, The Space Kat-ets, along with the major characters. Even Jesus Christ was 3-D-ized in the comic book *The First Christmas*, sporting a cover by Kelly Freas, later renowned for delineating Alfred E. Neuman on the covers of *Mad*.

In the *Starlog Photo Guidebook Fantastic 3-D*, editor Jack Adler told 3-D historian David Hutchison how the DC 3-D comics came about, "I was working with DC, which was then known as National Periodicals, doing color separations. There were rumors in the industry that someone was toying with the idea of 3-D for comics. Sol Harrison came over to me and asked if I had ever heard of such a thing and could I do it. I said yes it could be done. And he said do it. It was just as simple as that. My interests lay in the area of optics and photography, how and why it works. I took apart a panel and reassembled it on cels to show how it could be done... I think it was of two mice chasing each other, we used to do a lot of animal comics at DC."

Adler went on to note, "I worked out a formula that would allow you to create the illusion of correct relative size and distance. In other words, you could create the effect of something being ten inches or ten feet in front of you. Eventually, I applied for a patent for my method of creating 3-D drawings, but I was turned down on the premise that I used materials and methods from other things."

The *Superman* and *Batman* comics Adler produced for DC Comics weren't the only superhero comics during the 3-D mania. There was a superhero especially created for the 3-D comics medium by the co-creators of Captain America. The Simon and Kirby team conceived... Captain 3-D! Artists working with Joe Simon and Jack Kirby on this project included Mort Meskin and a young Steve Ditko, who was doing some of his very first work.

In his book *The Comic Book Makers,* Simon relates how Al Harvey of Harvey Comics called him on a rainy day one month after *Mighty Mouse* flew off the comic book racks. Harvey said he had a crash project and needed a team to tackle it. Simon said that his studio was booked, but was lured by Harvey's offer to pay double the standard page fee. Simon replied, "When do we start?"

Joe Simon, Jack Kirby, Mort Meskin, Steve Ditko, and other artists and letterers hoofed a few blocks over to Harvey Publications on Broadway in New York City. Harvey rented the entire 15th floor of a building to house the team who would quickly churn out the 3-D book. Harvey claimed that an artist had brought them an improved technique for creating the 3-D. The publisher walked the all-star team through the process. Simon relates that the time-sucking, tedious task proved to be a financial loss for the art shop.

Harvey also hired the Bob Powell Studio to produce 3-D books. Powell worked with Howard Nostrand, George

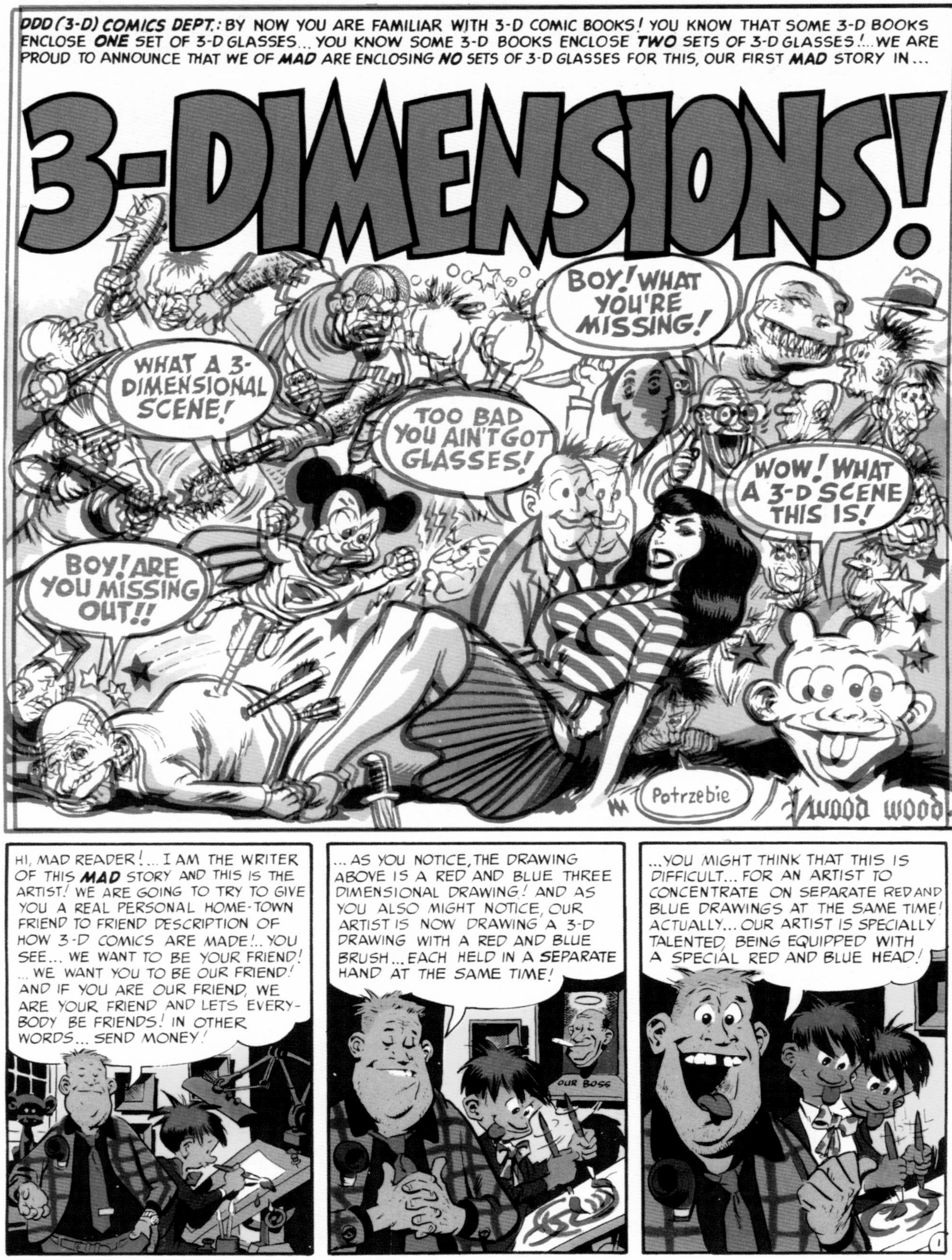
DDD (3-D) COMICS DEPT.: BY NOW YOU ARE FAMILIAR WITH 3-D COMIC BOOKS! YOU KNOW THAT SOME 3-D BOOKS ENCLOSE ONE SET OF 3-D GLASSES... YOU KNOW SOME 3-D BOOKS ENCLOSE TWO SETS OF 3-D GLASSES!...WE ARE PROUD TO ANNOUNCE THAT WE OF MAD ARE ENCLOSING NO SETS OF 3-D GLASSES FOR THIS, OUR FIRST MAD STORY IN...
3-DIMENSIONS!
BOY! WHAT YOU'RE MISSING!
WHAT A 3-DIMENSIONAL SCENE!
TOO BAD YOU AIN'T GOT GLASSES!
WOW! WHAT A 3-D SCENE THIS IS!
BOY! ARE YOU MISSING OUT!!
Potrzebie
wood wood
HI, MAD READER!... I AM THE WRITER OF THIS MAD STORY AND THIS IS THE ARTIST! WE ARE GOING TO TRY TO GIVE YOU A REAL PERSONAL HOME-TOWN FRIEND TO FRIEND DESCRIPTION OF HOW 3-D COMICS ARE MADE!.. YOU SEE... WE WANT TO BE YOUR FRIEND! ...WE WANT YOU TO BE OUR FRIEND! AND IF YOU ARE OUR FRIEND, WE ARE YOUR FRIEND AND LETS EVERY-BODY BE FRIENDS! IN OTHER WORDS... SEND MONEY!
...AS YOU NOTICE, THE DRAWING ABOVE IS A RED AND BLUE THREE DIMENSIONAL DRAWING! AND AS YOU ALSO MIGHT NOTICE, OUR ARTIST IS NOW DRAWING A 3-D DRAWING WITH A RED AND BLUE BRUSH... EACH HELD IN A SEPARATE HAND AT THE SAME TIME!
OUR BOSS
...YOU MIGHT THINK THAT THIS IS DIFFICULT... FOR AN ARTIST TO CONCENTRATE ON SEPARATE RED AND BLUE DRAWINGS AT THE SAME TIME! ACTUALLY... OUR ARTIST IS SPECIALLY TALENTED, BEING EQUIPPED WITH A SPECIAL RED AND BLUE HEAD!
1

350-320
Search Room
Oct. 13, 1936.
F. H. OWENS
2,057,051
METHOD OF DRAWING AND PHOTOGRAPHING STEREOSCOPIC PICTURES IN RELIEF
Filed Aug. 11, 1934
2 Sheets-Sheet 1
Freeman H. Owens.

Oct. 13, 1936.
F. H. OWENS
2,057,051
METHOD OF DRAWING AND PHOTOGRAPHING STEREOSCOPIC PICTURES IN RELIEF
Filed Aug. 11, 1934
2 Sheets-Sheet 2
Cells in register as set up for right eye
Plan of Camera (not moved)
Plan of Holder (not moved)
Cells in register as set up for left eye
Inventor.
Freeman H. Owens

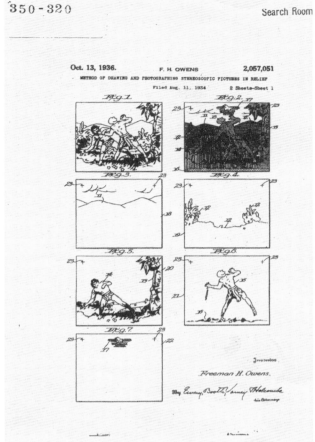

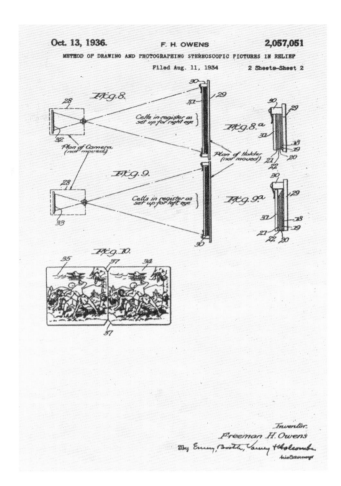

Siefringer, and Marty Epp to create some of the most fantastic 3-D comic stories. The plastic acetate used in the creation of the art could only be drawn on with a sticky, thick ink that Nostrand complained was like drawing "with tar." This team added the innovation of doing background shadings with Craftint paper wherein a chemical solution was applied to obtain a mechanical halftone, which made the far perspective details recede further. It was Powell and his associates that came up with *3-D Blinkey*, examples of which are reprinted in this book. The results of their enthusiastic contributions were spectacular.

Nostrand's grousing at the difficulty of producing art for 3-D was loudly echoed in an interview by Steven Ringgenberg with Angelo Torres. The artist says, "When I first met Al Williamson, he was working with George Evans on a 3-D EC science fiction job, *The Planetoid*. That's actually the first work I ever did for Al, and I did very little, some backgrounds, and I cleaned up some of the overlays. The pages were an absolute mess—each page had about three or four acetate overlays. The 3-D effect was done using layers of acetate over the art, and the acetate had to be whited-out from behind. The paint kept flaking off because the pages had sat around for so long. The acetate would buckle, and when the paint flaked off, we had to paint it in again. It was in a shambles. When Al delivered this, it was like bringing in the Dead Sea Scrolls. The thing was just falling apart. Beyond what little I did on this job, I know nothing else about it because I never saw it after that. I think they finally decided 3-D was dead and printed it flat."

There were many reasons why 3-D quickly died. It was a gimmick—a very good one, but a gimmick nonetheless. Often the printing and the paper weren't of good quality. Some publishers hurriedly converted existing art to 3-D, failing to make maximum use of the technique. In *Jungle Thrills* (Star Publications) there's even one page where the blue color didn't print in the rush and, of course, it fell... *flat!* There could be something lacking in not having comics in their usual full-color glory. Producing the art was laborious and the newsstand price high. And the books could be tedious to read, especially the dialogue balloons.

Above all there was oversaturation. Within a few short months, almost 100 3-D comics (including the non-anaglyph comics and the Cheerios/Disney premiums) were brought to market by nearly 15 different publishers, including some that sprang up just to capitalize on the fad. Artist Howard Nostrand said, "It all went for naught, because the whole thing died very rapidly."

LEFT-HAND PAGE **Harvey Kurtzman and Wally Wood send up the 3-D comic craze and the splash panel almost works in actual 3-D! (Though it reads better if you put the red lens on your right eye and the green lens on your left).** ***Mad*** **#12, June 1954.**

ABOVE **Freeman H. Owens' 1936 patent for drawing and photographing stereographic pictures was unearthed by comics historian Ken Quattro.**

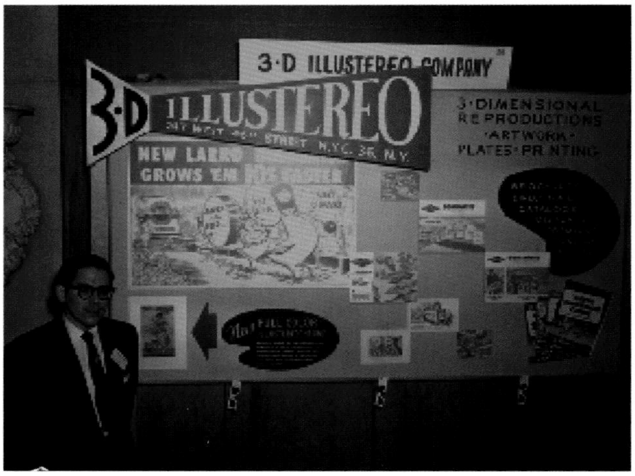
3-D ILLUSTEREO COMPANY
3-D ILLUSTEREO
3-DIMENSIONAL
REPRODUCTIONS
ARTWORK
PLATES PRINTING

The publisher there at the start invested the most—and lost the most. *The Three Stooges Scrapbook* details Archer St. John's rise and fall with 3-D comics. Norman Maurer recalled, "St. John wanted to put out 35 additional books in 3-D. He believed if he flooded the market it would generate millions for his company and him personally."

To maintain his increased production schedule, St. John expanded his New York offices on 230 West 42nd Street from one to two floors and rented hotel rooms for additional working space. Maurer recalls how St. John's super expansion turned into an unforgettable fiasco, "Joe and I warned him this was a temporary fad. He wouldn't listen. He put 50 girls to work inking and painting artwork. He dumped in every penny he had and borrowed to put a mess of 3-D books out. The demand stopped, he was stuck with the books, and lost a fortune, which eventually caused him to go bankrupt."

Rather than bringing lasting fortune, his trip into the 3-D realm eventually led St. John to Debt, Despair, and possibly self-inflicted Death. Archer failed to achieve substantial success with his subsequent publishing efforts and apparently had a troubled marriage. In August 1955, Archer St. John was found dead from an overdose of sleeping pills.

Ken Quattro uncovered the *The New York Times* obit of August 14, 1955, which Quattro comments "reads like the opening lines of a James M. Cain novel."

PUBLISHER FOUND DEAD
Archer St. John Succumbs in Friend's Penthouse

Archer St. John, 54 years old (sic), publisher of Secret Life *and other magazines, was found dead yesterday afternoon in the penthouse apartment of a friend, the police reported.*
The friend, Mrs. Frances Stratford of 170 East Seventy-Ninth Street, told the police he visited her Friday night in her six-room duplex penthouse and complained about 10:30 that he felt ill. "He lay down on the couch," she said. At 11:30 a.m. yesterday she found him still there and was unable to rouse him. Mrs. Stratford called a physician, who pronounced Mr.

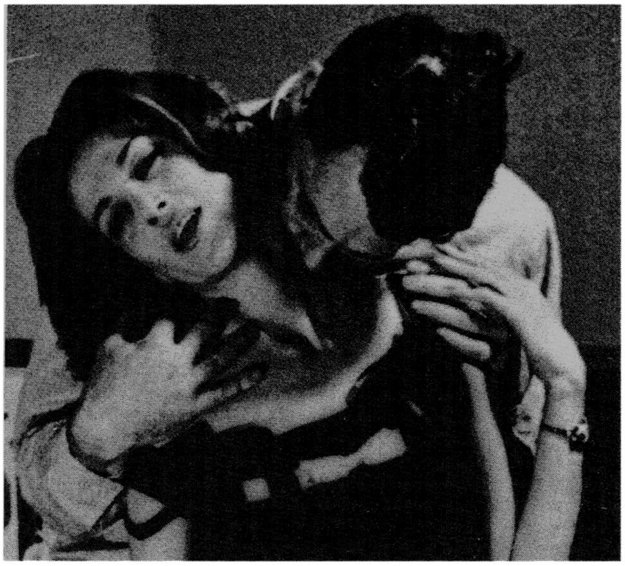

St. John dead. The police listed the cause as an apparent overdose of sleeping pills, pending an autopsy. Mr. St. John had been staying at the New York Athletic Club. He maintained an office at 545 Fifth Avenue.

St. John's demise may have been self-inflicted. In Stud Terkel's *Coming of Age* (1995), Archer's sibling Robert perfunctorily stated, "My brother had committed suicide." But some believe that Archer's death was accidental, arguing

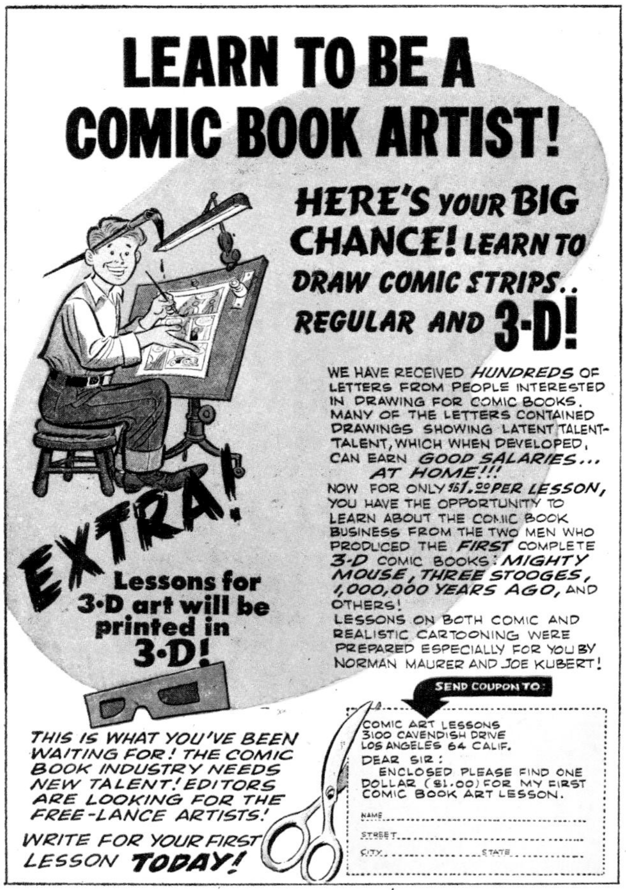
LEARN TO BE A
COMIC BOOK ARTIST!
HERE'S YOUR BIG CHANCE! LEARN TO DRAW COMIC STRIPS.. REGULAR AND 3-D!
WE HAVE RECEIVED HUNDREDS OF LETTERS FROM PEOPLE INTERESTED IN DRAWING FOR COMIC BOOKS. MANY OF THE LETTERS CONTAINED DRAWINGS SHOWING LATENT TALENT-TALENT, WHICH WHEN DEVELOPED, CAN EARN GOOD SALARIES... AT HOME!!!
NOW FOR ONLY $1.00 PER LESSON, YOU HAVE THE OPPORTUNITY TO LEARN ABOUT THE COMIC BOOK BUSINESS FROM THE TWO MEN WHO PRODUCED THE FIRST COMPLETE 3-D COMIC BOOKS: MIGHTY MOUSE, THREE STOOGES, 1,000,000 YEARS AGO, AND OTHERS!
LESSONS ON BOTH COMIC AND REALISTIC CARTOONING WERE PREPARED ESPECIALLY FOR YOU BY NORMAN MAURER AND JOE KUBERT!
EXTRA!
Lessons for 3-D art will be printed in 3-D!
SEND COUPON TO:
THIS IS WHAT YOU'VE BEEN WAITING FOR! THE COMIC BOOK INDUSTRY NEEDS NEW TALENT! EDITORS ARE LOOKING FOR THE FREE-LANCE ARTISTS!
WRITE FOR YOUR FIRST LESSON TODAY!
COMIC ART LESSONS
3100 CAVENDISH DRIVE
LOS ANGELES 64 CALIF.
DEAR SIR:
ENCLOSED PLEASE FIND ONE DOLLAR ($1.00) FOR MY FIRST COMIC BOOK ART LESSON.
NAME
STREET
CITY
STATE

LEFT-HAND PAGE, LEFT **Beyond comics! Leonard Maurer set up at a trade show to promote 3-D technology to the advertising community.**

LEFT-HAND PAGE, RIGHT **Comic book artist Howard Nostrand often used himself in reference photos for his artwork. "The reason I'm in them is 'cause I'm cheap!" Photo from Bill Spicer's *Graphic Story Magazine* #16, 1971.**

LEFT-HAND PAGE, BOTTOM **This correspondence course produced by Joe Kubert promised to teach comic book artistry and even how to do 3-D comics in *WHACK* #2, December 1953. While the course never got past lesson #1, Kubert today heads The Kubert School, an esteemed art institution in Dover, N.J.**

RIGHT **And in conclusion, *G.I. Jane* #5, 1953; artist, Bill Williams.**

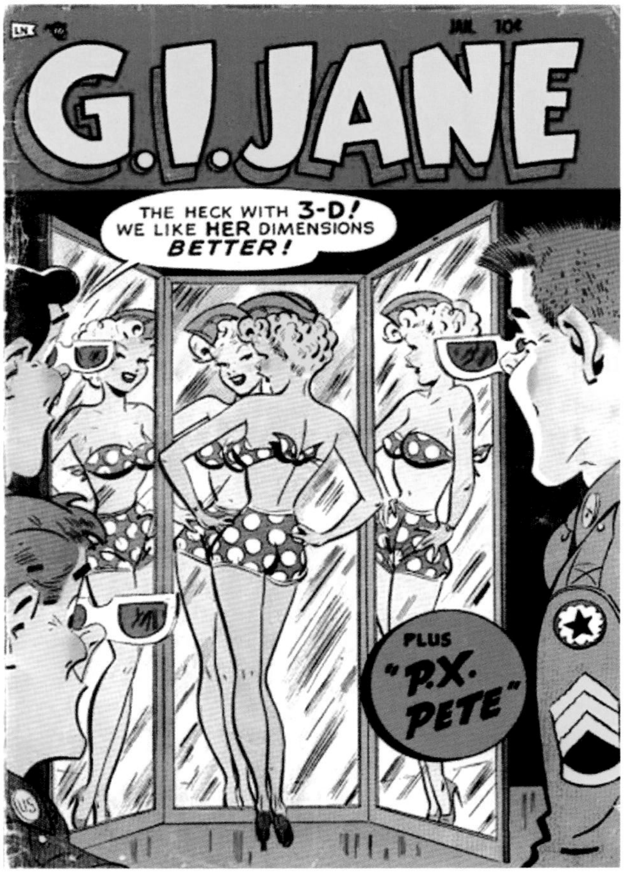
JAN. 10¢
G.I. JANE
THE HECK WITH 3-D! WE LIKE HER DIMENSIONS BETTER!
PLUS "P.X. PETE"

that he had much to live for. St. John had continued to publish some non 3-D comics. He was having success with the scandal magazine *Secret Life* and the best selling crime fiction periodical *Manhunt*. Additionally, the publisher was preparing to launch the literate *Playboy*-type men's magazine, *Nugget*.

It's no secret that the competition in the field of 3-D comics was fierce, even cutthroat. The publishers, who envisioned 3-D comics saving their sinking ships in the '50s, had attempted to grab all they could of the imagined life-preserver.

In the May 2001 issue of *3D News: The Newsletter of the Stereo Club of Southern California,* Leonard Maurer told Ray Zone (producer of many modern 3-D comics), "What eventually bankrupted St. John was his attempt to block all the other publishers by buying up, in carload quantities, all the factory output for over 6 months of dyed acetate (made to my specifications, and produced by Celanese Corporation). He also bought up carload quantities of comic book newsprint paper. He didn't succeed in blocking everybody, since there were other major acetate and paper manufacturers, but he did hold up a few..."

Leonard Maurer told Ray Zone that EC/*Mad* publisher William M. Gaines found Patent no. 2,057,051 filed on October 13, 1936 by Freeman H. Owens "a Method of Drawing and Photographing Stereoscopic Pictures in Relief." Maurer said, "A month before its expiration, Gaines bought the Freeman Owens patent—which never turned up in our patent search—from the dying inventor for a few hundred bucks." Then Gaines, according to Maurer, initiated suits for patent infringement on all the publishers of 3-D comics, including St. John.

"That suit," says Maurer, was "based on surreptitious individual tape recordings of meetings with Joe and Norman, where Gaines accused me of stealing the Owens patent out of the patent office. Big joke!"

There are differing accounts from all sides as to why editor Harvey Kurtzman left *Mad*. Maurer alleges the conflict over 3-D "triggered the resignation of Harvey Kurtzman and Bill Elder, who had gotten confidential disclosures of the entire process from me and felt betrayed by Gaines when phony accusations came out in court."

Leonard Maurer concluded, "The famous Judge Liebowitz threw the case out with the comment that the Gaines deposition read like a 'fantasy story out of *Mad* comics.'"

3-D comes and goes. 3-D movies are back in a big way. We're now well due for another 3-D comics craze.

The January 1954 issue of *Newsdealer* magazine breathlessly proclaimed 3-D as "the newest development in the presentation of pictures." The trade journal went on to say, "It is altogether likely that, whatever succeeding years may have in store, future students will find this a highly interesting and important milestone on a most important road. It is a far cry from crude, angular, flint scratch drawings on rock to printed pictures of naturally-rounded objects appearing on a magazine page in perspective, very much as they do in the world around us. Here, certainly, is another convincing evidence of mankind's eternal determination to progress; constantly to improve on earlier efforts; to do better, today, than the best of yesterday."

Amazing 3-D Comics' look back at the best of these initial forays into another dimension might provide inspiration for the future. So, don your Free Super-Sight Magic 3-D Eyepiece Viewer Space Goggles and experience, as the cover of *3-D Love* trumpeted, "VIVID... DYNAMIC... EXCITING... CLOSER-TO-LIFE STORIES IN CLOSER-TO-LIFE 3RD DIMENSION!"

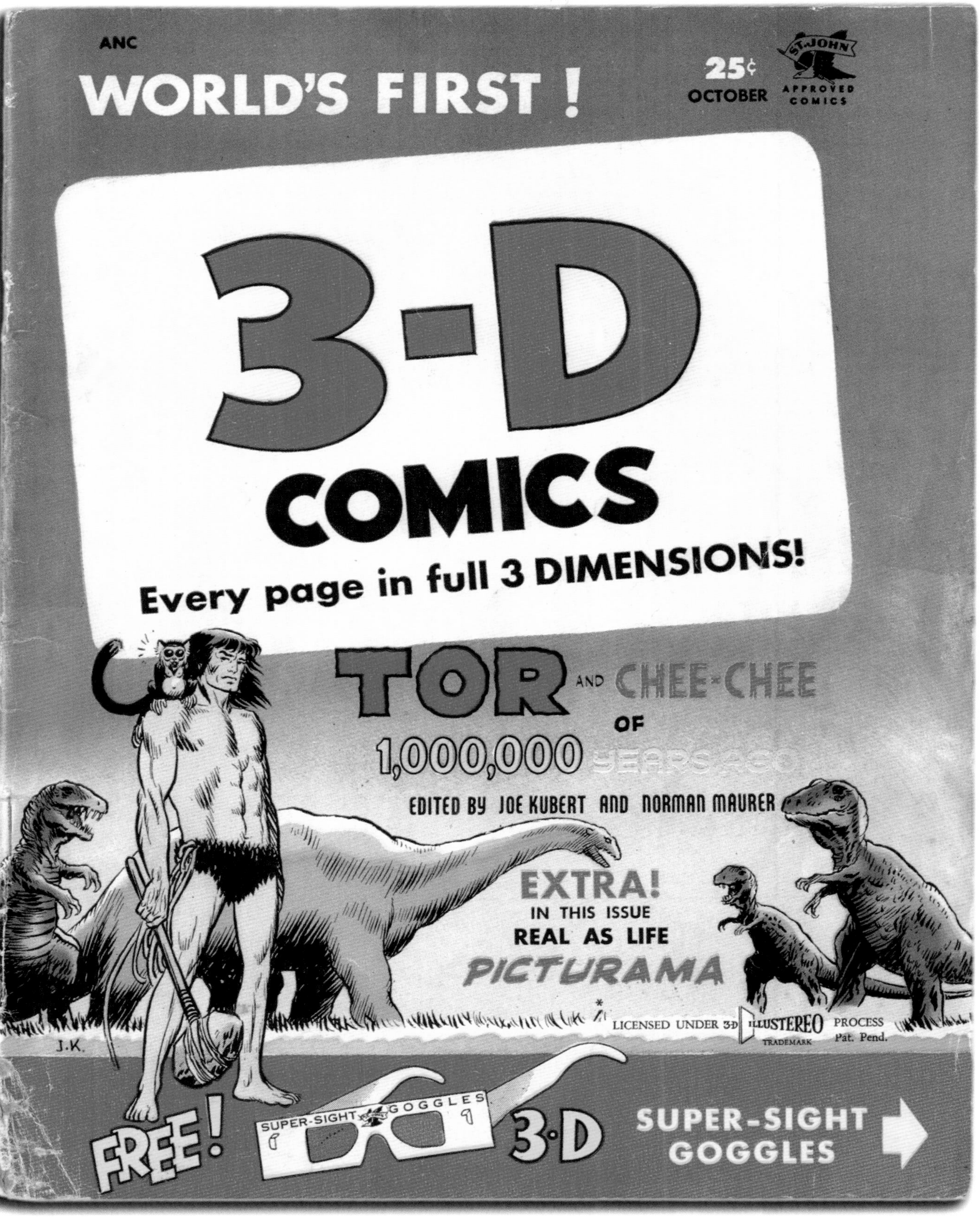
ANC
WORLD'S FIRST !
25¢
OCTOBER
ST. JOHN
APPROVED COMICS
3-D
COMICS
Every page in full 3 DIMENSIONS!
TOR AND CHEE-CHEE
OF
1,000,000 YEARS AGO
EDITED BY JOE KUBERT AND NORMAN MAURER
EXTRA!
IN THIS ISSUE
REAL AS LIFE
PICTURAMA
LICENSED UNDER 3-D ILLUSTEREO PROCESS
TRADEMARK
Pat. Pend.
J.K.
FREE!
SUPER-SIGHT GOGGLES
3-D
SUPER-SIGHT
GOGGLES

3-D Comics #2, October 1953; artist, Joe Kubert.

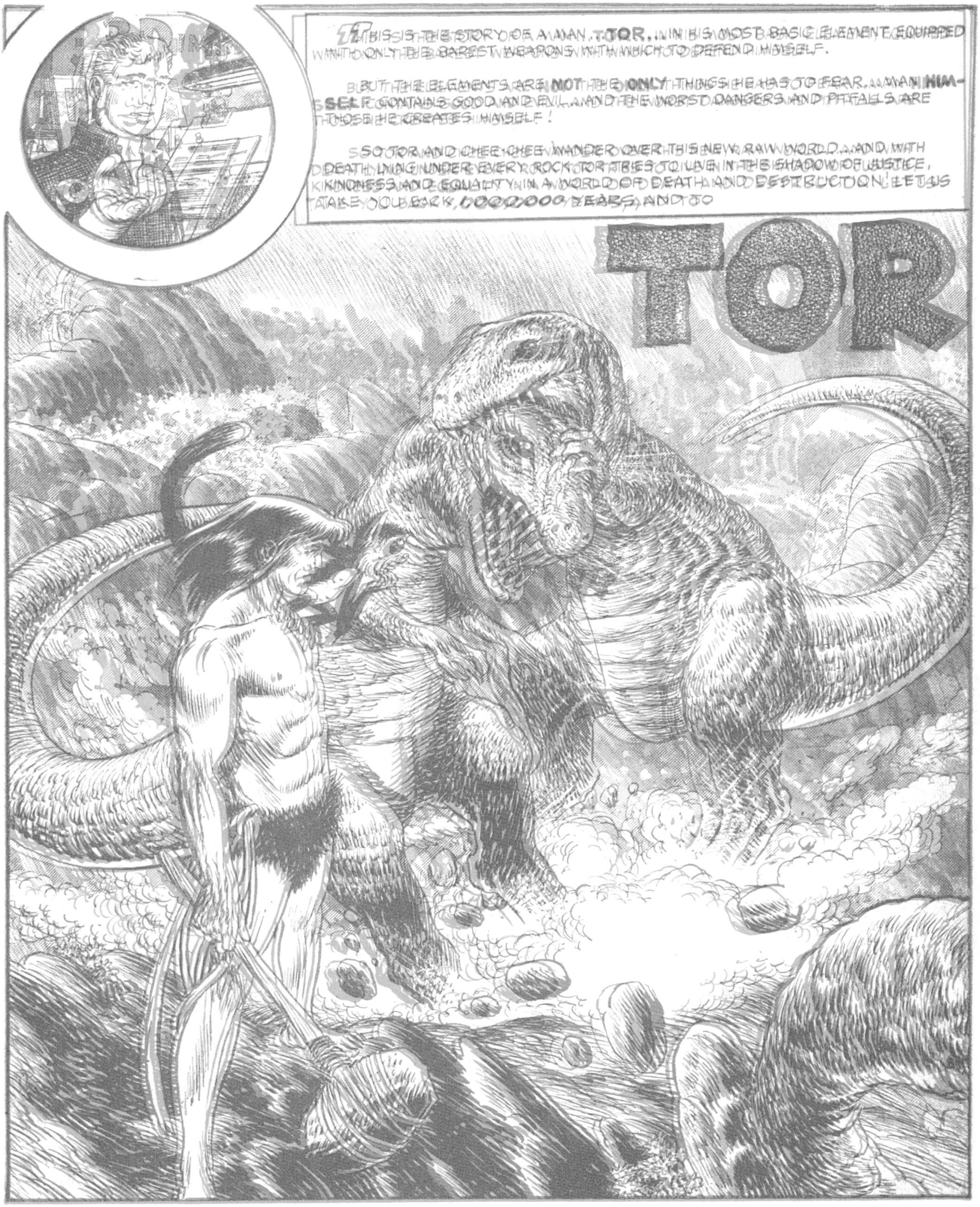
THIS IS THE STORY OF A MAN...TOR...IN HIS MOST BASIC ELEMENT EQUIPPED WITH ONLY THE BAREST WEAPONS WITH WHICH TO DEFEND HIMSELF.
BUT THE ELEMENTS ARE NOT THE ONLY THINGS HE HAS TO FEAR...MAN HIMSELF CONTAINS GOOD AND EVIL...AND THE WORST DANGERS AND PITFALLS ARE THOSE HE CREATES HIMSELF!
SO TOR AND CHEE-CHEE WANDER OVER THIS NEW, RAW WORLD...AND WITH DEATH LYING UNDER EVERY ROCK, TOR TRIES TO LIVE IN THE SHADOW OF JUSTICE, KINDNESS AND EQUALITY IN A WORLD OF DEATH AND DESTRUCTION! LET US TAKE YOU BACK 1,000,000 YEARS, AND TO
TOR

Joe Kubert himself introduces this tale of his signature character, Tor.

STEAMING LANDS, VOID OF ALL LIFE LIE BEFORE TOR... MOLTEN ROCK SPEWED FORTH ACRID VAPOR AS TOR SCANNED THE VAST DESOLATION...

CHEE-CHEE'S EXCITED CHATTERING BRINGS TOR TO THE MOUTH OF A CRATER...

WHAT IS IT, LITTLE ONE? IS SOMETHING DOWN THERE?

CHEE CHEE

HOLD FAST, LITTLE ONE...

...PERHAPS SOMEONE HAS FALLEN...

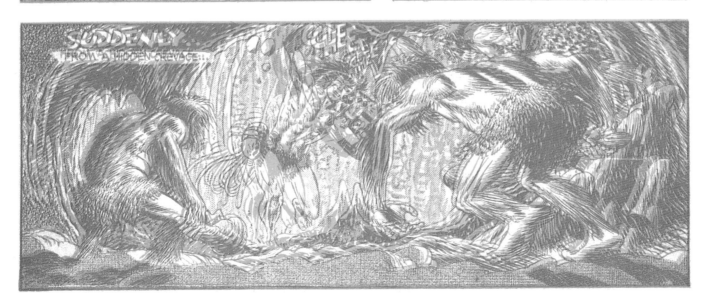

SUDDENLY... FROM A HIDDEN CREVICE...

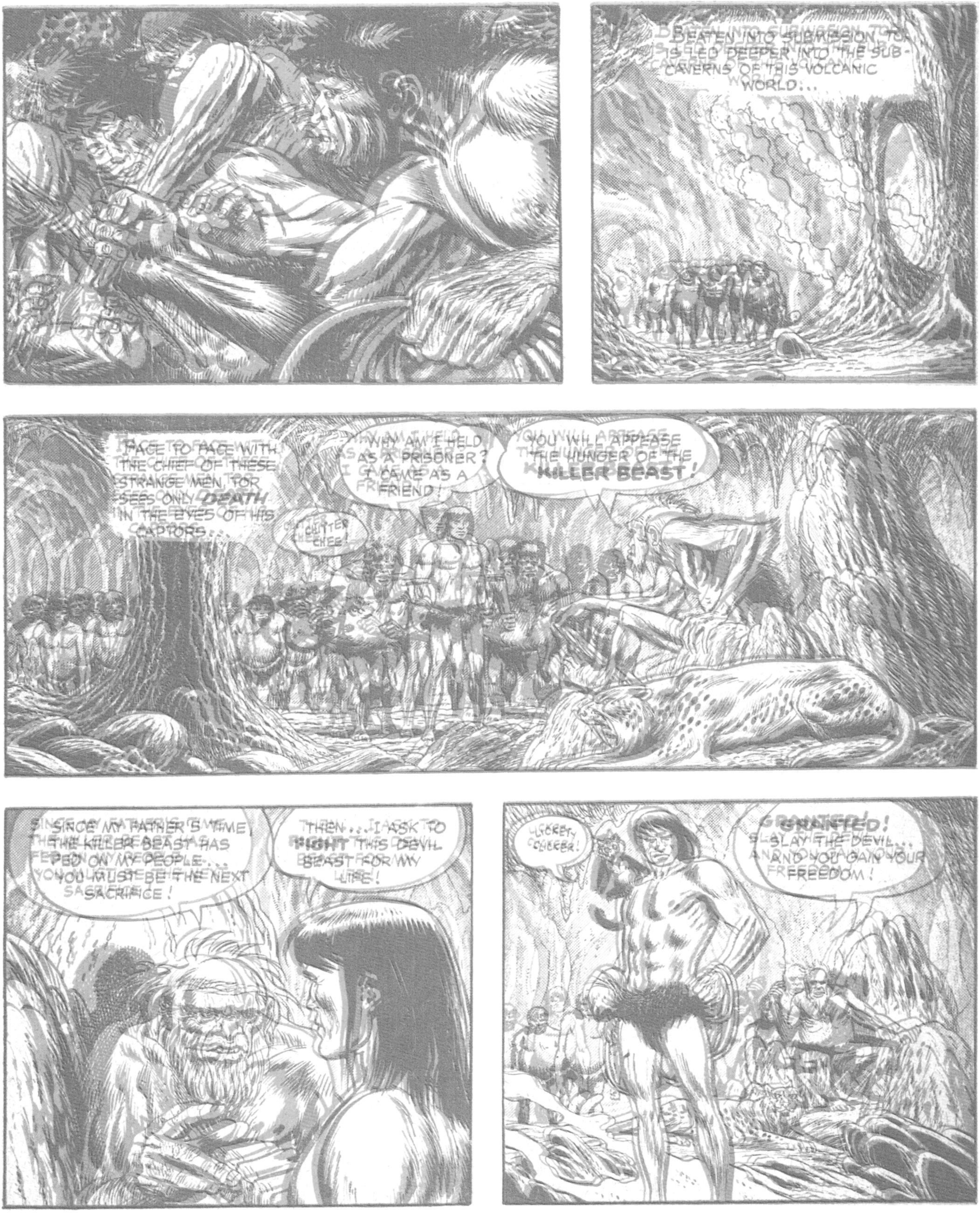
BEATEN INTO SUBMISSION TOR IS LED DEEPER INTO THE SUB-CAVERNS OF THIS VOLCANIC WORLD...
FACE TO FACE WITH THE CHIEF OF THESE STRANGE MEN, TOR SEES ONLY DEATH IN THE EYES OF HIS CAPTORS...
WHY AM I HELD AS A PRISONER? I CAME AS A FRIEND!
YOU WILL APPEASE THE HUNGER OF THE KILLER BEAST!
CHITTER CHEE!
SINCE MY FATHER'S TIME THE KILLER BEAST HAS FED ON MY PEOPLE... YOU MUST BE THE NEXT SACRIFICE!
THEN... I ASK TO FIGHT THIS DEVIL BEAST FOR MY LIFE!
LICKETY CLICKER!
GRANTED! SLAY THE DEVIL... AND YOU GAIN YOUR FREEDOM!

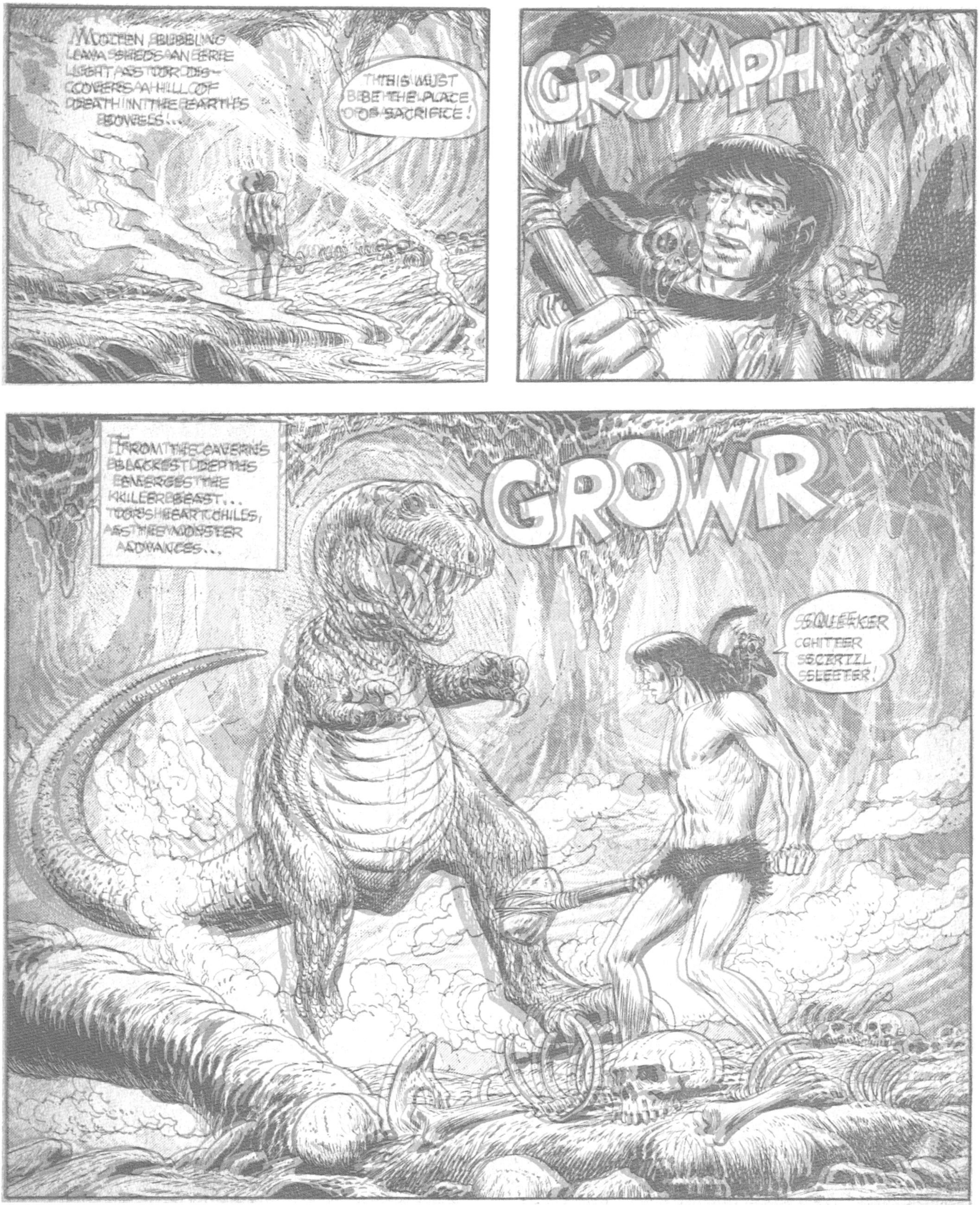
MOLTEN BUBBLING LAVA SHEDS AN EERIE LIGHT AS TOR DIS- COVERS A HILL OF DEATH IN THE EARTH'S BOWELS...
THIS MUST BE THE PLACE OF SACRIFICE!
GRUMPH
FROM THE CAVERN'S BLACKEST DEPTHS EMERGES THE KILLER BEAST... TOR'S HEART CHILLS, AS THE MONSTER ADVANCES...
GROWR
SQUEEKER CHITTER SCZRTZL SLEETER!

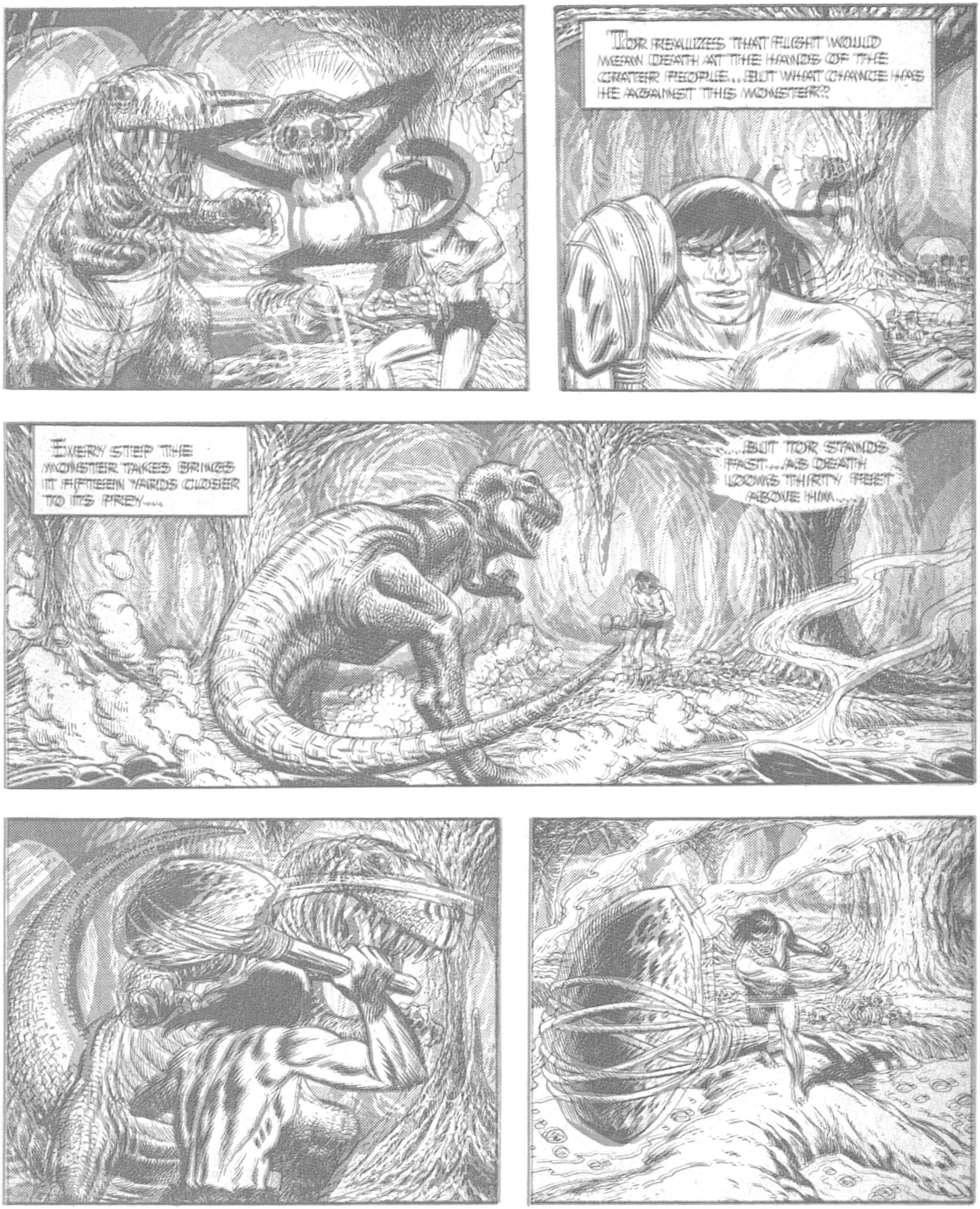

TOR REALIZES THAT FLIGHT WOULD MEAN DEATH AT THE HANDS OF THE CRATER PEOPLE... BUT WHAT CHANCE HAS HE AGAINST THIS MONSTER??
EVERY STEP THE MONSTER TAKES BRINGS IT FIFTEEN YARDS CLOSER TO ITS PREY....
...BUT TOR STANDS FAST...AS DEATH LOOMS THIRTY FEET ABOVE HIM....

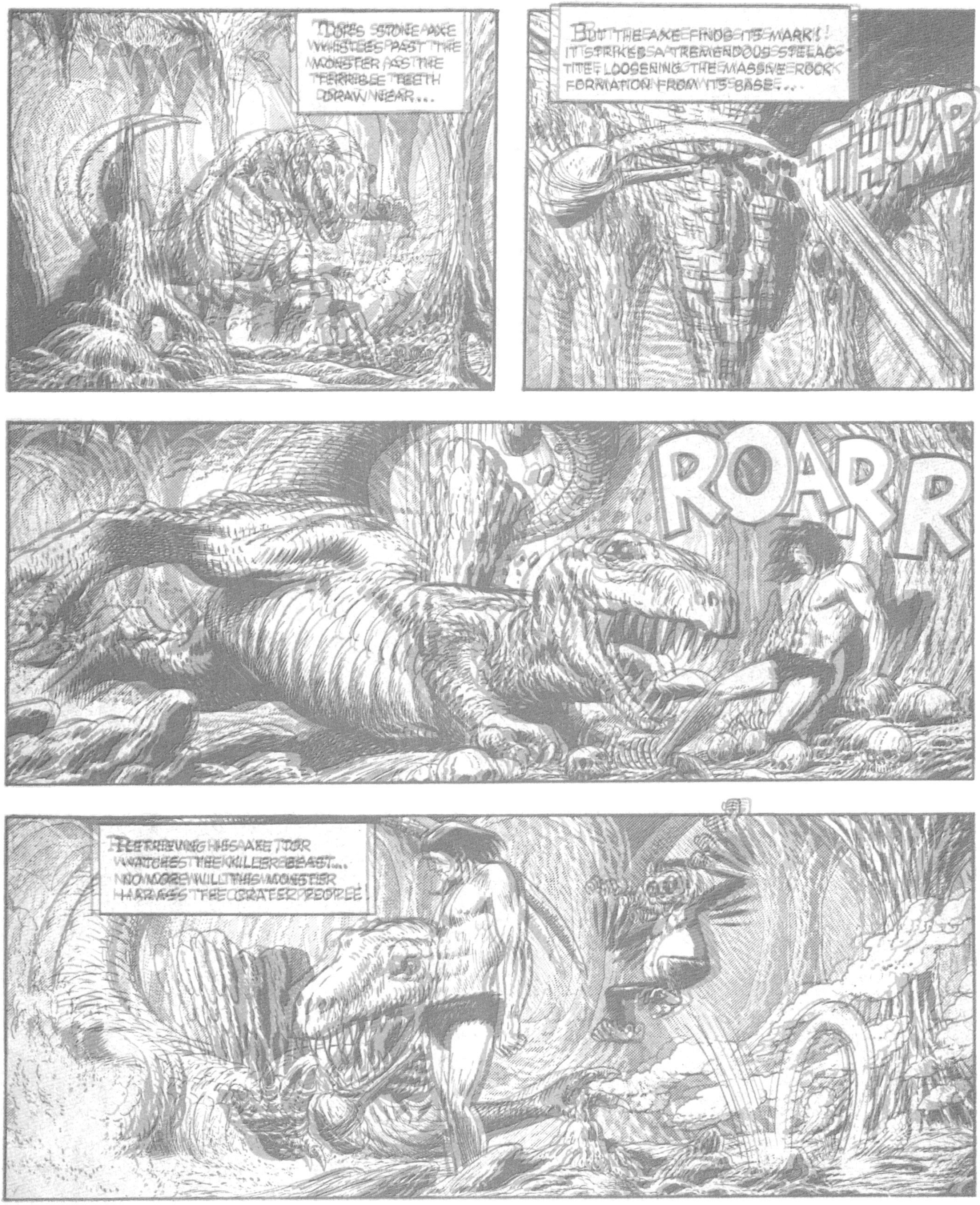
TOR'S STONE AXE WHISTLES PAST THE MONSTER AS THE TERRIBLE TEETH DRAW NEAR...
BUT THE AXE FINDS ITS MARK! IT STRIKES A TREMENDOUS STALAC-TITE, LOOSENING THE MASSIVE ROCK FORMATION FROM ITS BASE...
THUMP
ROARR
RETRIEVING HIS AXE, TOR WATCHES THE KILLER BEAST... NO MORE WILL THIS MONSTER HARASS THE CRATER PEOPLE!

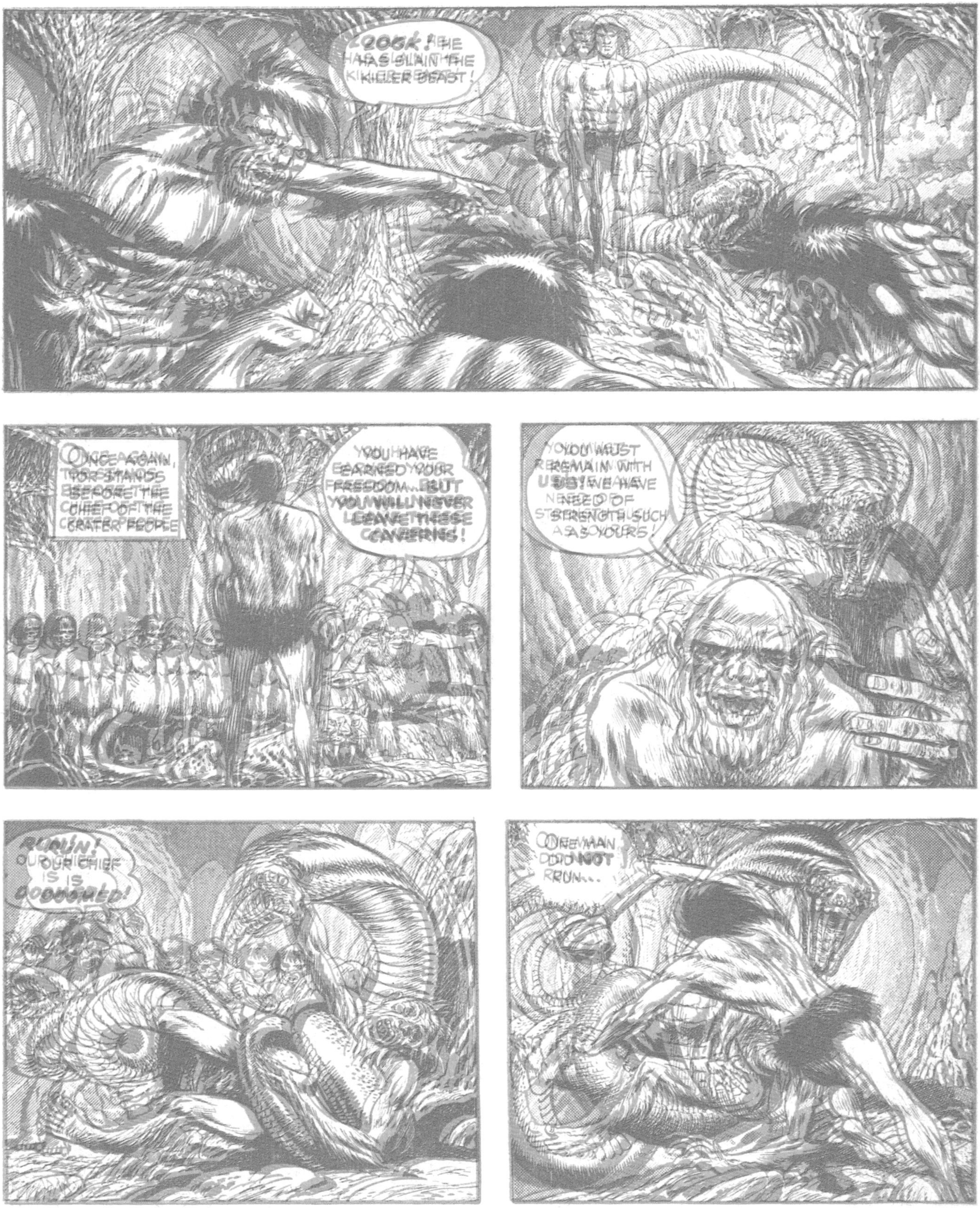
LOOK! HE HAS SLAIN THE KILLER BEAST!
ONCE AGAIN, TOR STANDS BEFORE THE CHIEF OF THE CRATER PEOPLE
YOU HAVE EARNED YOUR FREEDOM... BUT YOU WILL NEVER LEAVE THESE CAVERNS!
YOU MUST REMAIN WITH US! WE HAVE NEED OF STRENGTH SUCH AS YOURS!
RUN! OUR CHIEF IS DOOMED!
ONE MAN DID NOT RUN...

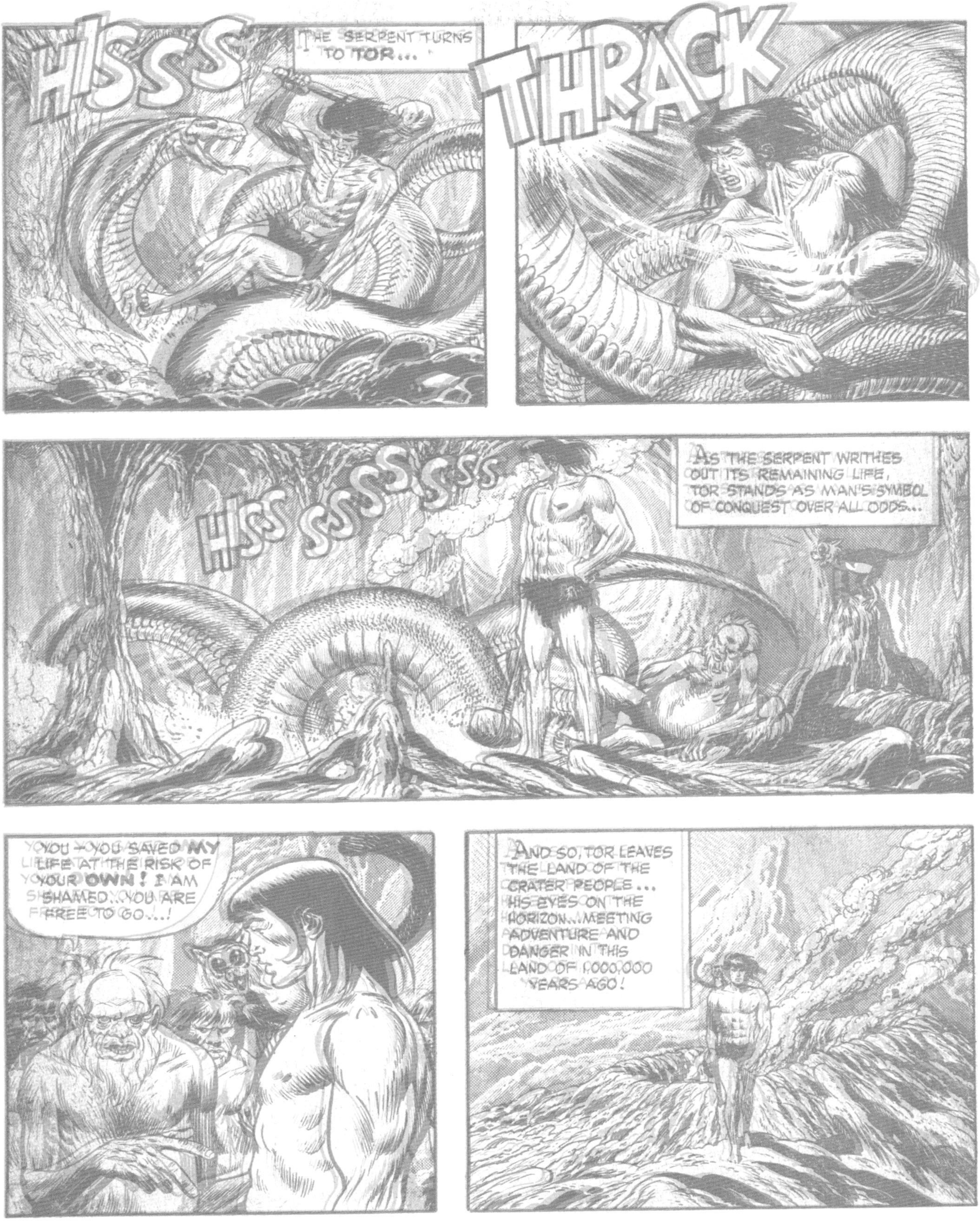
HISSS
THE SERPENT TURNS TO TOR...
THRACK
HISS SSSSSSSS
AS THE SERPENT WRITHES OUT ITS REMAINING LIFE, TOR STANDS AS MAN'S SYMBOL OF CONQUEST OVER ALL ODDS...
YOU -- YOU SAVED MY LIFE AT THE RISK OF YOUR OWN! I AM SHAMED... YOU ARE FREE TO GO...!
AND SO, TOR LEAVES THE LAND OF THE CRATER PEOPLE... HIS EYES ON THE HORIZON... MEETING ADVENTURE AND DANGER IN THIS LAND OF 1,000,000 YEARS AGO!

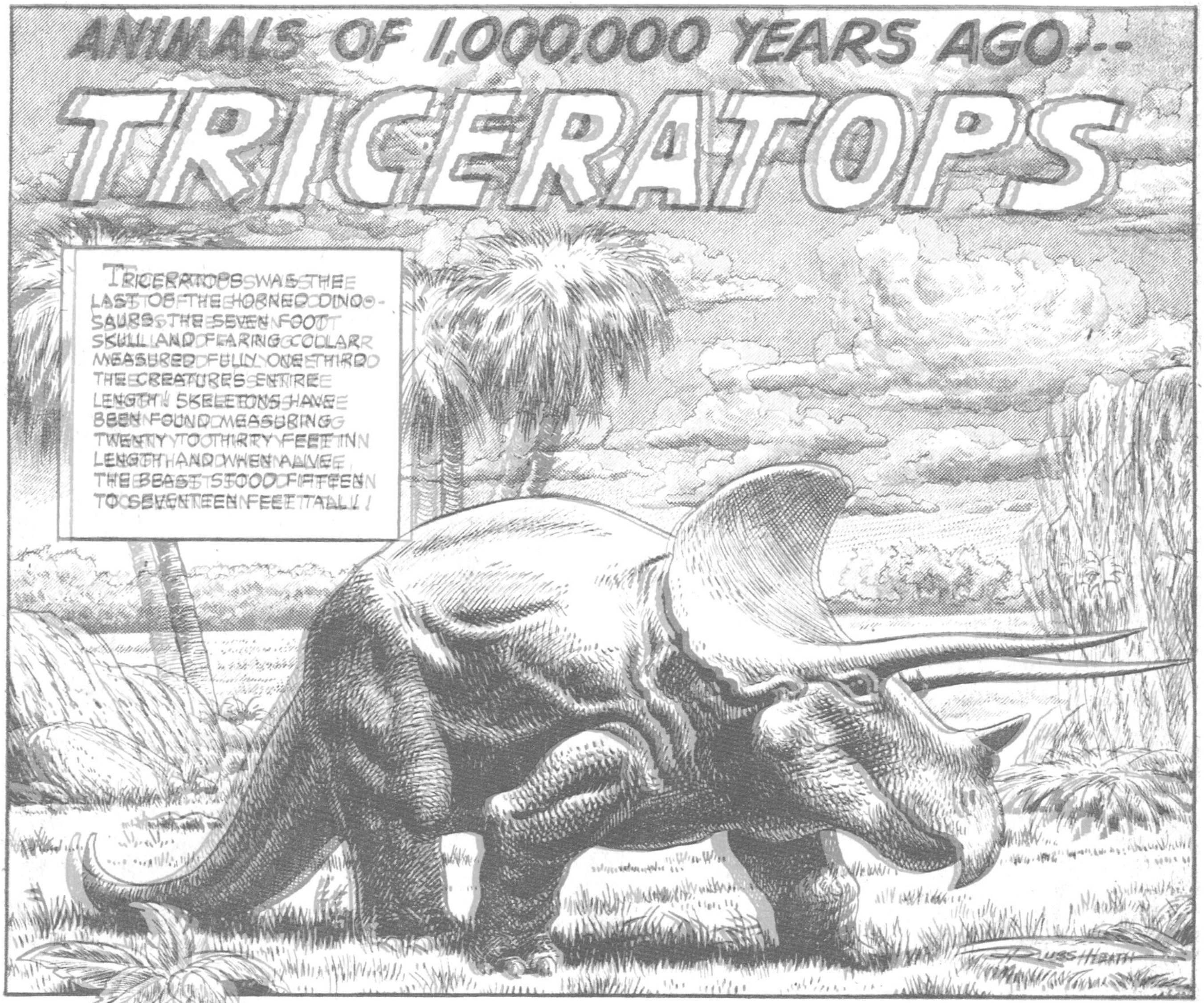
ANIMALS OF 1,000,000 YEARS AGO--
TRICERATOPS
TRICERATOPS WAS THE LAST OF THE HORNED DINO-SAURS. THE SEVEN FOOT SKULL AND FLARING COLLAR MEASURED FULLY ONE THIRD THE CREATURE'S ENTIRE LENGTH! SKELETONS HAVE BEEN FOUND MEASURING TWENTY TO THIRTY FEET IN LENGTH AND WHEN ALIVE THE BEAST STOOD FIFTEEN TO SEVENTEEN FEET TALL!
RUSS HEATH

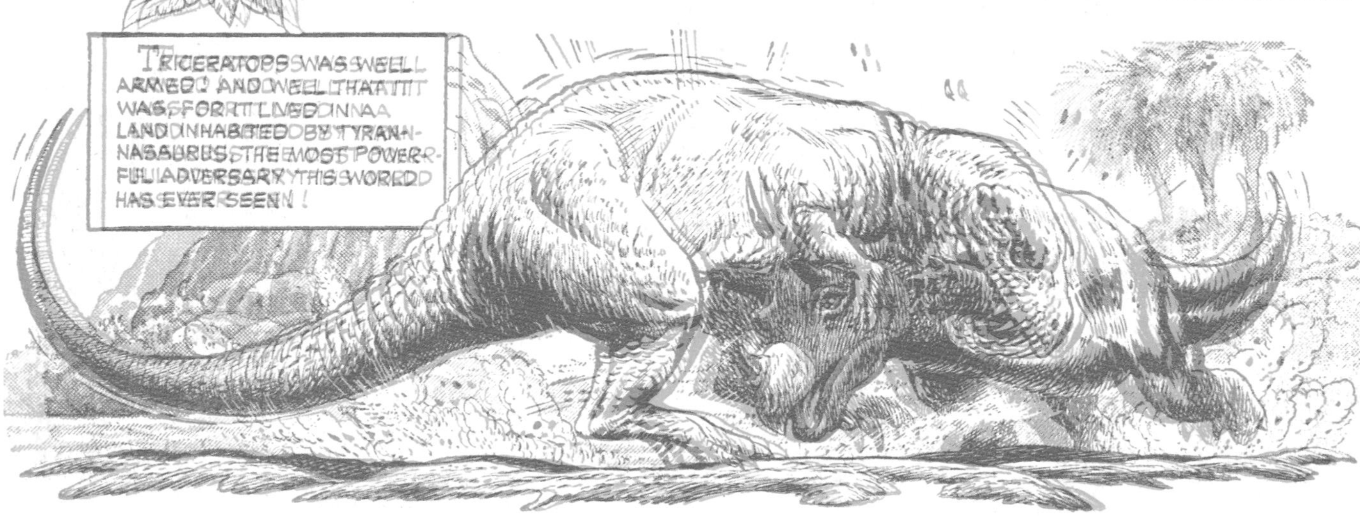
TRICERATOPS WAS WELL ARMED! AND WELL THAT IT WAS, FOR IT LIVED IN A LAND INHABITED BY TYRAN-NASAURUS, THE MOST POWER-FUL ADVERSARY THIS WORLD HAS EVER SEEN!

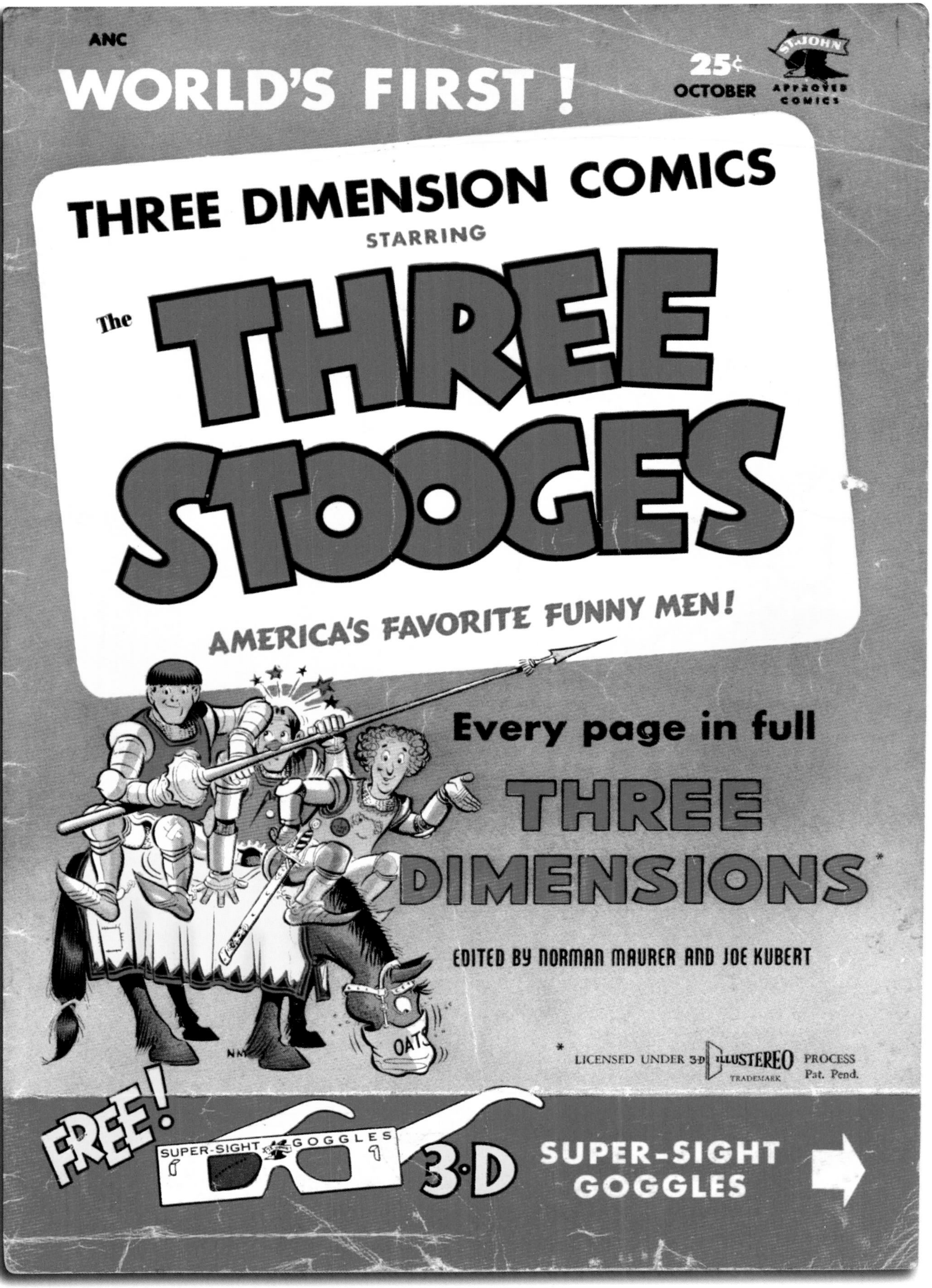
ANC
WORLD'S FIRST!
25¢
OCTOBER
ST. JOHN
APPROVED COMICS
THREE DIMENSION COMICS
STARRING
The THREE STOOGES
AMERICA'S FAVORITE FUNNY MEN!
Every page in full
THREE DIMENSIONS*
EDITED BY NORMAN MAURER AND JOE KUBERT
OATS
* LICENSED UNDER 3-D ILLUSTEREO PROCESS
TRADEMARK Pat. Pend.
FREE!
SUPER-SIGHT GOGGLES
3-D SUPER-SIGHT GOGGLES

The Three Stooges #2, October 1953; artist, Norman Maurer.

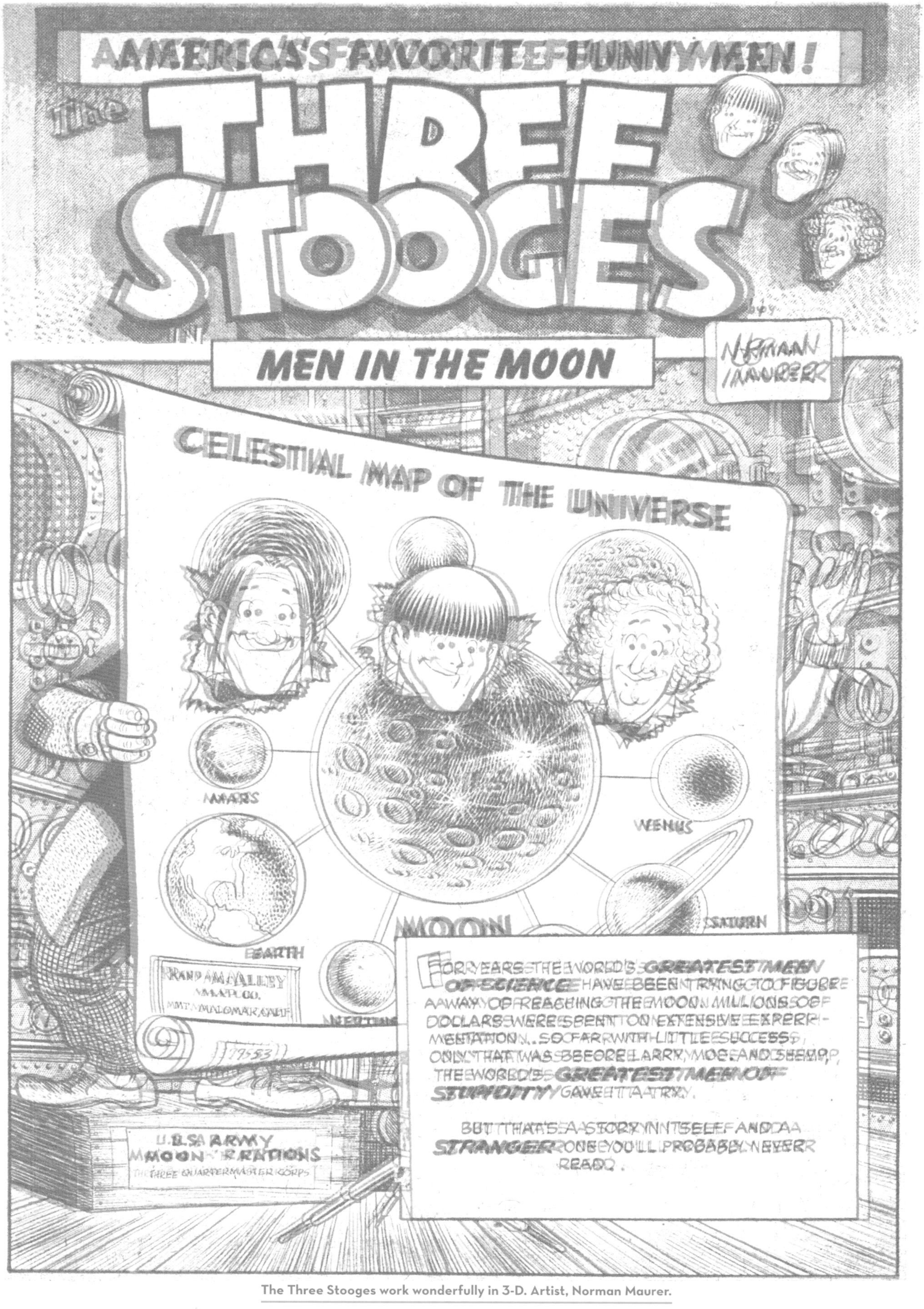
AMERICA'S FAVORITE FUNNY MEN!
THE THREE STOOGES
IN
MEN IN THE MOON
NORMAN MAURER
CELESTIAL MAP OF THE UNIVERSE
MARS
VENUS
EARTH
MOON
SATURN
FOR YEARS THE WORLD'S GREATEST MEN OF SCIENCE HAVE BEEN TRYING TO FIGURE A WAY OF REACHING THE MOON. MILLIONS OF DOLLARS WERE SPENT ON EXTENSIVE EXPERIMENTATION... SO FAR WITH LITTLE SUCCESS, ONLY THAT WAS BEFORE LARRY, MOE, AND SHEMP, THE WORLD'S GREATEST MEN OF STUPIDITY GAVE IT A TRY.
BUT THAT'S A STORY IN ITSELF AND A STRANGER ONE YOU'LL PROBABLY NEVER READ.
U.S. ARMY
MOON RATIONS
THREE QUARTERMASTER CORPS

The Three Stooges work wonderfully in 3-D. Artist, Norman Maurer.

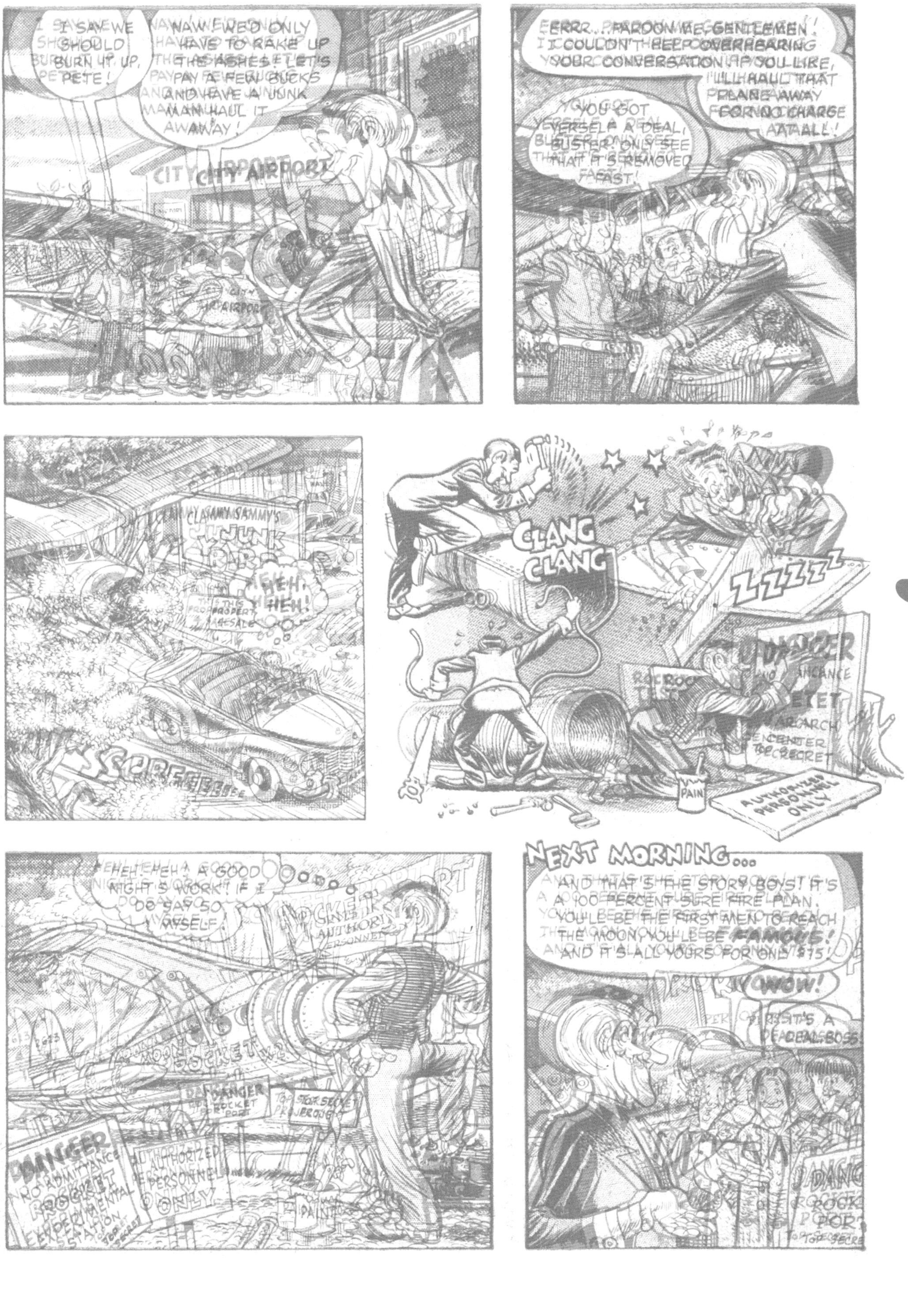
I SAY WE SHOULD BURN IT UP, PETE!
NAW! WE'D ONLY HAVE TO RAKE UP THE ASHES! LET'S PAY A FEW BUCKS AND HAVE A JUNK MAN HAUL IT AWAY!
CITY AIRPORT
ERRR... PARDON ME, GENTLEMEN! I COULDN'T HELP OVERHEARING YOUR CONVERSATION. IF YOU LIKE, I'LL HAUL THAT PLANE AWAY FOR NO CHARGE AT ALL!
YOU GOT YERSELF A DEAL, BUSTER. ONLY SEE THAT IT'S REMOVED FAST!
CLAMMY SAMMY'S JUNK YARD
HEH, HEH!
THIS PROPERTY FOR SALE
SCREEEE
CLANG CLANG
ZZZZZ
DANGER
TOP SECRET
PAINT
AUTHORIZED PERSONNEL ONLY
HEH, HEH! A GOOD NIGHT'S WORK! IF I DO SAY SO MYSELF.
ROCKET PORT
DANGER ROCKET PORT
TOP SECRET PROJECT
DANGER NO ADMITTANCE ROCKET EXPERIMENTAL STATION
AUTHORIZED PERSONNEL ONLY
PAINT
NEXT MORNING...
AND THAT'S THE STORY, BOYS! IT'S A 100 PERCENT SURE FIRE PLAN. YOU'LL BE THE FIRST MEN TO REACH THE MOON! YOU'LL BE FAMOUS! AND IT'S ALL YOURS FOR ONE $75!
WOW!
IT'S A DEAL, BOSS!

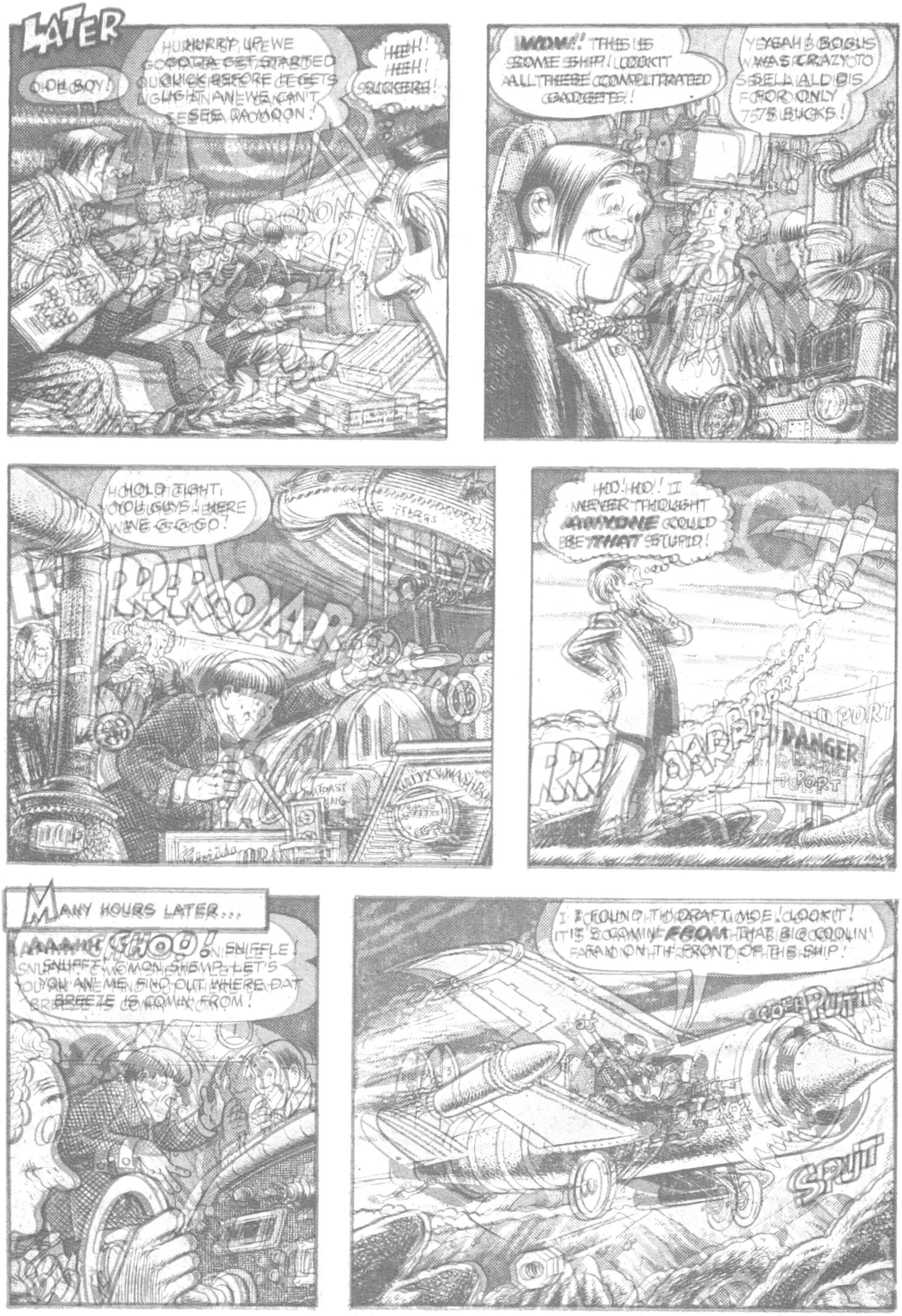
LATER
OH BOY!
HURRY UP, WE GOTTA GET STARTED QUICK BEFORE IT GETS LIGHT AN' WE CAN'T SEE DA MOON!
HEH! HEH! SUCKERS!
WOW! THIS IS SOME SHIP! LOOKIT ALL THESE COMPLITRATED GADGETS!
YEAH! BOGUS WAS CRAZY TO SELL AL DIS FOR ONLY 75 BUCKS!
HOLD TIGHT, YOU GUYS! HERE WE G-G-GO!
RRROAR
HO! HO! I NEVER THOUGHT ANYONE COULD BE THAT STUPID!
RRROARRR
DANGER ROCKET PORT
MANY HOURS LATER...
AAAH CHOO! SNIFFLE! SNUFF! C'MON SHEMP, LET'S YOU AN' ME FIND OUT WHERE DAT BREEZE IS COMIN' FROM!
I FOUND TH' DRAFT, MOE. LOOKIT! IT'S COMIN' FROM THAT BIG COOLIN' FAN ON TH' FRONT OF THE SHIP!
PUTT
SPUT

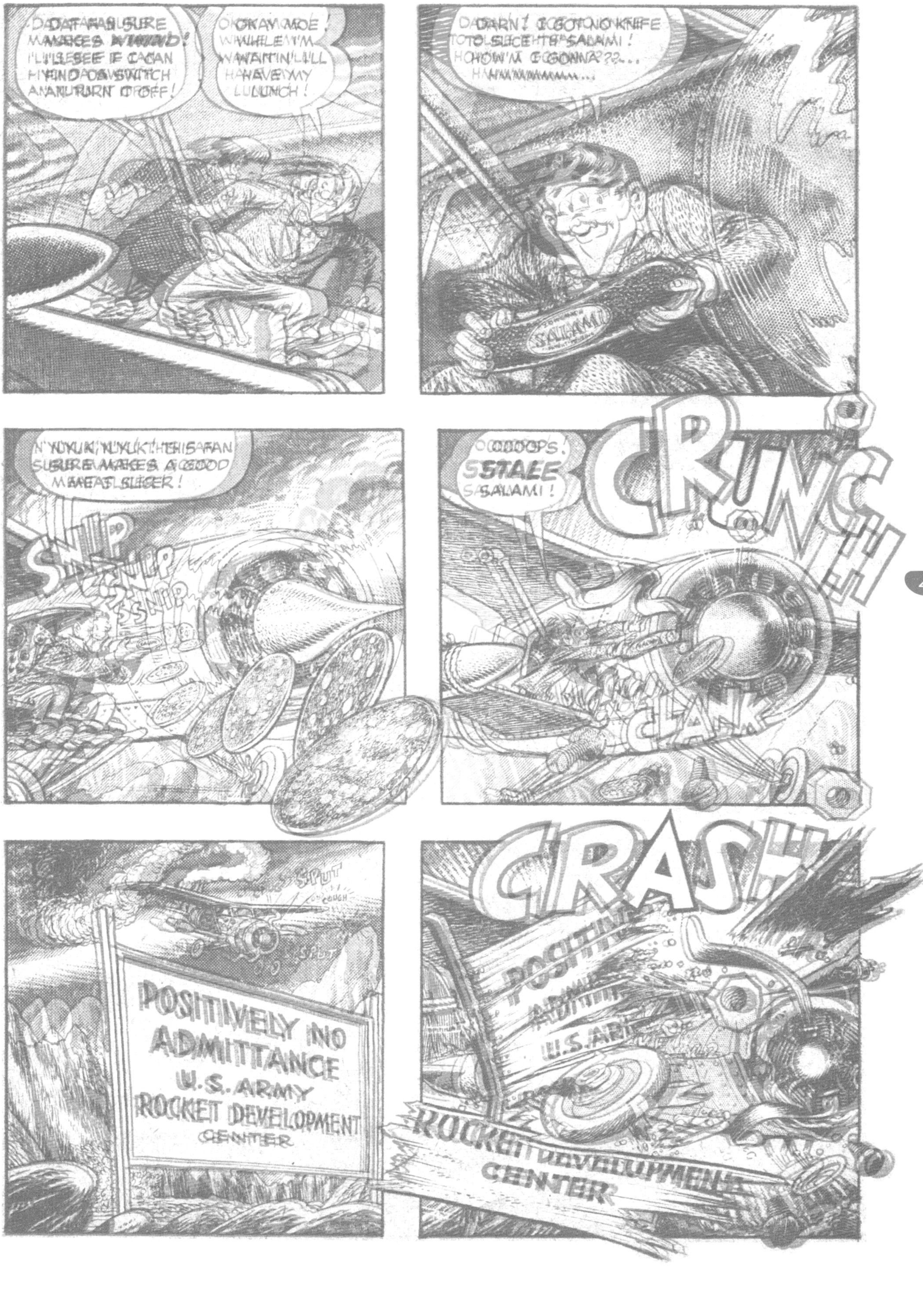
DAT FAN SURE MAKES WIND! I'LL SEE IF I CAN FIND DA SWITCH AN TURN IT OFF!
OKAY MOE! WHILE I'M WAITIN' I'LL HAVE MY LUNCH!
DARN! I GOT NO KNIFE TO SLICE TH' SALAMI! HOW'M I GONNA ??... HMMMMMMM...
SALAMI
N'YUK, N'YUK! THIS FAN SURE MAKES A GOOD MEAT SLICER!
SNIP
SNIP
SNIP
OOOOPS! STALE SALAMI!
CRUNCH
CLANK
POSITIVELY NO ADMITTANCE
U.S. ARMY
ROCKET DEVELOPMENT CENTER
CRASH
ROCKET DEVELOPMENT CENTER

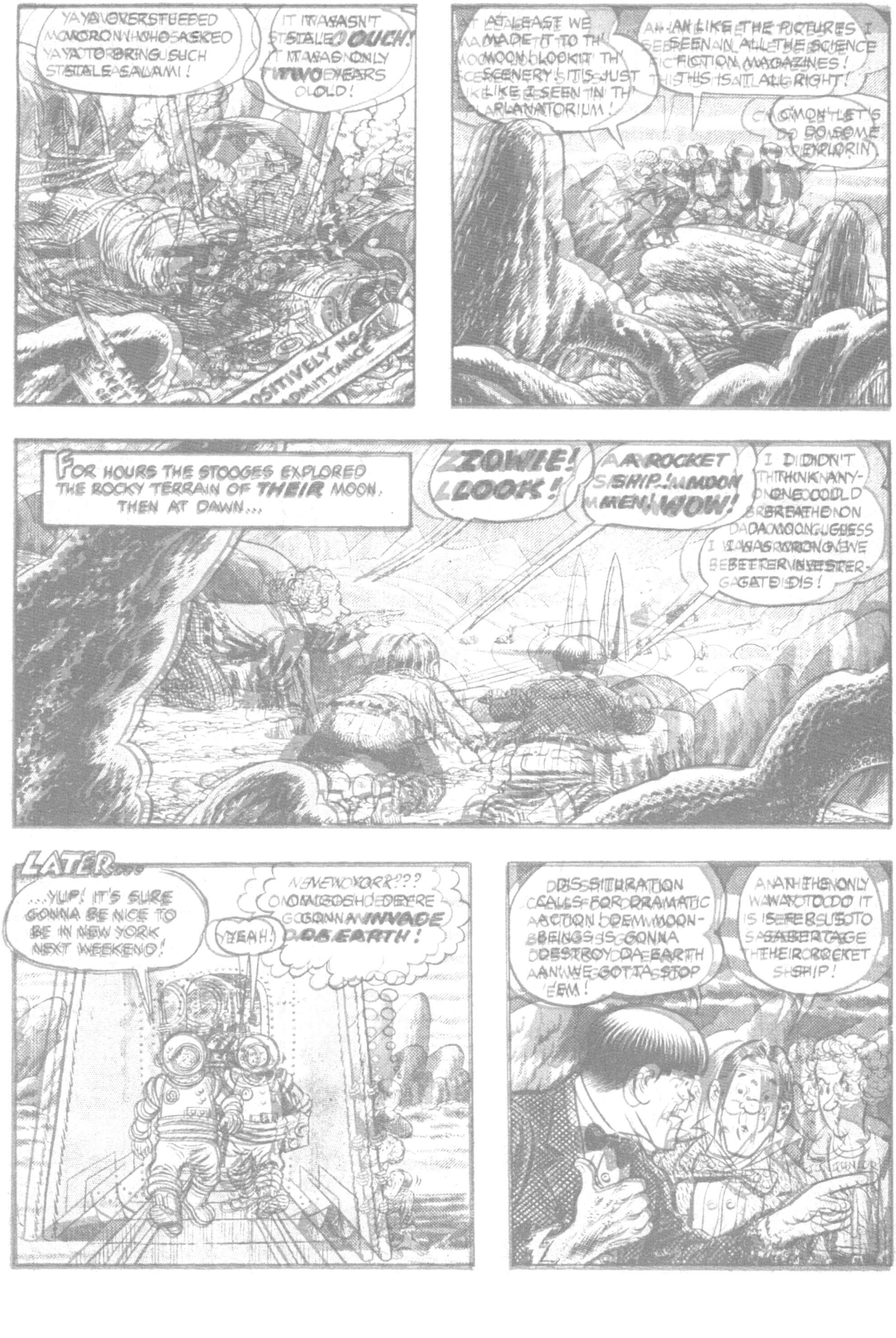
YA OVERSTUFFED MORON! WHO ASKED YA TO BRING SUCH STALE SALAMI!
IT WASN'T STALE! OUCH! IT WAS ONLY TWO YEARS OLD!
POSITIVELY NO ADMITTANCE
AT LEAST WE MADE IT TO TH' MOON! LOOKIT TH' SCENERY! IT'S JUST LIKE I SEEN IN TH' PLANATORIUM!
AN' LIKE THE PICTURES I SEEN IN ALL THE SCIENCE FICTION MAGAZINES! THIS IS IT ALL RIGHT!
C'MON! LET'S DO SOME EXPLORIN'!
FOR HOURS THE STOOGES EXPLORED THE ROCKY TERRAIN OF THEIR MOON. THEN AT DAWN...
ZOWIE! LOOK!
A ROCKET SHIP! MOON MEN! WOW!
I DIDN'T THINK ANYONE COULD BREATHE ON DA MOON. I GUESS I WAS WRONG. WE BETTER INVESTERGATE DIS!
LATER...
...YUP! IT'S SURE GONNA BE NICE TO BE IN NEW YORK NEXT WEEKEND!
YEAH!
NEW YORK??? OMIGOSH! DEY'RE GONNA INVADE DA EARTH!
DIS SITURATION CALLS FOR DRAMATIC ACTION! DEM MOON-BEINGS IS GONNA DESTROY DA EARTH AN' WE GOTTA STOP 'EM!
AN' THE ONLY WAY TO DO IT IS FER US TO SABERTAGE THEIR ROCKET SHIP!

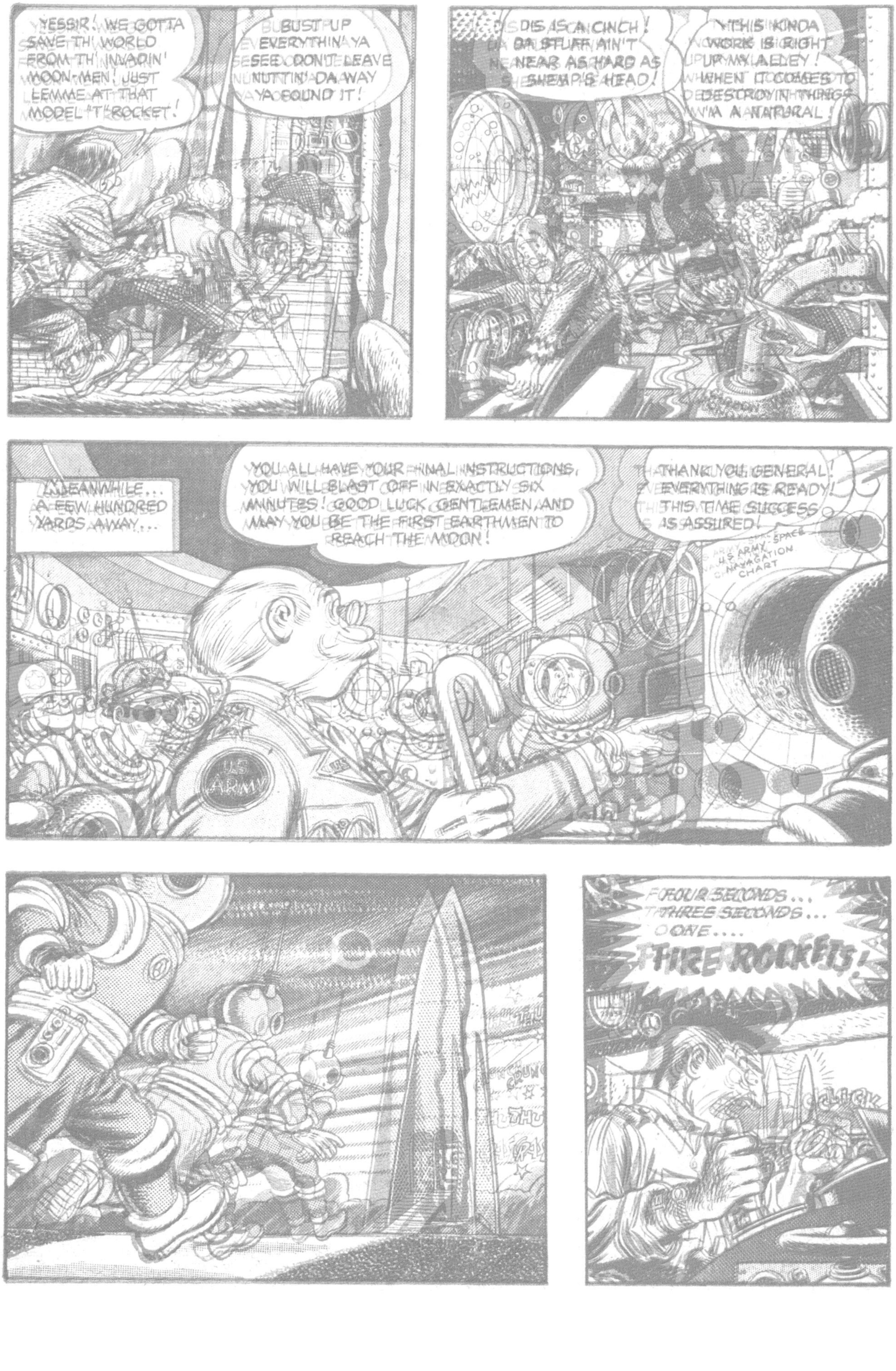
YESSIR! WE GOTTA SAVE TH' WORLD FROM TH' INVADIN' MOON-MEN! JUST LEMME AT THAT MODEL "T" ROCKET!
BUST UP EVERYTHIN YA SEE. DON'T LEAVE NUTTIN' DA WAY YA FOUND IT!
DIS AS A CINCH! DA STUFF AIN'T NEAR AS HARD AS SHEMP'S HEAD!
THIS KINDA WORK IS RIGHT UP MY ALLEY! WHEN IT COMES TO DESTROYIN THINGS I'M A NATURAL!
MEANWHILE... A FEW HUNDRED YARDS AWAY...
YOU ALL HAVE YOUR FINAL INSTRUCTIONS. YOU WILL BLAST OFF IN EXACTLY SIX MINUTES! GOOD LUCK GENTLEMEN AND MAY YOU BE THE FIRST EARTHMEN TO REACH THE MOON!
THANK YOU GENERAL! EVERYTHING IS READY! THIS TIME SUCCESS IS ASSURED!
U.S. ARMY NAVAGATION CHART
U.S. ARMY
FOUR SECONDS... THREE SECONDS... ONE....
FIRE ROCKETS!
CLICK

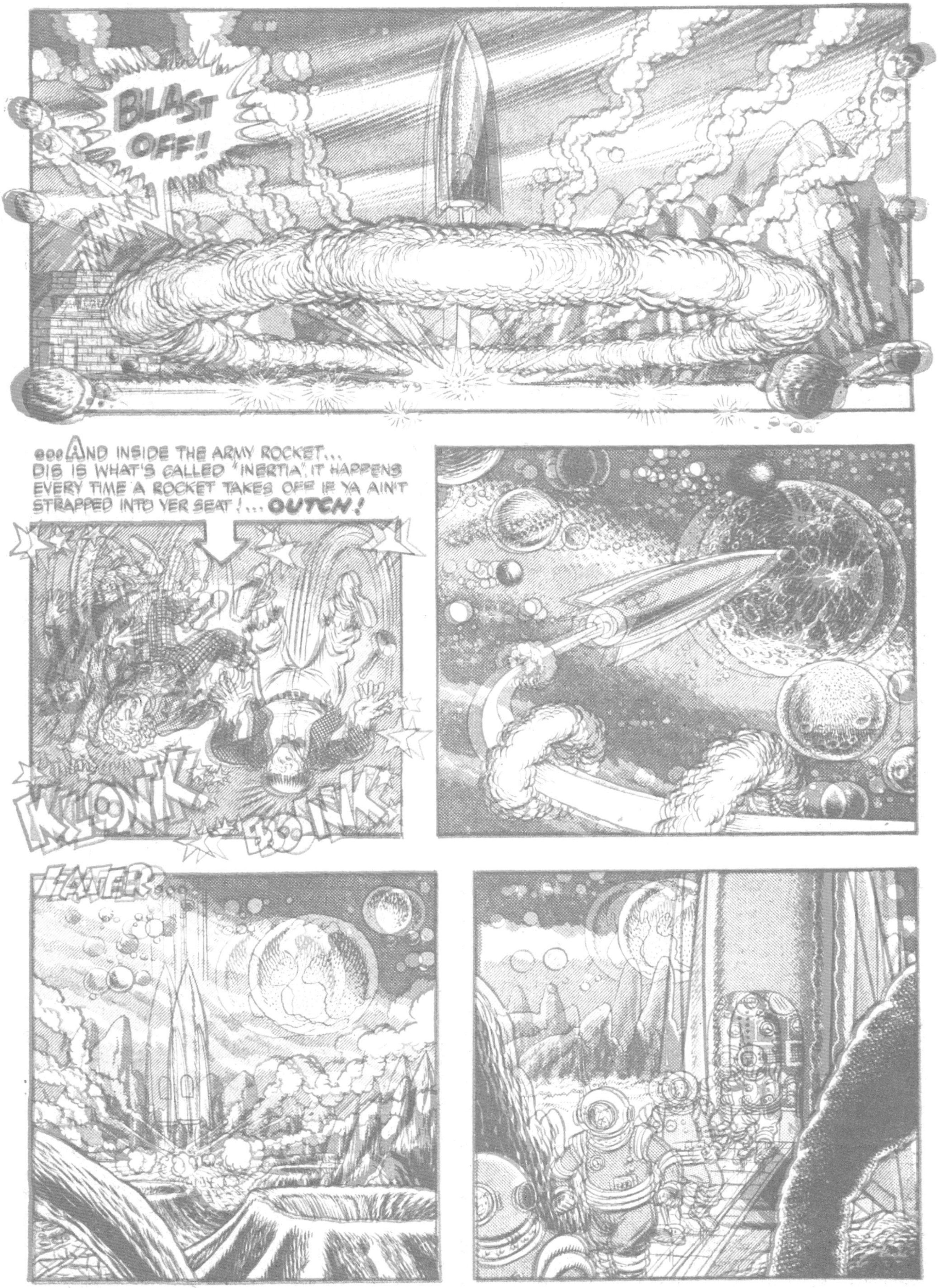
BLAST OFF!!
...AND INSIDE THE ARMY ROCKET...
DIS IS WHAT'S CALLED "INERTIA" IT HAPPENS EVERY TIME A ROCKET TAKES OFF IF YA AIN'T STRAPPED INTO YER SEAT!... OUTCH!
KLONK! BONK!
LATER...

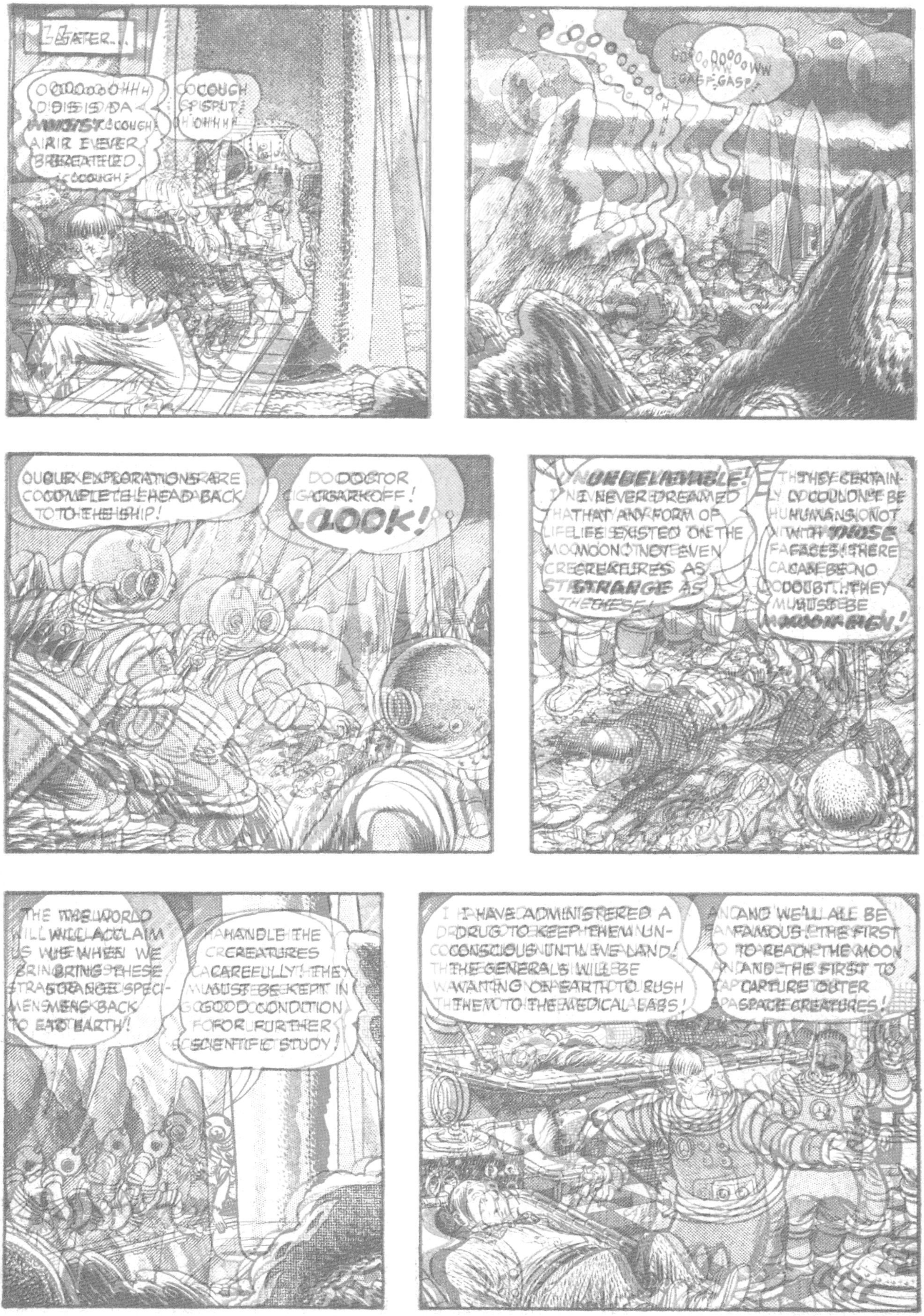
LATER...
OOOOOOOHHH DIS IS DA WORST *COUGH* AIR EVER BREATHED *COUGH*
COUGH SPUT OHHHH
OOOOOOOWW GASP GASP
OUR EXPLORATIONS ARE COMPLETE! HEAD BACK TO THE SHIP!
DOCTOR CIGARKOFF! LOOK!
UNBELIEVABLE! I NEVER DREAMED THAT ANY FORM OF LIFE EXISTED ON THE MOON! NOT EVEN CREATURES AS STRANGE AS THESE!
THEY CERTAINLY COULDN'T BE HUMANS, NOT WITH THOSE FACES! THERE CAN BE NO DOUBT! THEY MUST BE MOON-MEN!
THE WORLD WILL ACCLAIM US WHEN WE BRING THESE STRANGE SPECIMENS BACK TO EARTH!
HANDLE THE CREATURES CAREFULLY! THEY MUST BE KEPT IN GOOD CONDITION FOR FURTHER SCIENTIFIC STUDY!
I HAVE ADMINISTERED A DRUG TO KEEP THEM UNCONSCIOUS UNTIL WE LAND! THE GENERALS WILL BE WAITING ON EARTH TO RUSH THEM TO THE MEDICAL LABS!
AND WE'LL ALL BE FAMOUS! THE FIRST TO REACH THE MOON AND THE FIRST TO CAPTURE OUTER SPACE CREATURES!

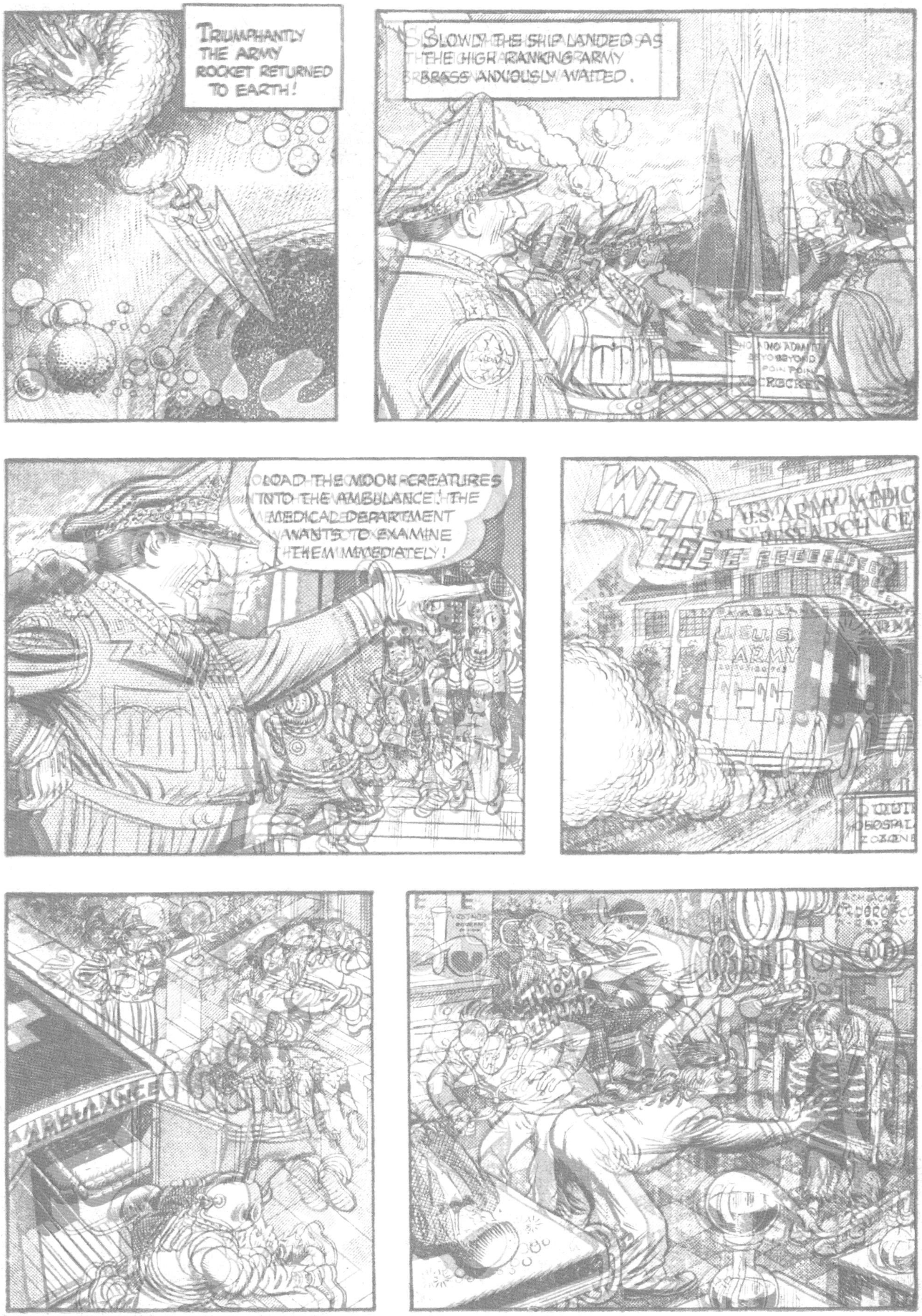
TRIUMPHANTLY THE ARMY ROCKET RETURNED TO EARTH!
SLOWLY THE SHIP LANDED AS THE HIGH RANKING ARMY BRASS ANXIOUSLY WAITED.
LOAD THE MOON CREATURES INTO THE AMBULANCE! THE MEDICAL DEPARTMENT WANTS TO EXAMINE THEM IMMEDIATELY!
U.S. ARMY
AMBULANCE
THUMP
THUMP

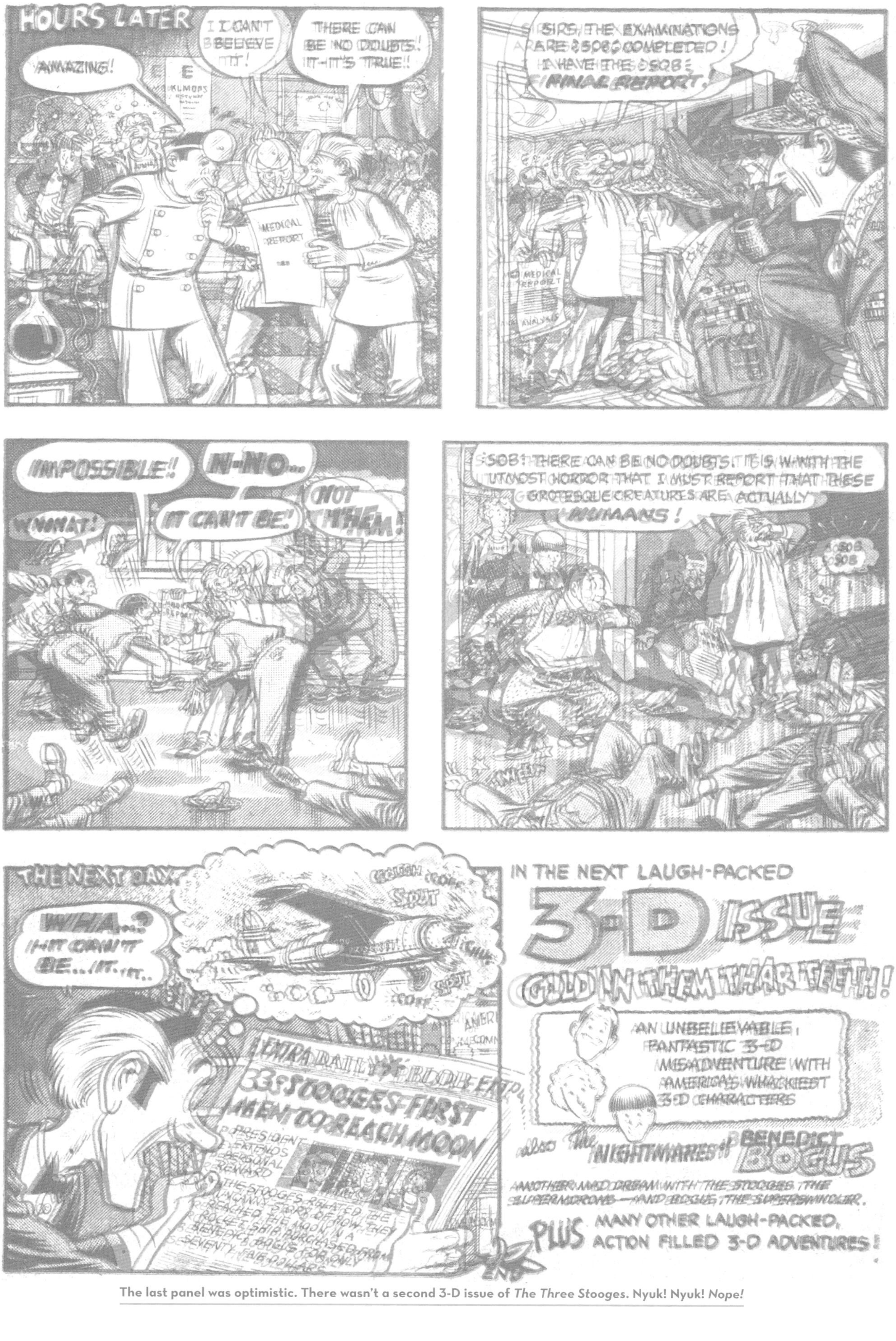
HOURS LATER
AMAZING!
I CAN'T BELIEVE IT!
THERE CAN BE NO DOUBTS! IT-IT'S TRUE!!
MEDICAL REPORT
SIRS, THE EXAMINATIONS ARE COMPLETED! I HAVE THE FINAL REPORT!
MEDICAL REPORT
IMPOSSIBLE!!
N-NO...
WHAT!
IT CAN'T BE!
NOT THEM!
SOB! THERE CAN BE NO DOUBTS. IT IS WITH THE UTMOST HORROR THAT I MUST REPORT THAT THESE GROTESQUE CREATURES ARE ACTUALLY HUMANS!
SOB SOB
THE NEXT DAY
WHA...? I-IT CAN'T BE...IT...IT...
SPUT
COFF
3 STOOGES FIRST MEN TO REACH MOON
PRESIDENT EXTENDS PERSONAL REWARD
THE STOOGES RELATED THE UNCANNY STORY OF HOW THEY REACHED THE MOON IN A ROCKET SHIP PURCHASED FROM BENEDICT BOGUS
IN THE NEXT LAUGH-PACKED
3-D ISSUE
GOLD IN THEM THAR TEETH!
AN UNBELIEVABLE, FANTASTIC 3-D MISADVENTURE WITH AMERICA'S WHACKIEST 3-D CHARACTERS
also The NIGHTMARES of BENEDICT BOGUS
ANOTHER MAD DREAM WITH THE STOOGES, THE SUPERMORONS—AND BOGUS, THE SUPERSWINDLER.
PLUS MANY OTHER LAUGH-PACKED, ACTION FILLED 3-D ADVENTURES!
END

The last panel was optimistic. There wasn't a second 3-D issue of *The Three Stooges*. Nyuk! Nyuk! *Nope!*

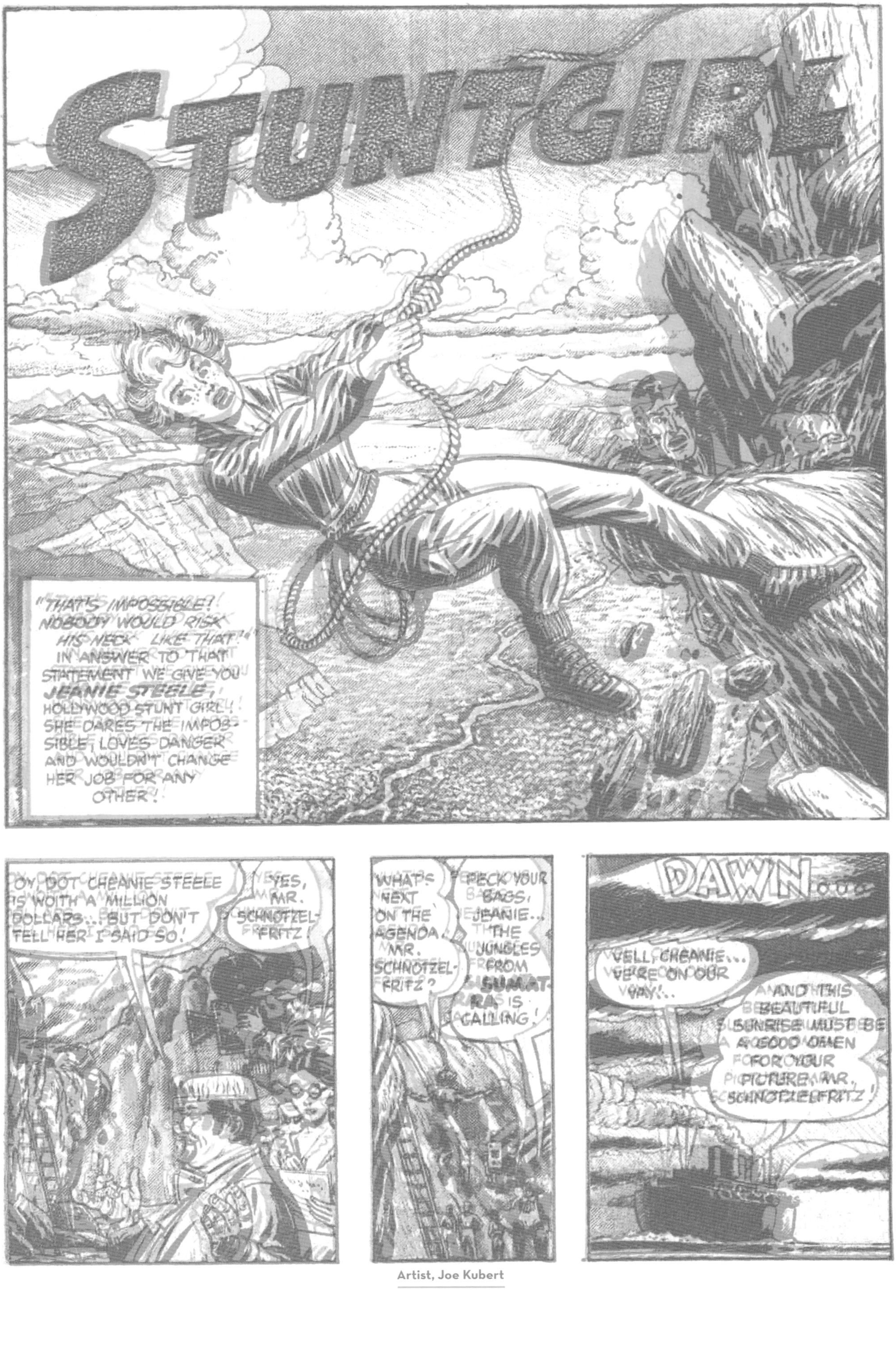
STUNTGIRL
"THAT'S IMPOSSIBLE! NOBODY WOULD RISK HIS NECK LIKE THAT!" IN ANSWER TO THAT STATEMENT WE GIVE YOU JEANIE STEELE, HOLLYWOOD STUNT GIRL! SHE DARES THE IMPOSSIBLE, LOVES DANGER AND WOULDN'T CHANGE HER JOB FOR ANY OTHER!
OY, DOT CHEANIE STEELE IS WOITH A MILLION DOLLARS... BUT DON'T TELL HER I SAID SO!
YES, MR. SCHNOTZELFRITZ!
WHAT'S NEXT ON THE AGENDA, MR. SCHNOTZELFRITZ?
PECK YOUR BAGS, JEANIE... THE JUNGLES FROM SUMATRA IS CALLING!
DAWN...
VELL, CHEANIE... VE'RE ON OUR VAY!..
AND THIS BEAUTIFUL SUNRISE MUST BE A GOOD OMEN FOR YOUR PICTURE, MR. SCHNOTZELFRITZ!

Artist, Joe Kubert

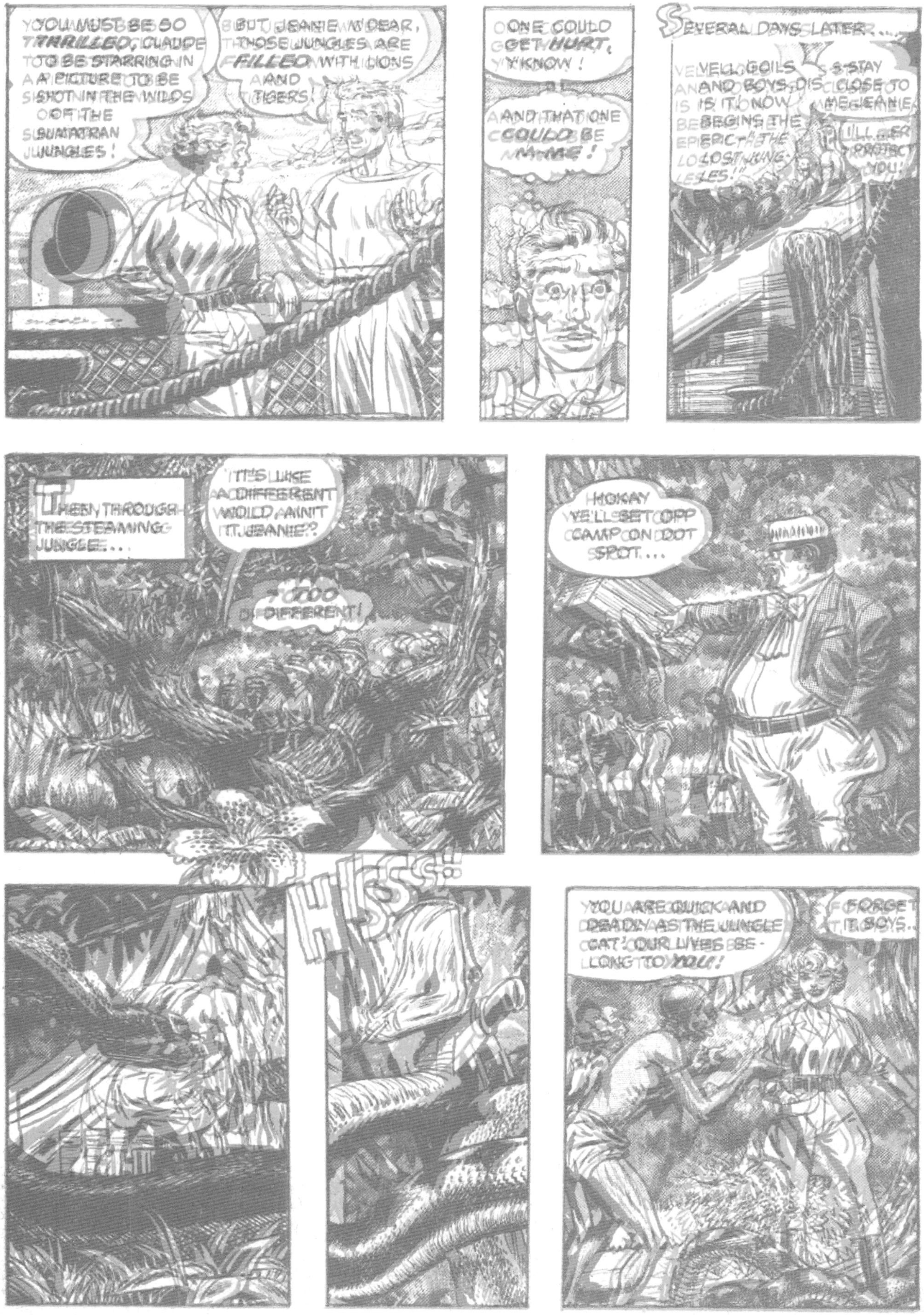

YOU MUST BE SO THRILLED, CLAUDE TO BE STARRING IN A PICTURE TO BE SHOT IN THE WILDS OF THE SUMATRAN JUNGLES!
BUT, JEANIE M'DEAR, THOSE JUNGLES ARE FILLED WITH LIONS AND TIGERS!
ONE COULD GET HURT, Y'KNOW!
AND THAT ONE COULD BE ME!
SEVERAL DAYS LATER...
VELL, GOILS AND BOYS, DIS IS IT! NOW BEGINS THE EPIC--"THE LOST JUNGLES!"
STAY CLOSE TO ME, JEANIE!
I'LL PROTECT YOU!
THEN, THROUGH THE STEAMING JUNGLE...
IT'S LIKE A DIFFERENT WORLD, AIN'T IT, JEANIE?
TOO DIFFERENT!
HOKAY. VE'LL SET OFF CAMP ON DOT SPOT...
HISSS!
YOU ARE QUICK AND DEADLY AS THE JUNGLE CAT! OUR LIVES BE-LONG TO YOU!
FORGET IT, BOYS...

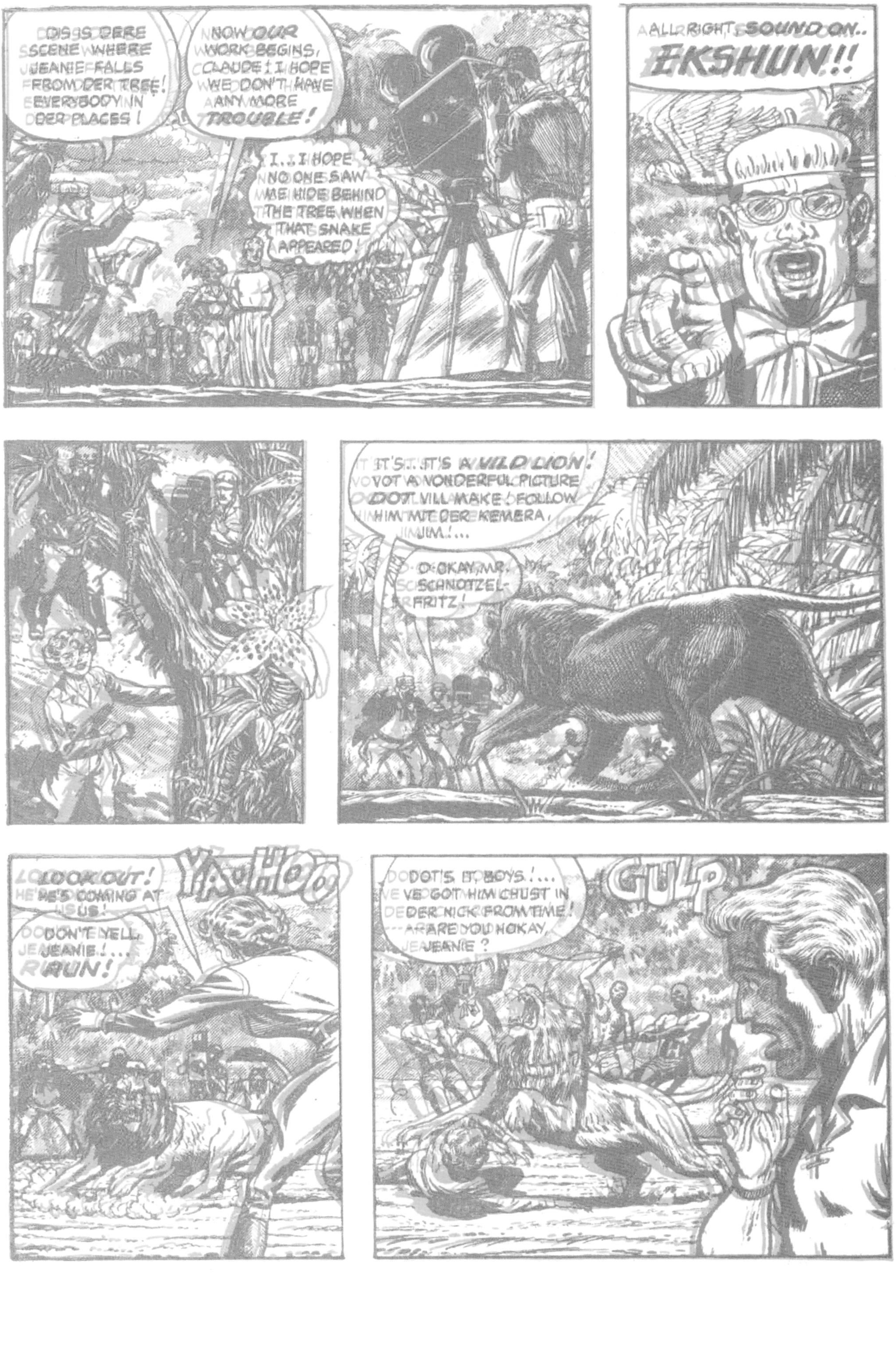
DIS IS DERE SCENE WHERE JEANIE FALLS FROM DER TREE! EVERYBODY IN DER PLACES!
NOW OUR WORK BEGINS, CLAUDE! I HOPE WE DON'T HAVE ANY MORE TROUBLE!
I...I HOPE NO ONE SAW ME HIDE BEHIND THE TREE WHEN THAT SNAKE APPEARED!
ALL RIGHT, SOUND ON.. EKSHUN!!
IT'S.. IT'S A VILD LION! VOT A VONDERFUL PICTURE DOT VILL MAKE! FOLLOW HIM MIT DER KEMERA, JIM!...
O-OKAY, MR. SCHNOTZELFRITZ!
LOOK OUT! HE'S COMING AT US!
DON'T YELL, JEANIE!... RUN!
DOT'S IT, BOYS!... VE GOT HIM CHUST IN DER NICK FROM TIME! ...ARE YOU HOKAY, JEANIE?
GULP

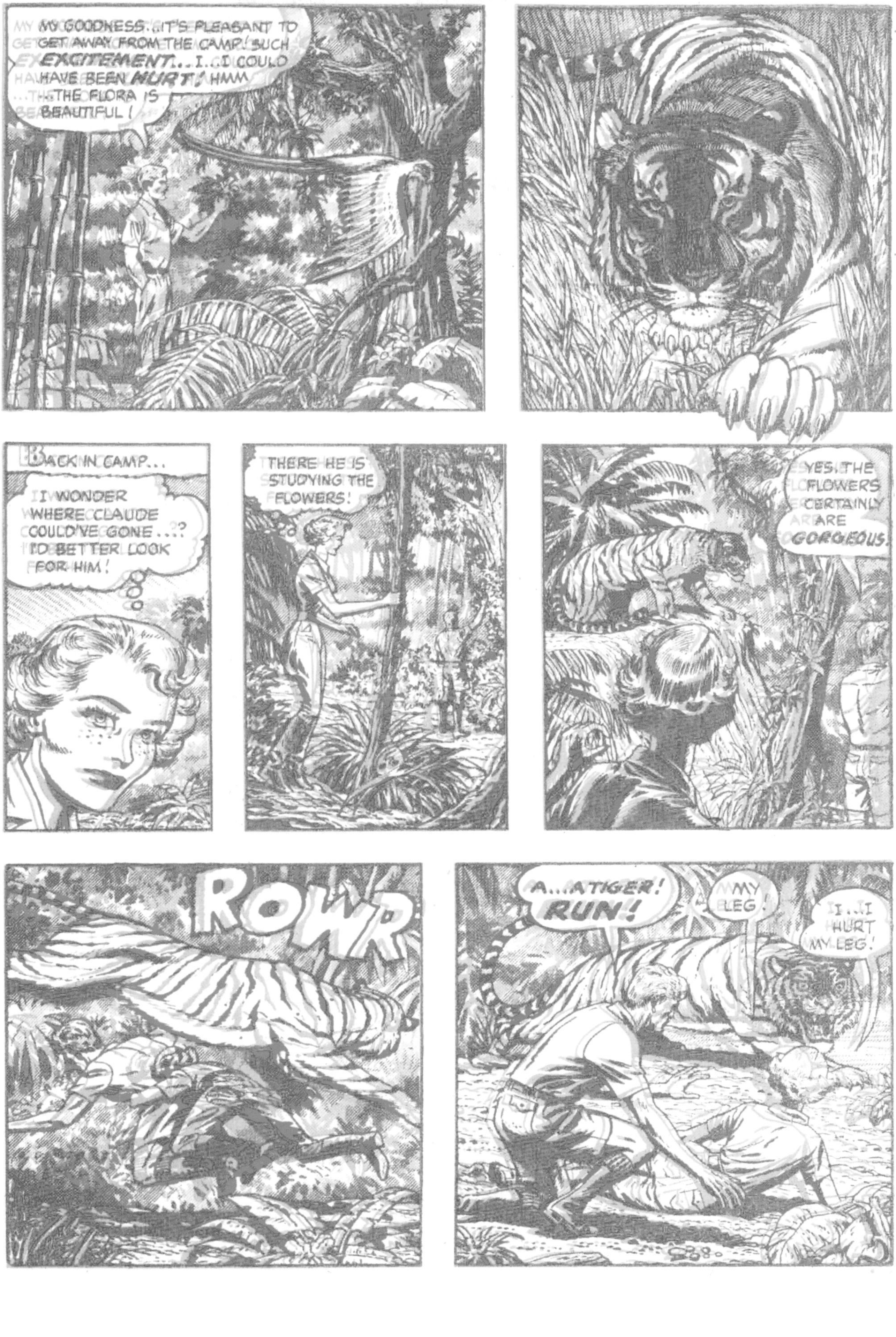
MY GOODNESS...IT'S PLEASANT TO GET AWAY FROM THE CAMP! SUCH EXCITEMENT...I...I COULD HAVE BEEN HURT! HMM ...THE FLORA IS BEAUTIFUL!
BACK IN CAMP...
I WONDER WHERE CLAUDE COULD'VE GONE...?? I'D BETTER LOOK FOR HIM!
THERE HE IS STUDYING THE FLOWERS!
YES, THE FLOWERS CERTAINLY ARE GORGEOUS!
ROWR
A...A TIGER! RUN!
MY LEG!
I...I HURT MY LEG!

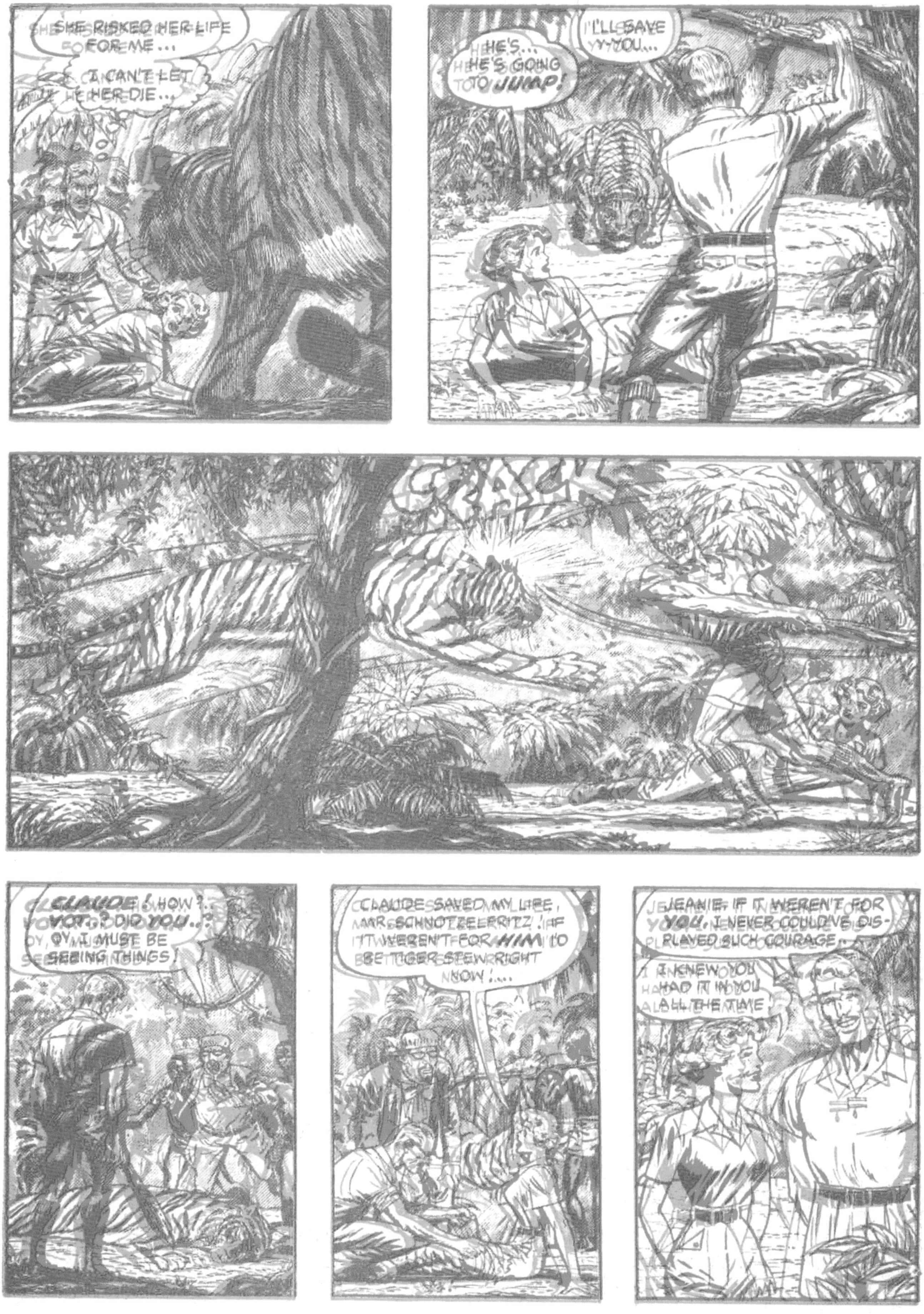

SHE RISKED HER LIFE FOR ME...
I CAN'T LET HER DIE...
HE'S... HE'S GOING TO JUMP!
I'LL SAVE Y-YOU...
CLAUDE! HOW? VOT? DID YOU..? OY, I MUST BE SEEING THINGS!
CLAUDE SAVED MY LIFE, MR. SCHNOTZEEFRITZ! IF IT WEREN'T FOR HIM I'D BE TIGER STEW RIGHT NOW!...
JEANIE, IF IT WEREN'T FOR YOU, I NEVER COULD'VE DISPLAYED SUCH COURAGE...
I KNEW YOU HAD IT IN YOU ALL THE TIME

54

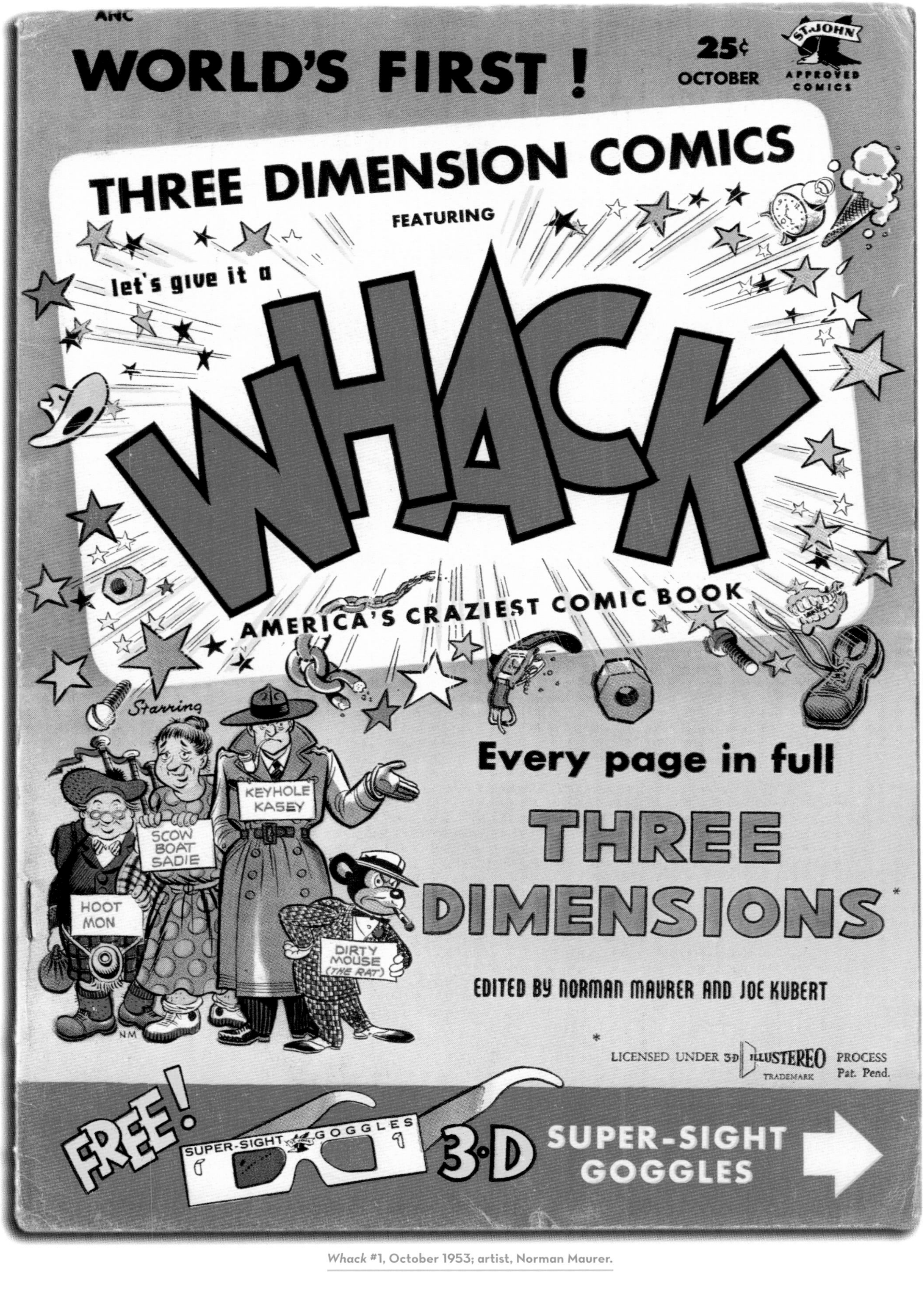
ANC
WORLD'S FIRST !
25¢
OCTOBER
ST. JOHN
APPROVED COMICS
THREE DIMENSION COMICS
FEATURING
let's give it a
WHACK
AMERICA'S CRAZIEST COMIC BOOK
Starring
KEYHOLE KASEY
SCOW BOAT SADIE
HOOT MON
DIRTY MOUSE (THE RAT)
NM
Every page in full
THREE DIMENSIONS*
EDITED BY NORMAN MAURER AND JOE KUBERT
* LICENSED UNDER 3-D ILLUSTEREO PROCESS
TRADEMARK
Pat. Pend.
FREE!
SUPER-SIGHT GOGGLES
3-D
SUPER-SIGHT GOGGLES

Whack #1, October 1953; artist, Norman Maurer.

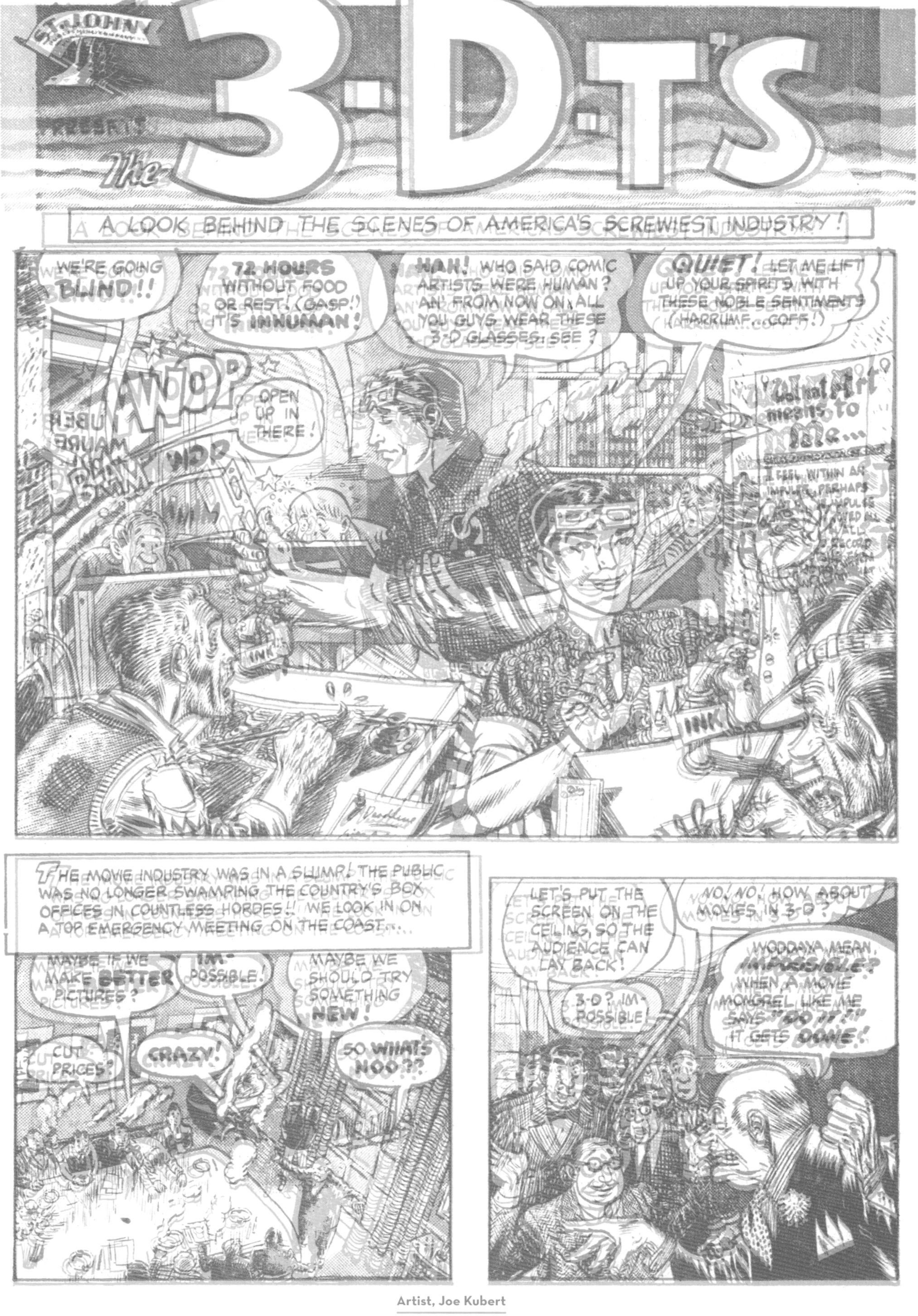
ST. JOHN
PRESENTS
the 3-D-T's
A LOOK BEHIND THE SCENES OF AMERICA'S SCREWIEST INDUSTRY!
WE'RE GOING BLIND!!
72 HOURS WITHOUT FOOD OR REST! (GASP!) IT'S INHUMAN!
HAH! WHO SAID COMIC ARTISTS WERE HUMAN? AN' FROM NOW ON, ALL YOU GUYS WEAR THESE 3-D GLASSES, SEE?
QUIET! LET ME LIFT UP YOUR SPIRITS WITH THESE NOBLE SENTIMENTS (HARRUMF... COFF!)
WOP
OPEN UP IN THERE!
INK
THE MOVIE INDUSTRY WAS IN A SLUMP! THE PUBLIC WAS NO LONGER SWAMPING THE COUNTRY'S BOX OFFICES IN COUNTLESS HORDES!! WE LOOK IN ON A TOP EMERGENCY MEETING ON THE COAST...
MAYBE IF WE MAKE BETTER PICTURES?
IM-POSSIBLE!
MAYBE WE SHOULD TRY SOMETHING NEW!
CUT PRICES?
CRAZY!
SO WHATS NOO??
LET'S PUT THE SCREEN ON THE CEILING, SO THE AUDIENCE CAN LAY BACK!
NO! NO! HOW ABOUT MOVIES IN 3-D?
3-D? IM-POSSIBLE!
WODDAYA MEAN, IMPOSSIBLE? WHEN A MOVIE MONGREL LIKE ME SAYS "DO IT!" IT GETS DONE!

Artist, Joe Kubert

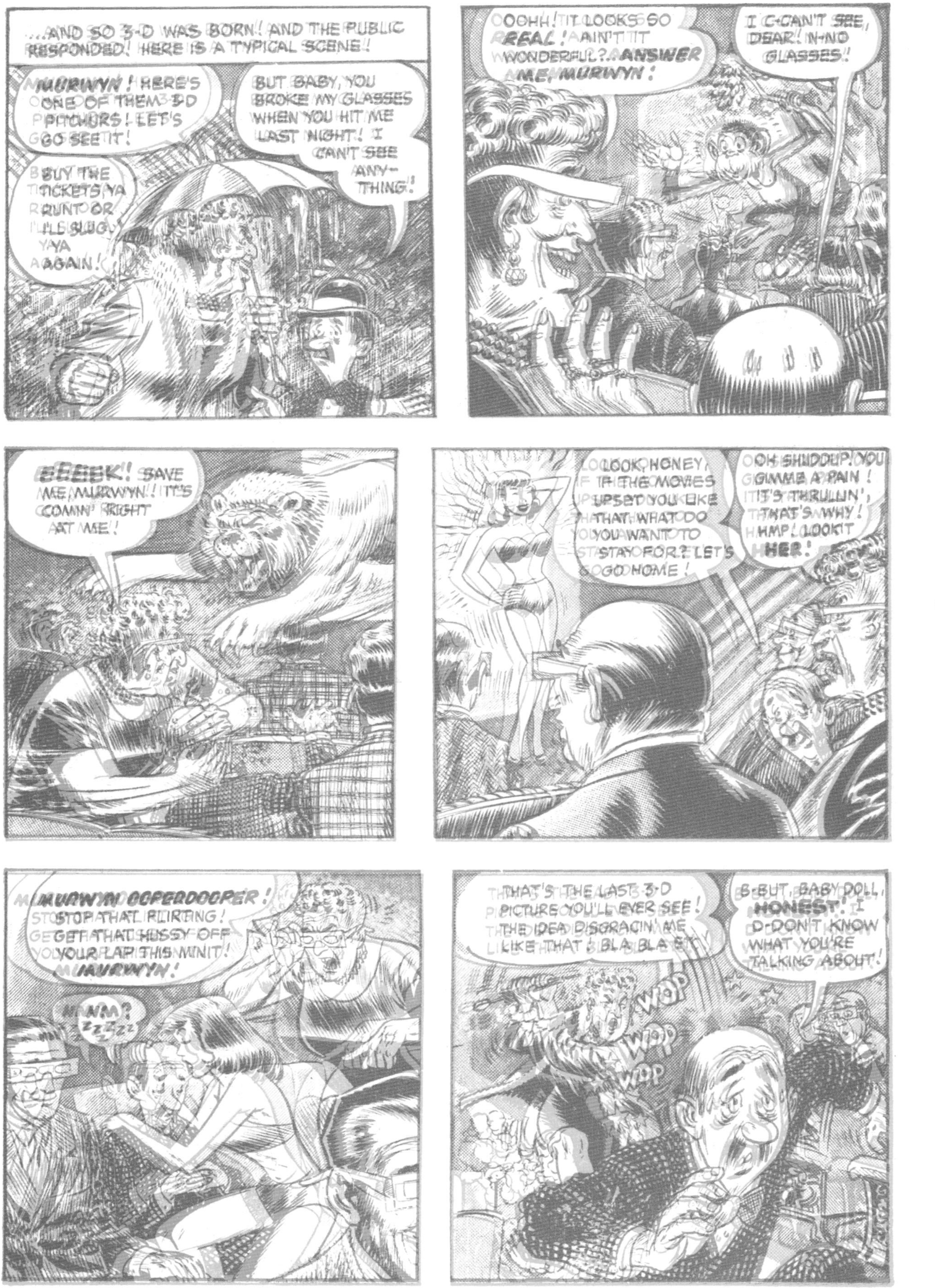
...AND SO 3-D WAS BORN! AND THE PUBLIC RESPONDED! HERE IS A TYPICAL SCENE!
MURWYN! HERE'S ONE OF THEM 3-D PITCHURS! LET'S GO SEE IT!
BUT BABY, YOU BROKE MY GLASSES WHEN YOU HIT ME LAST NIGHT! I CAN'T SEE ANY-THING!
BUY THE TICKETS, YA RUNT OR I'LL SLUG YA AGAIN!
OOHH! IT LOOKS SO REAL! AIN'T IT WONDERFUL?... ANSWER ME, MURWYN!
I C-CAN'T SEE, DEAR! N-NO GLASSES!
EEEEK! SAVE ME, MURWYN! IT'S COMIN' RIGHT AT ME!
LOOK, HONEY, IF THE MOVIES UPSET YOU LIKE THAT, WHAT DO YOU WANT TO STAY FOR? LET'S GO HOME!
OH SHUDDUP! YOU GIMME A PAIN! IT'S THRILLIN', THAT'S WHY! HMP! LOOKIT HER!
MURWYN OOPERDOOPER! STOP THAT FLIRTING! GET THAT HUSSY OFF YOUR LAP THIS MINIT! MURWYN!
HMM? ZZZZZ
THAT'S THE LAST 3-D PICTURE YOU'LL EVER SEE! THE IDEA DISGRACIN' ME LIKE THAT! BLA BLA ETC!
B-BUT, BABY DOLL, HONEST! I D-DON'T KNOW WHAT YOU'RE TALKING ABOUT!
WOP
WOP
WOP

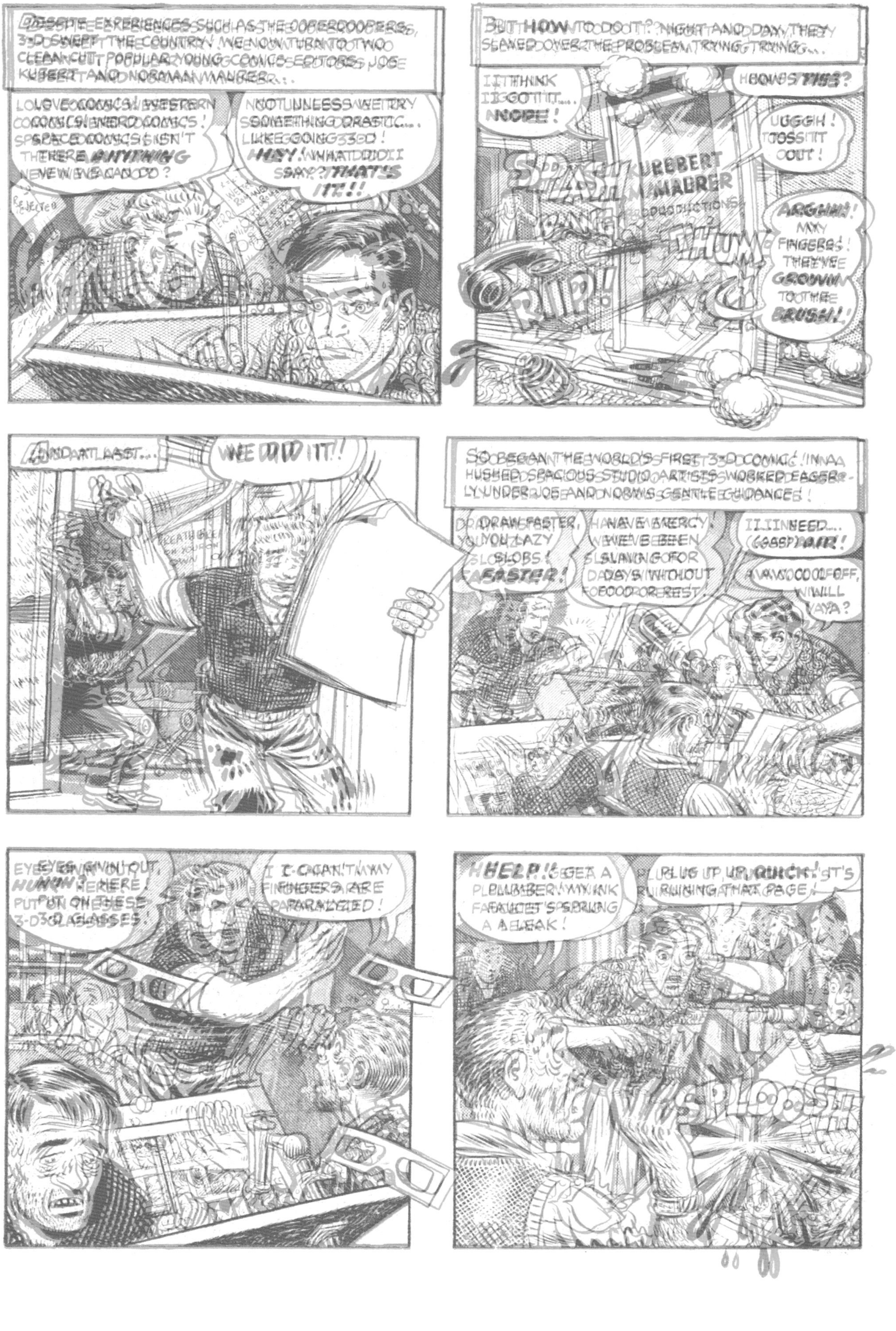
DESPITE EXPERIENCES SUCH AS THE OOPERDOOPERS, 3-D SWEPT THE COUNTRY! WE NOW TURN TO TWO CLEAN-CUT, POPULAR YOUNG COMICS EDITORS, JOE KUBERT AND NORMAN MAURER...
LOVE COMICS! WESTERN COMICS! WEIRD COMICS! SPACE COMICS! ISN'T THERE ANYTHING NEW WE CAN DO?
NOT UNLESS WE TRY SOMETHING DRASTIC... LIKE GOING 3-D! HEY! WHAT DID I SAY? THAT'S IT!!
BUT HOW TO DO IT? NIGHT AND DAY, THEY SLAVED OVER THE PROBLEM, TRYING, TRYING...
I THINK I GOT IT... NOPE!
HOW'S THIS?
UGGH! TOSS IT OUT!
KUBERT MAURER PRODUCTIONS
ARGHH! MY FINGERS! THEY'VE GROWN TO THE BRUSH!
AND AT LAST...
WE DID IT!!
SO BEGAN THE WORLD'S FIRST 3-D COMIC! IN A HUSHED, SPACIOUS STUDIO, ARTISTS WORKED EAGERLY UNDER JOE AND NORM'S GENTLE GUIDANCE!
DRAW FASTER, YOU LAZY SLOBS! FASTER!
HAVE MERCY! WE'VE BEEN SLAVING FOR DAYS WITHOUT FOOD OR REST!
I NEED... (GASP) AIR!
AW, COOL OFF, WILL YA?
EYES GIVIN' OUT, HUH? HERE! PUT ON THESE 3-D GLASSES!
I C-CAN'T! MY FINGERS ARE PARALYZED!
HELP! GET A PLUMBER! MY INK FAUCET'S SPRUNG A LEAK!
PLUG IT UP, QUICK! IT'S RUINING THAT PAGE!
SPLOOSH

58

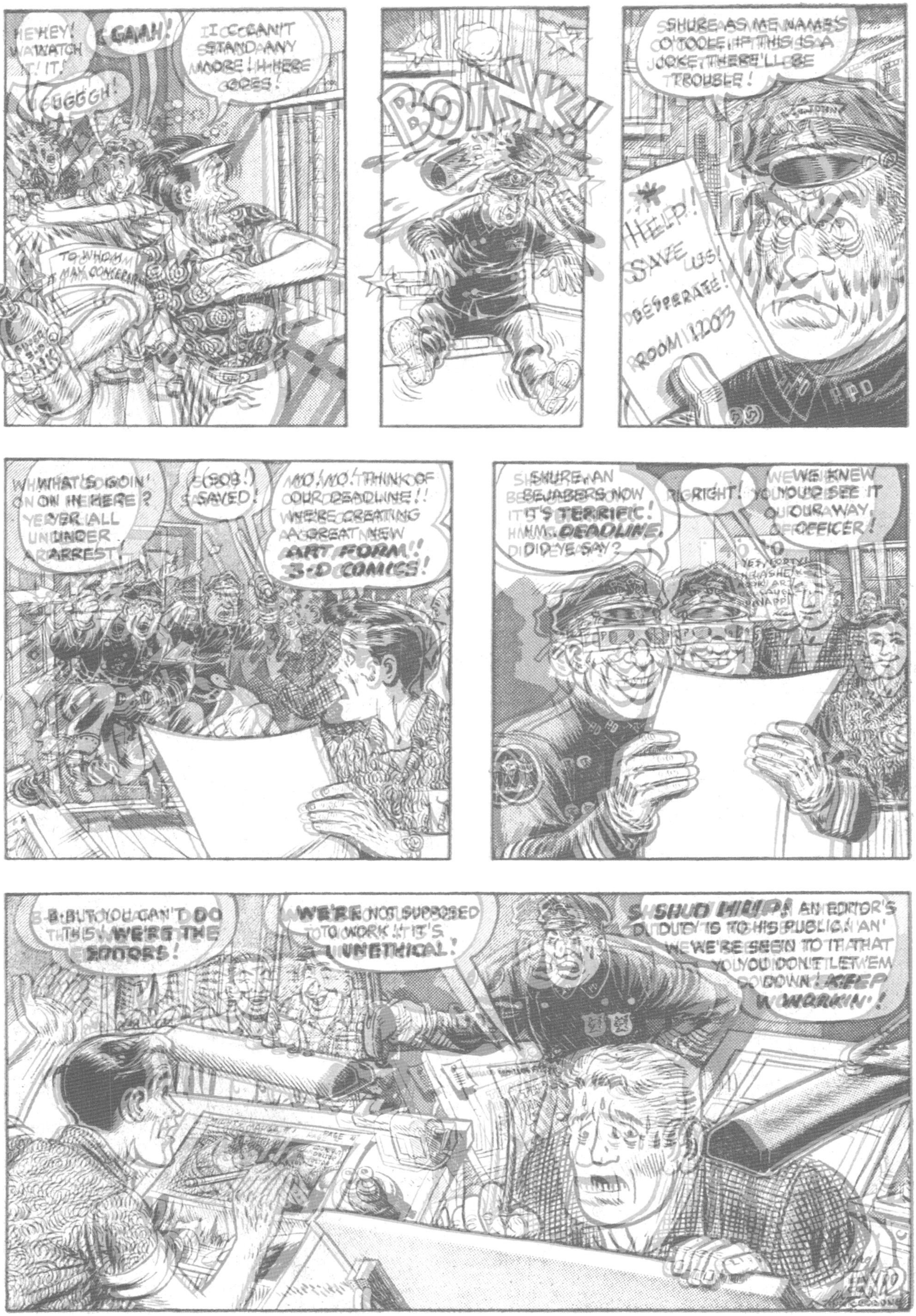
HEY! WATCH IT!
G-GAAH!
I C-CAN'T STAND ANY MORE! H-HERE GOES!
UGGGH!
TO WHOM IT MAY CONCERN
BOINK!!
SHURE AS ME NAME'S O'TOOLE, IF THIS IS A JOKE, THERE'LL BE TROUBLE!
HELP! SAVE US! DESPERATE! ROOM 1203
WHAT'S GOIN' ON IN HERE? YER ALL UNDER ARREST!
(SOB!) SAVED!
NO! NO! THINK OF OUR DEADLINE!! WE'RE CREATING A GREAT NEW ART FORM!! 3-D COMICS!
SHURE, AN BEJABERS NOW IT'S TERRIFIC! HM... DEADLINE, DID YE SAY?
RIGHT!
WE KNEW YOU'D SEE IT OUR WAY, OFFICER!
B-BUT YOU CAN'T DO THIS! WE'RE THE EDITORS!
WE'RE NOT SUPPOSED TO WORK! IT'S UNETHICAL!
SHUD HUP! AN EDITOR'S DUTY IS TO HIS PUBLIC! AN' WE'RE SEEIN TO IT THAT YOU DON'T LET 'EM DOWN! KEEP WORKIN'!
END

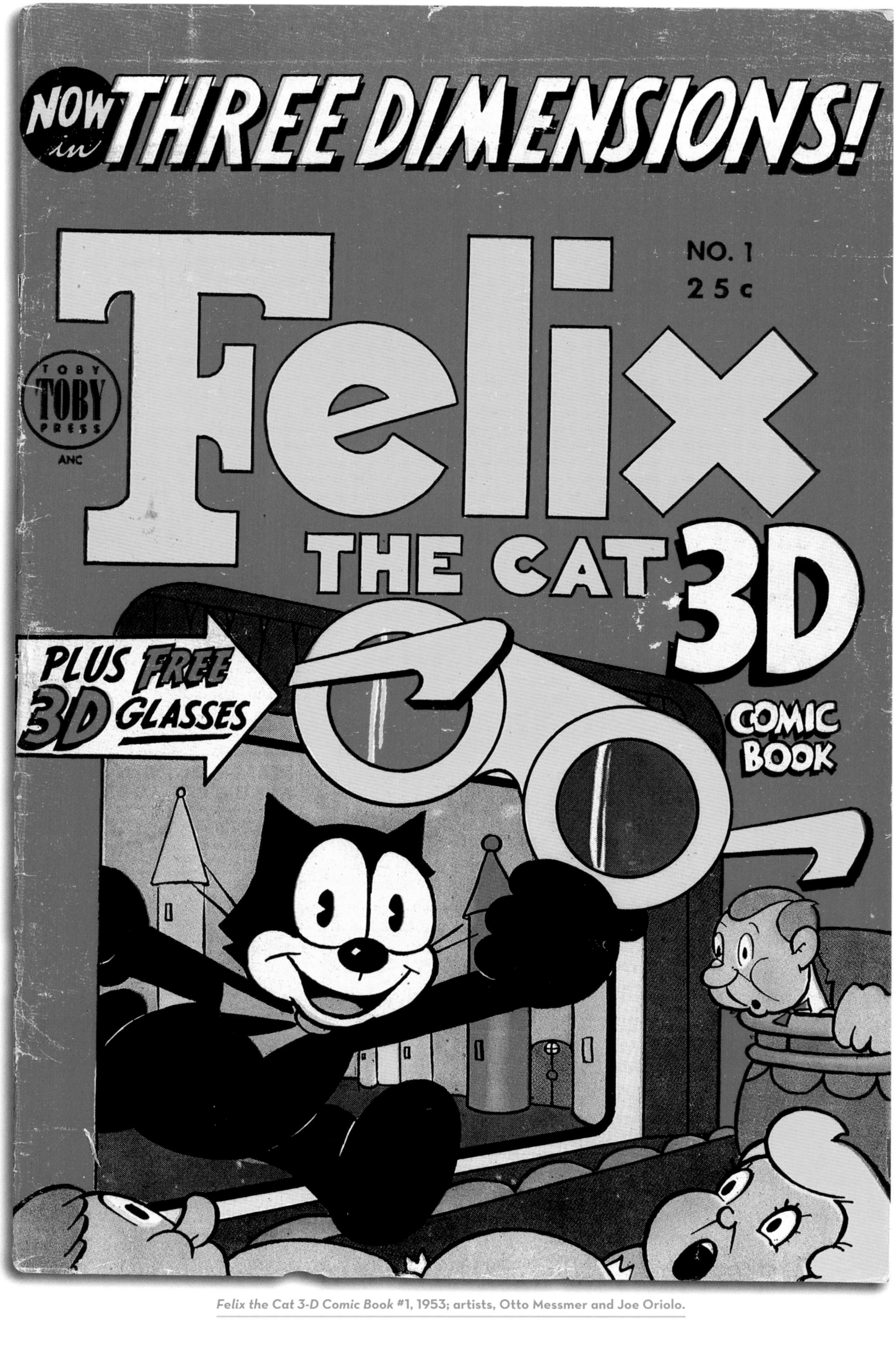
NOW in THREE DIMENSIONS!
NO. 1
25c
TOBY PRESS
ANC
Felix
THE CAT 3D
COMIC BOOK
PLUS FREE 3D GLASSES

Felix the Cat 3-D Comic Book #1, 1953; artists, Otto Messmer and Joe Oriolo.

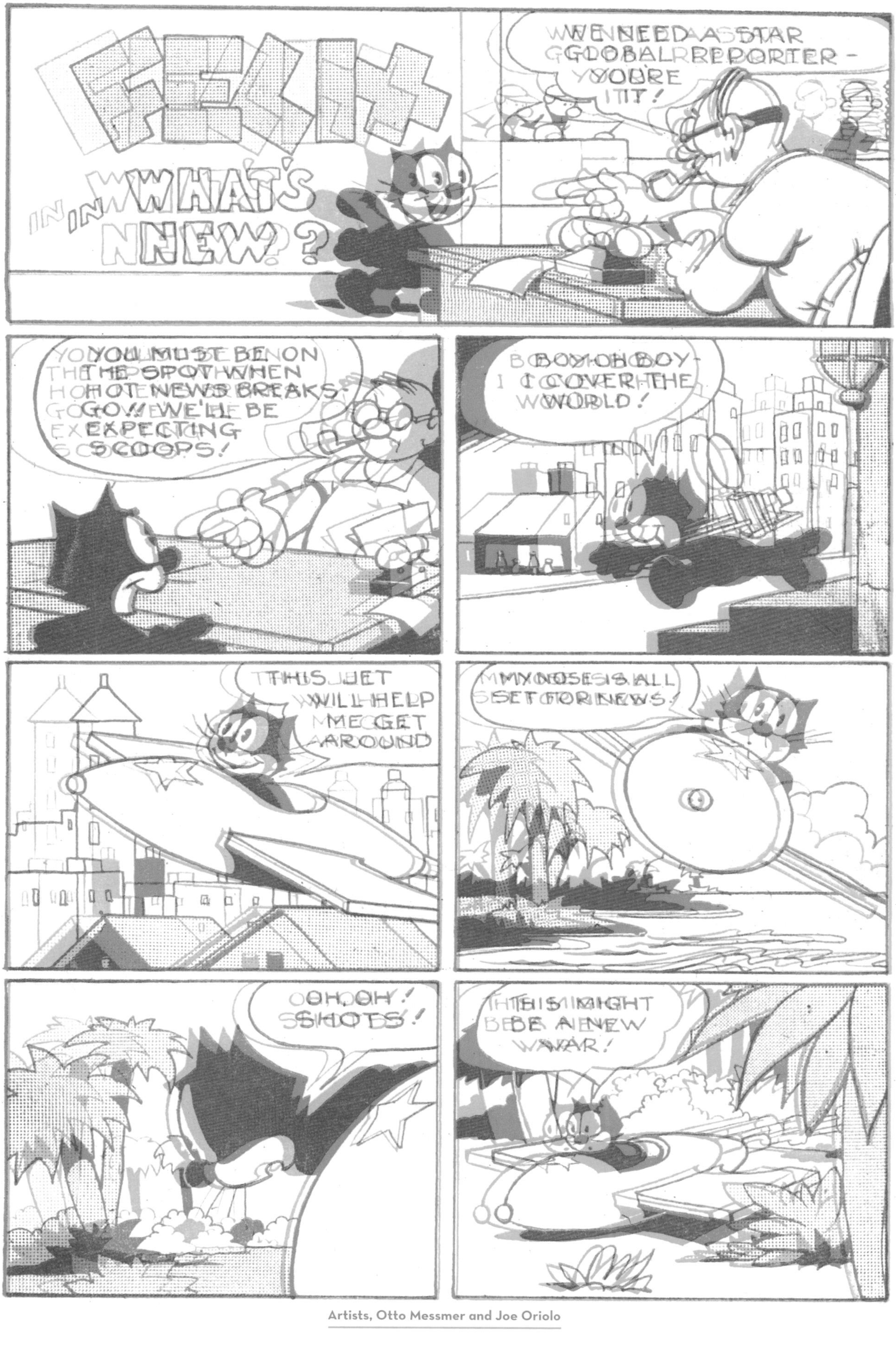
FELIX
in WHAT'S NEW?
WE NEED A STAR GLOBAL REPORTER - YOU'RE IT!
YOU MUST BE ON THE SPOT WHEN HOT NEWS BREAKS: GO!! WE'LL BE EXPECTING SCOOPS!
BOY OH BOY - I COVER THE WORLD!
THIS JET WILL HELP ME GET AROUND
MY NOSE IS ALL SET FOR NEWS!
OH, OH! SHOTS!
THIS MIGHT BE A NEW WAR!

Artists, Otto Messmer and Joe Oriolo

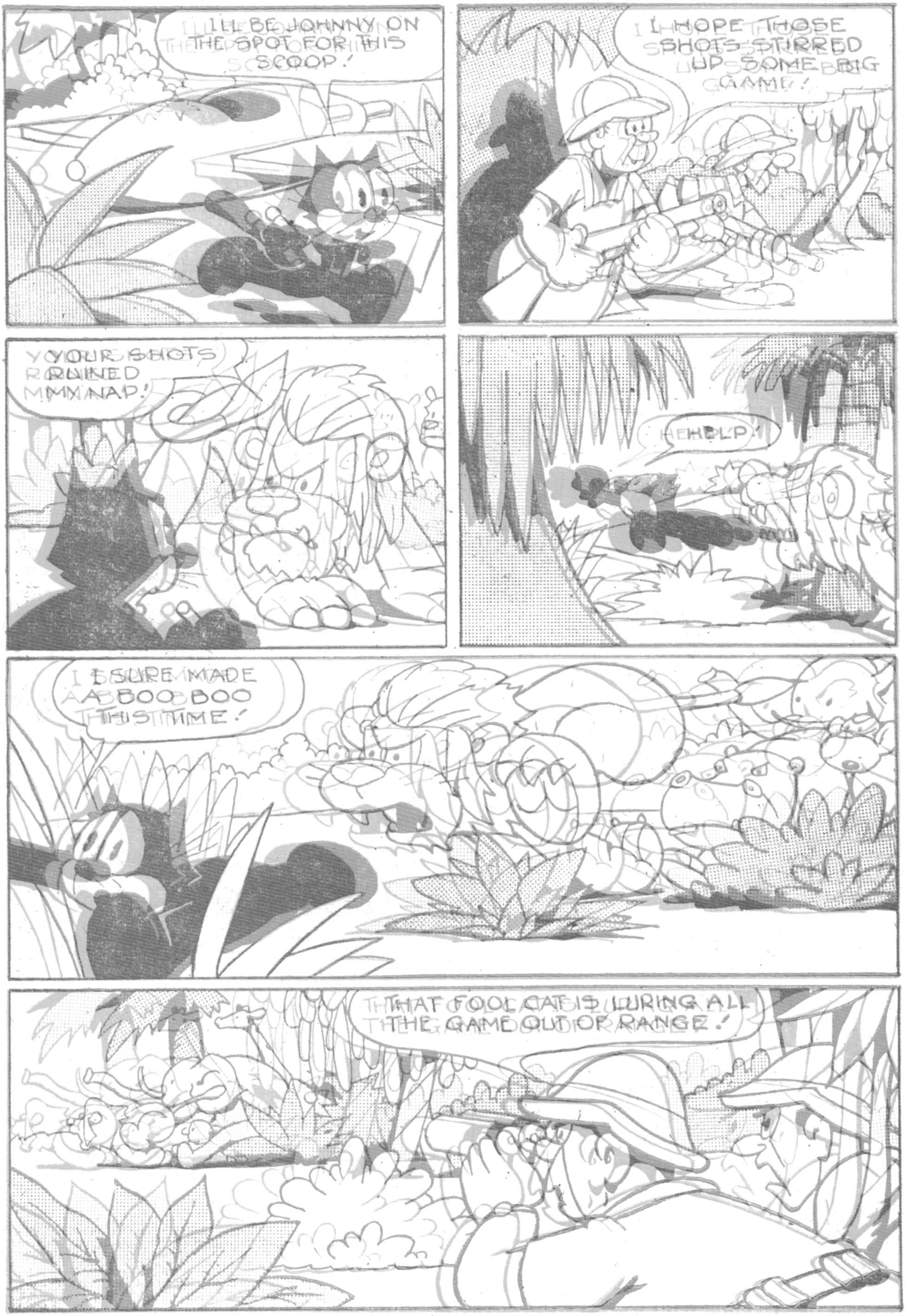
I'LL BE JOHNNY ON THE SPOT FOR THIS SCOOP!
I HOPE THOSE SHOTS STIRRED UP SOME BIG GAME!
YOUR SHOTS RUINED MY NAP!
HELP!
I SURE MADE A BOO BOO THIS TIME!
THAT FOOL CAT IS LURING ALL THE GAME OUT OF RANGE!

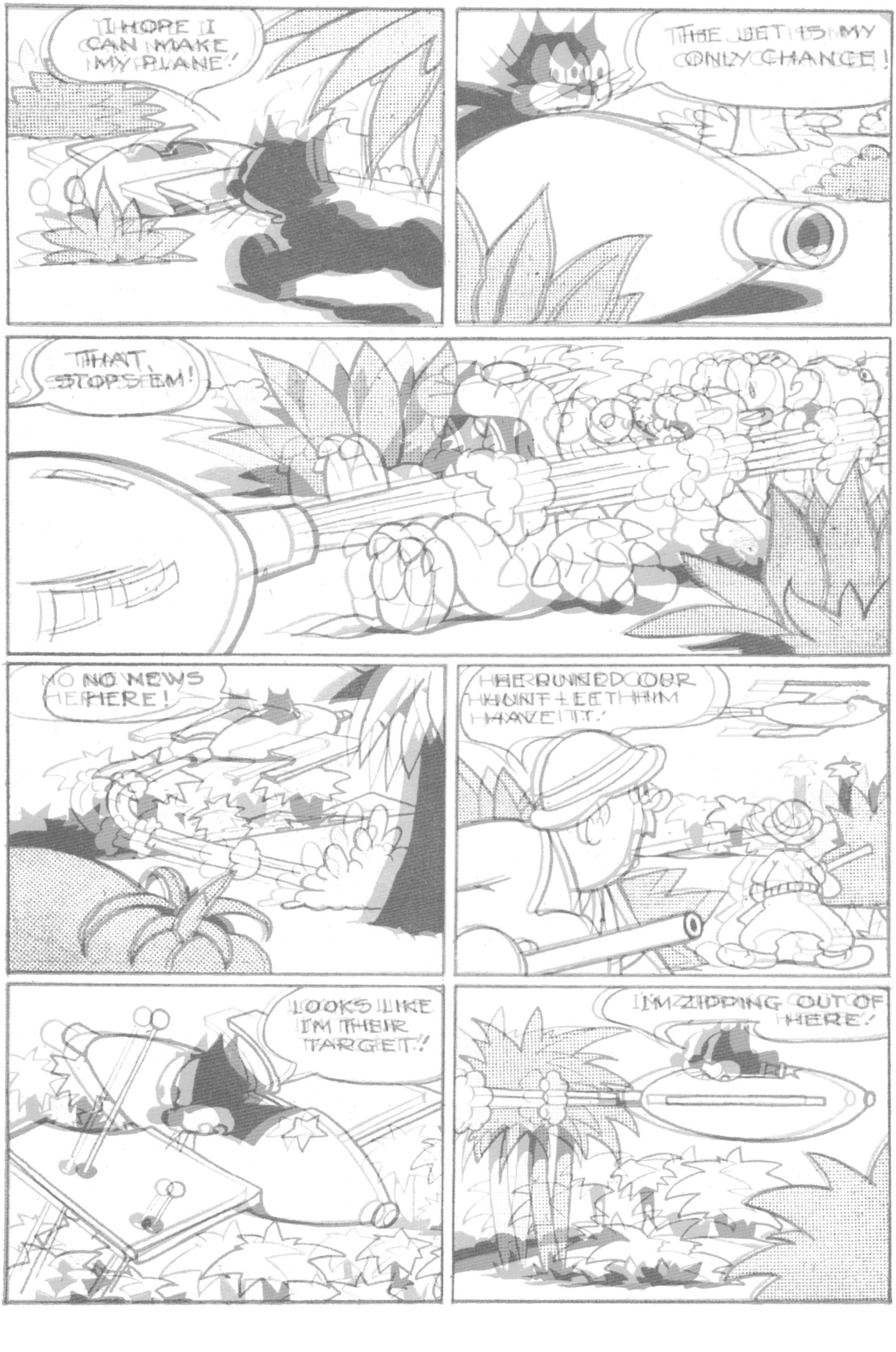
I HOPE I CAN MAKE MY PLANE!
THE JET IS MY ONLY CHANCE!
THAT STOPS 'EM!
NO NEWS HERE!
HE RUINED OUR HUNT - LET HIM HAVE IT!
LOOKS LIKE I'M THEIR TARGET!
I'M ZIPPING OUT OF HERE!

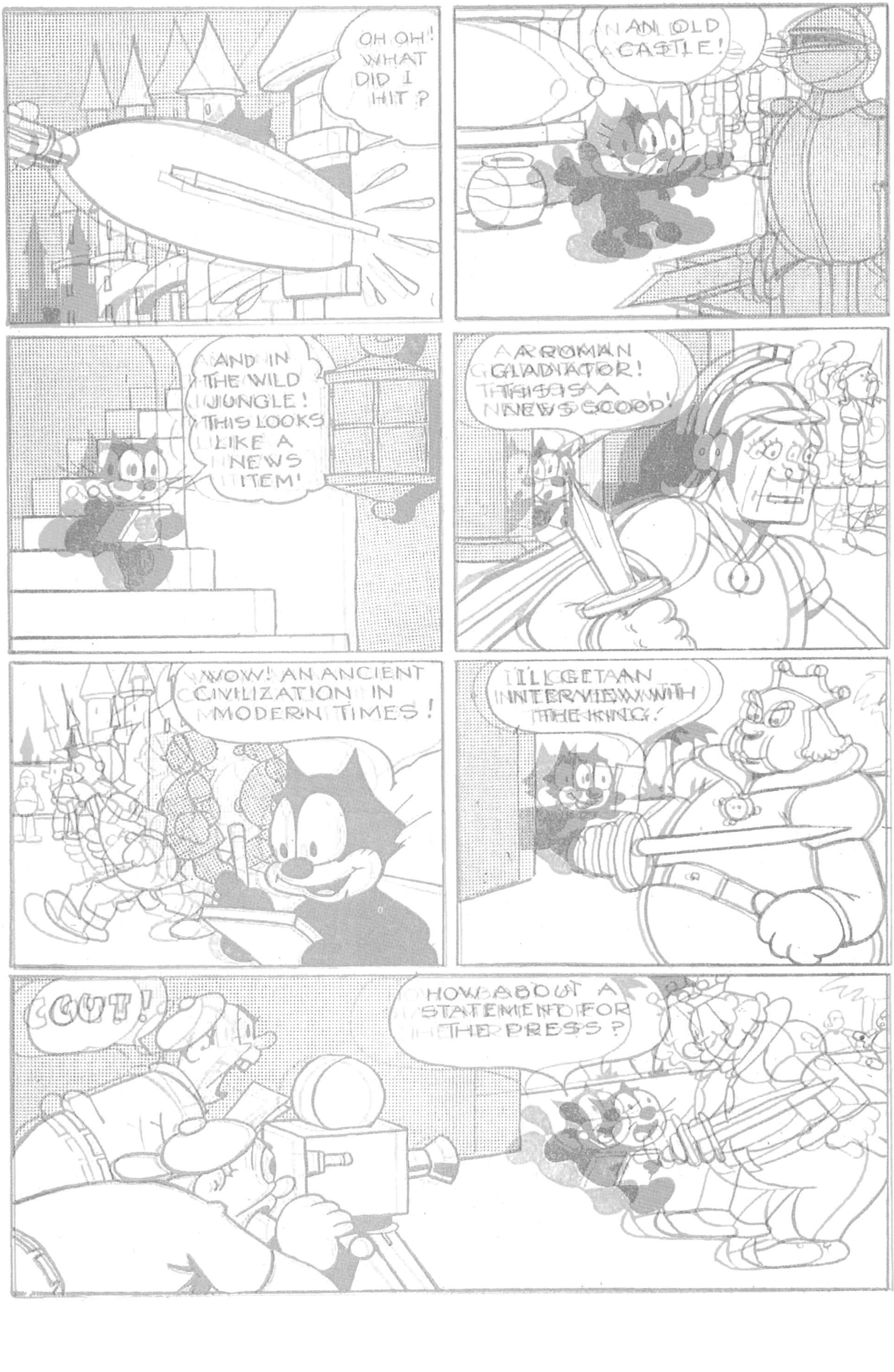
OH OH! WHAT DID I HIT?
AN OLD CASTLE!
AND IN THE WILD JUNGLE! THIS LOOKS LIKE A NEWS ITEM!
A ROMAN GLADIATOR! THIS IS A NEWS SCOOP!
WOW! AN ANCIENT CIVILIZATION IN MODERN TIMES!
I'LL GET AN INTERVIEW WITH THE KING!
CUT!
HOW ABOUT A STATEMENT FOR THE PRESS?

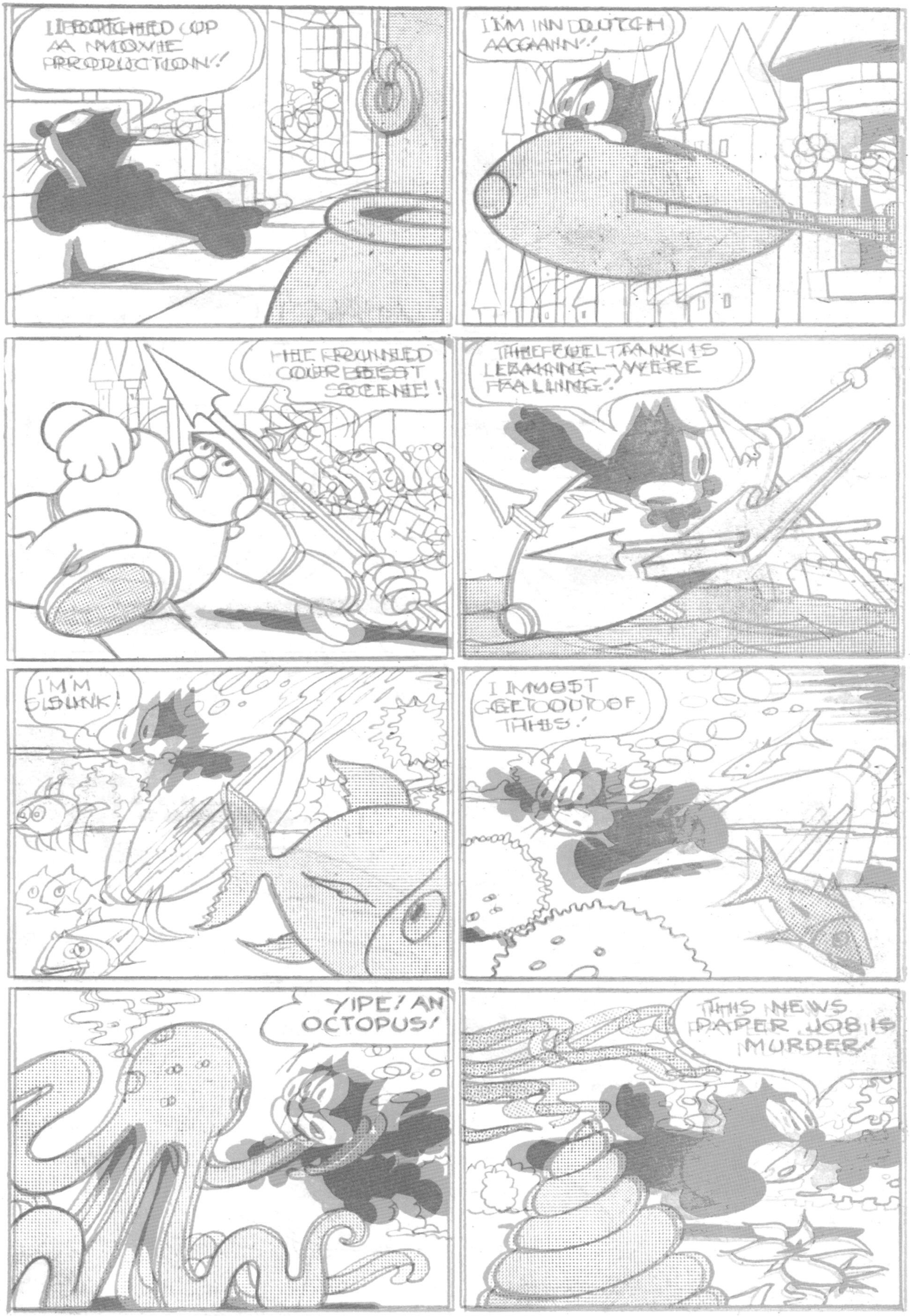
I BOTCHED UP A MOVIE PRODUCTION!
I'M IN DUTCH AGAIN!
HE RUINED OUR BEST SCENE!
THE FUEL TANK IS LEAKING—WE'RE FALLING!
I'M SUNK!
I MUST GET OUT OF THIS!
YIPE! AN OCTOPUS!
THIS NEWS PAPER JOB IS MURDER!

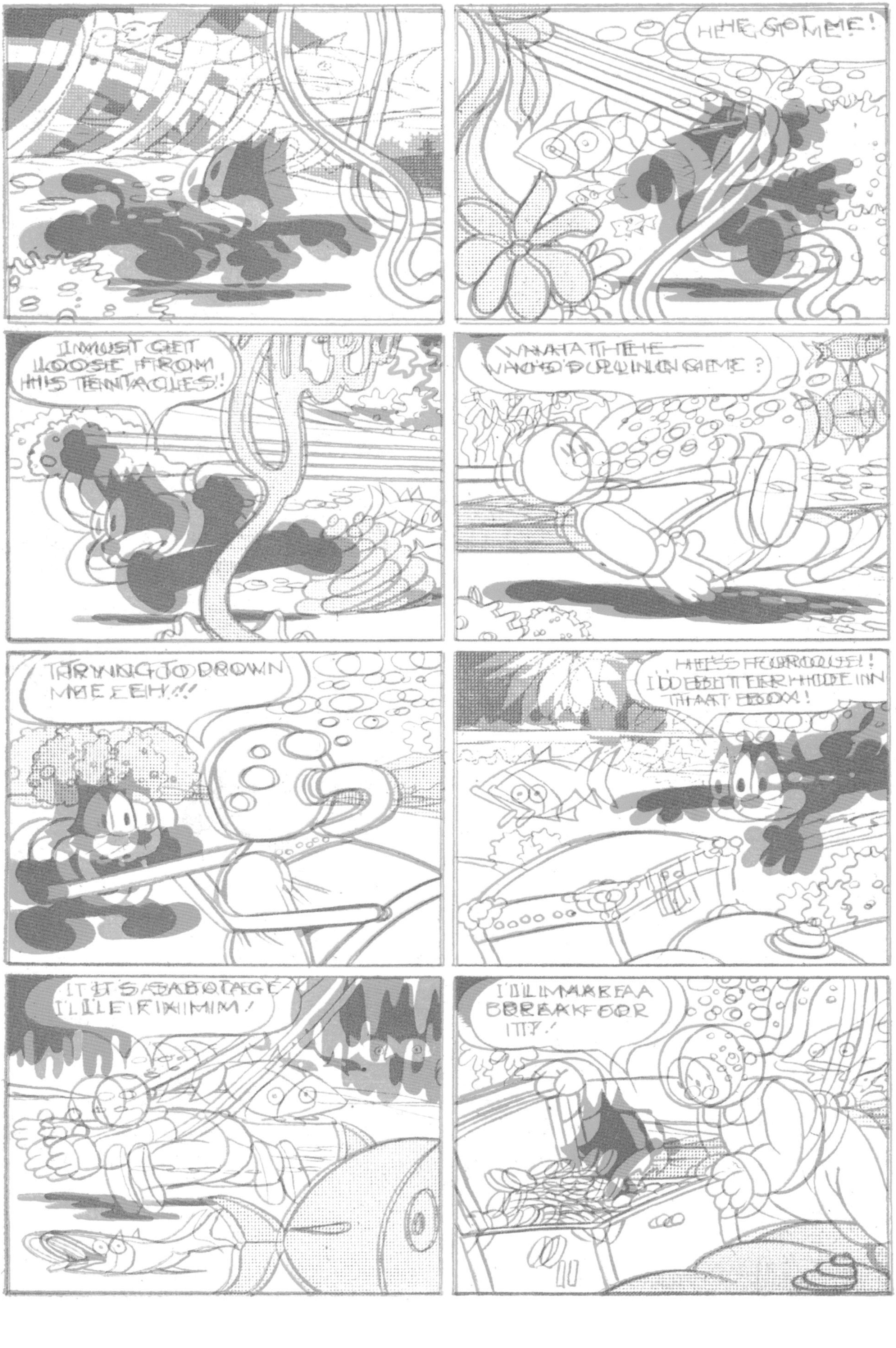

HE GOT ME!
I MUST GET LOOSE FROM HIS TENTACLES!!
WHAT THE— WHO'S PULLING ME?
TRYING TO DROWN MEEEH!!!
I'D BETTER HIDE IN THAT BOX!
IT'S SABOTAGE— I'LL FIX HIM!
I'LL MAKE A BREAK FOR IT!

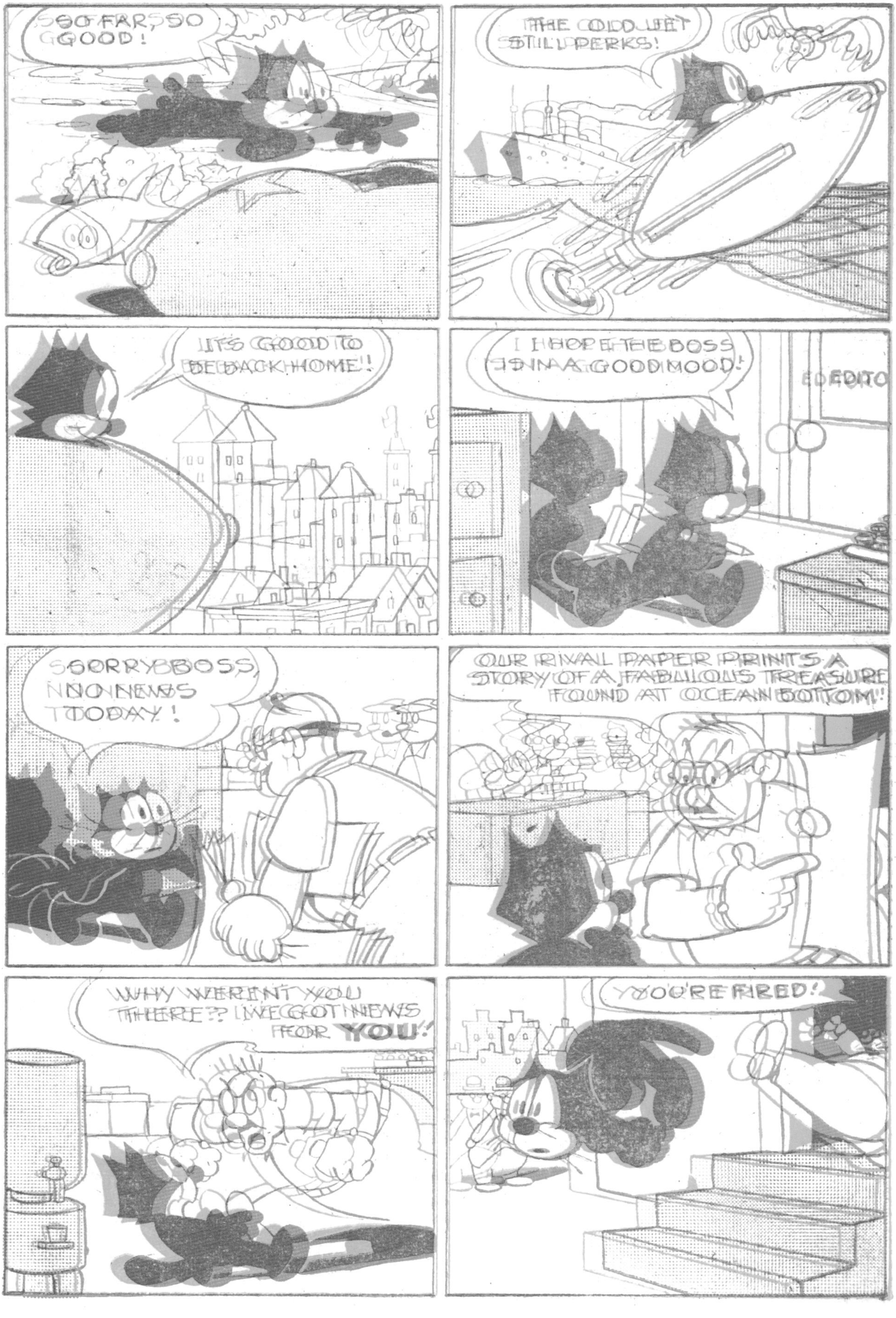
SO FAR, SO GOOD!
THE OLD JET STILL PERKS!
IT'S GOOD TO BE BACK HOME!
I HOPE THE BOSS IS IN A GOOD MOOD!
EDITO
SORRY BOSS, NO NEWS TODAY!
OUR RIVAL PAPER PRINTS A STORY OF A FABULOUS TREASURE FOUND AT OCEAN BOTTOM!
WHY WEREN'T YOU THERE?? I'VE GOT NEWS FOR YOU!
YOU'RE FIRED!

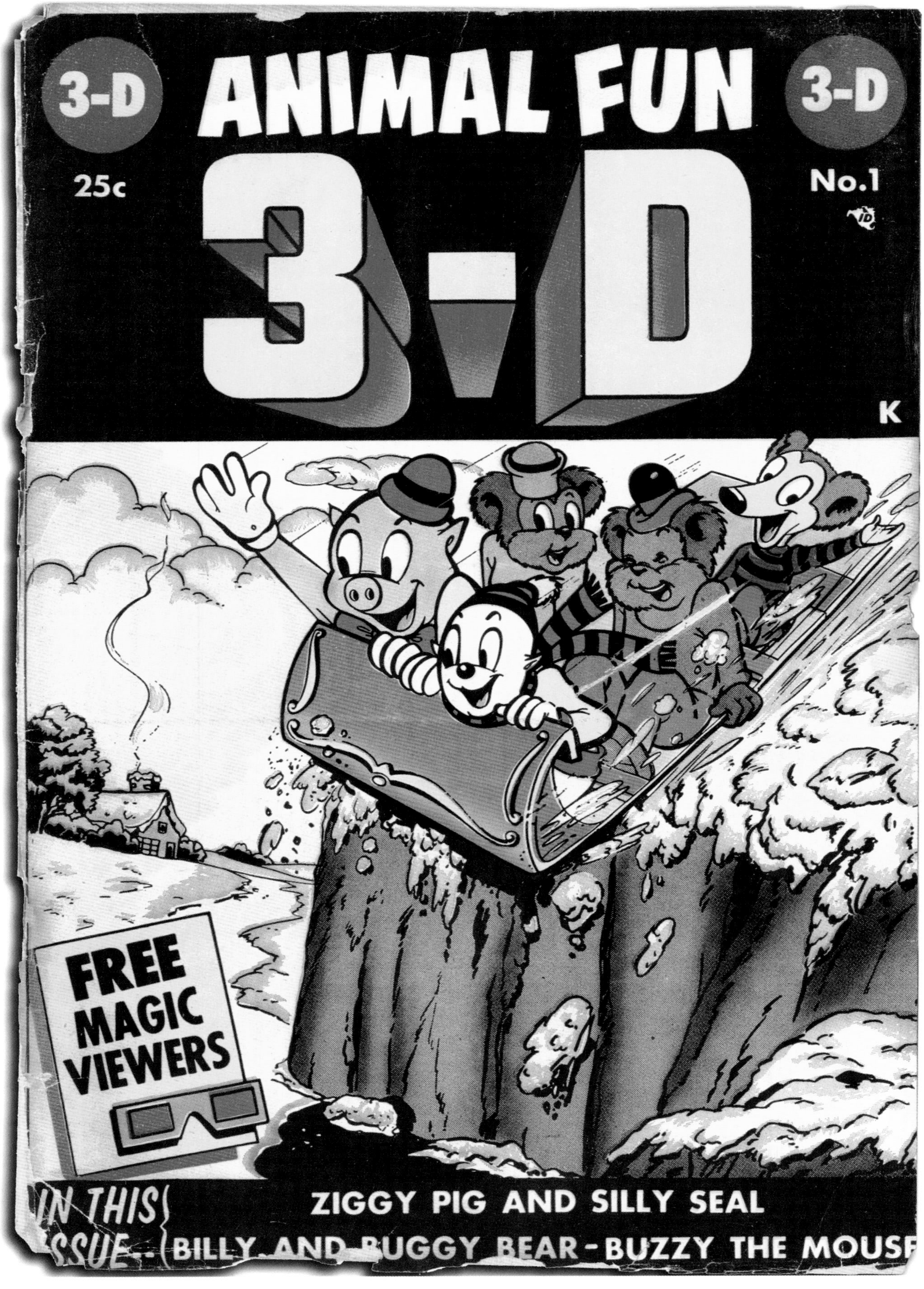
3-D
ANIMAL FUN
3-D
25c
No.1
3-D
K
FREE MAGIC VIEWERS
IN THIS ISSUE--
ZIGGY PIG AND SILLY SEAL
BILLY AND BUGGY BEAR-BUZZY THE MOUSE

Animal Fun 3-D #1, 1953; artist, Al Jaffee.

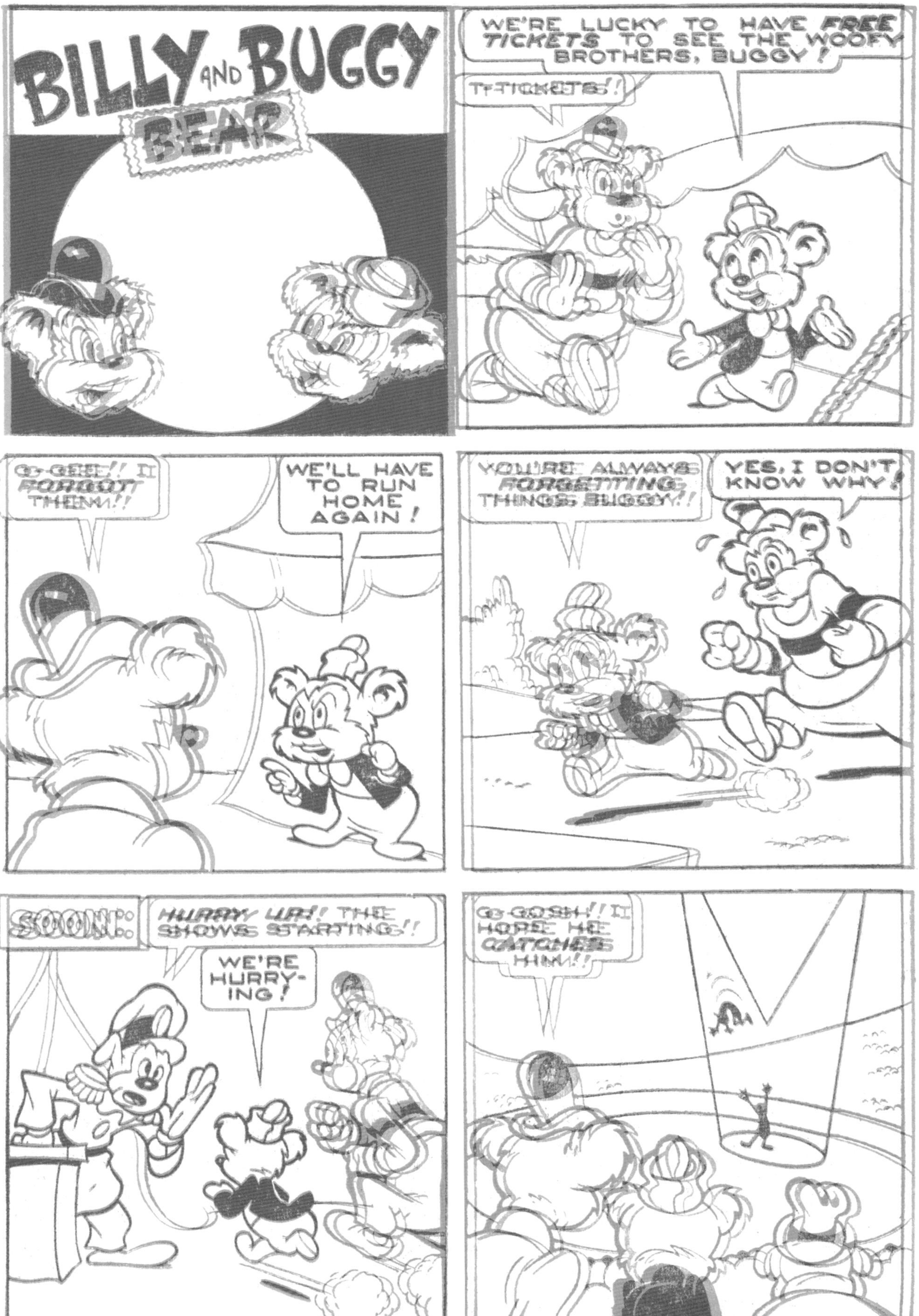
BILLY AND BUGGY BEAR
WE'RE LUCKY TO HAVE FREE TICKETS TO SEE THE WOOFY BROTHERS, BUGGY!
T-TICKETS!
G-GEE!! I FORGOT THEM!!
WE'LL HAVE TO RUN HOME AGAIN!
YOU'RE ALWAYS FORGETTING THINGS, BUGGY!!
YES, I DON'T KNOW WHY!
SOON...
HURRY UP!! THE SHOWS STARTING!!
WE'RE HURRY-ING!
G-GOSH!! I HOPE HE CATCHES HIM!!

Artist, Milton Stein

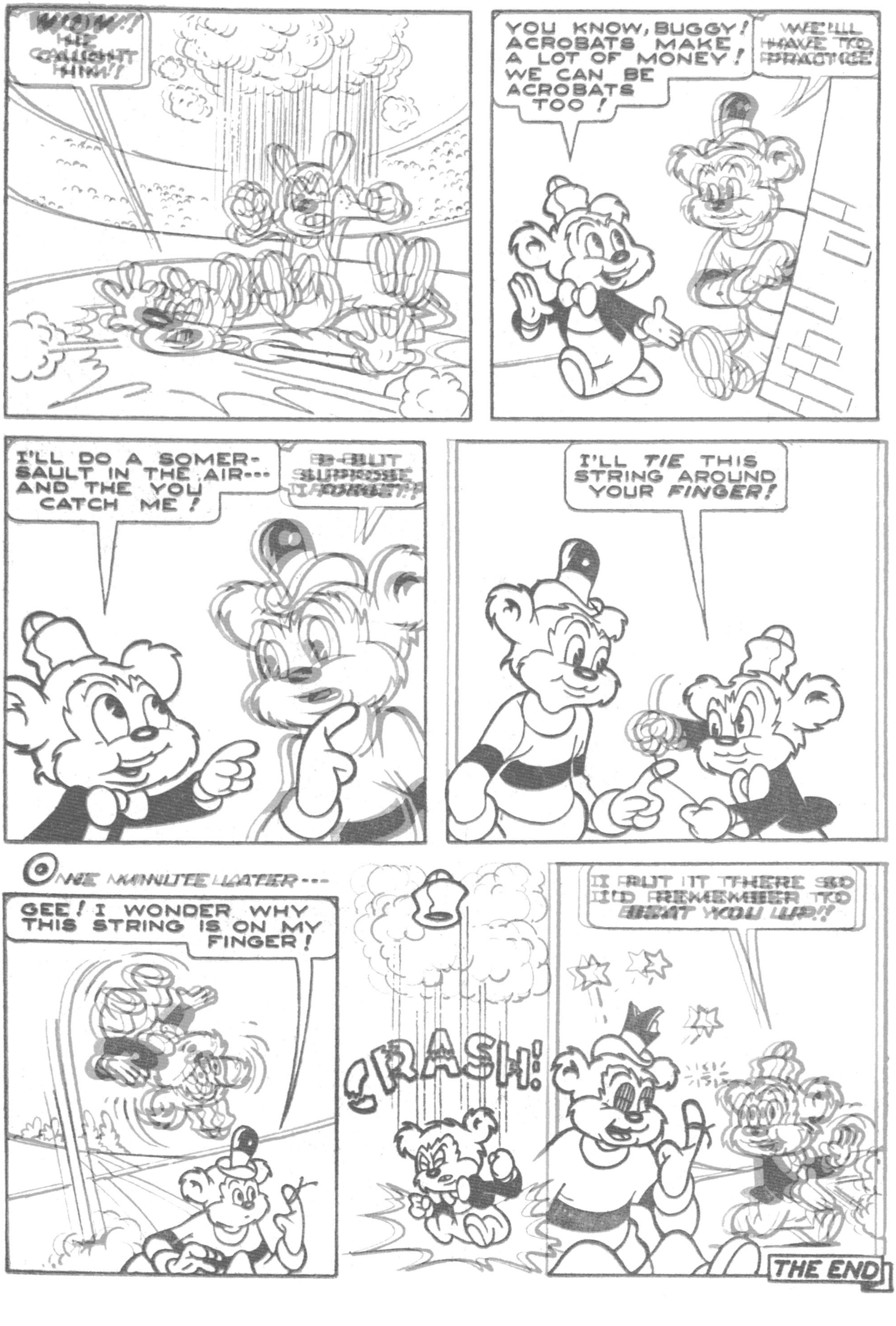
WOW!! HE CAUGHT HIM!!
YOU KNOW, BUGGY! ACROBATS MAKE A LOT OF MONEY! WE CAN BE ACROBATS TOO!
WE'LL HAVE TO PRACTICE!
I'LL DO A SOMER-SAULT IN THE AIR--- AND THE YOU CATCH ME!
B-BUT SUPPOSE I FORGET!?
I'LL TIE THIS STRING AROUND YOUR FINGER!
ONE MINUTE LATER---
GEE! I WONDER WHY THIS STRING IS ON MY FINGER!
CRASH!
I PUT IT THERE SO I'D REMEMBER TO BEAT YOU UP!!
THE END

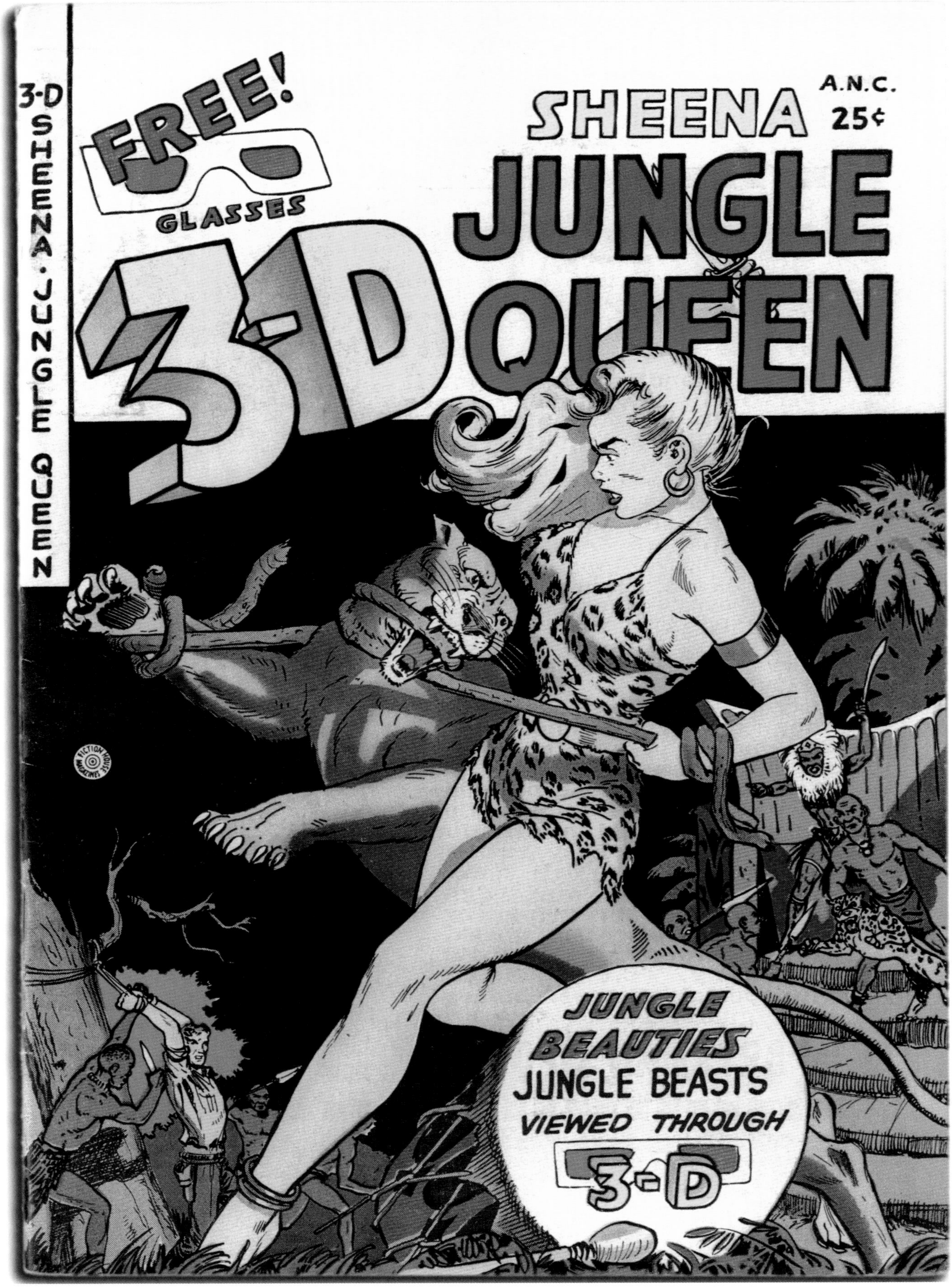
3-D SHEENA · JUNGLE QUEEN
FREE!
GLASSES
3-D
SHEENA
JUNGLE QUEEN
A.N.C.
25¢
JUNGLE BEAUTIES
JUNGLE BEASTS
VIEWED THROUGH
3-D

3-D Sheena, Jungle Queen #1, 1953; artist, Maurice Whitman.

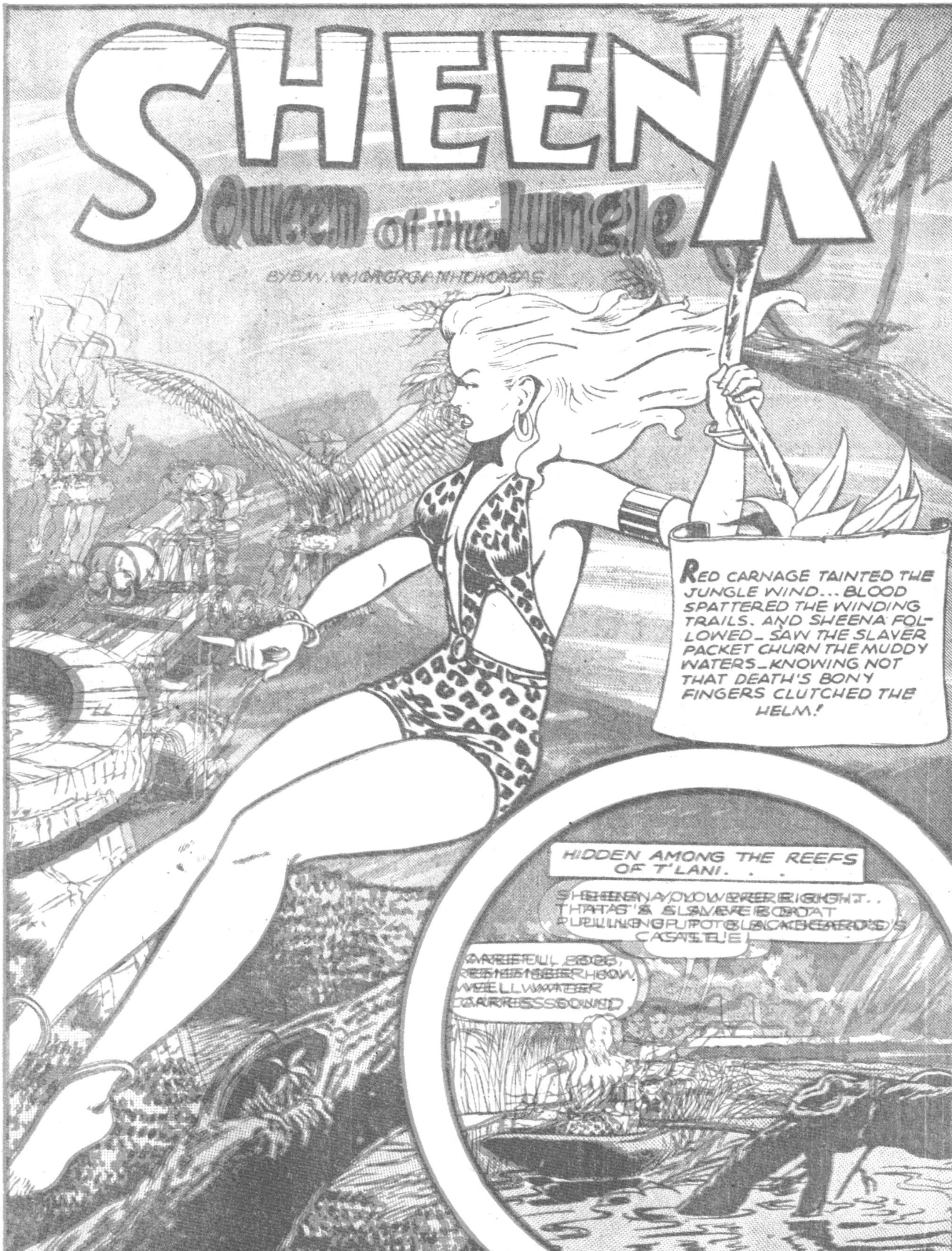
SHEENA
Queen of the Jungle
RED CARNAGE TAINTED THE JUNGLE WIND... BLOOD SPATTERED THE WINDING TRAILS. AND SHEENA FOLLOWED_ SAW THE SLAVER PACKET CHURN THE MUDDY WATERS_KNOWING NOT THAT DEATH'S BONY FINGERS CLUTCHED THE HELM!
HIDDEN AMONG THE REEFS OF T'LANI. . .
SHEENA, YOU WERE RIGHT.. THAT'S A SLAVE BOAT PULLING UP TO BLACKBEARD'S CASTLE!
CAREFUL, BOB, REMEMBER HOW WELL WATER CARRIES SOUND.

Artist unknown

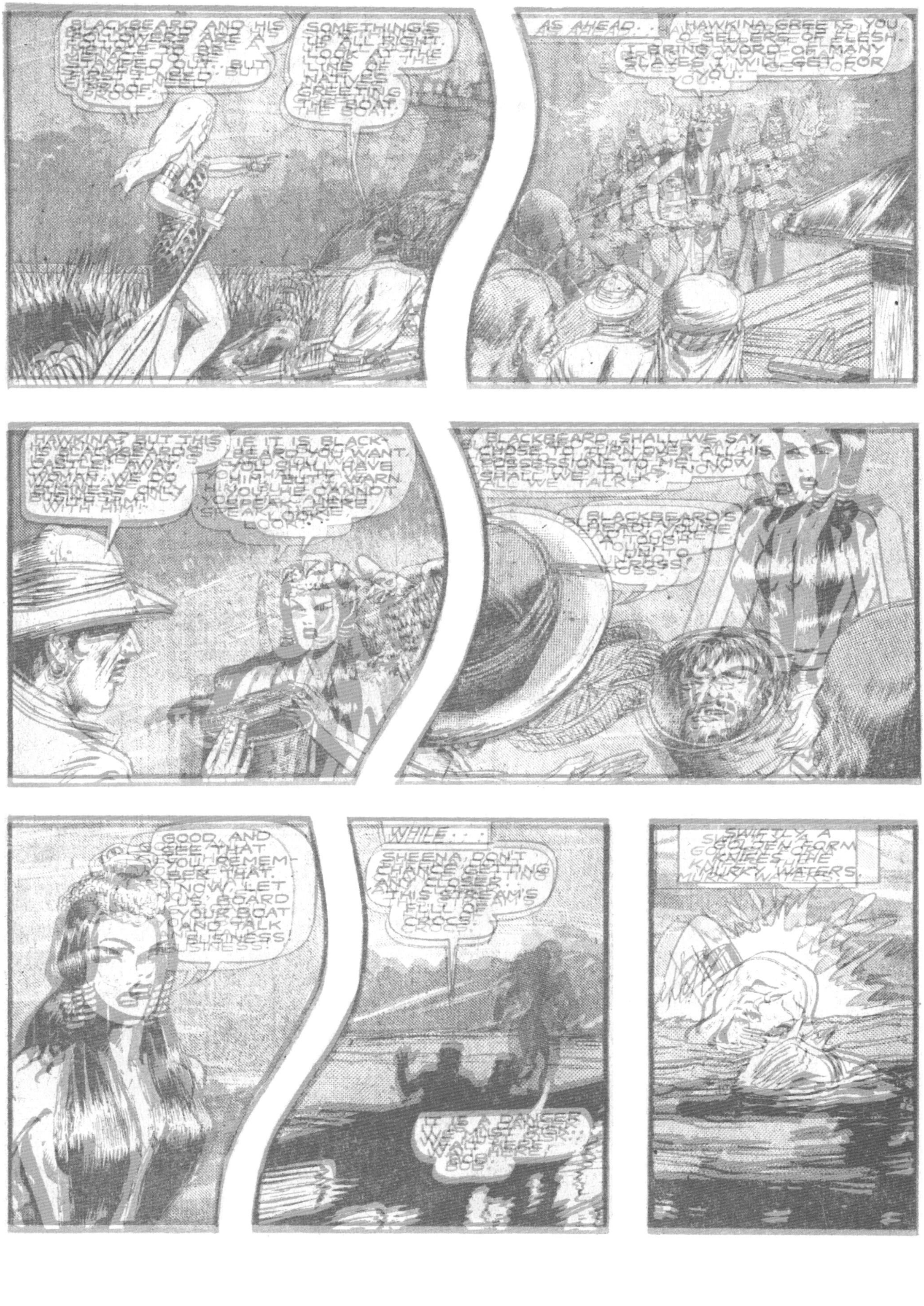
BLACKBEARD AND HIS FOLLOWERS ARE A MENACE TO BE STAMPED OUT. BUT FIRST I NEED PROOF.
SOMETHING'S UP ALL RIGHT. LOOK AT THE LINE OF NATIVES GREETING THE BOAT.
AS AHEAD...
HAWKINA GREETS YOU, O SELLERS OF FLESH. I BRING WORD OF MANY SLAVES I WILL GET FOR YOU.
HAWKINA? BUT THIS IS BLACKBEARD'S CASTLE! AWAY, WOMAN! WE DO BUSINESS ONLY WITH HIM!
IF IT IS BLACKBEARD YOU WANT YOU SHALL HAVE HIM. BUT I WARN YOU! HE CANNOT SPEAK! LOOK!
BLACKBEARD SHALL WE SAY CHOSE TO TURN OVER ALL HIS POSSESSIONS TO ME! NOW SHALL WE TALK?
BLACKBEARD'S DEAD! YOU'RE A TOUGH UN' TO CROSS!
GOOD, AND SEE THAT YOU REMEMBER THAT. NOW, LET US BOARD YOUR BOAT AND TALK BUSINESS!
WHILE...
SHEENA, DON'T CHANCE GETTING ANY CLOSER. THIS STREAM'S FULL OF CROCS.
IT IS A DANGER WE MUST RISK. WAIT HERE, BOB.
SWIFTLY A GOLDEN FORM KNIFES THE MURKY WATERS.

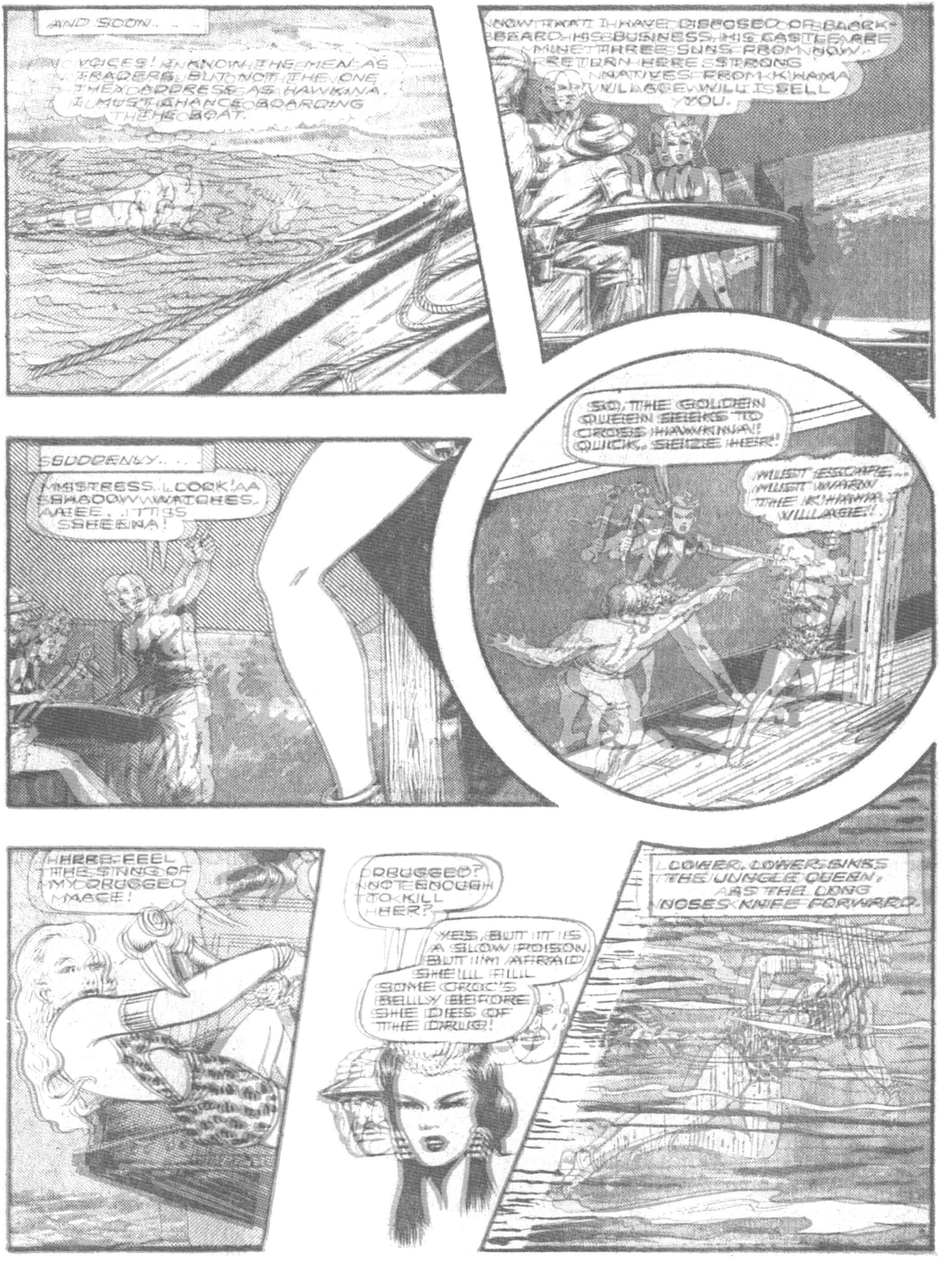

AND SOON...
VOICES! I KNOW THE MEN AS TRADERS, BUT NOT THE ONE THEY ADDRESS AS HAWKANA. I MUST CHANCE BOARDING THE BOAT.
NOW THAT I HAVE DISPOSED OF BLACK-BEARD, HIS BUSINESS, HIS CASTLE ARE MINE! THREE SUNS FROM NOW, RETURN HERE. STRONG NATIVES FROM KHAMA VILLAGE WILL I SELL YOU.
SUDDENLY...
MISTRESS, LOOK! A SHADOW WATCHES. AIEE, IT IS SHEENA!
SO, THE GOLDEN QUEEN SEEKS TO CROSS HAWKANA! QUICK, SEIZE HER!
MUST ESCAPE... MUST WARN THE KHAMA VILLAGE!
HERE! FEEL THE STING OF MY DRUGGED MACE!
DRUGGED? NOT ENOUGH TO KILL HER?
YES, BUT IT IS A SLOW POISON. BUT I'M AFRAID SHE'LL FILL SOME CROC'S BELLY BEFORE SHE DIES OF THE DRUG!
LOWER, LOWER SINKS THE JUNGLE QUEEN, AS THE LONG NOSES KNIFE FORWARD.

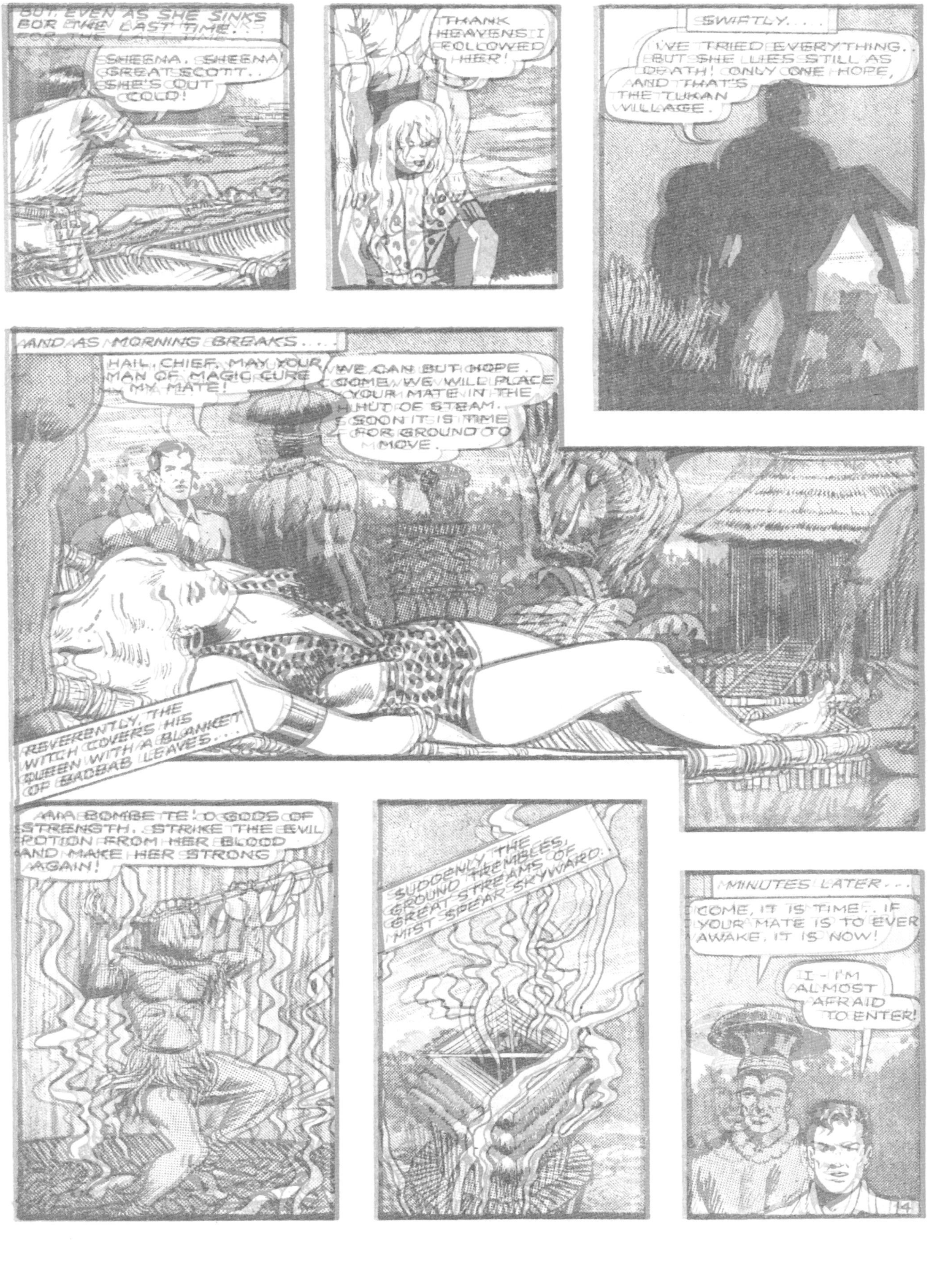
BUT, EVEN AS SHE SINKS FOR THE LAST TIME...
SHEENA, SHEENA! GREAT SCOTT... SHE'S OUT COLD!
THANK HEAVENS I FOLLOWED HER!
SWIFTLY...
WE TRIED EVERYTHING. BUT SHE LIES STILL AS DEATH! ONLY ONE HOPE, AND THAT'S THE TUKAN VILLAGE.
AND AS MORNING BREAKS...
HAIL, CHIEF, MAY YOUR MAN OF MAGIC CURE MY MATE!
WE CAN BUT HOPE. COME, WE WILL PLACE YOUR MATE IN THE HUT OF STEAM. SOON IT IS TIME FOR GROUND TO MOVE.
REVERENTLY, THE WITCH COVERS HIS QUEEN WITH A BLANKET OF BAOBAB LEAVES...
MA BOMBETE! O GODS OF STRENGTH, STRIKE THE EVIL POTION FROM HER BLOOD AND MAKE HER STRONG AGAIN!
SUDDENLY THE GROUND TREMBLES, GREAT STREAMS OF MIST SPEAR SKYWARD.
MINUTES LATER...
COME, IT IS TIME. IF YOUR MATE IS TO EVER AWAKE, IT IS NOW!
I-I'M ALMOST AFRAID TO ENTER!
14

YOU'VE FAILED.. YOU'VE.. NO, SHE AWAKES! SHEENA, SPEAK TO ME, IT'S BOB!

TAKE IT EASY. EVERYTHING'S ALRIGHT NOW..

BOB, NOW I REMEMBER! HAWKINA, SHE SPOKE OF ATTACKING THE K'HAMA VILLAGE! COME, WE MUST TREK SWIFTLY!

AS, OUTSIDE THE HIGH STOCKADE SURROUNDING THE K'HAMA VILLAGE...

O HAWKINA THE NATIVES WITHIN TURN OUR TERRIS, THEY OPEN NOT THE GATES.

NO MATTER. READY THE GIANT BOWS!

SWIFTLY, THE BIRD NATIVES PLACE THEMSELVES ON THE PRIMITIVE CATAPULTS...

A SHARP TWANG, AND SUDDENLY THEY SOAR SKYWARD...

AND GRACEFULLY DIVE DOWN INTO THE BARRICADED VILLAGE, FLAMING FIGURES OF VENGEANCE...

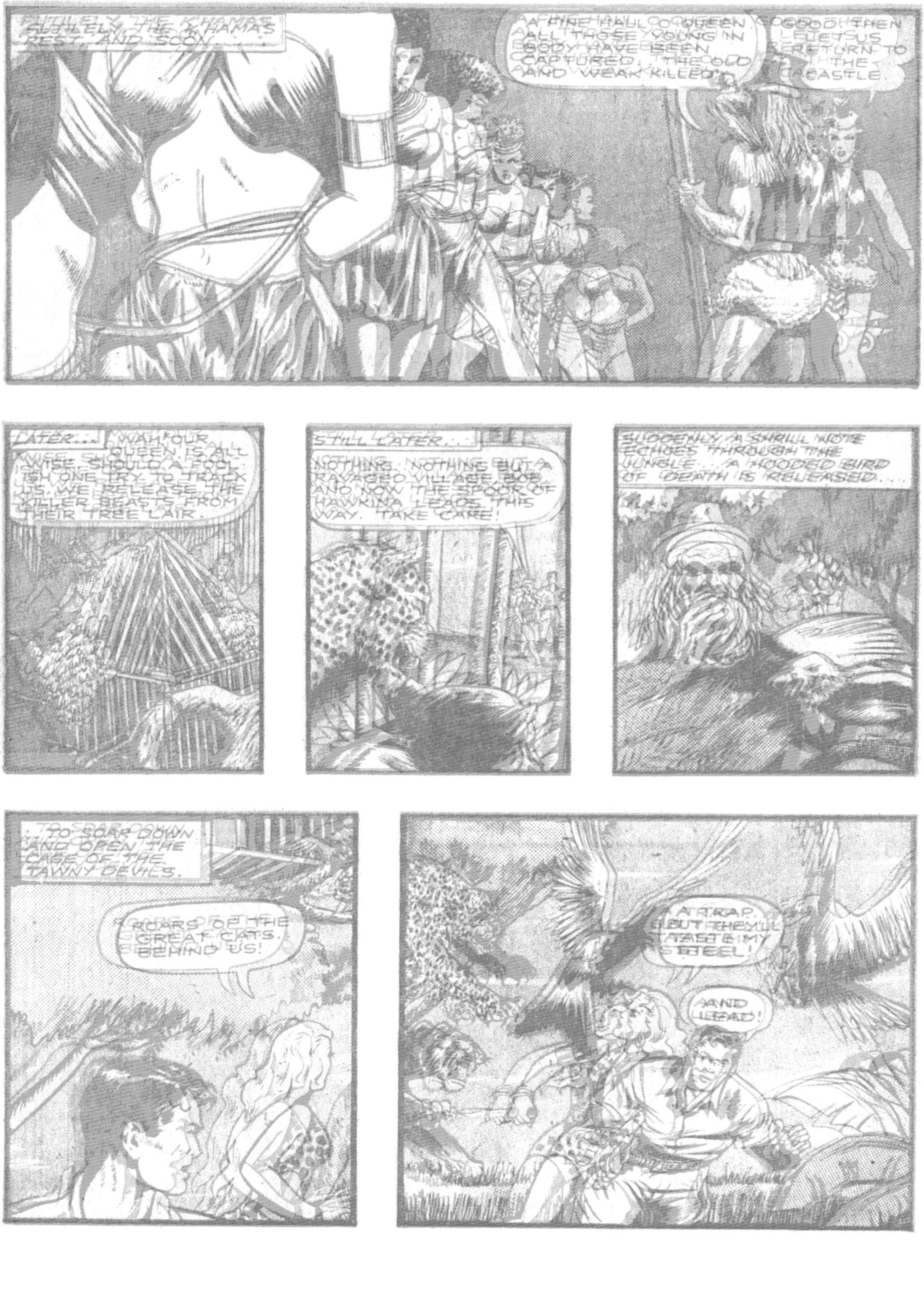
SUBTLELY, THE KHAMAS REST, AND SOON . . .
A FINE HAUL, O QUEEN. ALL THOSE YOUNG IN BODY HAVE BEEN CAPTURED, THE OLD AND WEAK KILLED!
GOOD! THEN LET US RETURN TO THE CASTLE.
LATER . . .
WAH! OUR QUEEN IS ALL WISE. SHOULD A FOOLISH ONE TRY TO TRACK US, WE RELEASE THE KILLER BEASTS FROM THEIR TREE LAIR.
STILL LATER . . .
NOTHING. NOTHING BUT A RAVAGED VILLAGE BOB. AND NOW THE SPOOR OF HAWKINA LEADS THIS WAY. TAKE CARE!
SUDDENLY A SHRILL NOTE ECHOES THROUGH THE JUNGLE . . . A HOODED BIRD OF DEATH IS RELEASED . . .
. . . TO SOAR DOWN AND OPEN THE CAGE OF THE TAWNY DEVILS.
ROARS OF THE GREAT CATS. BEHIND US!
A TRAP. BUT THEY'LL TASTE MY STEEL!
AND LEAD!

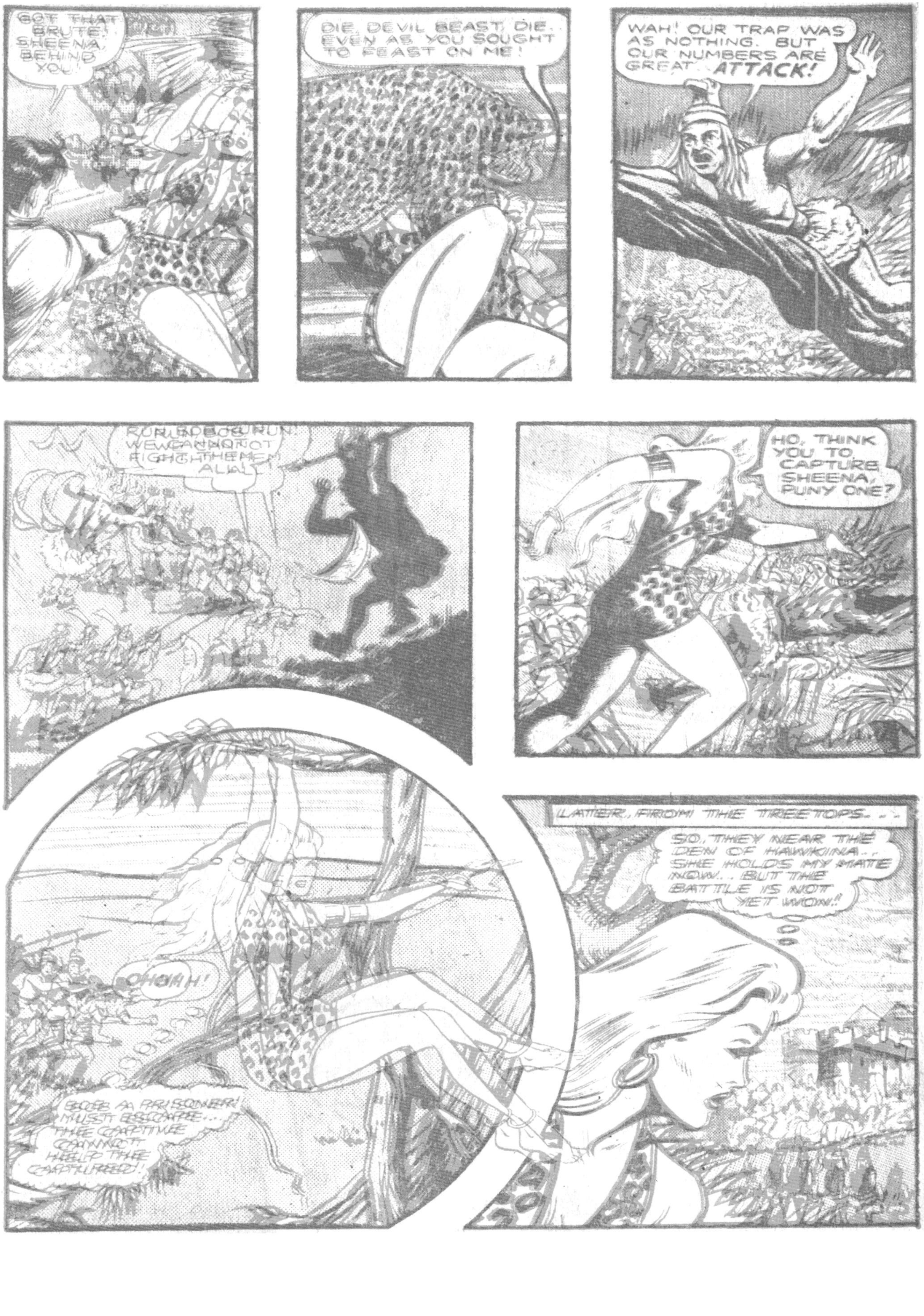
GOT THAT BRUTE! SHEENA, BEHIND YOU!
DIE, DEVIL BEAST! DIE, EVEN AS YOU SOUGHT TO FEAST ON ME!
WAH! OUR TRAP WAS AS NOTHING. BUT OUR NUMBERS ARE GREAT. ATTACK!
RUN, BOB, RUN! WE CANNOT FIGHT THEM ALL!
HO, THINK YOU TO CAPTURE SHEENA, PUNY ONE?
OHHHH!
BOB A PRISONER! MUST ESCAPE... THE CAPTIVE CANNOT HELP THE CAPTURED!
LATER, FROM THE TREETOPS...
SO, THEY NEAR THE DEN OF HAWKINA... SHE HOLDS MY MATE NOW... BUT THE BATTLE IS NOT YET WON!!

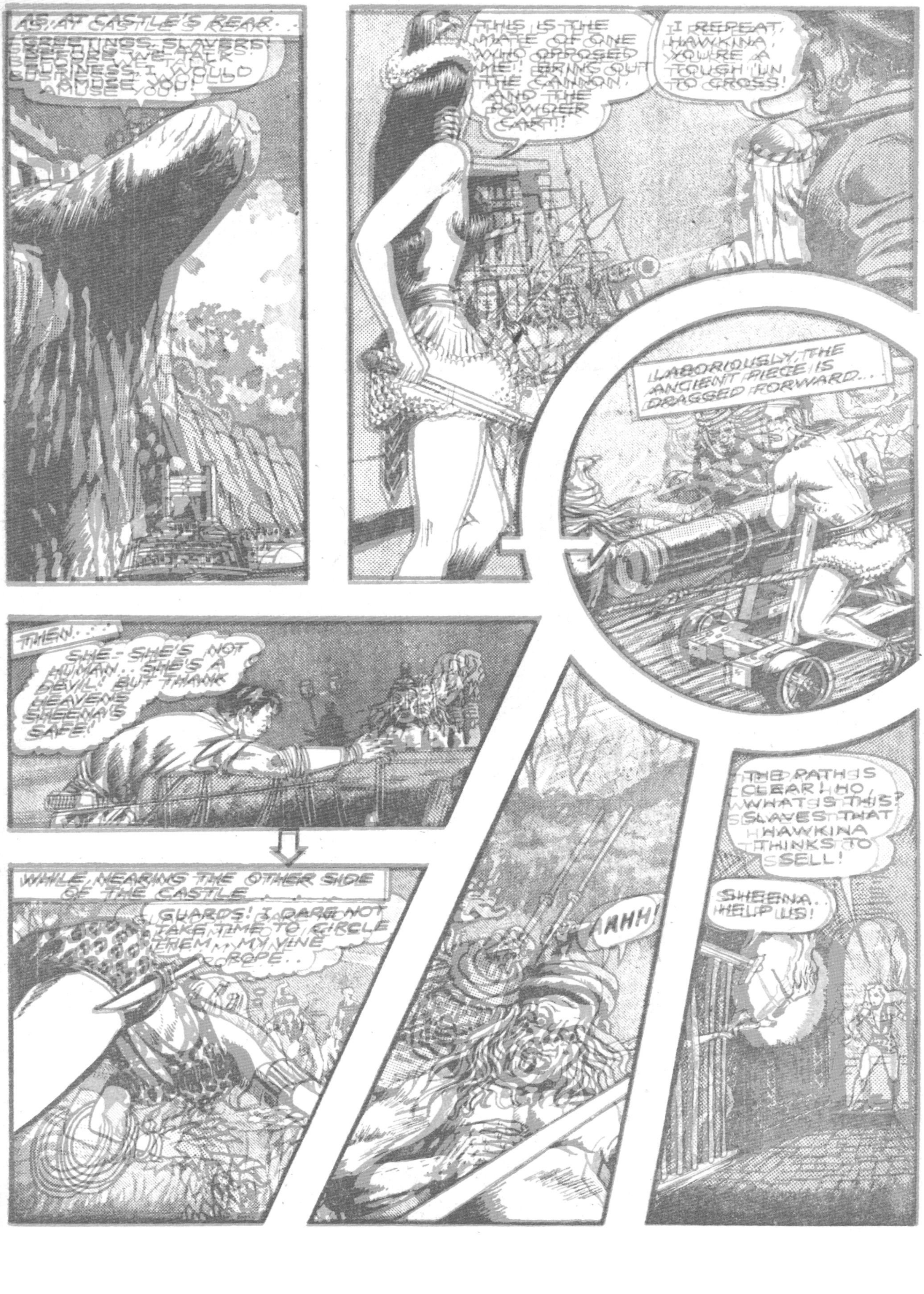
AS AT CASTLE'S REAR
GREETINGS, SLAVERS! BEFORE WE TALK BUSINESS, I WOULD AMUSE YOU!
THIS IS THE MATE OF ONE WHO OPPOSED ME! BRING OUT THE CANNON AND THE POWDER CART!
I REPEAT, HAWKINA, YOU'RE A TOUGH 'UN TO CROSS!
LABORIOUSLY, THE ANCIENT PIECE IS DRAGGED FORWARD...
THEN
SHE-SHE'S NOT HUMAN. SHE'S A DEVIL! BUT THANK HEAVENS SHEENA'S SAFE!
WHILE NEARING THE OTHER SIDE OF THE CASTLE
GUARDS! I DARE NOT TAKE TIME TO CIRCLE THEM... MY VINE ROPE...
AHHH!
THE PATH IS CLEAR! HO, WHAT IS THIS? SLAVES THAT HAWKINA THINKS TO SELL!
SHEENA.. HELP US!

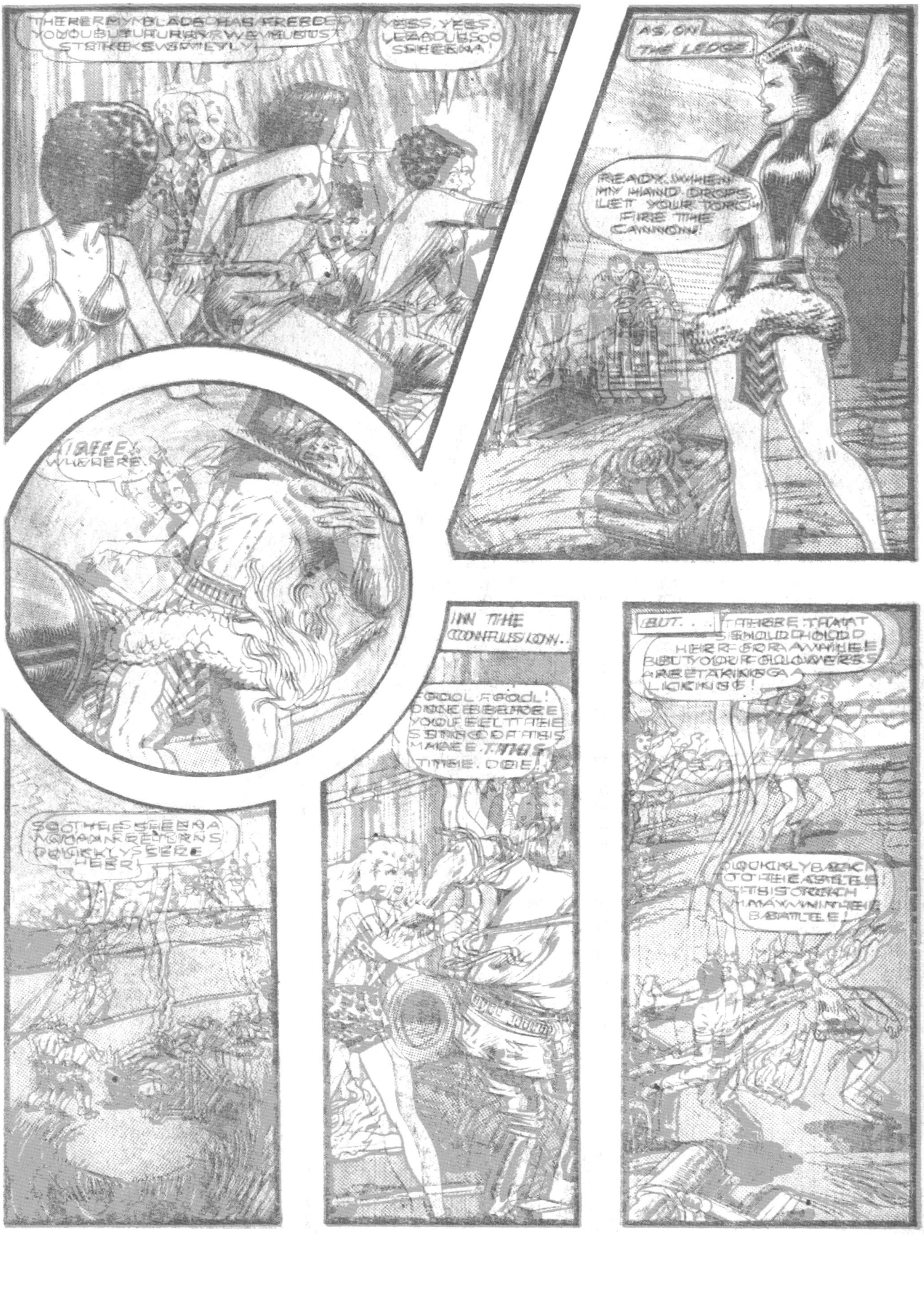
AS, ON THE LEDGE
READY, WHEN MY HAND DROPS, LET YOUR TORCH FIRE THE CANNON!
BUT. . .

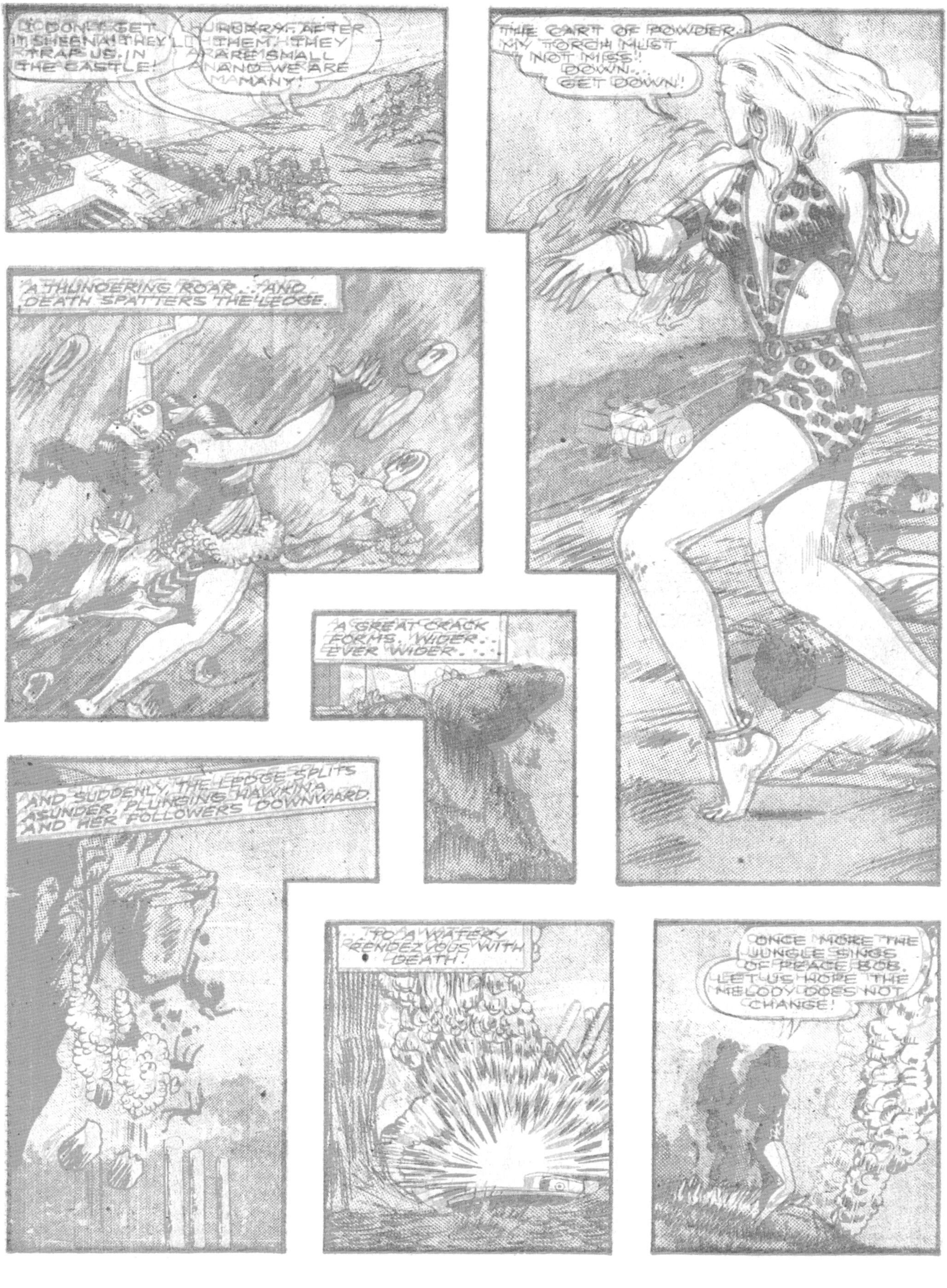
I DON'T GET IT SHEENA! THEY TRAP US IN THE CASTLE!
HURRY! AFTER THEM! THEY ARE SMALL AND WE ARE MANY!
THE CART OF POWDER... MY TORCH MUST NOT MISS!! DOWN... GET DOWN!
A THUNDERING ROAR... AND DEATH SPATTERS THE LEDGE.
A GREAT CRACK FORMS. WIDER... EVER WIDER...
AND SUDDENLY, THE LEDGE SPLITS ASUNDER, PLUNGING HAWKINA AND HER FOLLOWERS DOWNWARD.
TO A WATERY RENDEZVOUS WITH DEATH.
ONCE MORE THE JUNGLE SINGS OF PEACE BOB. LET US HOPE THE MELODY DOES NOT CHANGE!

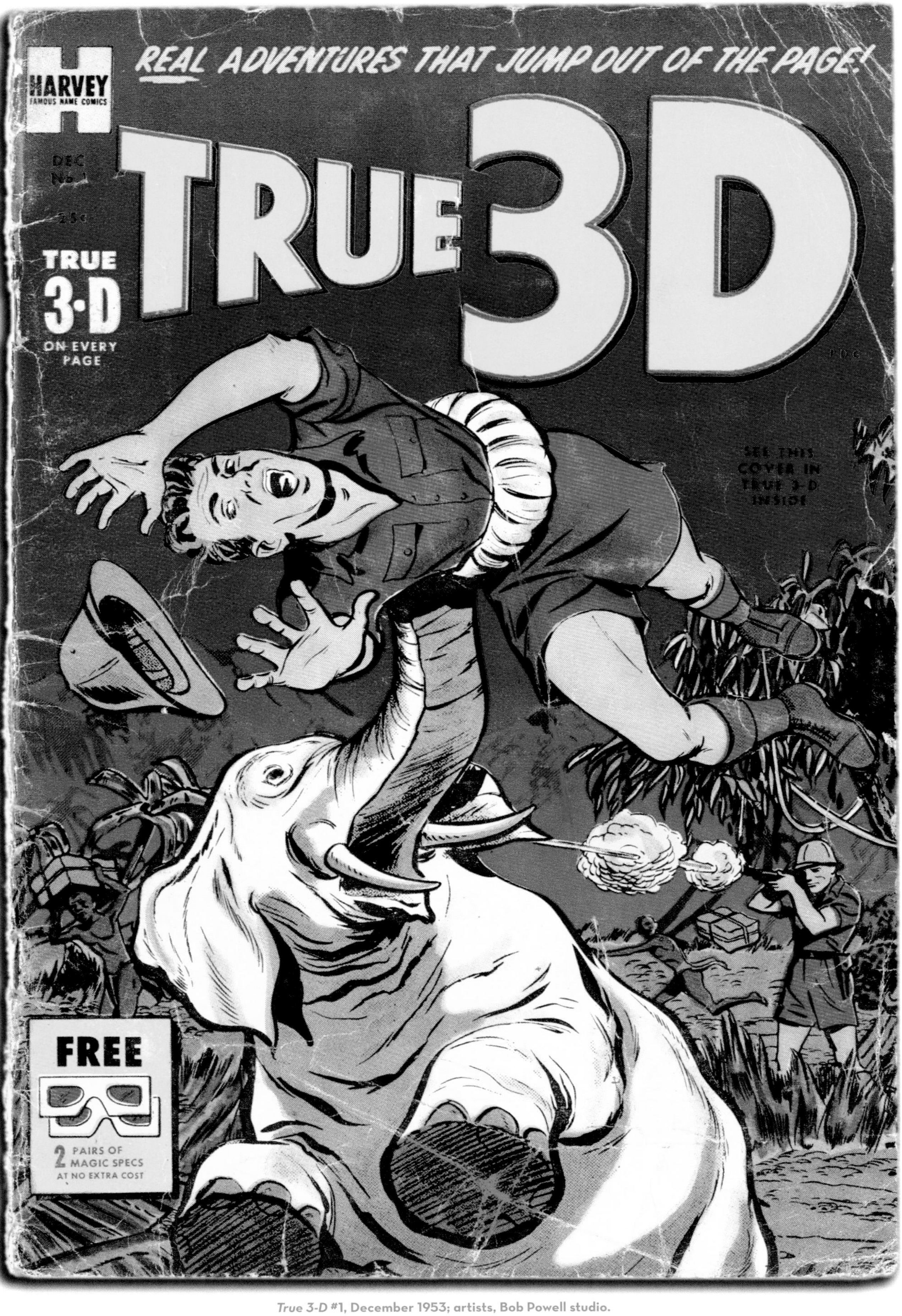
REAL ADVENTURES THAT JUMP OUT OF THE PAGE!
HARVEY
FAMOUS NAME COMICS
DEC
No. 1
25¢
TRUE 3D
TRUE 3-D ON EVERY PAGE
SEE THIS COVER IN TRUE 3-D INSIDE
FREE
2 PAIRS OF MAGIC SPECS AT NO EXTRA COST

True 3-D #1, December 1953; artists, Bob Powell studio.

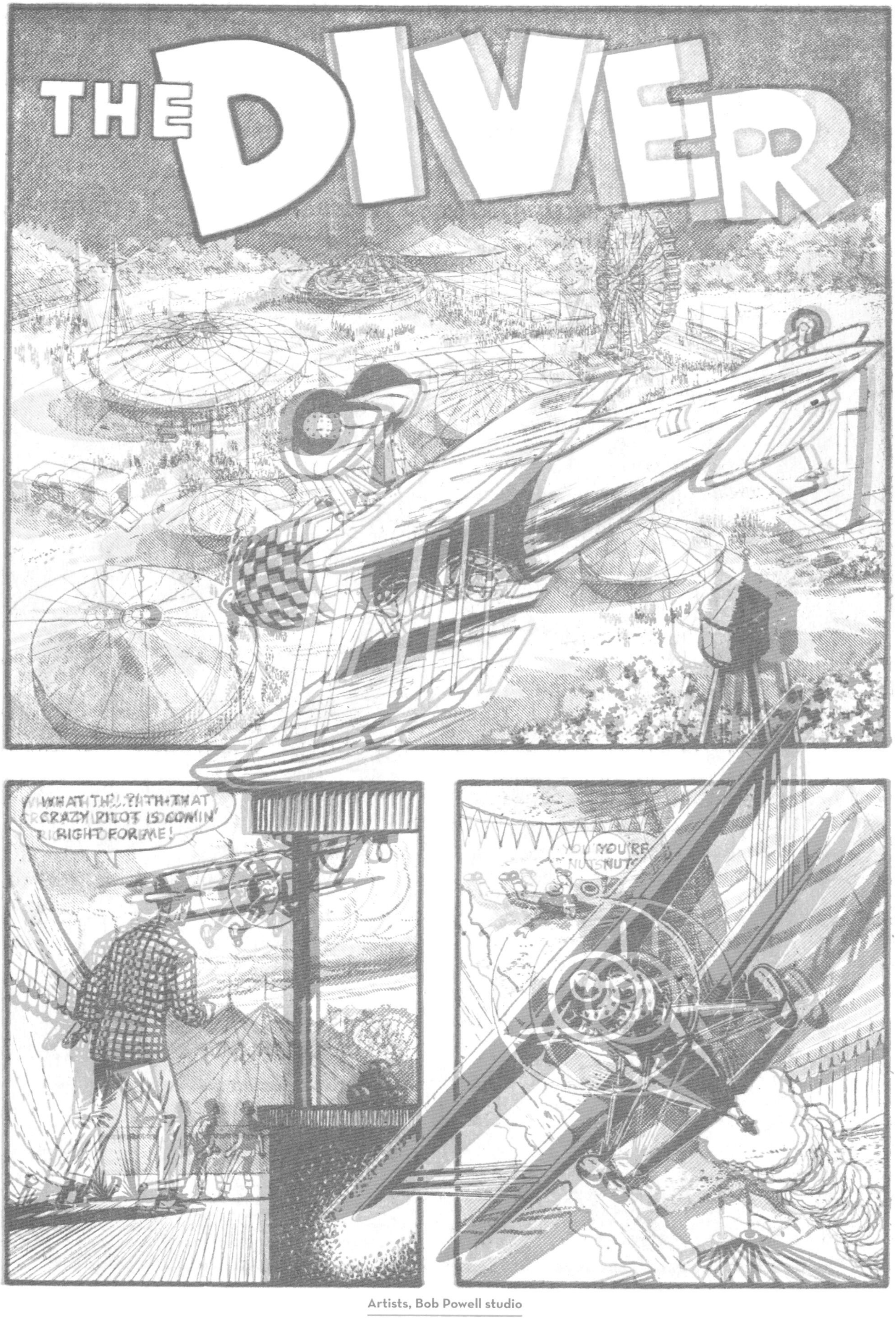

THE DIVER
WHAT TH..?! THAT CRAZY PILOT IS COMIN' RIGHT FOR ME!
YOU'RE NUTS

Artists, Bob Powell studio

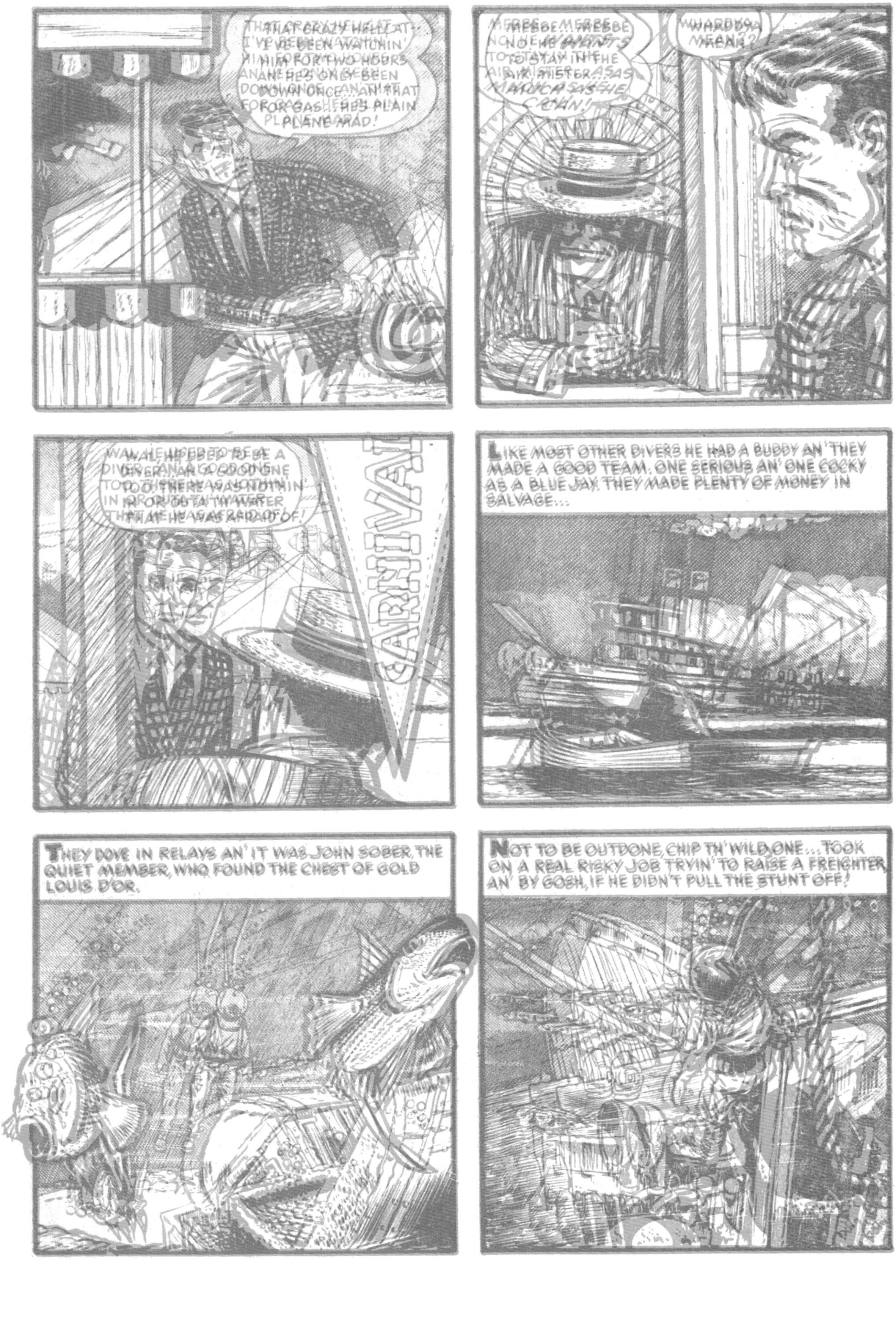

THAT CRAZY HELLCAT... I'VE BEEN WATCHIN' HIM FOR TWO HOURS AN' HE'S ONLY BEEN DOWN ONCE... AN' THAT FOR GAS... HE'S PLAIN PLANE MAD!
MEBBE... MEBBE NO! HE WANTS TO STAY IN THE AIR, MISTER... AS
CAN!
WHADDYA MEAN??
WAL, HE USED TO BE A DIVER... AN' A GOOD ONE TOO. THERE WAS NOTHIN' IN OR OUTA TH' WATER THAT HE WAS AFRAID OF!
CARNIVAL
LIKE MOST OTHER DIVERS HE HAD A BUDDY AN' THEY MADE A GOOD TEAM. ONE SERIOUS AN' ONE COCKY AS A BLUE JAY. THEY MADE PLENTY OF MONEY IN SALVAGE...
THEY DOVE IN RELAYS AN' IT WAS JOHN SOBER, THE QUIET MEMBER, WHO FOUND THE CHEST OF GOLD LOUIS D'OR.
NOT TO BE OUTDONE, CHIP TH' WILD ONE... TOOK ON A REAL RISKY JOB TRYIN' TO RAISE A FREIGHTER AN' BY GOSH, IF HE DIDN'T PULL THE STUNT OFF!

84

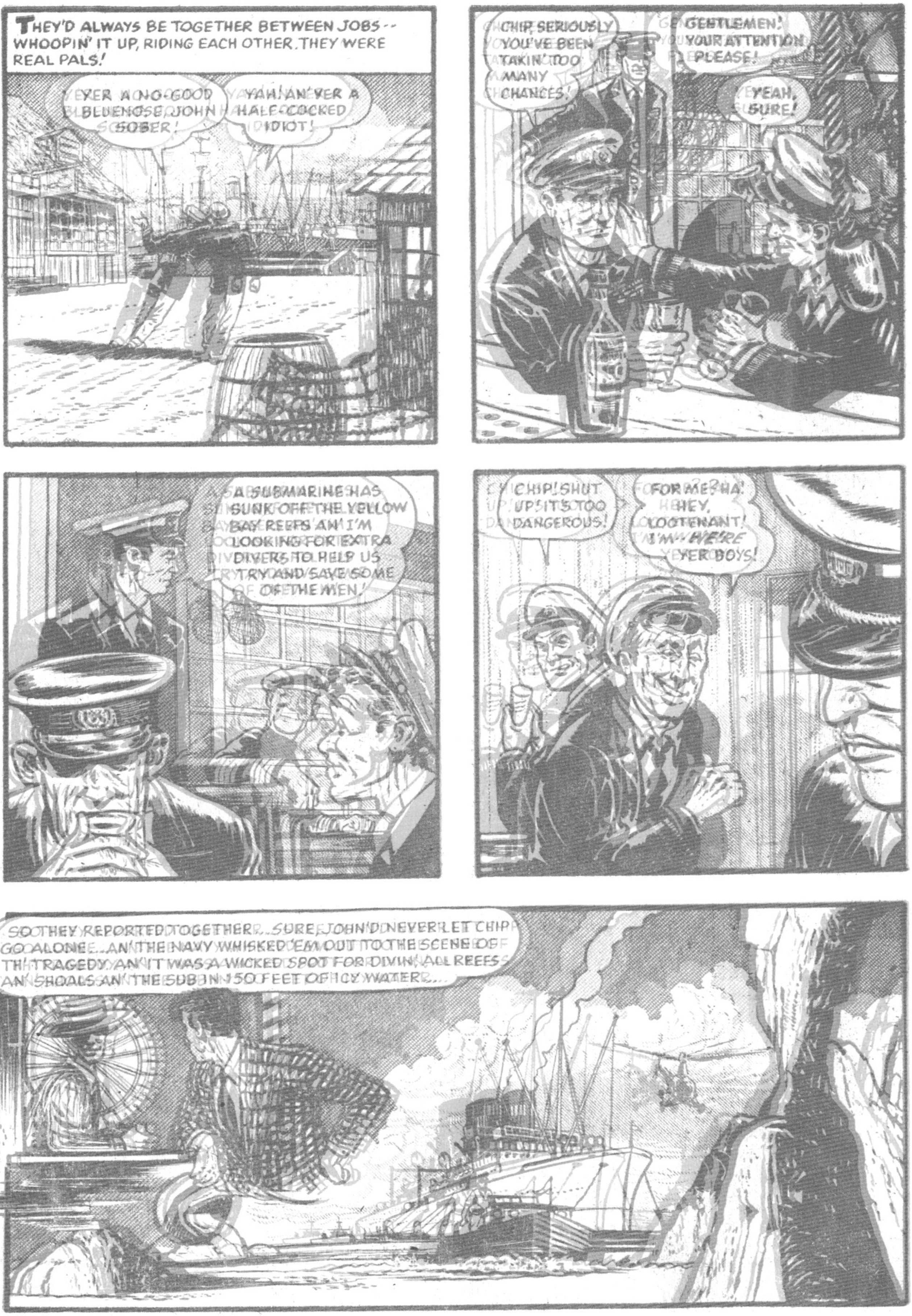
THEY'D ALWAYS BE TOGETHER BETWEEN JOBS-- WHOOPIN' IT UP, RIDING EACH OTHER. THEY WERE REAL PALS!
YER A NO-GOOD BLUENOSE, JOHN SOBER!
YAH! AN' YER A HALF-COCKED IDIOT!
CHIP, SERIOUSLY YOU'VE BEEN TAKIN' TOO MANY CHANCES!
GENTLEMEN! YOUR ATTENTION PLEASE!
YEAH, SURE!
A SUBMARINE HAS SUNK OFF THE YELLOW BAY REEFS AN' I'M LOOKING FOR EXTRA DIVERS TO HELP US TRY AND SAVE SOME OF THE MEN!
CHIP! SHUT UP! IT'S TOO DANGEROUS!
FOR ME? HA! HEY, LOOTENANT! I'M--WE'RE YER BOYS!
SO THEY REPORTED TOGETHER... SURE, JOHN'D NEVER LET CHIPP GO ALONE... AN' THE NAVY WHISKED 'EM OUT TO THE SCENE OF TH' TRAGEDY. AN' IT WAS A WICKED SPOT FOR DIVIN'. ALL REEFS AN' SHOALS AN' THE SUB IN 150 FEET OF ICY WATER...

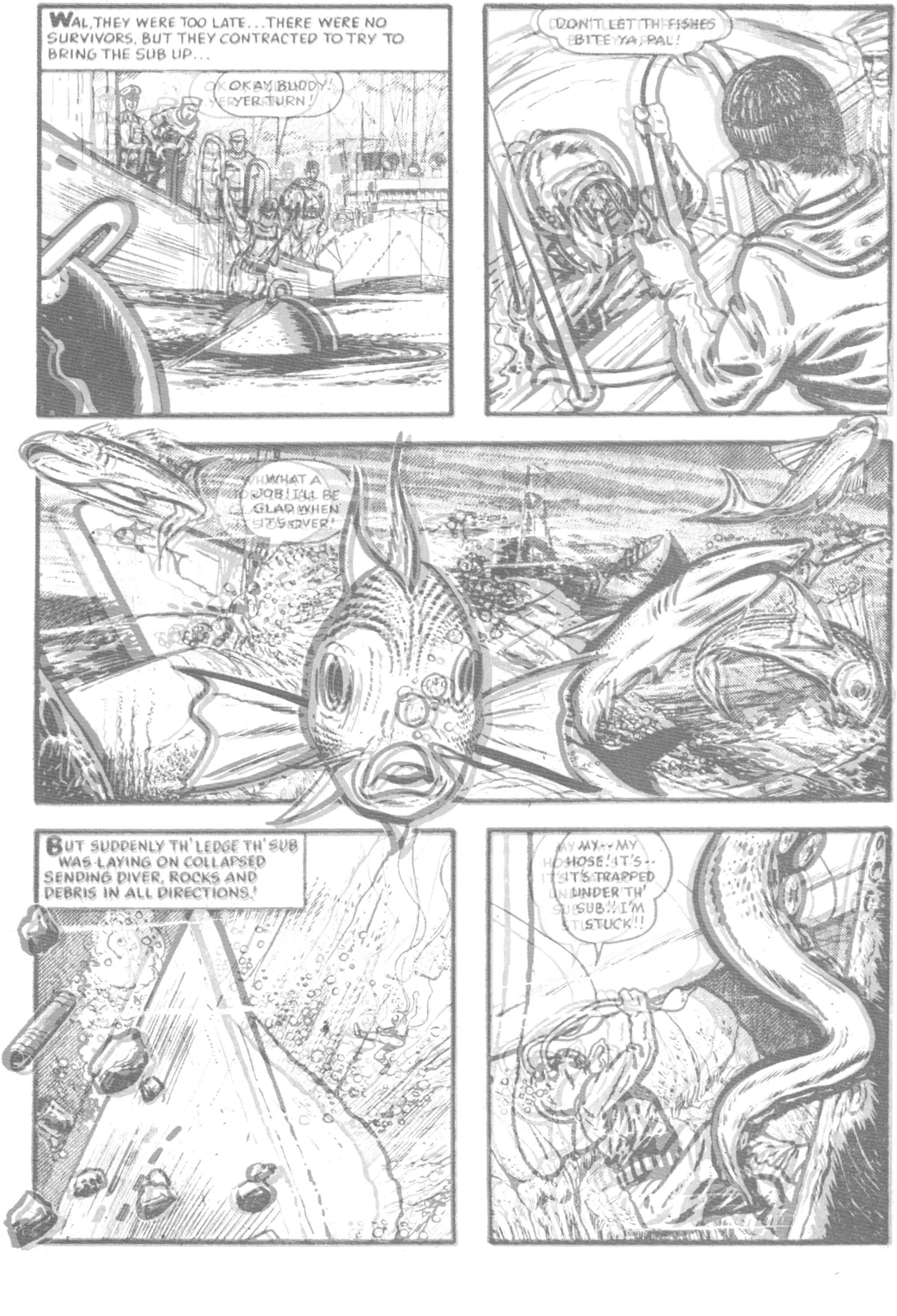
WAL, THEY WERE TOO LATE... THERE WERE NO SURVIVORS, BUT THEY CONTRACTED TO TRY TO BRING THE SUB UP...
OKAY, BUDDY! YER TURN!
DON'T LET TH' FISHES BITE YA, PAL!
WHAT A JOB! I'LL BE GLAD WHEN IT'S OVER!
BUT SUDDENLY TH' LEDGE TH' SUB WAS LAYING ON COLLAPSED SENDING DIVER, ROCKS AND DEBRIS IN ALL DIRECTIONS!
MY--MY HOSE! IT'S--IT'S TRAPPED UNDER TH' SUB!! I'M STUCK!!

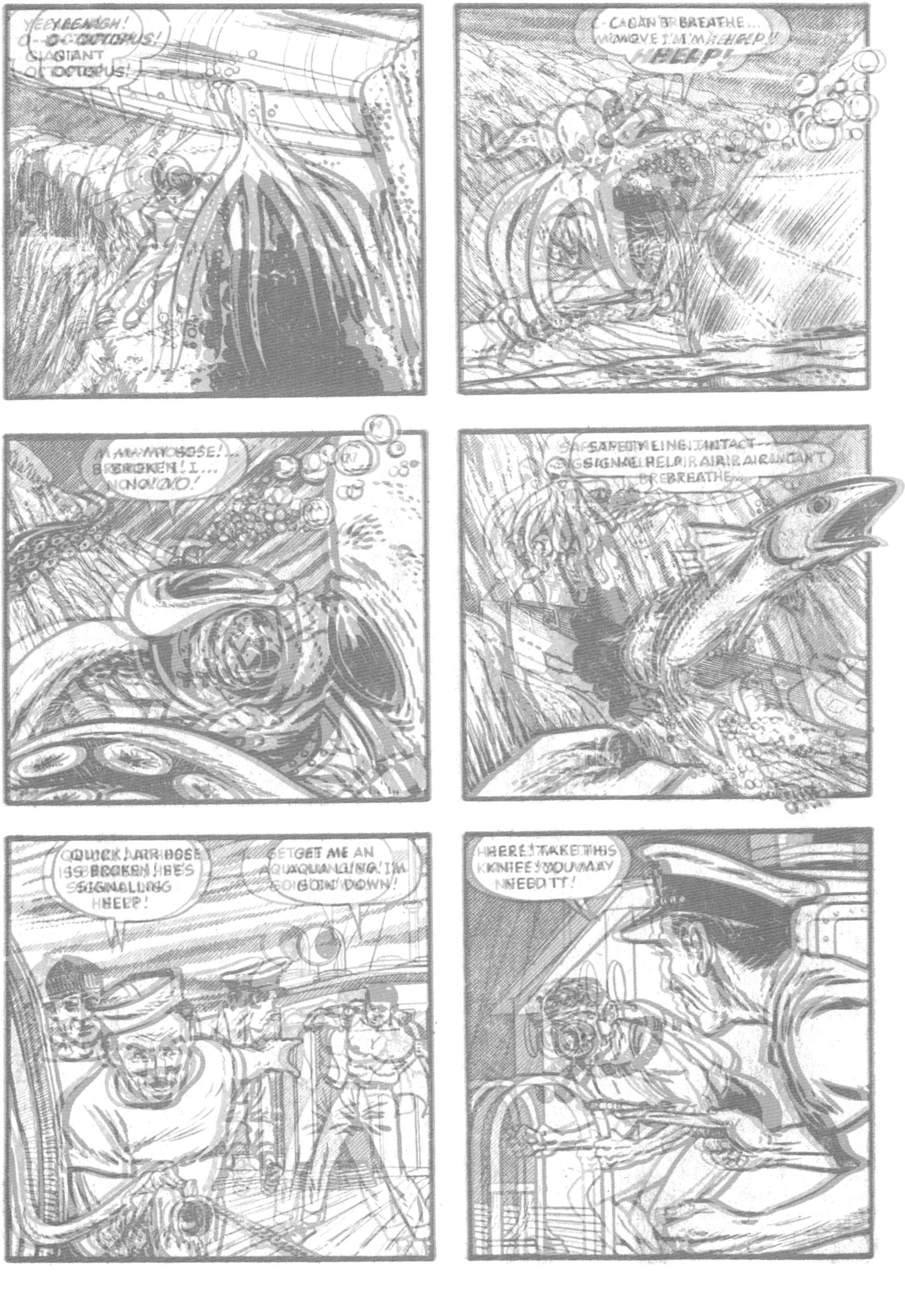
YEEAAGH! O-OCTOPUS! GIANT OCTOPUS!
C-CAN'T BREATHE... HELP!! HELP!
MY HOSE!... BROKEN! I... NO! NO!
SAFETY LINE INTACT -- SIGNAL... AIR... CAN'T BREATHE...
QUICK! AIR HOSE IS BROKEN! HE'S SIGNALLING HELP!
GET ME AN AQUALUNG! I'M GOIN' DOWN!
HERE! TAKE THIS KNIFE! YOU MAY NEED IT!

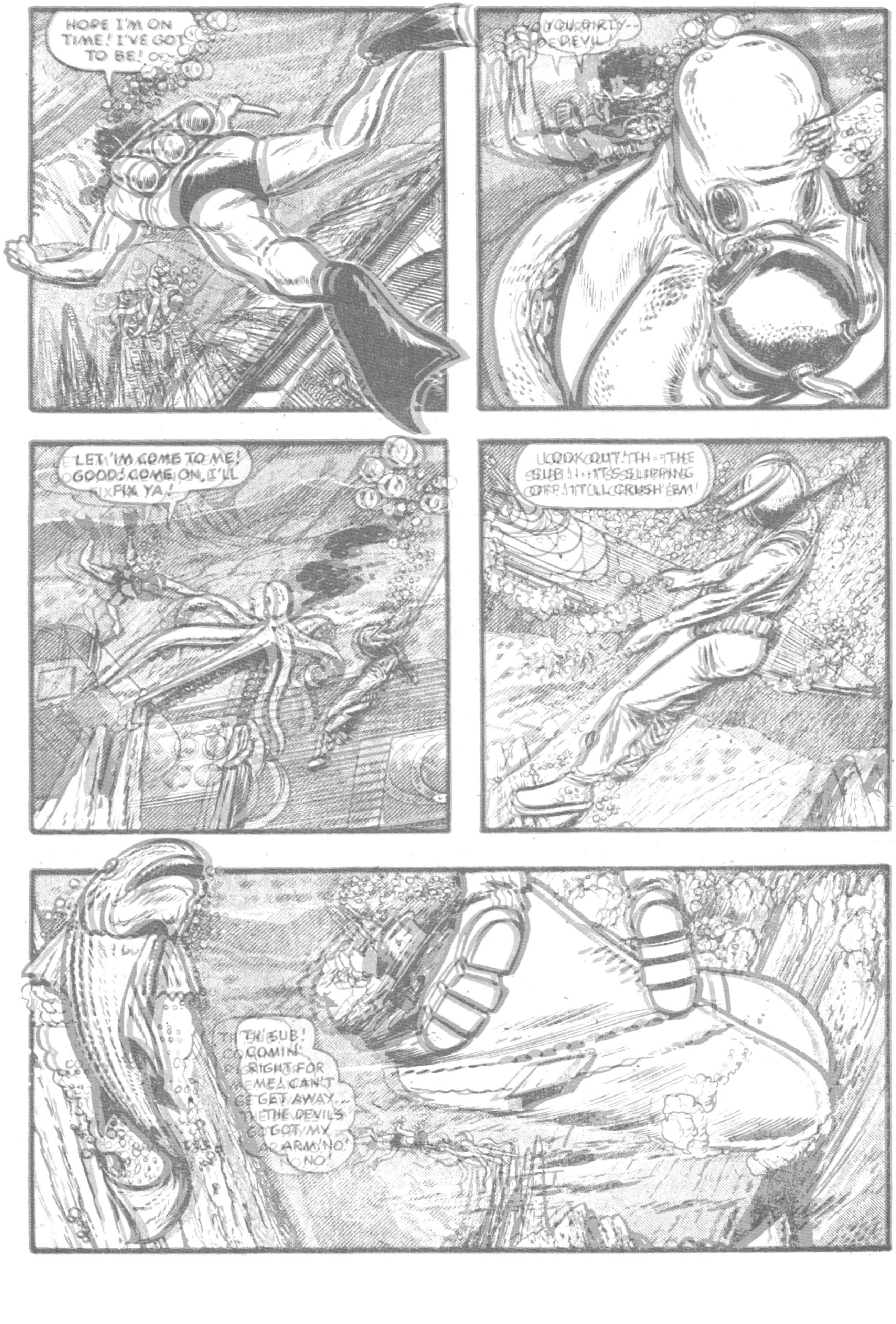
HOPE I'M ON TIME! I'VE GOT TO BE!
YOU DIRTY-- DEVIL!
LET 'IM COME TO ME! GOOD! COME ON, I'LL FIX YA!
LOOK OUT! TH-- THE SUB! IT'S SLIPPING OFF! IT'LL CRUSH 'EM!
TH' SUB! COMIN' RIGHT FOR ME! I CAN'T GET AWAY... THE DEVIL'S GOT MY ARM! NO! NO!

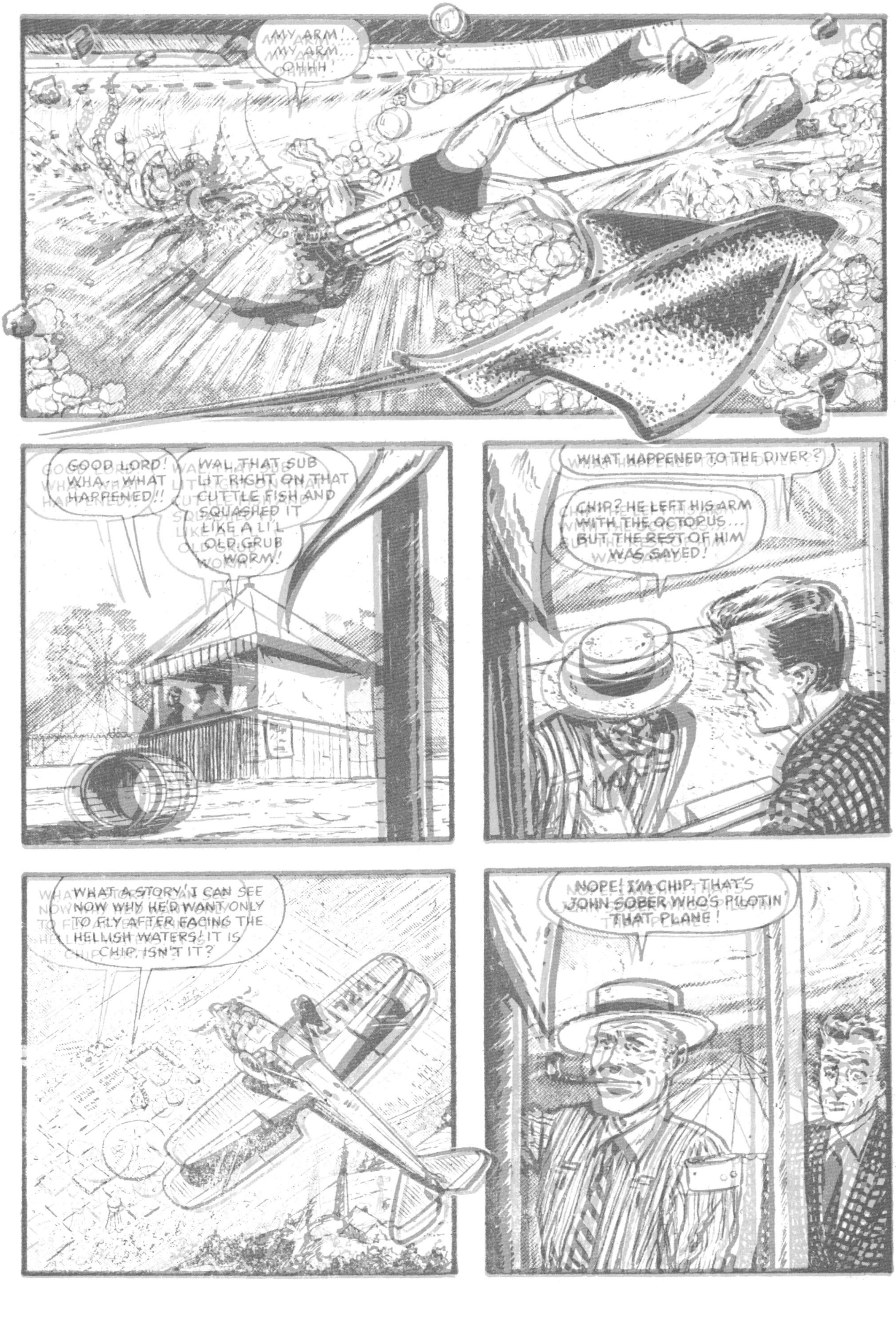

MY ARM! MY ARM... OHHH!
GOOD LORD! WHA-- WHAT HAPPENED!!
WAL, THAT SUB LIT RIGHT ON THAT CUTTLE FISH AND SQUASHED IT LIKE A LI'L OLD GRUB WORM!
WHAT HAPPENED TO THE DIVER?
CHIP? HE LEFT HIS ARM WITH THE OCTOPUS... BUT THE REST OF HIM WAS SAVED!
WHAT A STORY! I CAN SEE NOW WHY HE'D WANT ONLY TO FLY AFTER FACING THE HELLISH WATERS! IT IS CHIP, ISN'T IT?
NOPE! I'M CHIP. THAT'S JOHN SOBER WHO'S PILOTIN' THAT PLANE!

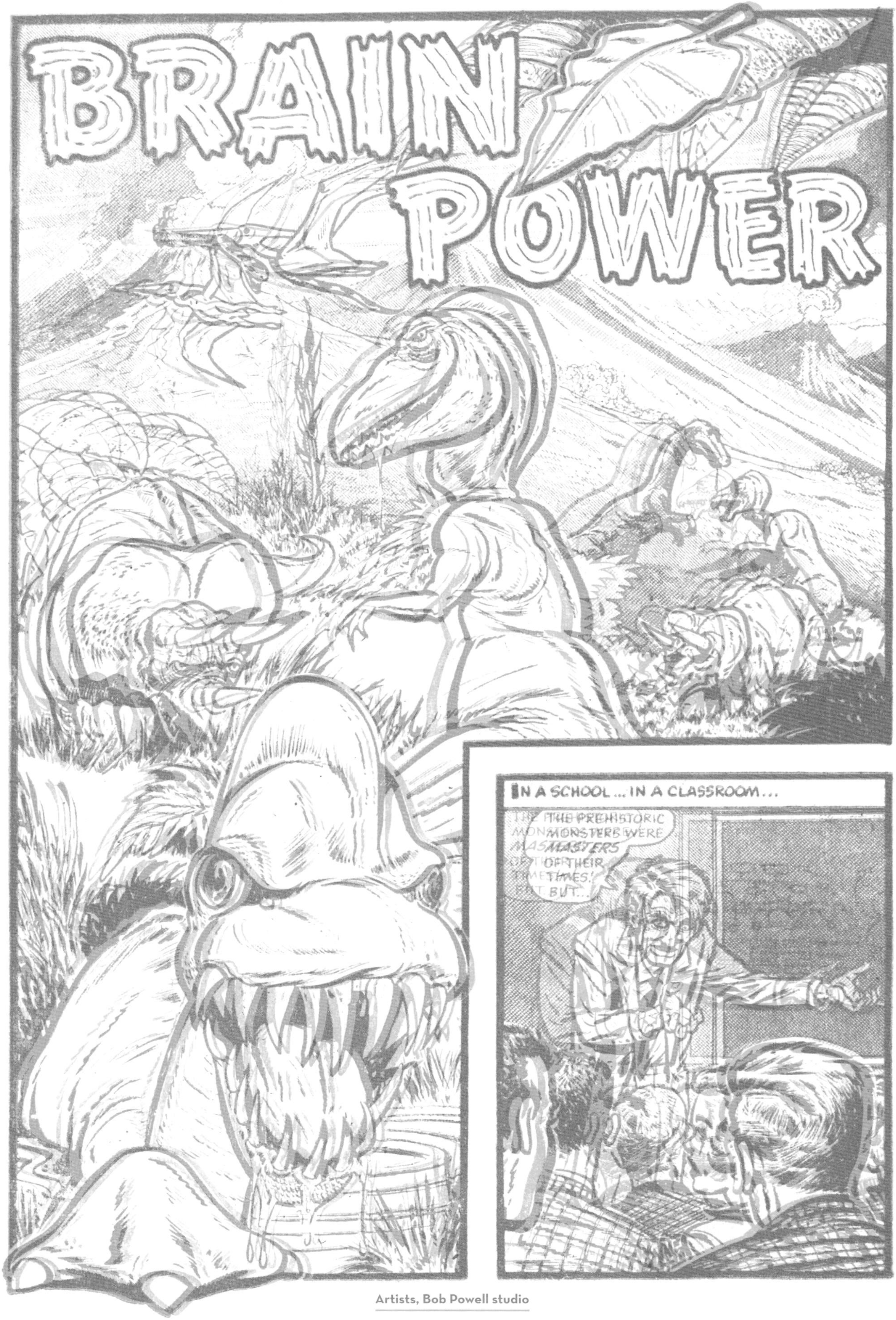
BRAIN POWER
IN A SCHOOL ... IN A CLASSROOM ...
THE PREHISTORIC MONSTERS WERE MASTERS OF THEIR TIMES! BUT...

Artists, Bob Powell studio

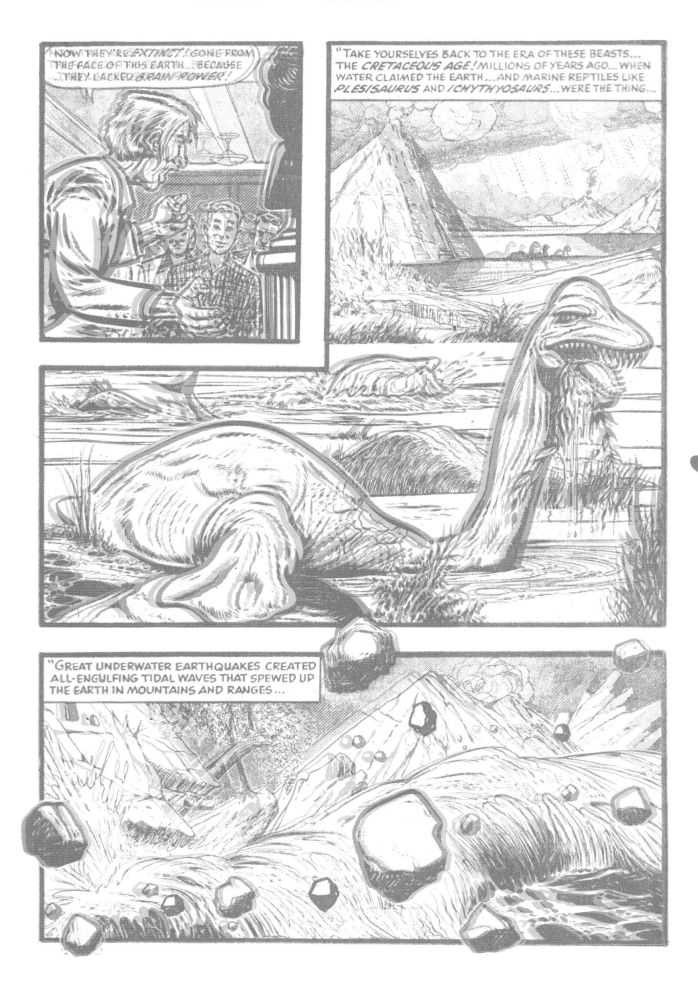

NOW THEY'RE *EXTINCT!* GONE FROM THE FACE OF THIS EARTH...BECAUSE ...THEY LACKED *BRAIN POWER!*

"TAKE YOURSELVES BACK TO THE ERA OF THESE BEASTS... THE *CRETACEOUS AGE!* MILLIONS OF YEARS AGO...WHEN WATER CLAIMED THE EARTH...AND MARINE REPTILES LIKE *PLESISAURUS* AND *ICHYTHYOSAURS*...WERE THE THING...

"GREAT UNDERWATER EARTHQUAKES CREATED ALL-ENGULFING TIDAL WAVES THAT SPEWED UP THE EARTH IN MOUNTAINS AND RANGES...

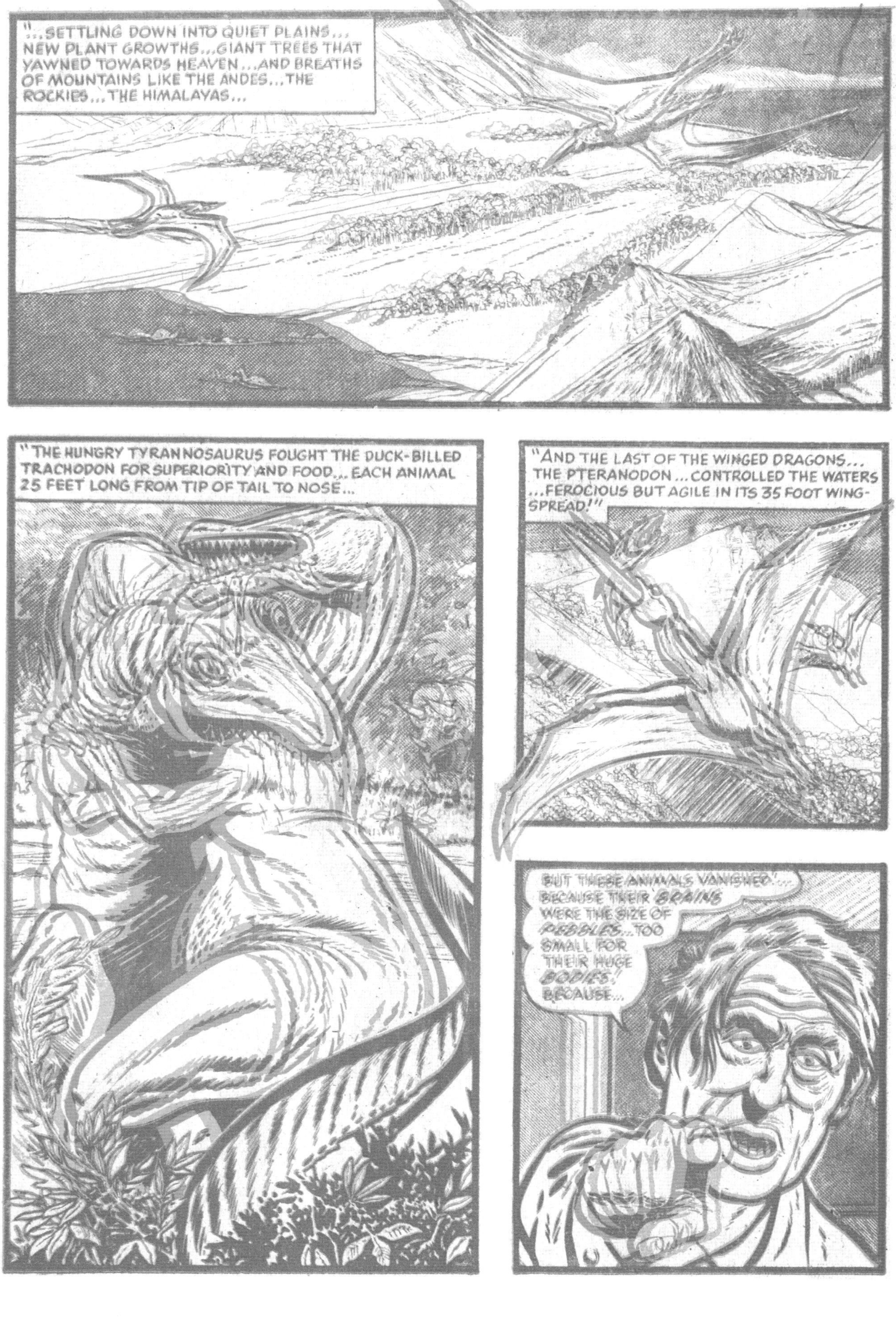
"...SETTLING DOWN INTO QUIET PLAINS... NEW PLANT GROWTHS...GIANT TREES THAT YAWNED TOWARDS HEAVEN...AND BREATHS OF MOUNTAINS LIKE THE ANDES...THE ROCKIES...THE HIMALAYAS...
"THE HUNGRY TYRANNOSAURUS FOUGHT THE DUCK-BILLED TRACHODON FOR SUPERIORITY AND FOOD... EACH ANIMAL 25 FEET LONG FROM TIP OF TAIL TO NOSE...
"AND THE LAST OF THE WINGED DRAGONS... THE PTERANODON...CONTROLLED THE WATERS ...FEROCIOUS BUT AGILE IN ITS 35 FOOT WING-SPREAD!"
BUT THESE ANIMALS VANISHED!... BECAUSE THEIR BRAINS WERE THE SIZE OF PEBBLES...TOO SMALL FOR THEIR HUGE BODIES! BECAUSE...

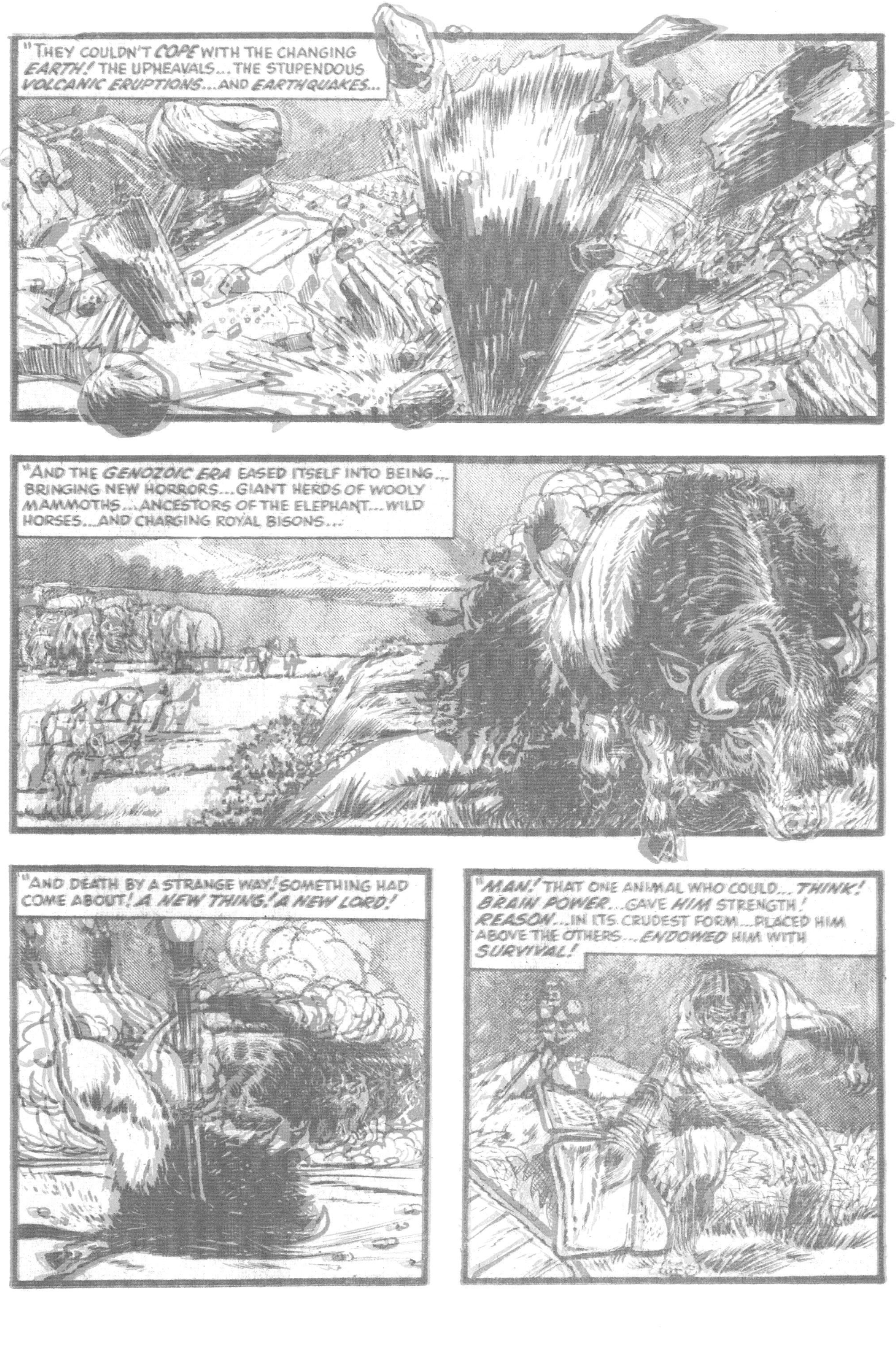
"THEY COULDN'T COPE WITH THE CHANGING EARTH! THE UPHEAVALS... THE STUPENDOUS VOLCANIC ERUPTIONS... AND EARTHQUAKES...
"AND THE GENOZOIC ERA EASED ITSELF INTO BEING... BRINGING NEW HORRORS... GIANT HERDS OF WOOLY MAMMOTHS... ANCESTORS OF THE ELEPHANT... WILD HORSES... AND CHARGING ROYAL BISONS...
"AND DEATH BY A STRANGE WAY! SOMETHING HAD COME ABOUT! A NEW THING! A NEW LORD!
"MAN! THAT ONE ANIMAL WHO COULD... THINK! BRAIN POWER... GAVE HIM STRENGTH! REASON... IN ITS CRUDEST FORM... PLACED HIM ABOVE THE OTHERS... ENDOWED HIM WITH SURVIVAL!

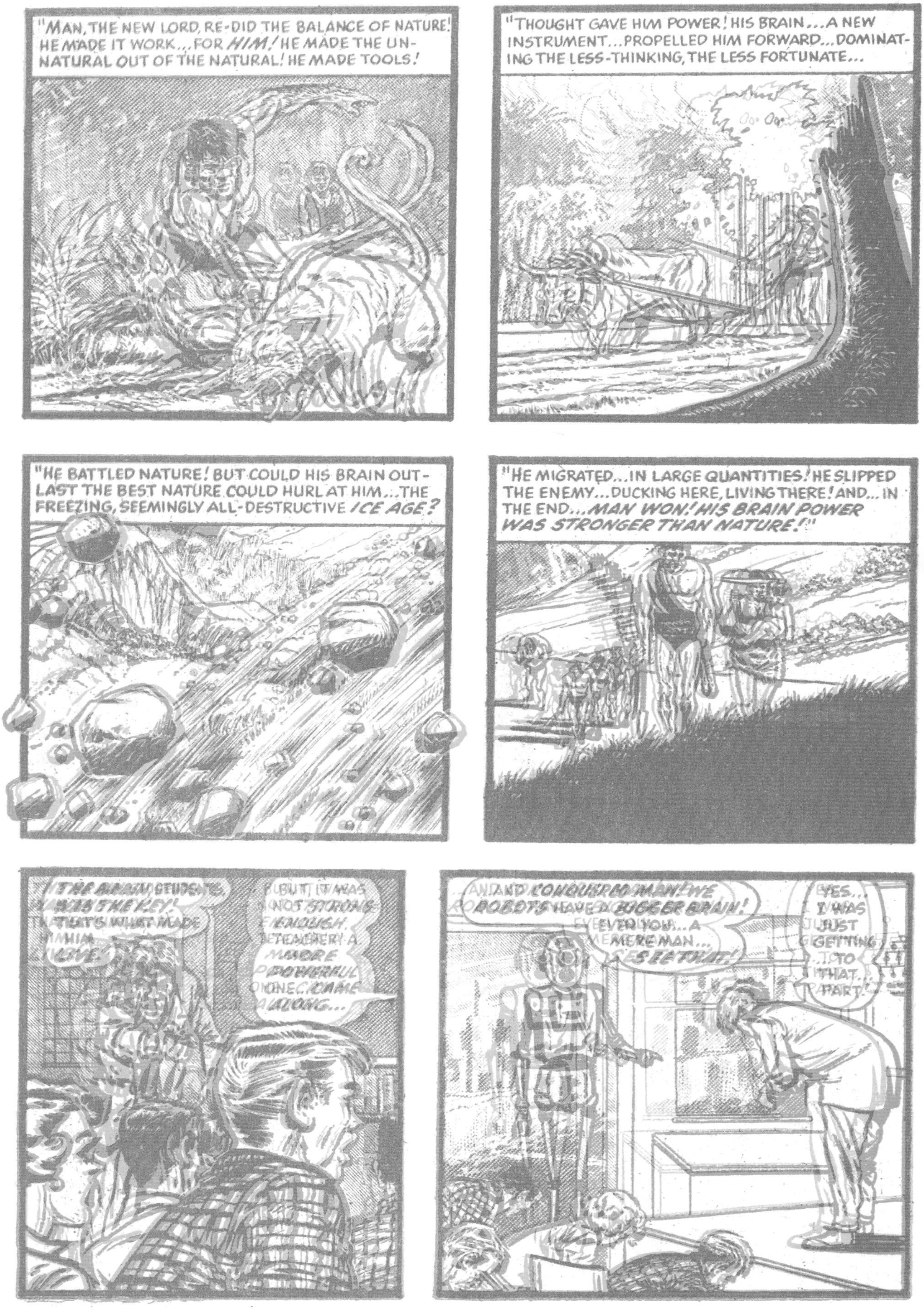
"MAN, THE NEW LORD, RE-DID THE BALANCE OF NATURE! HE MADE IT WORK... FOR HIM! HE MADE THE UN-NATURAL OUT OF THE NATURAL! HE MADE TOOLS!
"THOUGHT GAVE HIM POWER! HIS BRAIN... A NEW INSTRUMENT... PROPELLED HIM FORWARD... DOMINATING THE LESS-THINKING, THE LESS FORTUNATE...
"HE BATTLED NATURE! BUT COULD HIS BRAIN OUT-LAST THE BEST NATURE COULD HURL AT HIM... THE FREEZING, SEEMINGLY ALL-DESTRUCTIVE ICE AGE?
"HE MIGRATED... IN LARGE QUANTITIES! HE SLIPPED THE ENEMY... DUCKING HERE, LIVING THERE! AND... IN THE END... MAN WON! HIS BRAIN POWER WAS STRONGER THAN NATURE!"
THE BRAIN, STUDENTS, WAS THE KEY! THAT'S WHAT MADE HIM LIVE!
BUT IT WAS NOT STRONG ENOUGH, TEACHER! A MORE POWERFUL ONE CAME ALONG...
...AND CONQUERED MAN! WE ROBOTS HAVE A BIGGER BRAIN!
EVEN YOU... A MERE MAN... SEE THAT!
YES... I WAS JUST GETTING TO THAT PART!

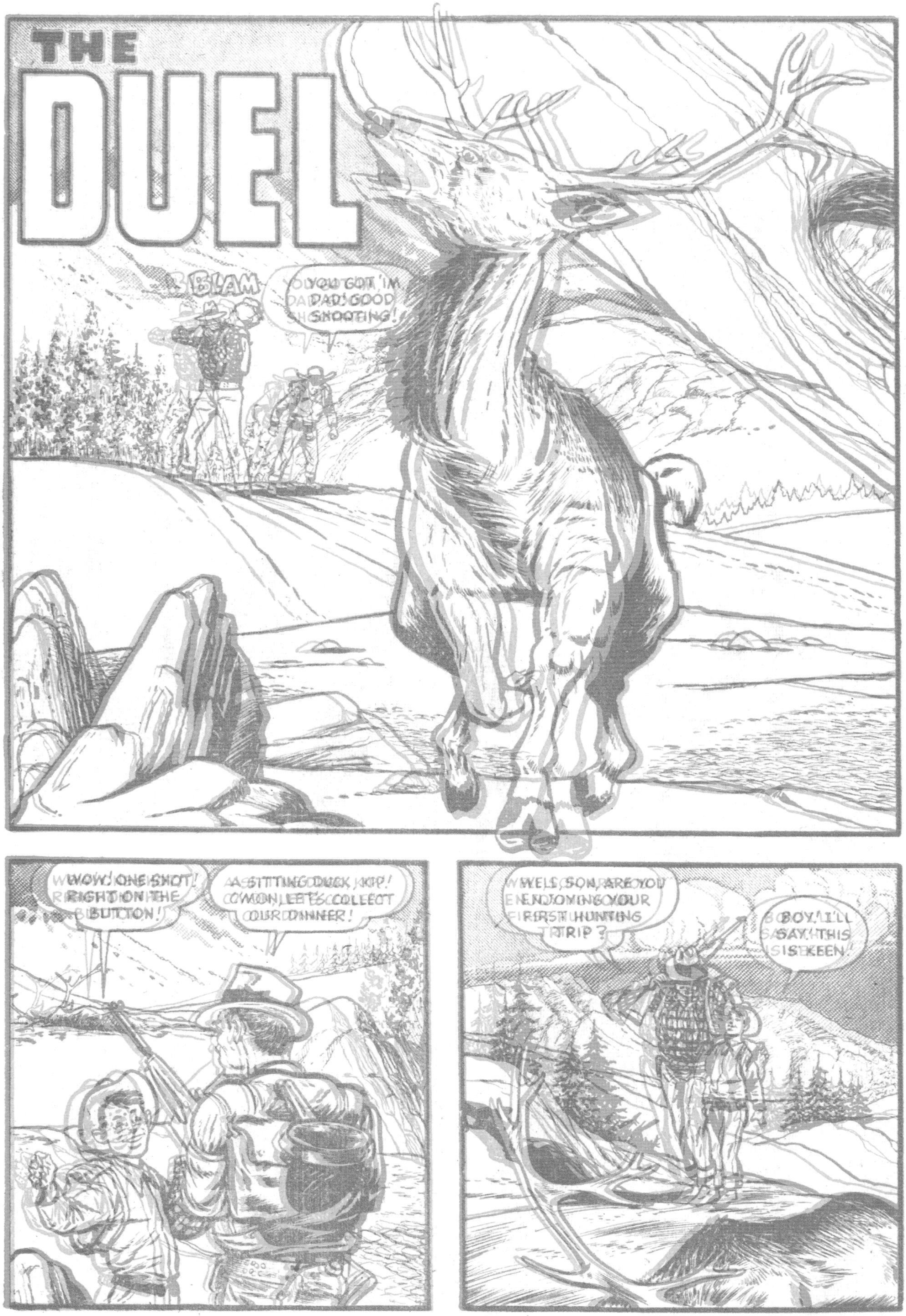
THE DUEL
BLAM
YOU GOT 'IM DAD! GOOD SHOOTING!
WOW! ONE SHOT! RIGHT ON THE BUTTON!
A SITTING DUCK, KIP! C'MON, LET'S COLLECT OUR DINNER!
WELL, SON, ARE YOU ENJOYING YOUR FIRST HUNTING TRIP?
BOY, I'LL SAY, THIS IS KEEN!

Artists, Bob Powell studio

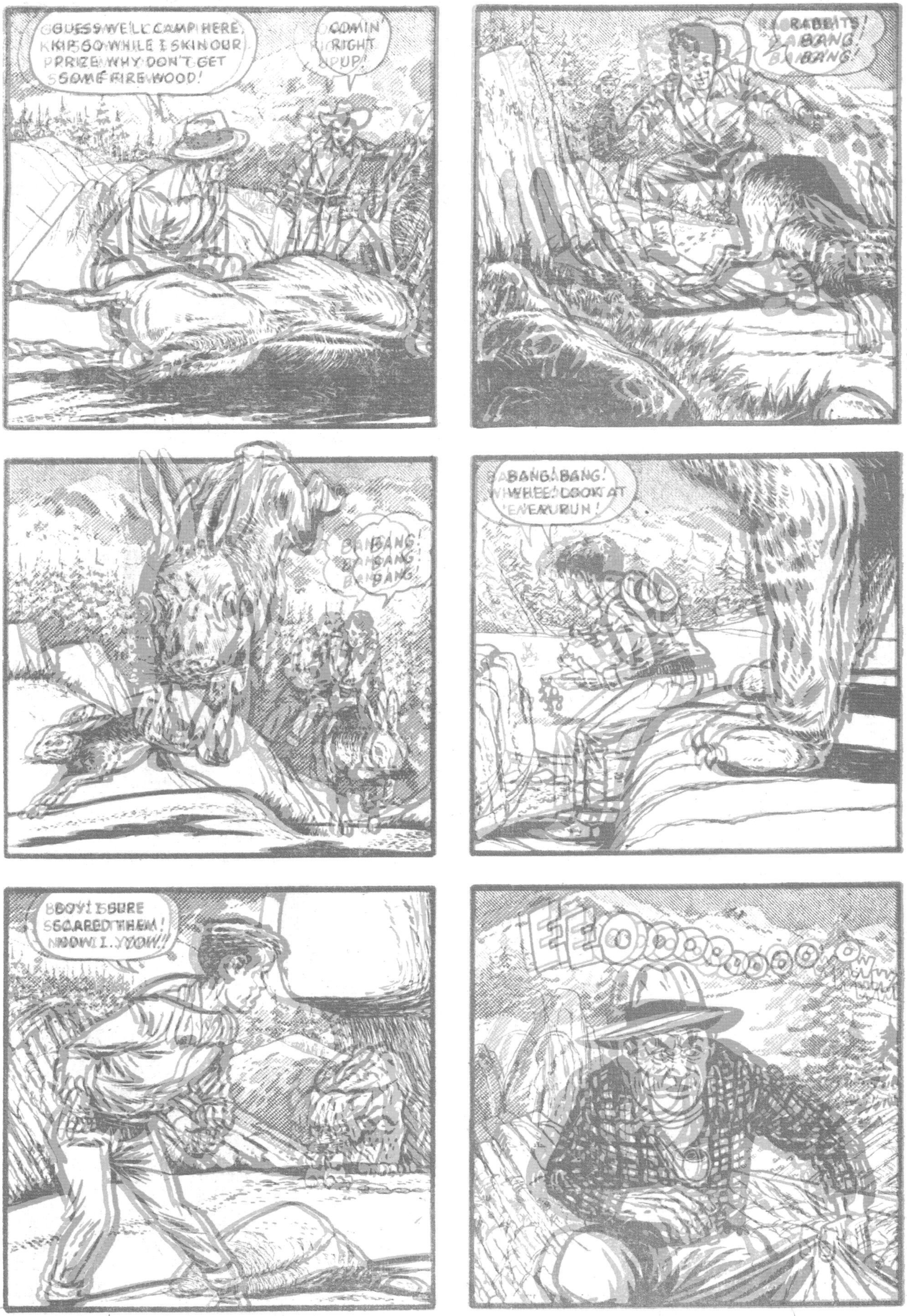
GUESS WE'LL CAMP HERE, KIP, SO WHILE I SKIN OUR PRIZE WHY DON'T GET SOME FIRE WOOD!
COMIN' RIGHT UP!
RABBITS! BANG! BANG!
BANG! BANG! BANG!
BANG! BANG! WHEE! LOOK AT 'EM RUN!
BOY! I SURE SCARED THEM! NOW I... YOW!
EEOOOOOOOOOOW

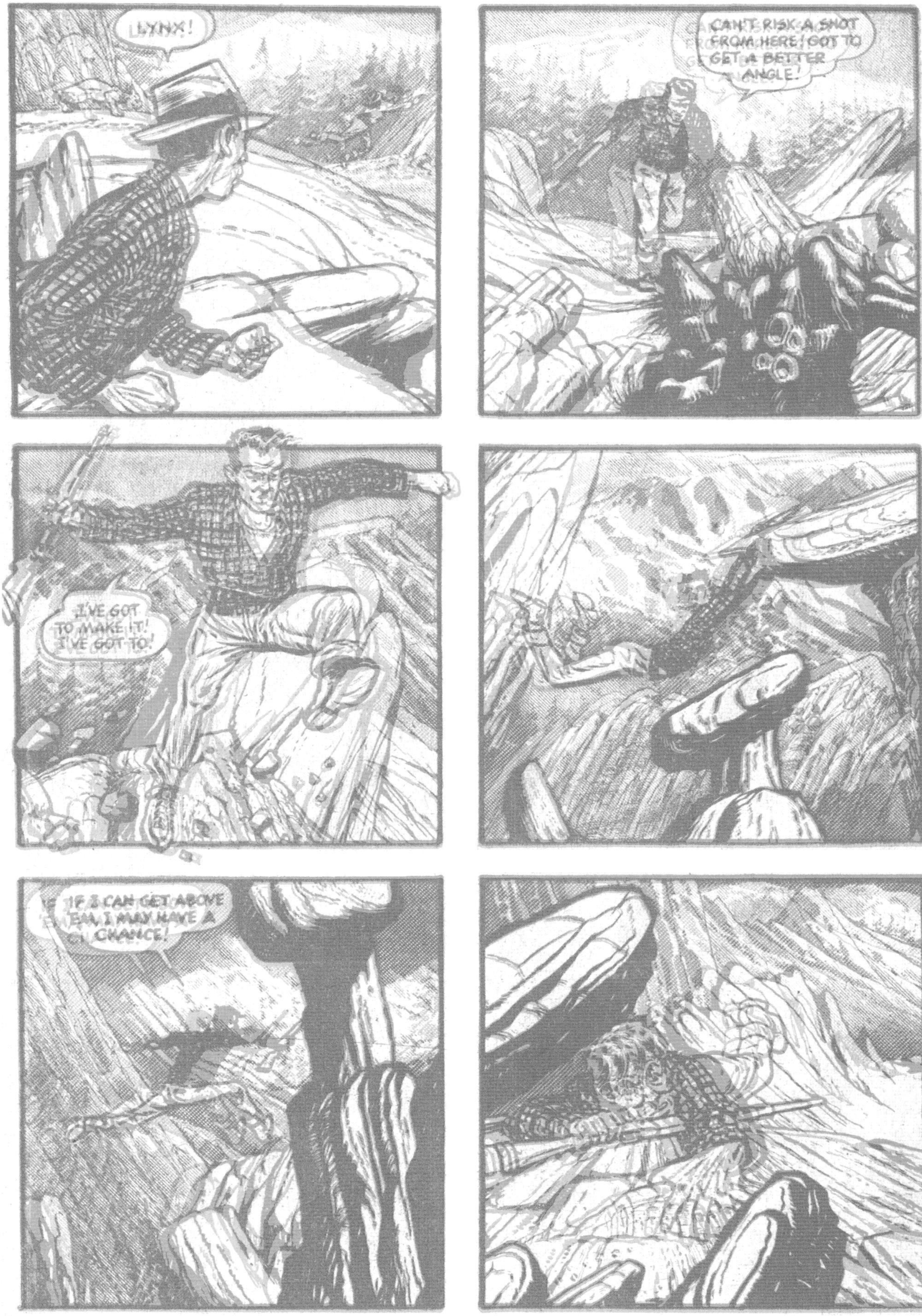
LYNX!
CAN'T RISK A SHOT FROM HERE! GOT TO GET A BETTER ANGLE!
I'VE GOT TO MAKE IT! I'VE GOT TO!
IF I CAN GET ABOVE 'EM, I MAY HAVE A CHANCE!

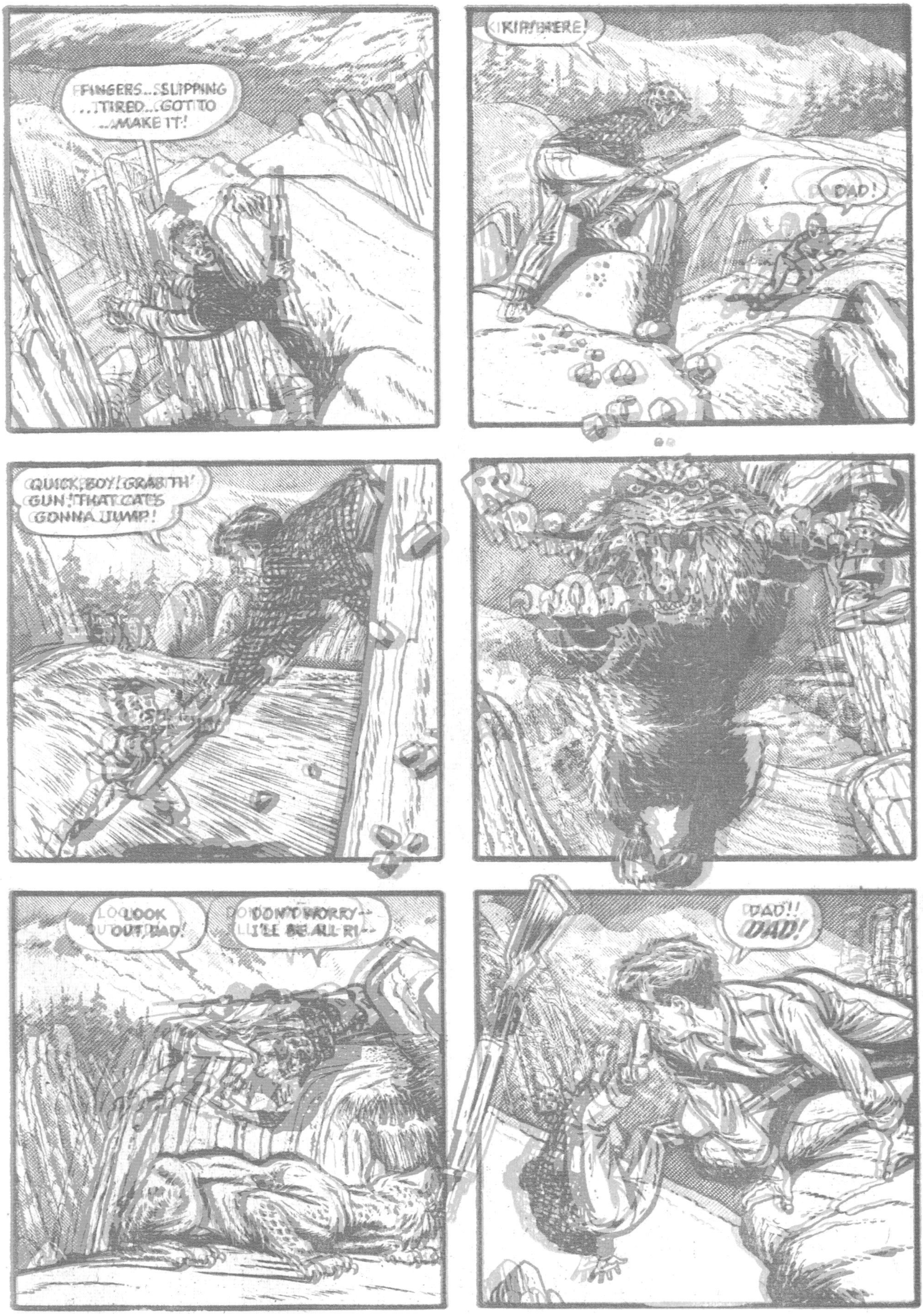
FINGERS...SLIPPING ...TIRED...GOT TO ...MAKE IT!
KIP! HERE!
DAD!
QUICK, BOY! GRAB TH' GUN! THAT CAT'S GONNA JUMP!
LOOK OUT, DAD!
DON'T WORRY-- I'LL BE ALL RI--
DAD!! DAD!

CLUMSY FOOL! NOW I'M IN FOR IT-- WITH NO WEAPON! -- STAY THERE, KIP, I'LL BE ALL RIGHT!
--I HOPE! HA! YOU MISSED ME, CAT!
I'VE GOT TO HELP HIM! IF I HAD SOMETHING ... ROCKS! MAYBE...?!
IF I CAN MAKE THAT LYNX LEAVE DAD ALONE FOR AWHILE, MAYBE HE CAN GET UP HERE!
GOOD WORK, KIP! NOW IF I CAN GET UP--

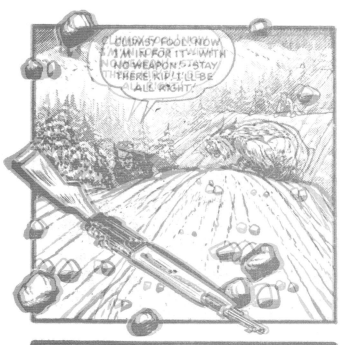

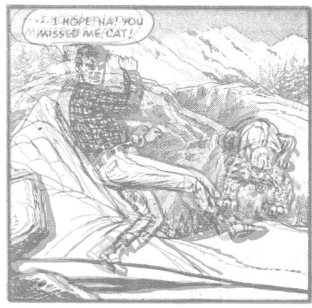

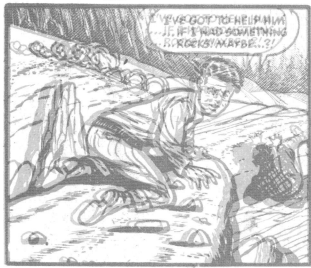

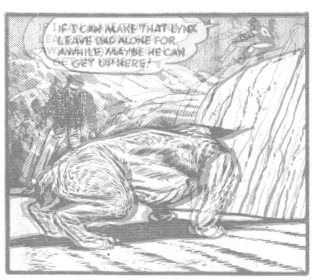

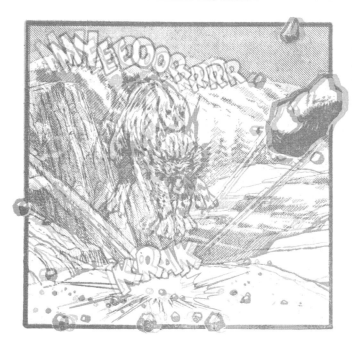

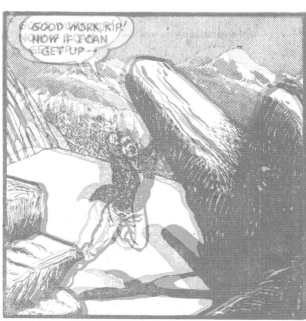

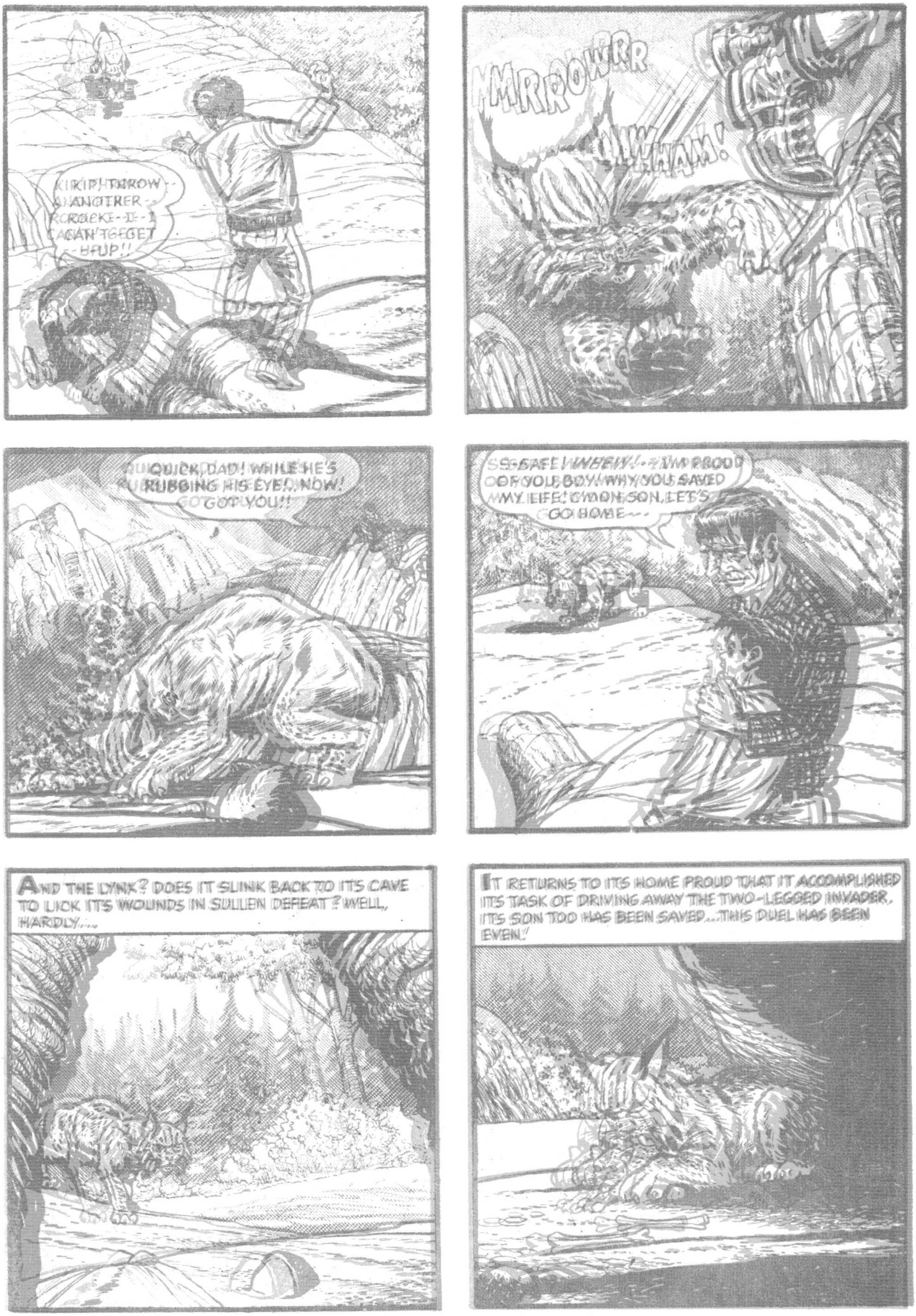
KIP! THROW ANOTHER ROCK-- I-- I CAN'T GET UP!!
MMRROWRR
WHAM!
QUICK, DAD! WHILE HE'S RUBBING HIS EYE! NOW!
GOT YOU!!
S-SAFE! WHEW!-- I'M PROUD OF YOU, BOY! WHY, YOU SAVED MY LIFE! C'MON, SON, LET'S GO HOME...
AND THE LYNX? DOES IT SLINK BACK TO ITS CAVE TO LICK ITS WOUNDS IN SULLEN DEFEAT? WELL, HARDLY....
IT RETURNS TO ITS HOME PROUD THAT IT ACCOMPLISHED ITS TASK OF DRIVING AWAY THE TWO-LEGGED INVADER. ITS SON TOO HAS BEEN SAVED... THIS DUEL HAS BEEN EVEN!

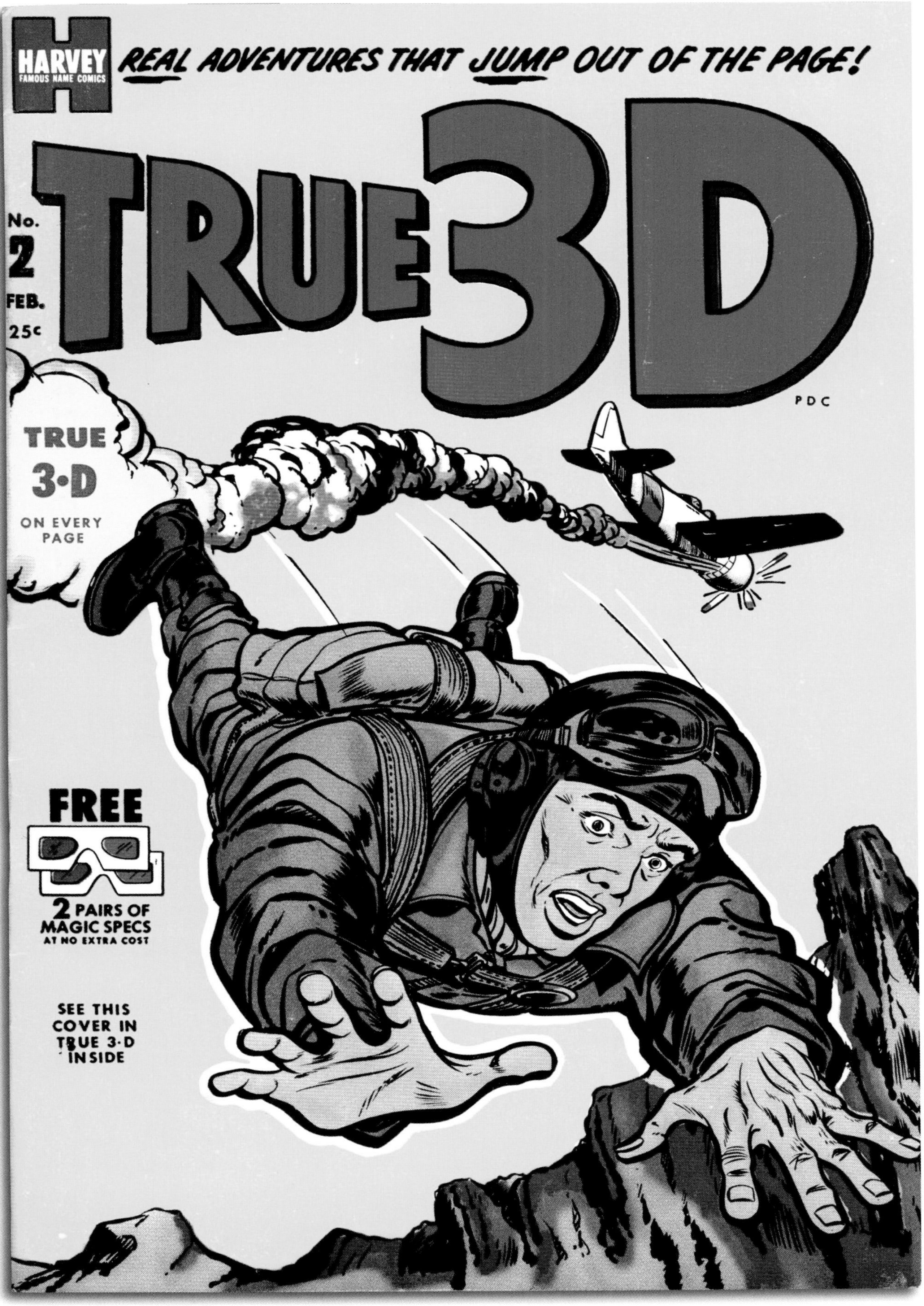
HARVEY
FAMOUS NAME COMICS
REAL ADVENTURES THAT JUMP OUT OF THE PAGE!
No. 2
FEB.
25¢
TRUE 3D
PDC
TRUE 3-D ON EVERY PAGE
FREE
2 PAIRS OF MAGIC SPECS AT NO EXTRA COST
SEE THIS COVER IN TRUE 3-D INSIDE

True 3-D #2, February 1954; artist, Howard Nostrand.

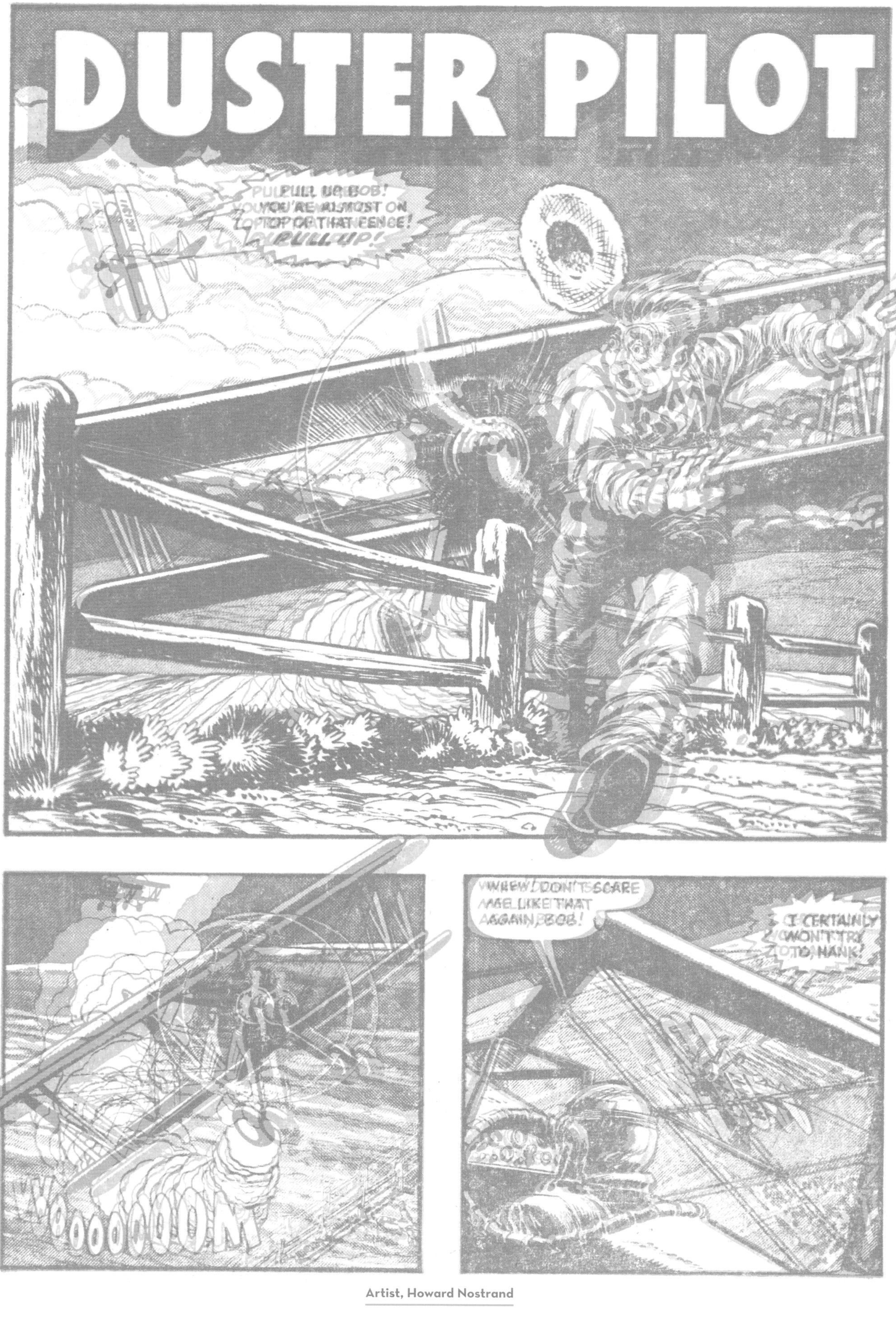
DUSTER PILOT
PULL UP, BOB! YOU'RE ALMOST ON TOP OF THAT FENCE! PULL UP!
WOOOOOOOM
WHEW! DON'T SCARE ME LIKE THAT AGAIN, BOB!
I CERTAINLY WON'T TRY TO, HANK!

Artist, Howard Nostrand

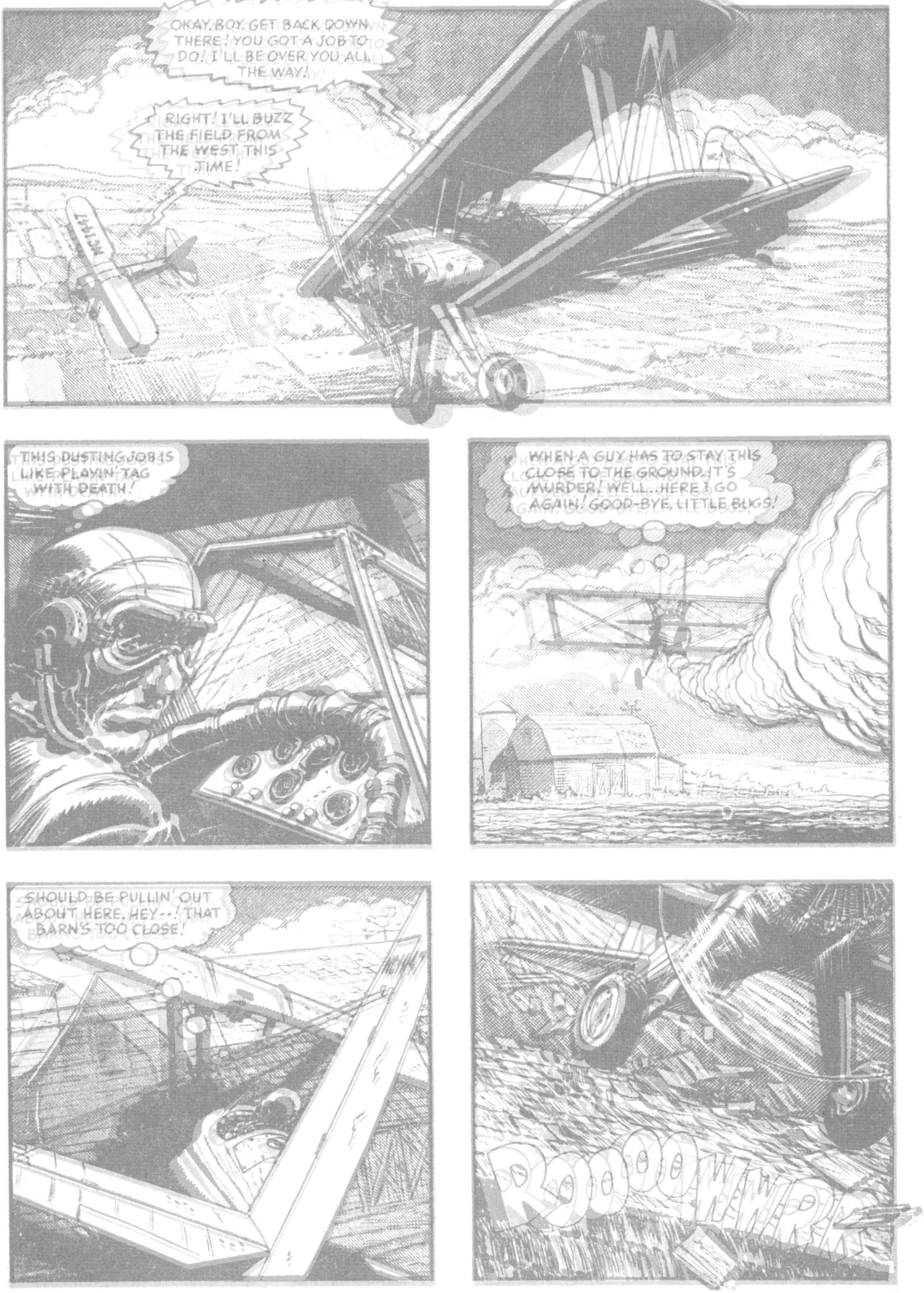
OKAY, BOY, GET BACK DOWN THERE! YOU GOT A JOB TO DO! I'LL BE OVER YOU ALL THE WAY!
RIGHT! I'LL BUZZ THE FIELD FROM THE WEST THIS TIME!
THIS DUSTING JOB IS LIKE PLAYIN' TAG WITH DEATH!
WHEN A GUY HAS TO STAY THIS CLOSE TO THE GROUND, IT'S MURDER! WELL... HERE I GO AGAIN! GOOD-BYE, LITTLE BUGS!
SHOULD BE PULLIN' OUT ABOUT HERE. HEY--! THAT BARN'S TOO CLOSE!
ROOOOOAWWRR

WELL, NOW TO DUST...
WHAT'S WRONG, BOB?
SPRAY TANK'S WORKED LOOSE! SMOKE'S POURIN' INTO MY COCKPIT!
GOT TO PUSH THE TANK BACK INTO PLACE! MEBBE A NOSE DIVE'LL DO THE TRICK!

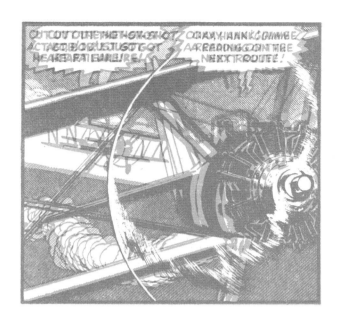

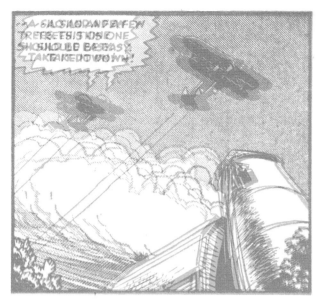

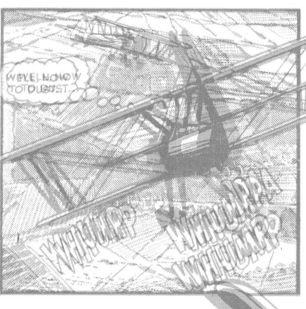

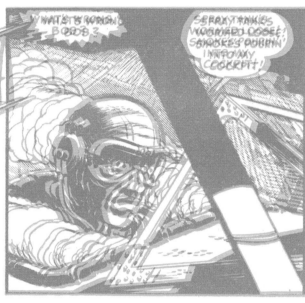

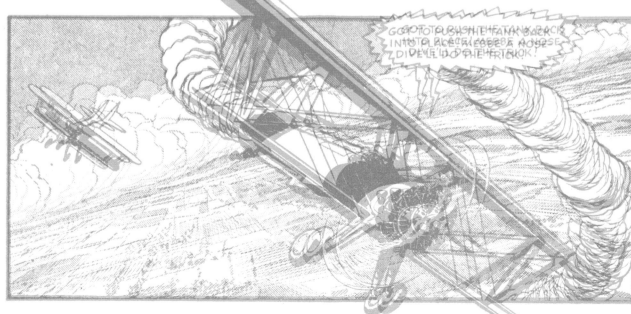

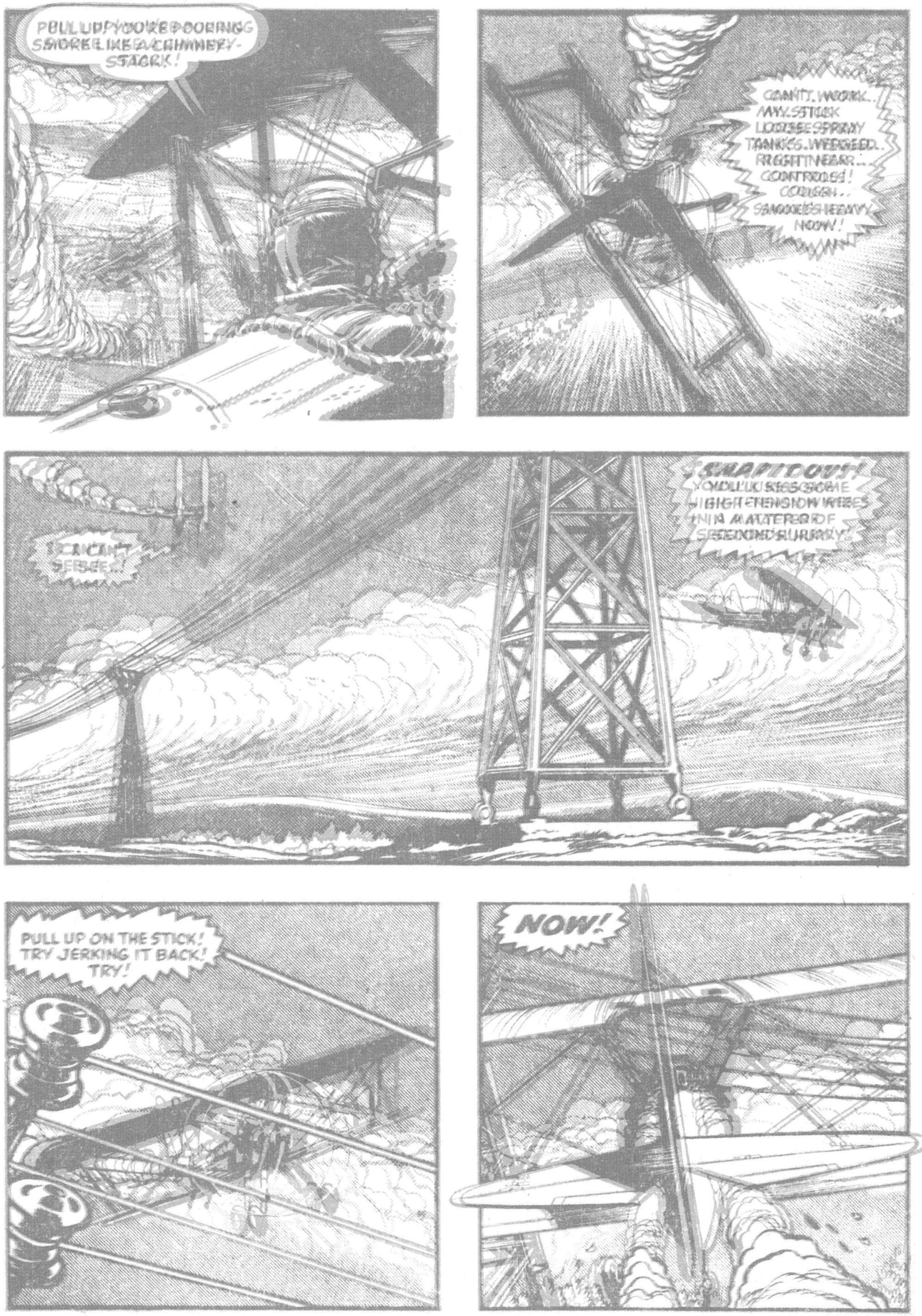
PULL UP! YOU'RE POURING SMOKE LIKE A CHIMNEY-STACK!
CAN'T. WORK.. MY STICK LOOSE SPRAY TANKS.. WEDGED.. RIGHT NEAR.. CONTROLS! COUGH.. SMOKE'S HEAVY NOW!
I CAN'T SEE..!
SNAP OUT! YOU'LL MISS SOME HIGH-TENSION WIRES IN A MATTER OF SECONDS! HURRY!
PULL UP ON THE STICK! TRY JERKING IT BACK! TRY!
NOW!

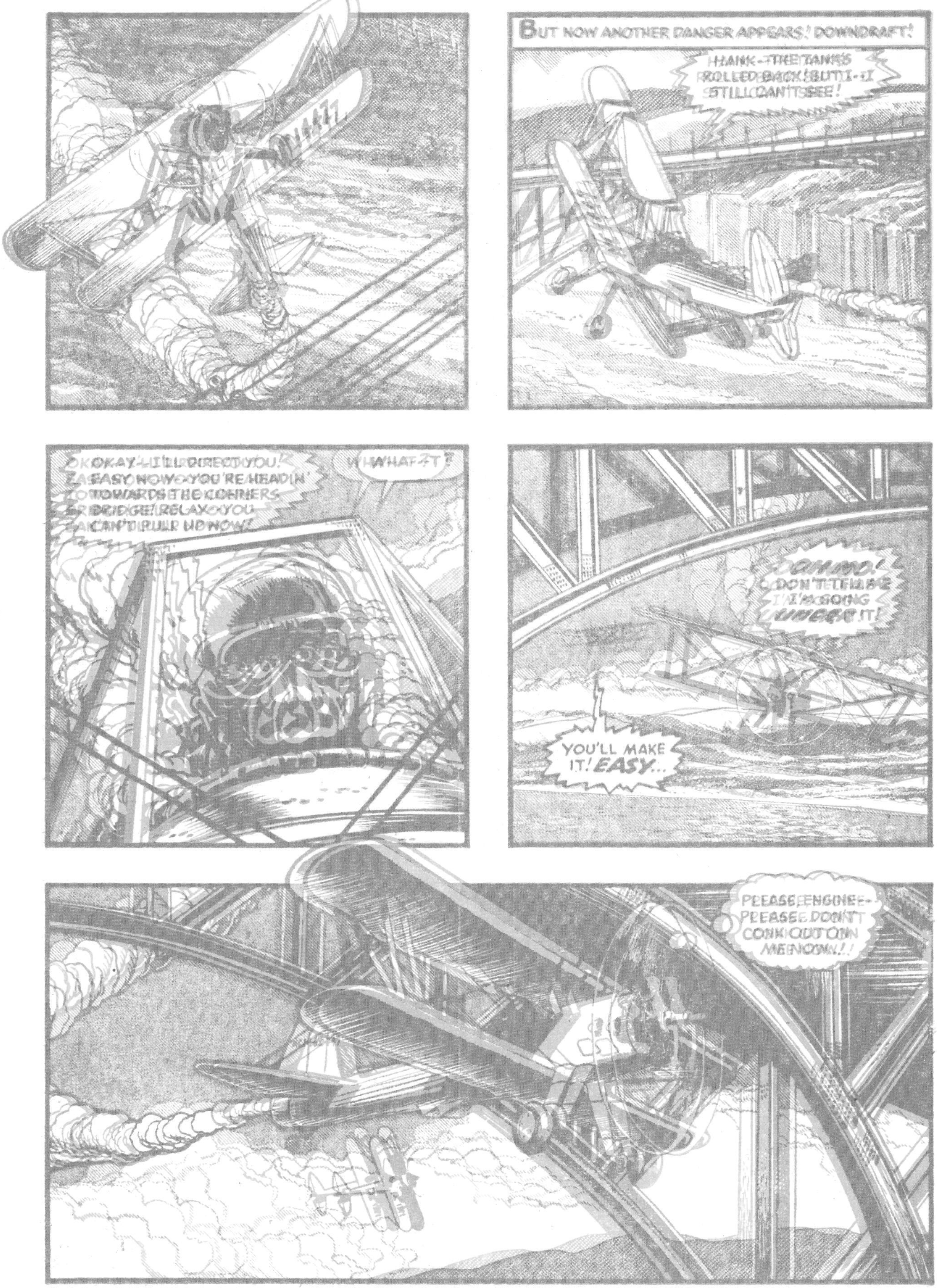
BUT NOW ANOTHER DANGER APPEARS! DOWNDRAFT!
HANK -- THE TANKS ROLLED BACK! BUT I-I STILL CAN'T SEE!
OKAY -- I'LL DIRECT YOU! EASY NOW -- YOU'RE HEADIN' TOWARDS THE CONNERS BRIDGE! RELAX -- YOU CAN'T PULL UP NOW!
WHAT -?
DON'T TELL ME I'M GOING
IT!
YOU'LL MAKE IT! EASY...
PLEASE, ENGINE -- PLEASE DON'T CONK OUT ON ME NOW!!

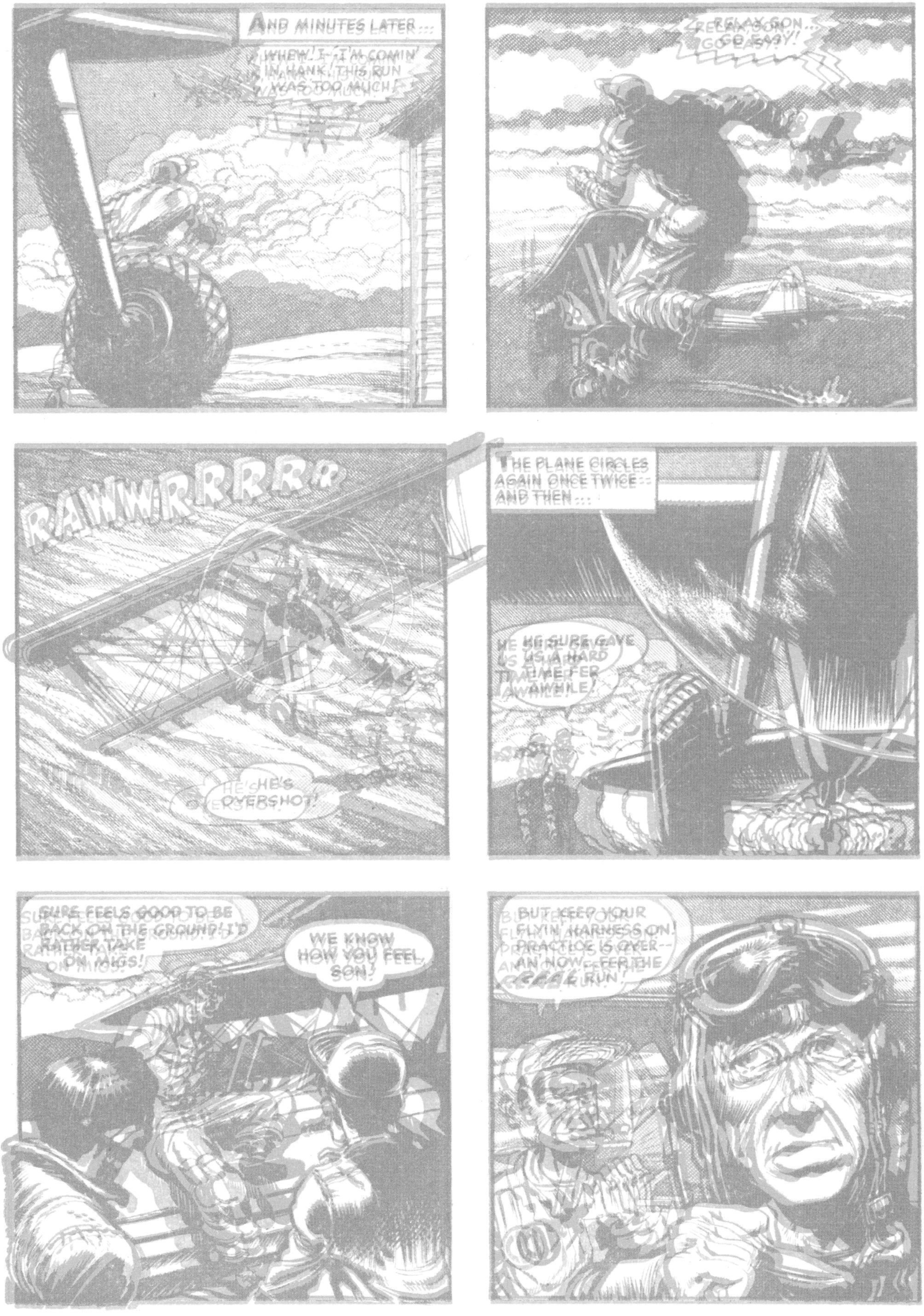
AND MINUTES LATER:::
WHEW! I--I'M COMIN' IN HANK. THIS RUN WAS TOO MUCH!
RELAX SON... GO EASY!
RAWWRRRRR
HE'S OVERSHOT!
THE PLANE CIRCLES AGAIN ONCE TWICE:: AND THEN:::
HE SURE GAVE US A HARD TIME FER AWHILE!
SURE FEELS GOOD TO BE BACK ON THE GROUND! I'D RATHER TAKE ON MIGS!
WE KNOW HOW YOU FEEL, SON!
BUT KEEP YOUR FLYIN' HARNESS ON! PRACTICE IS OVER-- AN' NOW... FER THE REAL RUN!

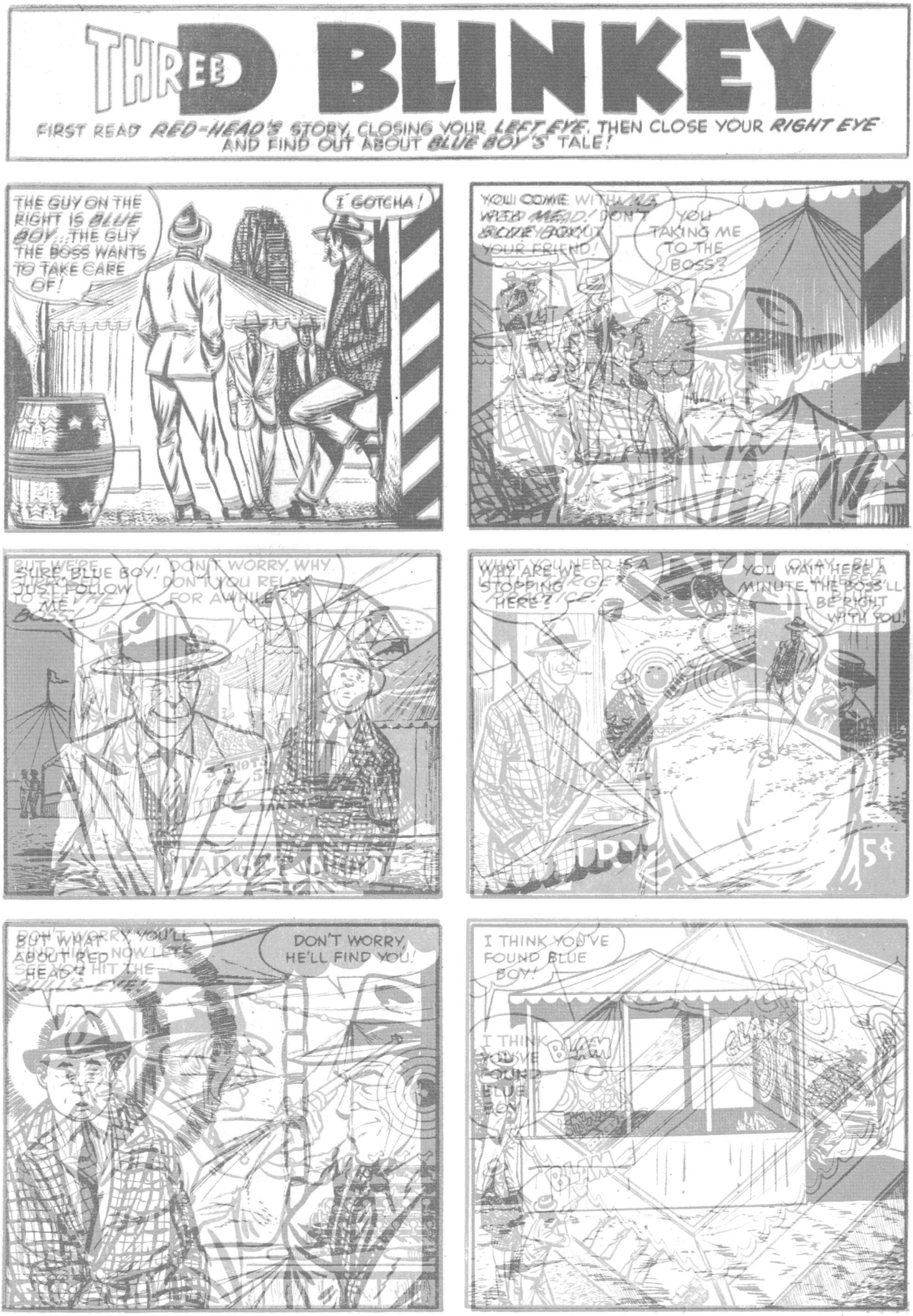
THREE D BLINKEY
FIRST READ RED-HEAD'S STORY, CLOSING YOUR LEFT EYE, THEN CLOSE YOUR RIGHT EYE AND FIND OUT ABOUT BLUE BOY'S TALE!
THE GUY ON THE RIGHT IS BLUE BOY... THE GUY THE BOSS WANTS TO TAKE CARE OF!
I GOTCHA!
YOU TAKING ME TO THE BOSS?
SURE, BLUE BOY! JUST FOLLOW ME.
DON'T WORRY. WHY DON'T YOU RELAX FOR AWHILE?
WHY ARE WE STOPPING HERE?
YOU WAIT HERE A MINUTE. THE BOSS'LL BE RIGHT WITH YOU!
5¢
BUT WHAT ABOUT RED-HEAD?
DON'T WORRY, HE'LL FIND YOU!
I THINK YOU'VE FOUND BLUE BOY!

Artists, Bob Powell studio

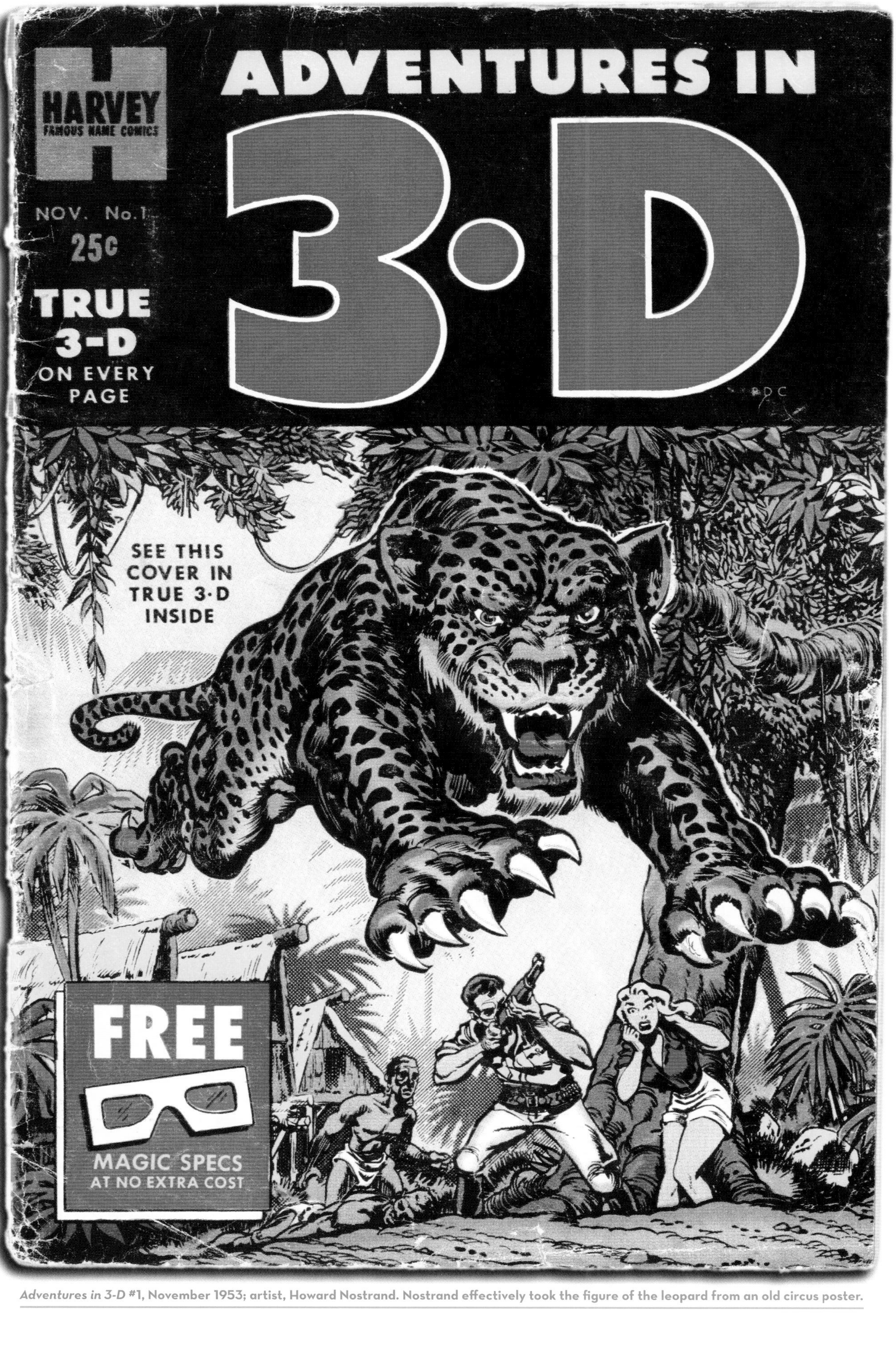
HARVEY
FAMOUS NAME COMICS
ADVENTURES IN
3-D
NOV. No.1
25¢
TRUE
3-D
ON EVERY
PAGE
SEE THIS
COVER IN
TRUE 3-D
INSIDE
FREE
MAGIC SPECS
AT NO EXTRA COST

Adventures in 3-D #1, November 1953; artist, Howard Nostrand. Nostrand effectively took the figure of the leopard from an old circus poster.

HERE IS THE COVER IN 3-D MAGIC. COMPARE
IT WITH THE FRONT COVER AND SEE THE
STARTLING EFFECTS.
SEE HOW THE LEOPARD JUMPS OUT OF THE
PICTURE AND INTO YOUR LAP! SEE THE
DEPTH OF THE JUNGLE BACKGROUND THAT
GOES RIGHT THROUGH THE PAGE! MOVE THE
PICTURE SLIGHTLY FROM SIDE TO SIDE AND
SEE THE PICTURE COME TO LIFE!

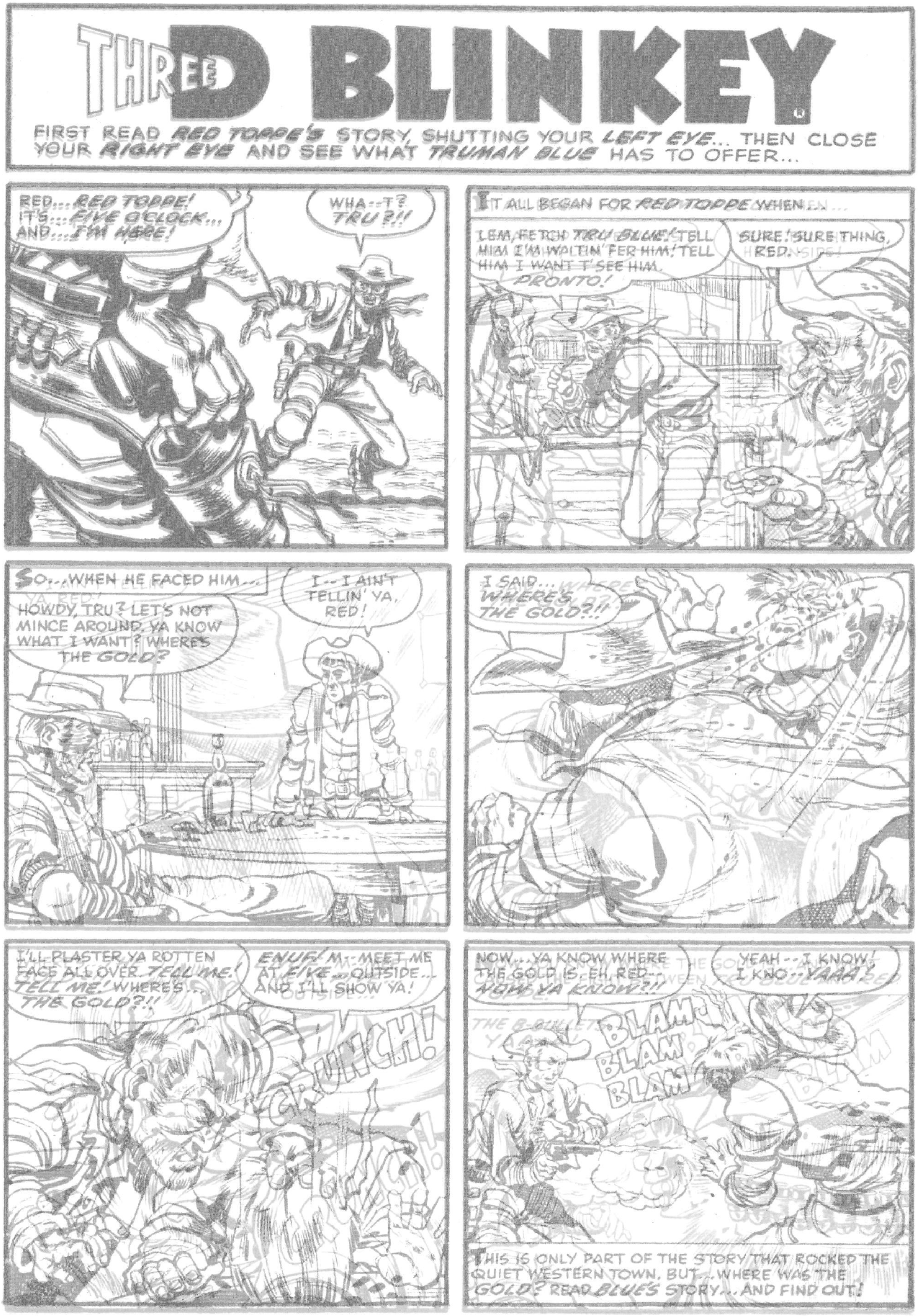
THREE D BLINKEY
FIRST READ RED TOPPE'S STORY, SHUTTING YOUR LEFT EYE... THEN CLOSE YOUR RIGHT EYE AND SEE WHAT TRUMAN BLUE HAS TO OFFER...
RED... RED TOPPE! IT'S... FIVE O'CLOCK... AND... I'M HERE!
WHA--T? TRU?!!
IT ALL BEGAN FOR RED TOPPE WHEN...
LEM, FETCH TRU BLUE! TELL HIM I'M WAITIN' FER HIM! TELL HIM I WANT T'SEE HIM. PRONTO!
SURE! SURE THING, RED.
SO... WHEN HE FACED HIM...
HOWDY, TRU? LET'S NOT MINCE AROUND, YA KNOW WHAT I WANT? WHERES THE GOLD?
I -- I AIN'T TELLIN' YA, RED!
I SAID... WHERE'S THE GOLD?!!
I'LL PLASTER YA ROTTEN FACE ALL OVER. TELL ME! TELL ME! WHERE'S... THE GOLD?!!
ENUF! M--MEET ME AT FIVE... OUTSIDE... AND I'LL SHOW YA!
CRUNCH!
NOW... YA KNOW WHERE THE GOLD IS, EH, RED-- NOW YA KNOW?!!
YEAH -- I KNOW! I KNO--YAAA!
BLAM BLAM BLAM
THIS IS ONLY PART OF THE STORY THAT ROCKED THE QUIET WESTERN TOWN, BUT... WHERE WAS THE GOLD? READ BLUE'S STORY... AND FIND OUT!

Artists, Bob Powell studio

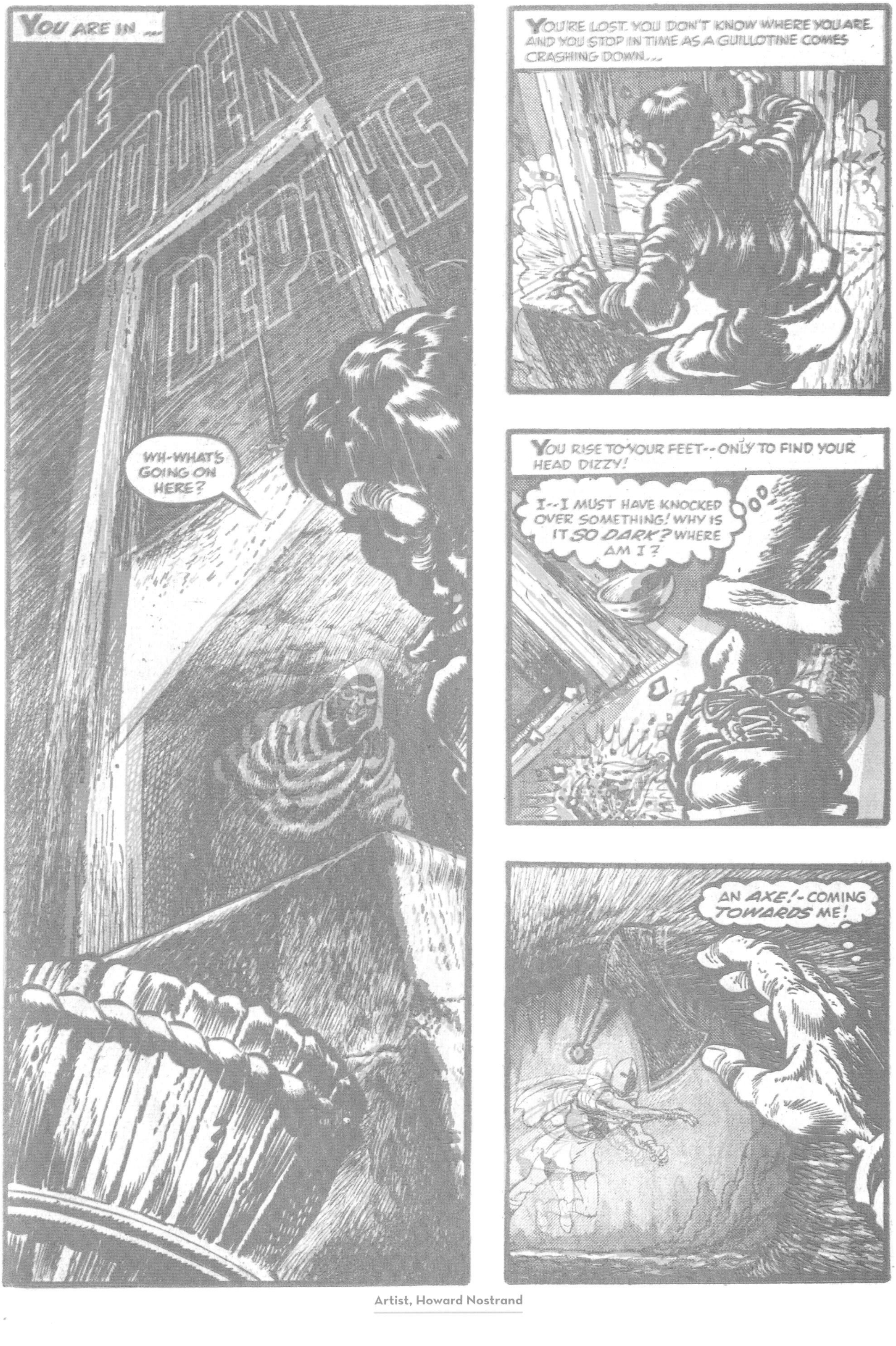
YOU ARE IN ...
THE HIDDEN DEPTHS
WH-WHAT'S GOING ON HERE?
YOU'RE LOST. YOU DON'T KNOW WHERE YOU ARE. AND YOU STOP IN TIME AS A GUILLOTINE COMES CRASHING DOWN...
YOU RISE TO YOUR FEET--ONLY TO FIND YOUR HEAD DIZZY!
I--I MUST HAVE KNOCKED OVER SOMETHING! WHY IS IT SO DARK? WHERE AM I?
AN AXE!-COMING TOWARDS ME!

Artist, Howard Nostrand

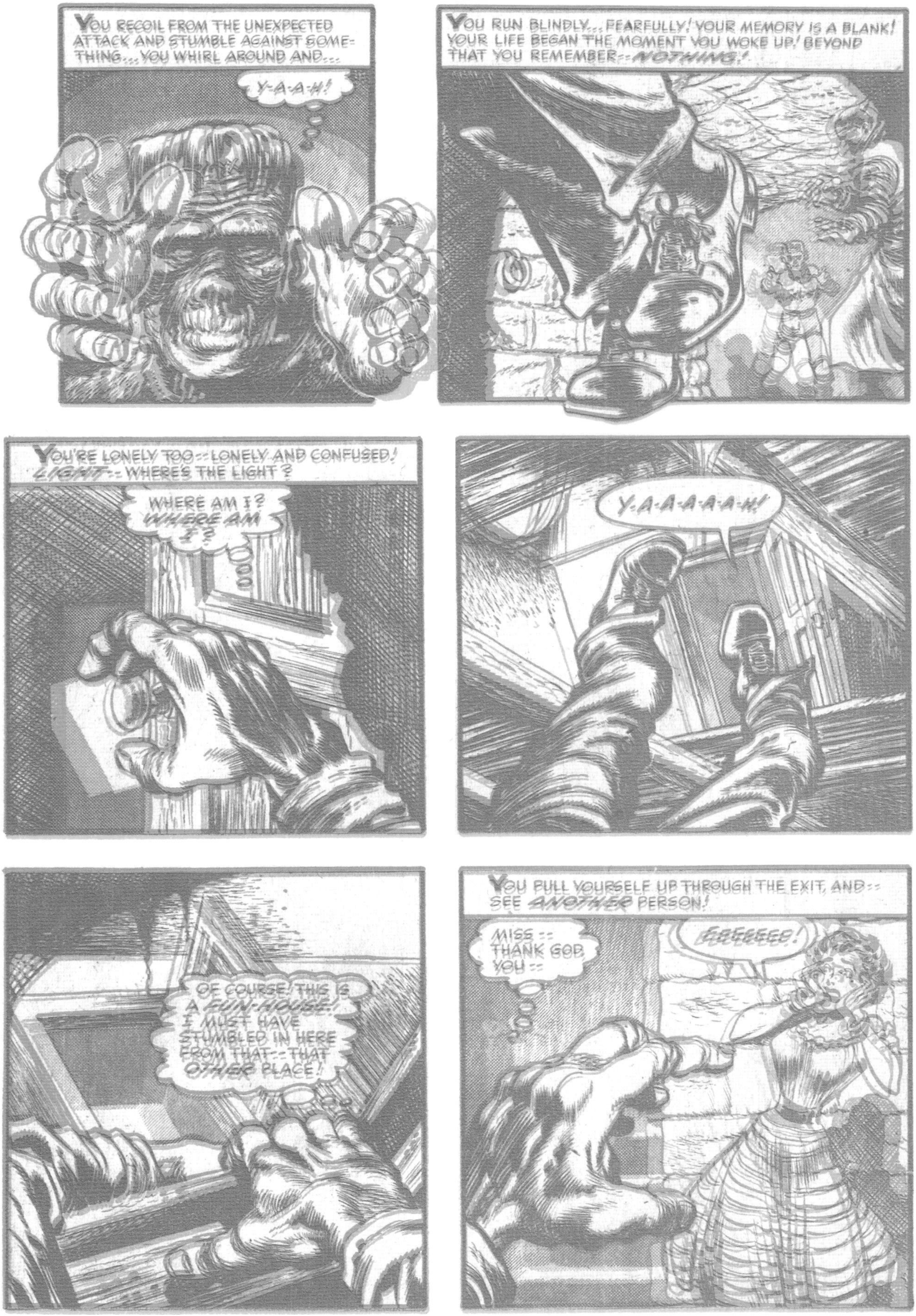
YOU RECOIL FROM THE UNEXPECTED ATTACK AND STUMBLE AGAINST SOME-THING... YOU WHIRL AROUND AND...
Y-A-A-H!
YOU RUN BLINDLY... FEARFULLY! YOUR MEMORY IS A BLANK! YOUR LIFE BEGAN THE MOMENT YOU WOKE UP! BEYOND THAT YOU REMEMBER--NOTHING!
YOU'RE LONELY TOO--LONELY AND CONFUSED! LIGHT--WHERE'S THE LIGHT?
WHERE AM I? WHERE AM I?
Y-A-A-A-A-A-H!
OF COURSE! THIS IS A FUN-HOUSE! I MUST HAVE STUMBLED IN HERE FROM THAT--THAT OTHER PLACE!
YOU PULL YOURSELF UP THROUGH THE EXIT, AND--SEE ANOTHER PERSON!
MISS--THANK GOD YOU--
EEEEEEE!

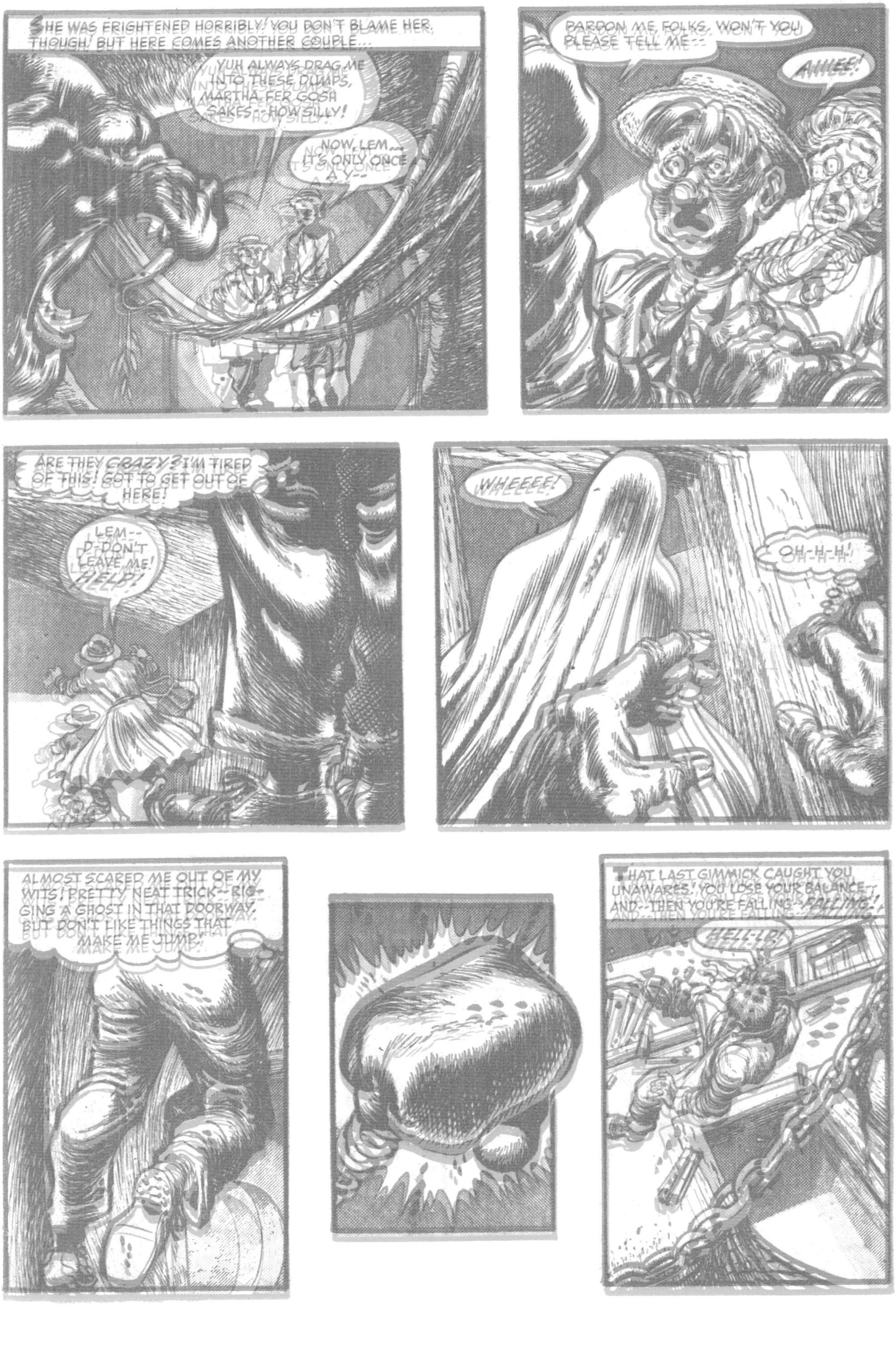
SHE WAS FRIGHTENED HORRIBLY! YOU DON'T BLAME HER, THOUGH! BUT HERE COMES ANOTHER COUPLE...
YUH ALWAYS DRAG ME INTO THESE DUMPS, MARTHA-FER GOSH SAKES--HOW SILLY!
NOW, LEM... IT'S ONLY ONCE A Y--
PARDON ME, FOLKS, WON'T YOU PLEASE TELL ME--
AIIEE!
ARE THEY CRAZY? I'M TIRED OF THIS! GOT TO GET OUT OF HERE!
LEM-- D-DON'T LEAVE ME! HELP!
WHEEEE!
OH-H-H!
ALMOST SCARED ME OUT OF MY WITS! PRETTY NEAT TRICK--RIGGING A GHOST IN THAT DOORWAY. BUT DON'T LIKE THINGS THAT MAKE ME JUMP.
THAT LAST GIMMICK CAUGHT YOU UNAWARES! YOU LOSE YOUR BALANCE-- AND--THEN YOU'RE FALLING--FALLING!
HELL-LP!

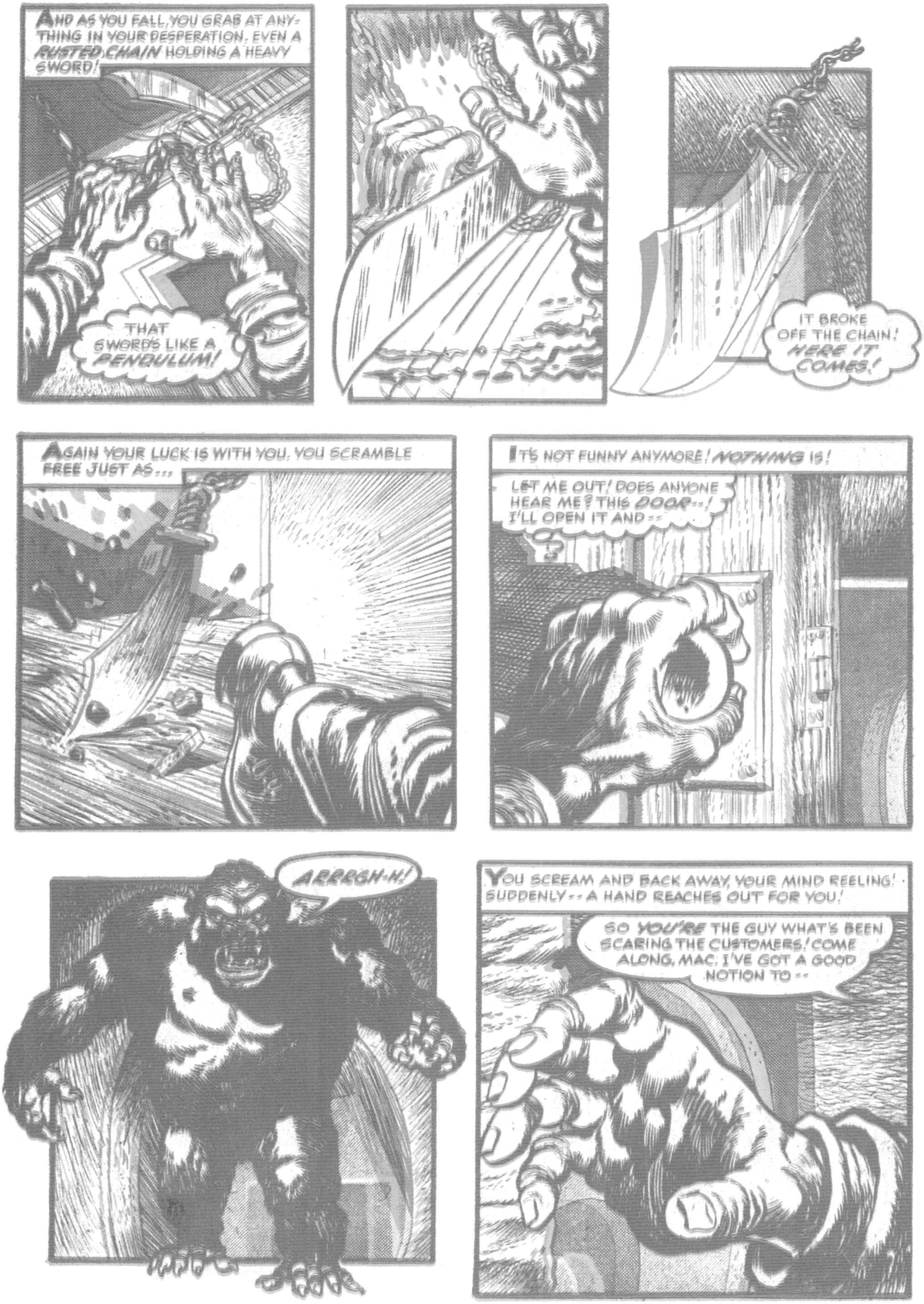

AND AS YOU FALL, YOU GRAB AT ANYTHING IN YOUR DESPERATION, EVEN A RUSTED CHAIN HOLDING A HEAVY SWORD!
THAT SWORD'S LIKE A PENDULUM!
IT BROKE OFF THE CHAIN! HERE IT COMES!
AGAIN YOUR LUCK IS WITH YOU. YOU SCRAMBLE FREE JUST AS...
IT'S NOT FUNNY ANYMORE! NOTHING IS!
LET ME OUT! DOES ANYONE HEAR ME? THIS DOOR--! I'LL OPEN IT AND--
ARRRGH-H!
YOU SCREAM AND BACK AWAY, YOUR MIND REELING! SUDDENLY-- A HAND REACHES OUT FOR YOU!
SO YOU'RE THE GUY WHAT'S BEEN SCARING THE CUSTOMERS! COME ALONG, MAC. I'VE GOT A GOOD NOTION TO--

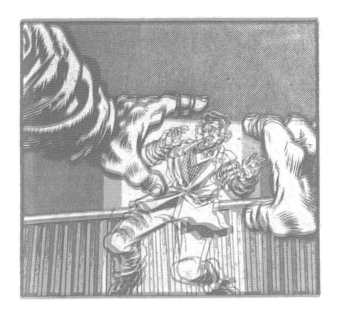

HE VANISHES INTO A DOORWAY AND YOU LOSE HIM. YOU REEL AND FLOUNDER! YOU'RE DIZZY! YOU'RE LOST! YOU TURN INTO....

A SPOOK TROLLEY.... COMING RIGHT AT ME....

YOU CLIMB A NARROW LEDGE! YOU'RE IN A COLD SWEAT.... AND EVEN THE DOOR FEELS CLAMMY! BUT WHAT'S BEHIND IT?

THAT'S HIM OR OTHER YOU OR SOMETHING!

GET HIM! THERE HE IS!

YOU'RE CONFUSED.... BEWILDERED! YOU'RE THE TARGET IN A CHASE! STAGGERINGLY, YOU RETREAT INTO THE HOUSE OF HORRORS!

HE'S RUNNING THROUGH THAT OTHER ROOM! DON'T LET HIM OUT OF YOUR SIGHT!

YOU STUMBLE TOWARDS A REAR-STAIRWAY THAT SUDDENLY POPS INTO YOUR MEMORY. THEN-- AS YOU THROW OPEN THE DOOR AND LOOK DOWN AT A CELLAR-- EVERY-THING BECOMES CRYSTAL-CLEAR!

NO ONE WANTS TO LOOK AT ME.... TALK TO ME! IT'S BETTER TO GO BACK HERE WHERE I BELONG!

SO YOU THROW YOURSELF INTO THE BUBBLING VAT--INTO THE MOTHER MATRIX THAT GAVE YOU LIFE--FOR YOU ARE A LUMP OF WAX THAT CAME TO LIFE--ONLY TO FIND THAT DEATH WAS BETTER THAN HATE AND LONELINESS!

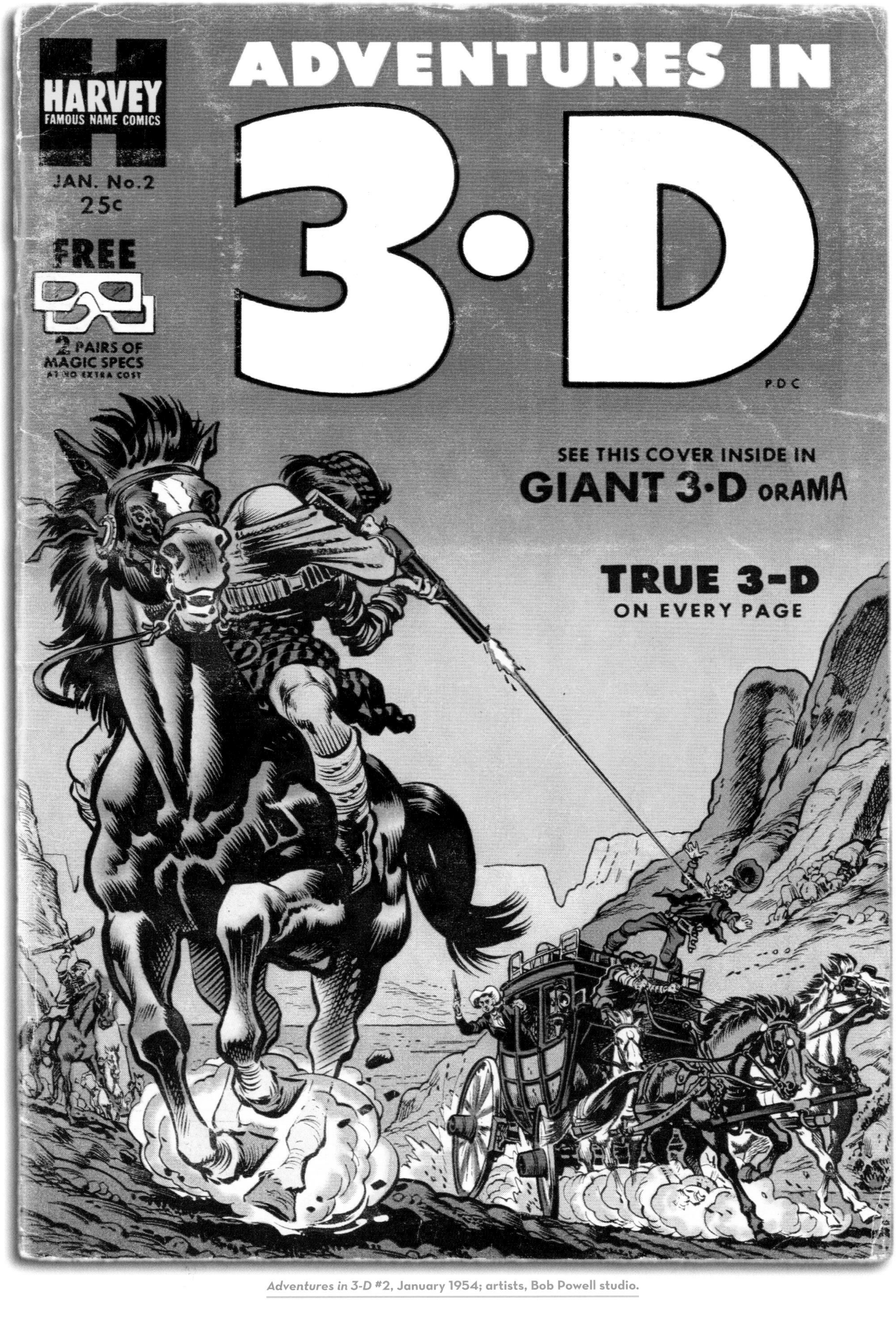
ADVENTURES IN
3-D
HARVEY
FAMOUS NAME COMICS
JAN. No.2
25c
FREE
2 PAIRS OF
MAGIC SPECS
AT NO EXTRA COST
P.D.C
SEE THIS COVER INSIDE IN
GIANT 3-D ORAMA
TRUE 3-D
ON EVERY PAGE

Adventures in 3-D #2, January 1954; artists, Bob Powell studio.

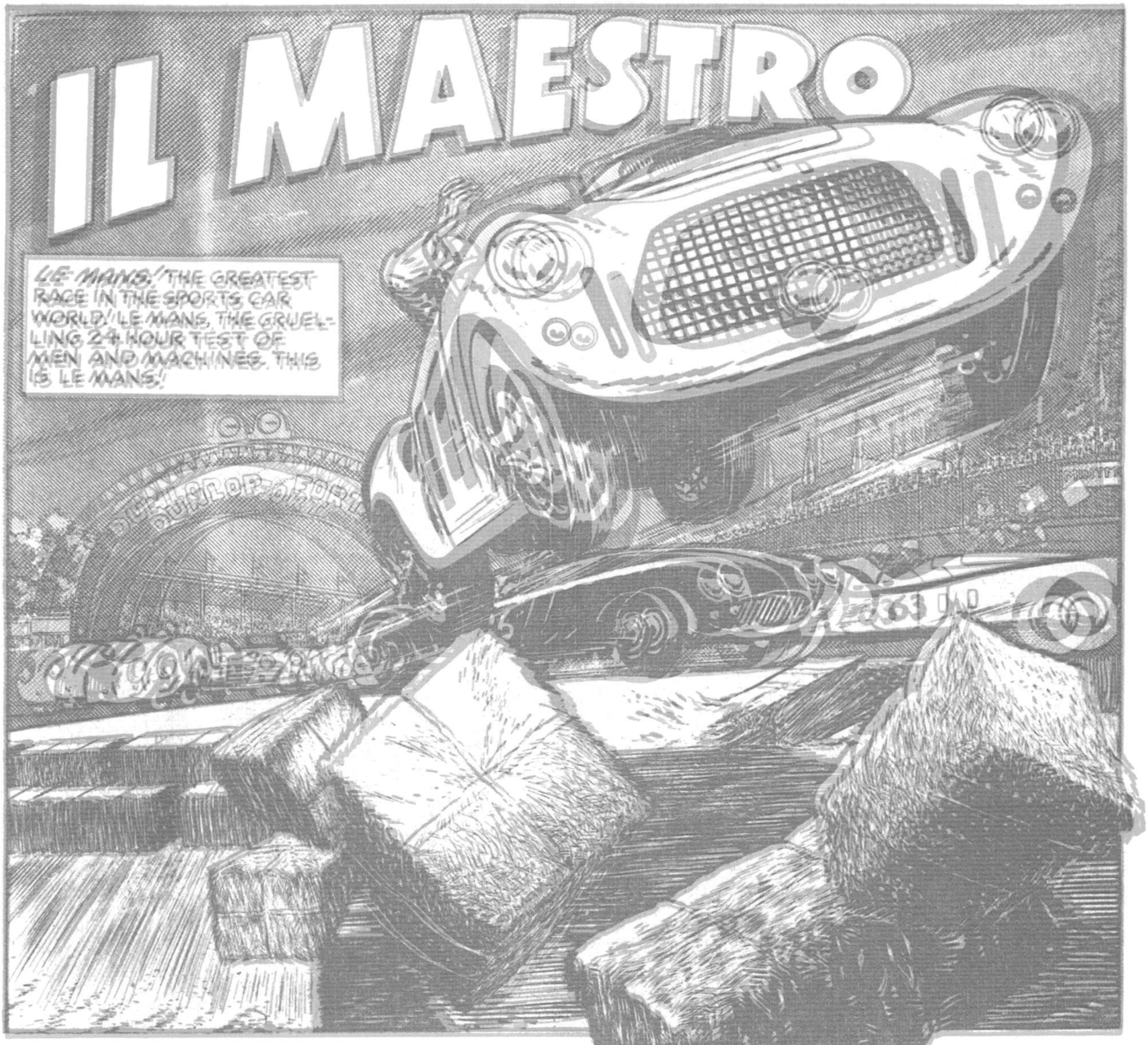
IL MAESTRO
LE MANS! THE GREATEST RACE IN THE SPORTS CAR WORLD! LE MANS, THE GRUELLING 24 HOUR TEST OF MEN AND MACHINES. THIS IS LE MANS!

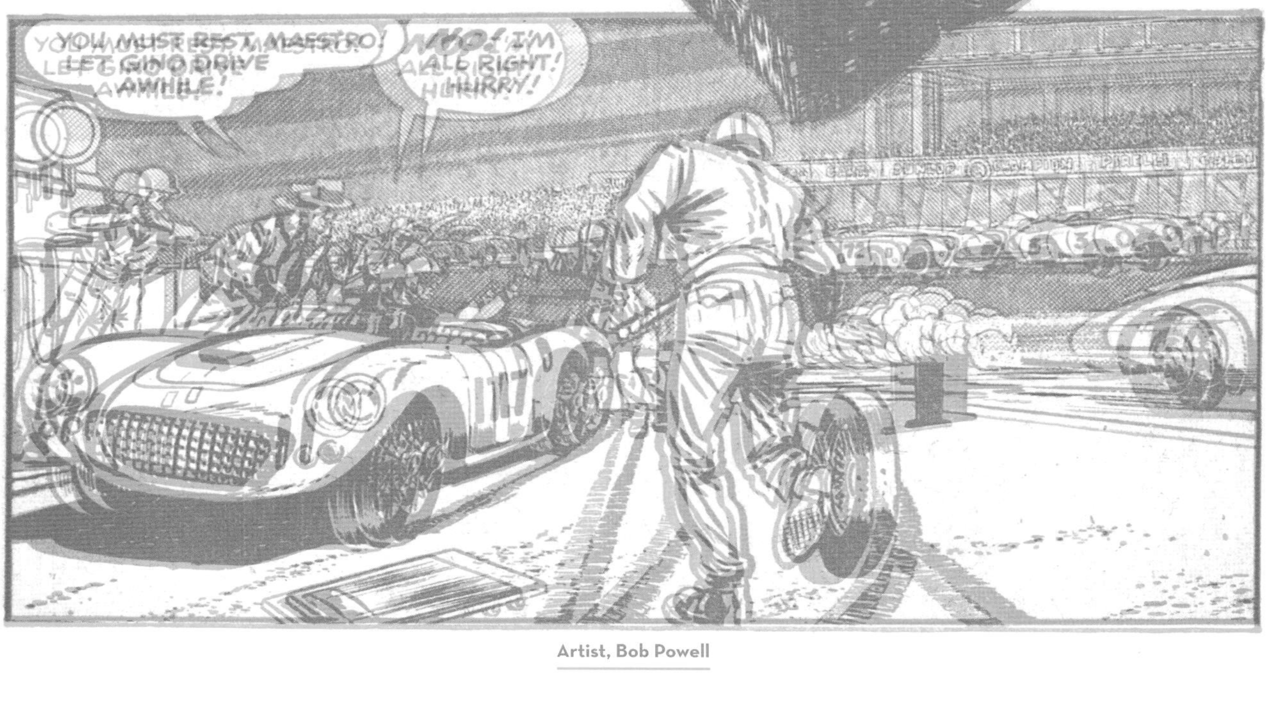
YOU MUST REST, MAESTRO! LET GINO DRIVE AWHILE!
NO! I'M ALL RIGHT! HURRY!

Artist, Bob Powell

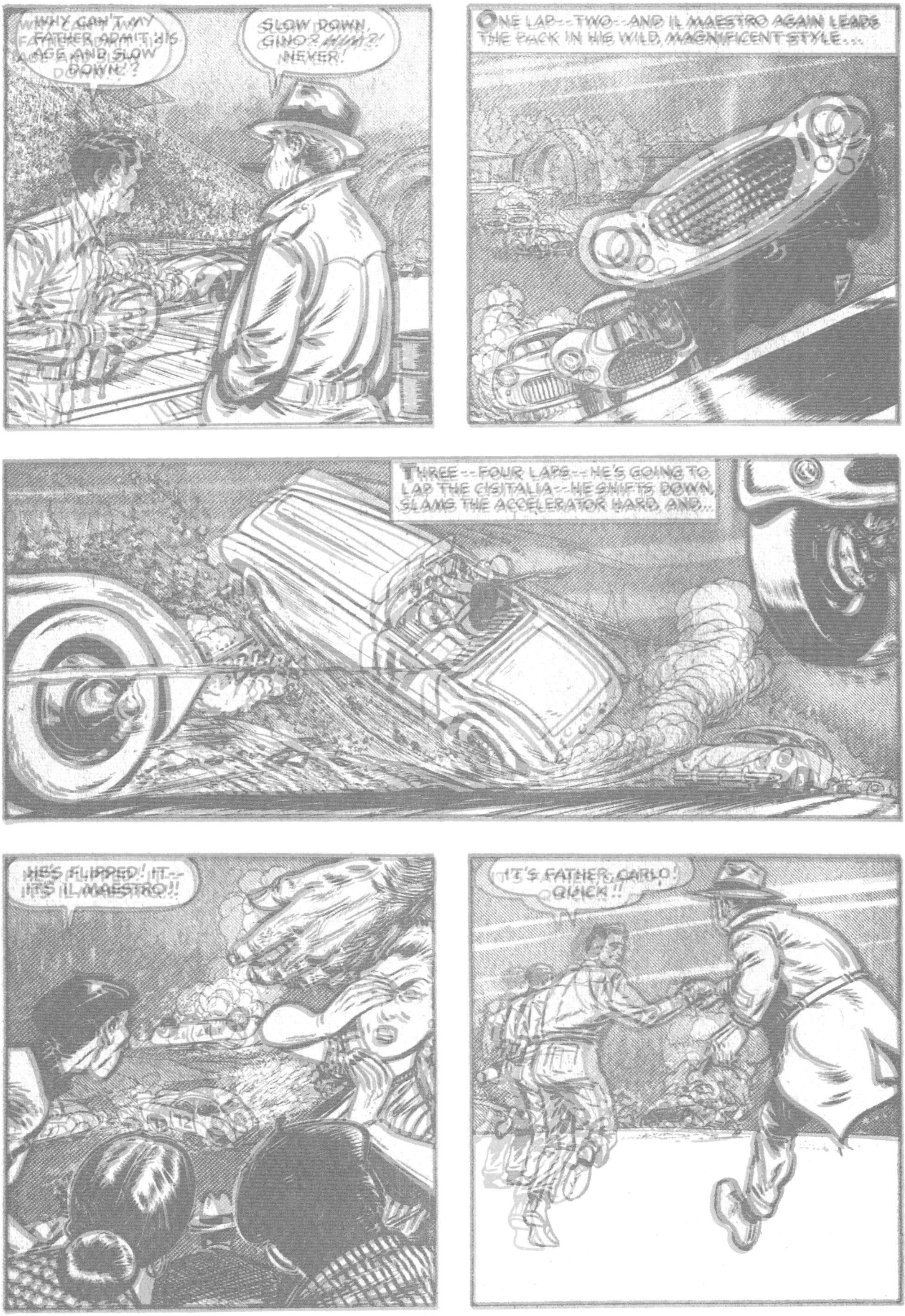
WHY CAN'T MY FATHER ADMIT HIS AGE AND SLOW DOWN?
SLOW DOWN, GINO? NEVER!
ONE LAP--TWO--AND IL MAESTRO AGAIN LEADS THE PACK IN HIS WILD MAGNIFICENT STYLE...
THREE--FOUR LAPS--HE'S GOING TO LAP THE CISITALIA--HE SHIFTS DOWN, SLAMS THE ACCELERATOR HARD AND...
HE'S FLIPPED! IT--IT'S IL MAESTRO!!
IT'S FATHER CARLO! QUICK!!

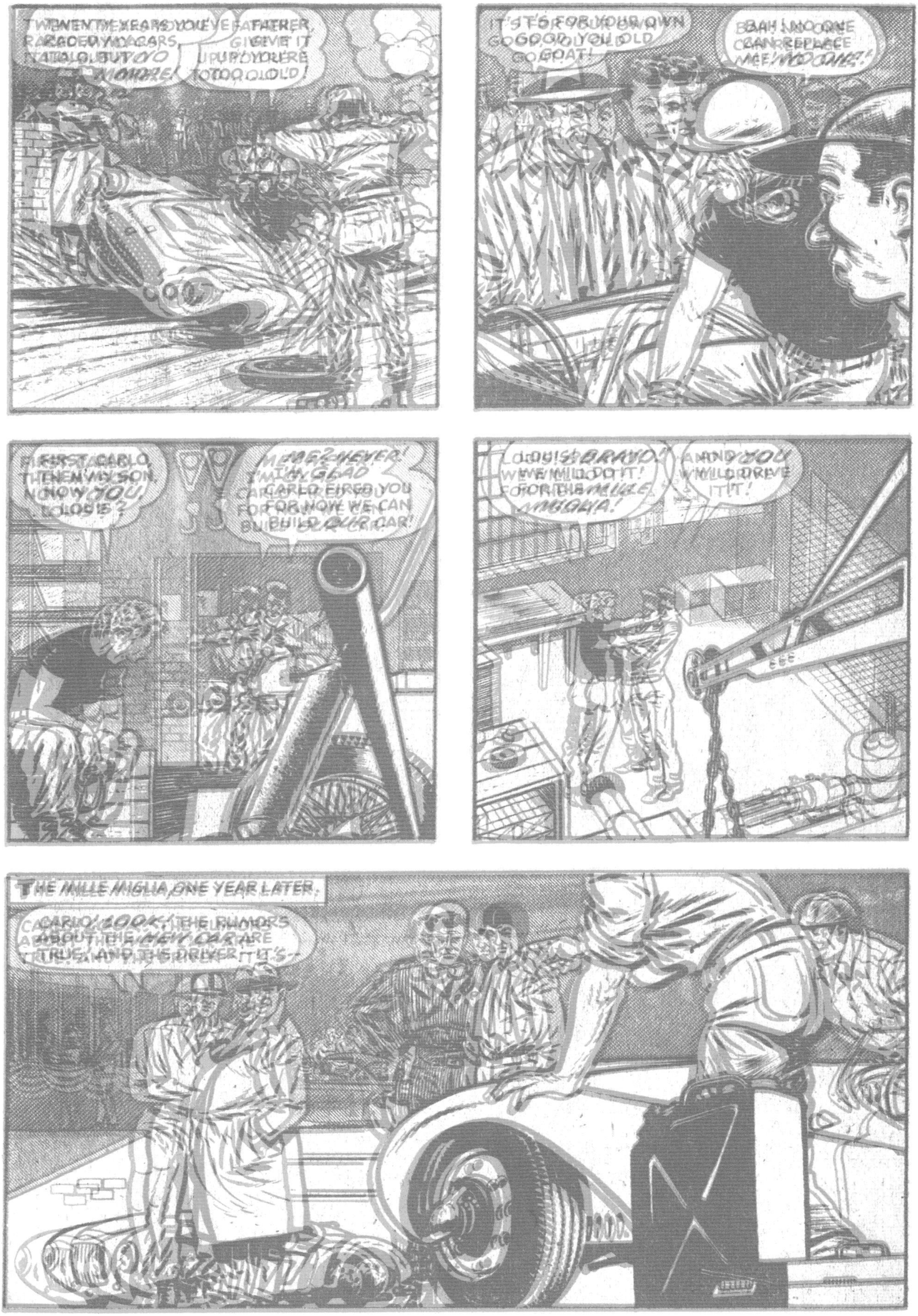
TWENTY YEARS YOU'VE RACED MY CARS, ITALO, BUT NO MORE!
FATHER, GIVE IT UP. YOU'RE TOO OLD!
IT'S FOR YOUR OWN GOOD, YOU OLD GOAT!
BAH! NO ONE CAN REPLACE ME! NO ONE!
FIRST CARLO, THEN MY SON, NOW YOU, LOUIS?
ME? NEVER! I'M GLAD CARLO FIRED YOU FOR NOW WE CAN BUILD OUR CAR!
LOUIS! BRAVO! WE WILL DO IT! FOR THE MILLE MIGLIA!
AND YOU WILL DRIVE IT!
THE MILLE MIGLIA, ONE YEAR LATER.
CARLO! LOOK! THE RUMORS ABOUT THE NEW CAR ARE TRUE, AND THE DRIVER...IT'S--

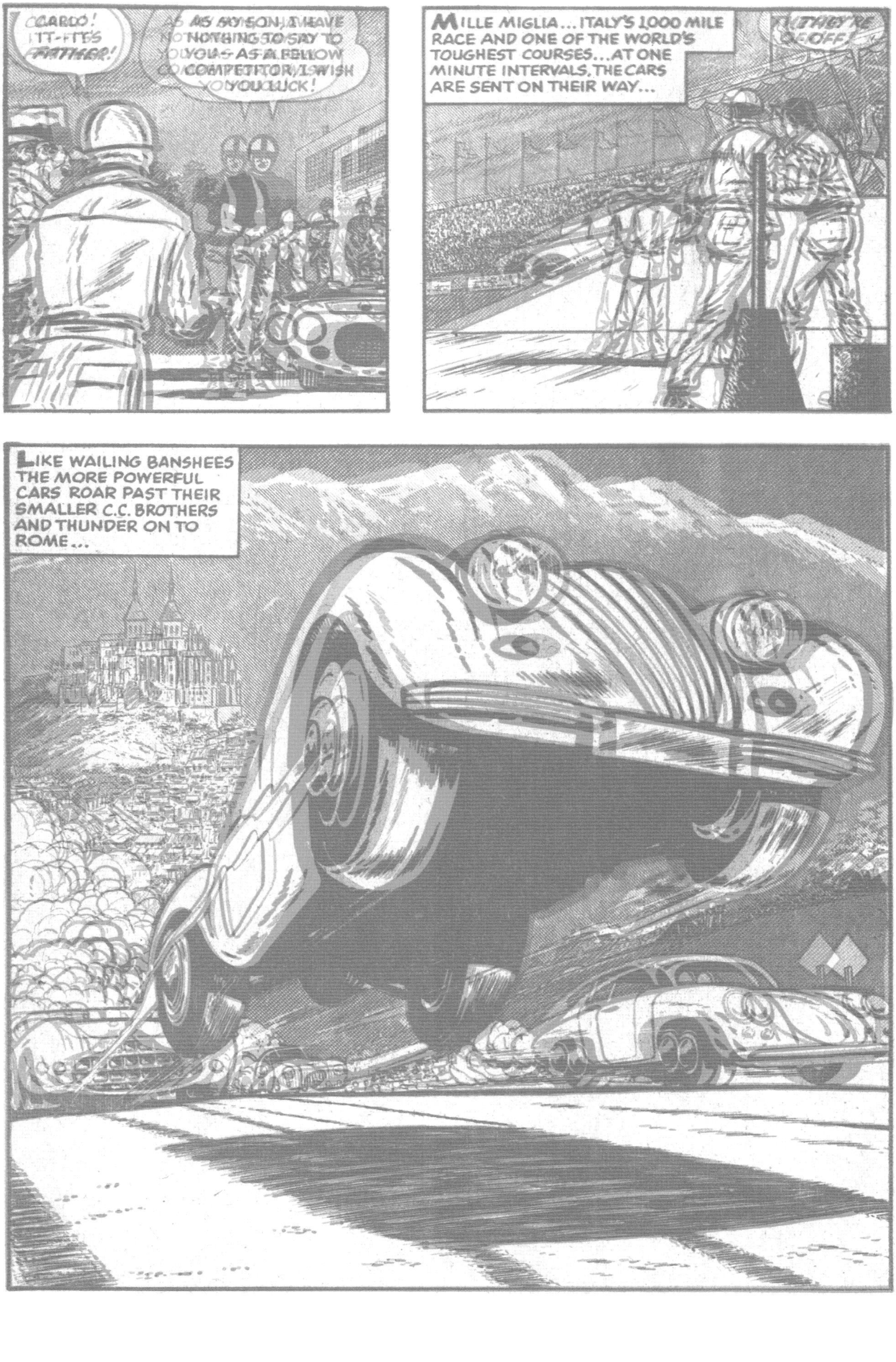

CARLO! IT-IT'S FATHER!
AS MY SON, I HAVE NOTHING TO SAY TO YOU! AS A FELLOW COMPETITOR, I WISH YOU LUCK!
MILLE MIGLIA... ITALY'S 1,000 MILE RACE AND ONE OF THE WORLD'S TOUGHEST COURSES... AT ONE MINUTE INTERVALS, THE CARS ARE SENT ON THEIR WAY...
THEY'RE OFF!
LIKE WAILING BANSHEES THE MORE POWERFUL CARS ROAR PAST THEIR SMALLER C.C. BROTHERS AND THUNDER ON TO ROME...

121

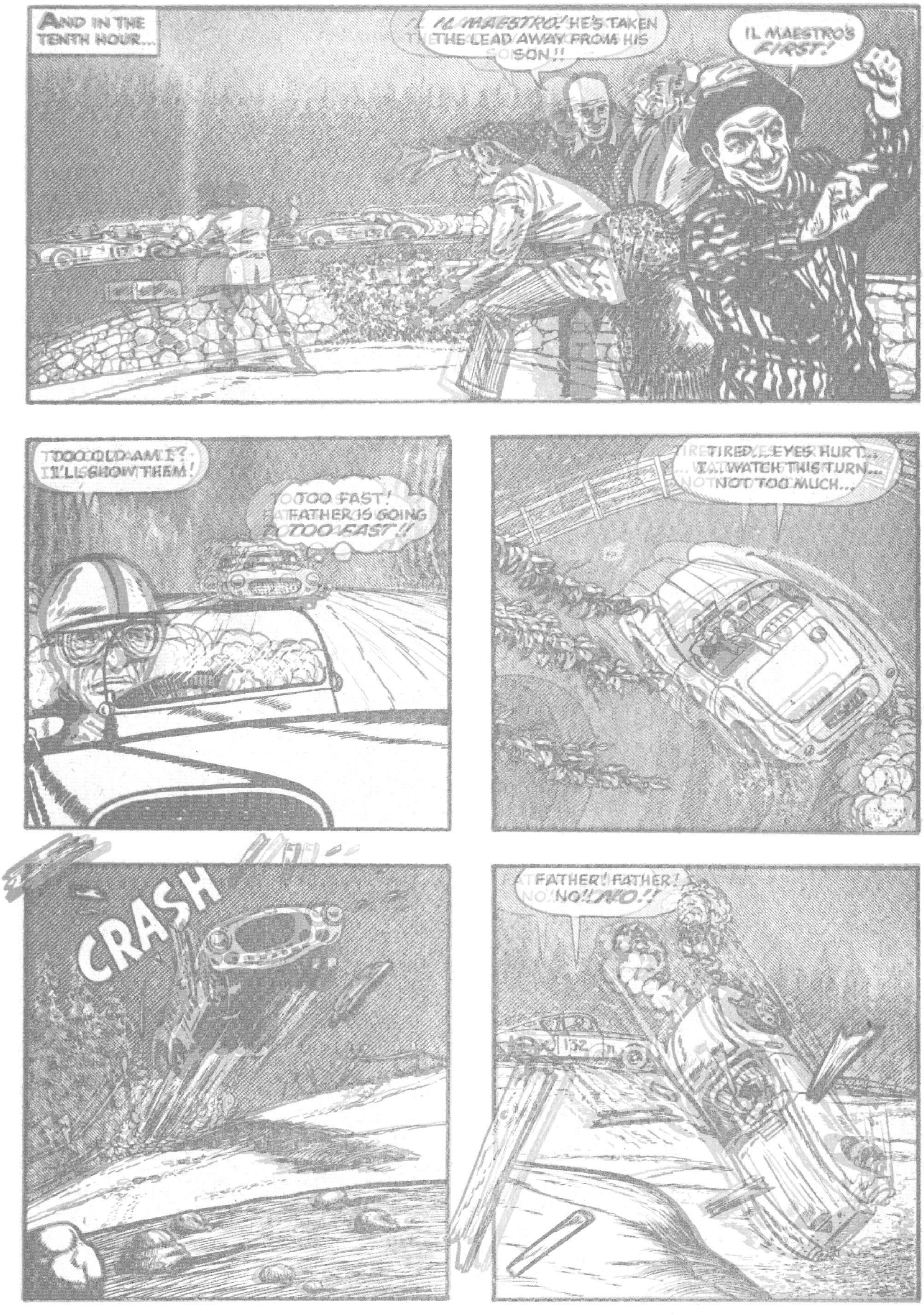
AND IN THE TENTH HOUR...
IL MAESTRO! HE'S TAKEN THE LEAD AWAY FROM HIS SON!!
IL MAESTRO'S FIRST!
TOO OLD AM I? I'LL SHOW THEM!
TOO FAST! FATHER IS GOING TOO FAST!!
TIRED... EYES HURT... WATCH THIS TURN... NOT TOO MUCH...
CRASH
FATHER! FATHER! NO!! NO!!

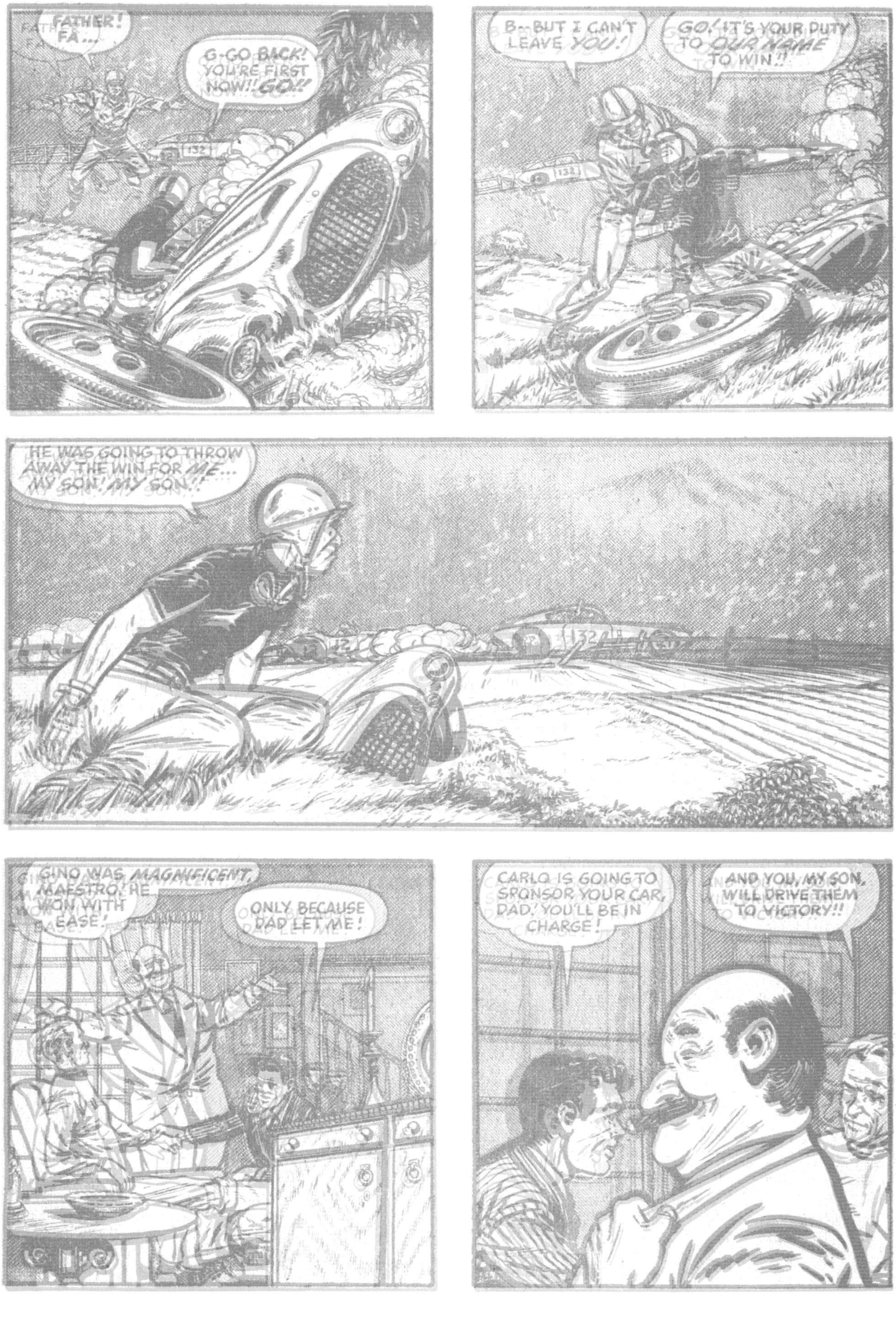

FATHER! FA...
G-GO BACK! YOU'RE FIRST NOW!! GO!!
B-BUT I CAN'T LEAVE YOU!
GO! IT'S YOUR DUTY TO OUR NAME TO WIN!!
HE WAS GOING TO THROW AWAY THE WIN FOR ME... MY SON! MY SON!!
GINO WAS MAGNIFICENT, MAESTRO! HE WON WITH EASE!
ONLY BECAUSE DAD LET ME!
CARLO IS GOING TO SPONSOR YOUR CAR, DAD! YOU'LL BE IN CHARGE!
AND YOU, MY SON, WILL DRIVE THEM TO VICTORY!!

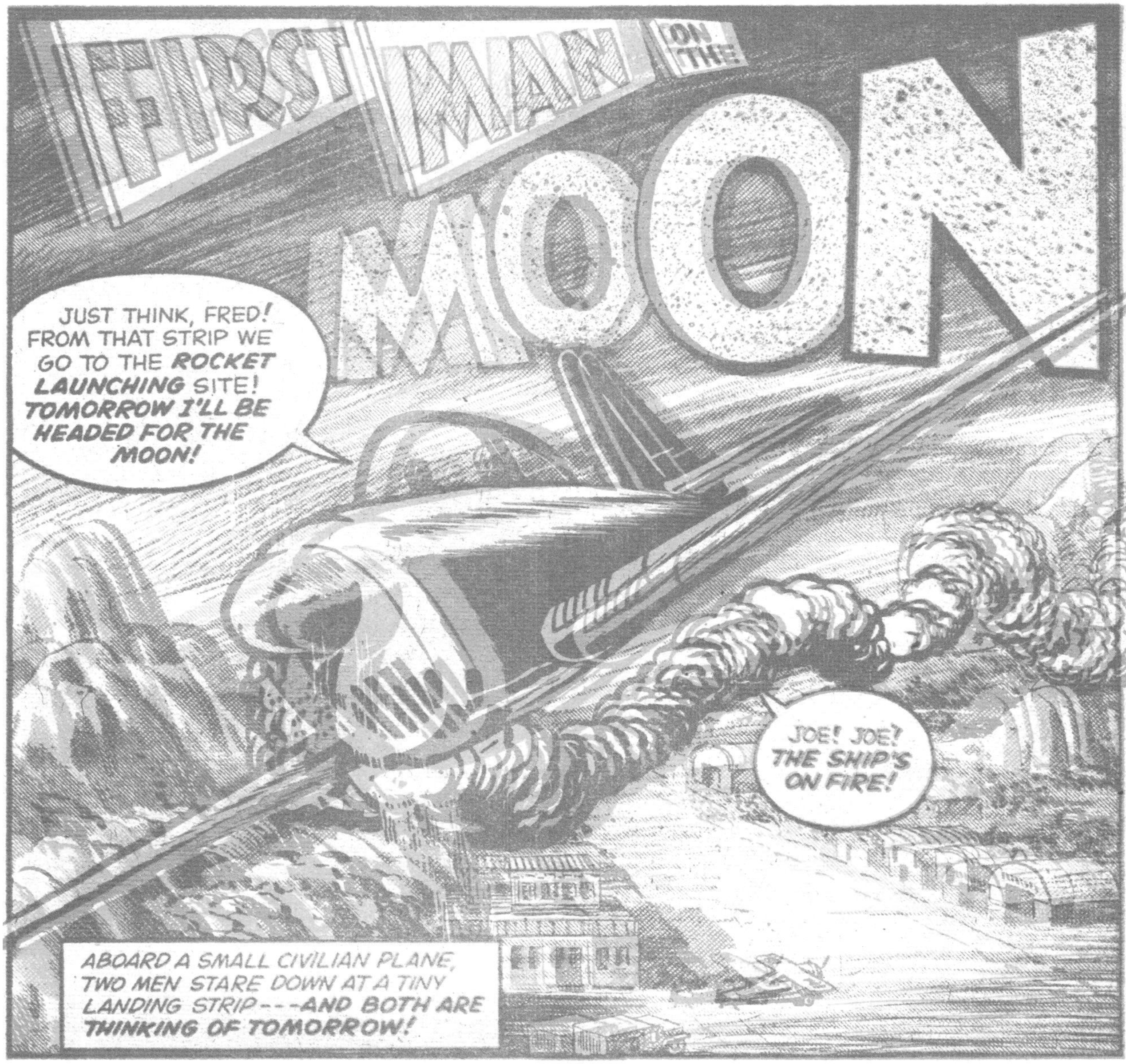
FIRST MAN ON THE MOON
JUST THINK, FRED! FROM THAT STRIP WE GO TO THE ROCKET LAUNCHING SITE! TOMORROW I'LL BE HEADED FOR THE MOON!
JOE! JOE! THE SHIP'S ON FIRE!
ABOARD A SMALL CIVILIAN PLANE, TWO MEN STARE DOWN AT A TINY LANDING STRIP---AND BOTH ARE THINKING OF TOMORROW!

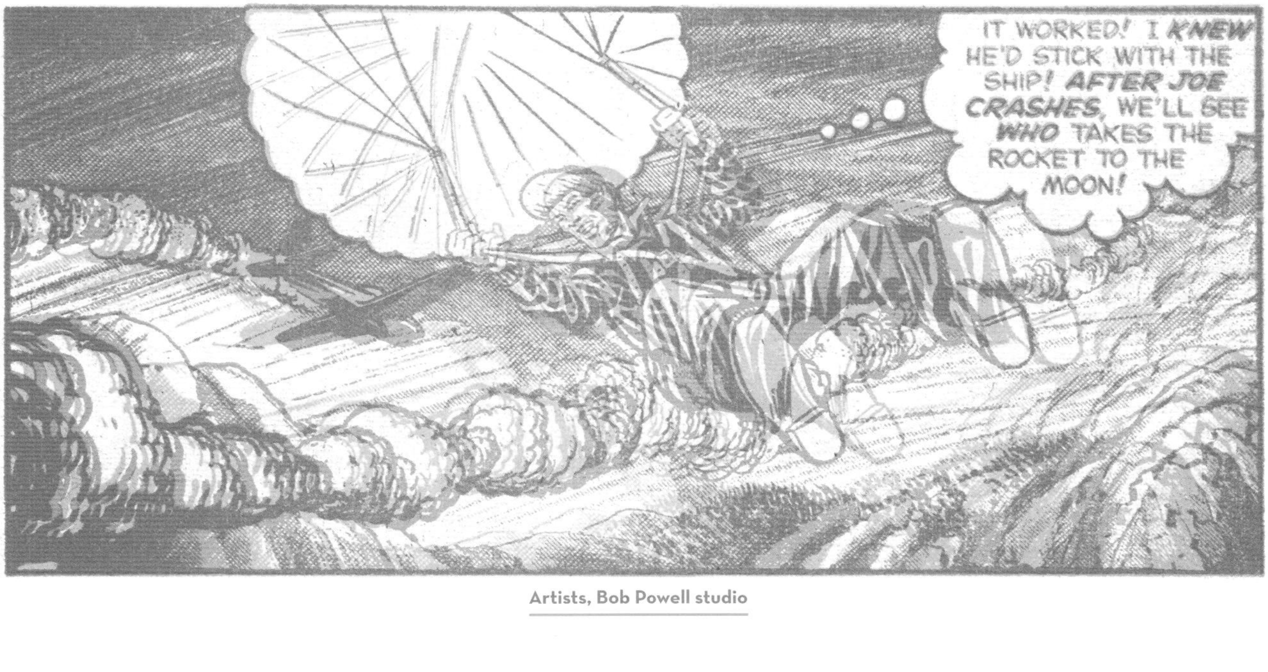
IT WORKED! I KNEW HE'D STICK WITH THE SHIP! AFTER JOE CRASHES, WE'LL SEE WHO TAKES THE ROCKET TO THE MOON!

Artists, Bob Powell studio

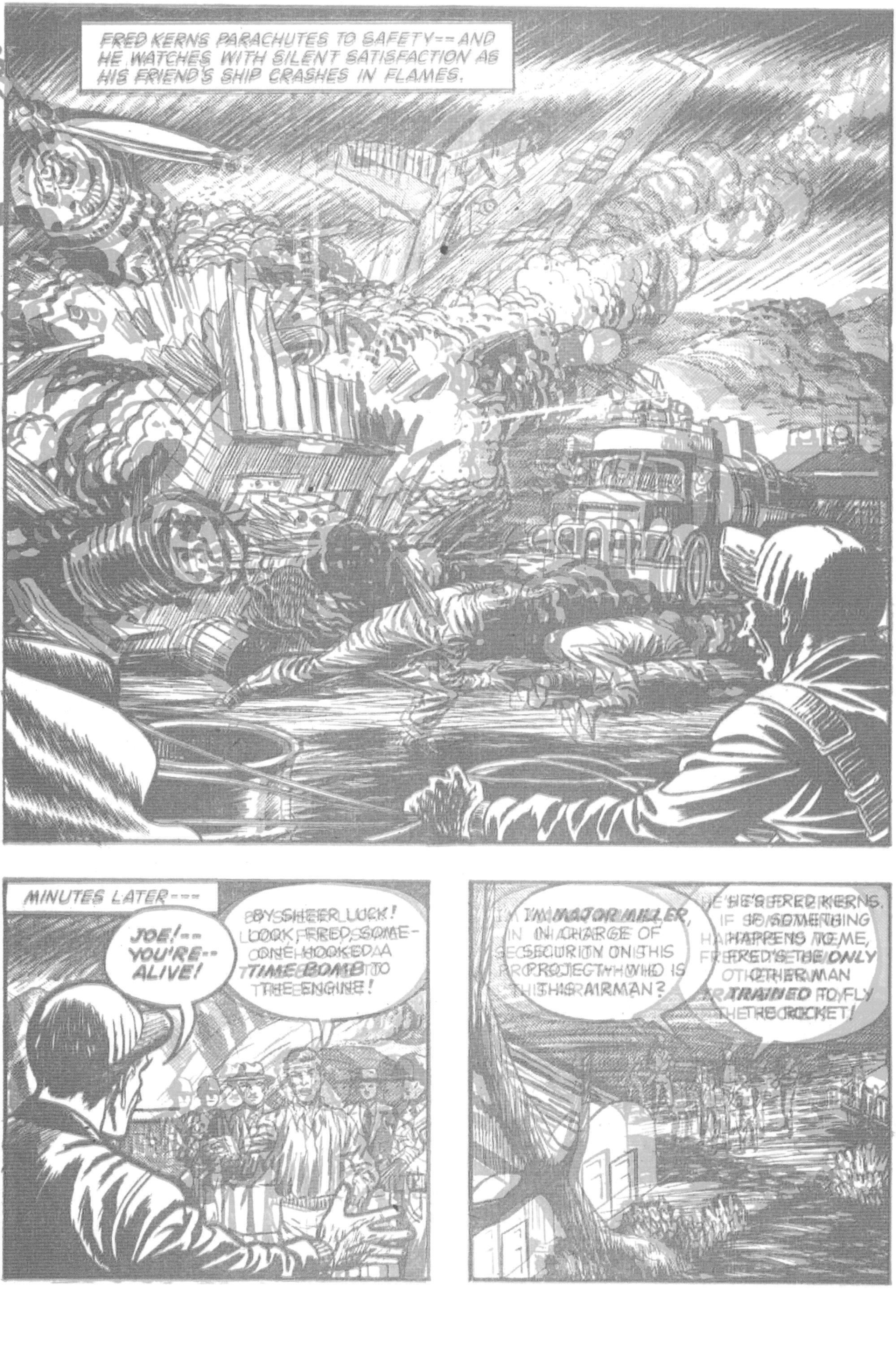
FRED KERNS PARACHUTES TO SAFETY-- AND HE WATCHES WITH SILENT SATISFACTION AS HIS FRIEND'S SHIP CRASHES IN FLAMES.
MINUTES LATER---
JOE!-- YOU'RE-- ALIVE!
BY SHEER LUCK! LOOK, FRED, SOMEONE HOOKED A TIME BOMB TO THE ENGINE!
I'M MAJOR MILLER, IN CHARGE OF SECURITY ON THIS PROJECT. WHO IS THIS AIRMAN?
HE'S FRED KERNS. IF SOMETHING HAPPENS TO ME, FRED'S THE ONLY OTHER MAN TRAINED TO FLY THE ROCKET!

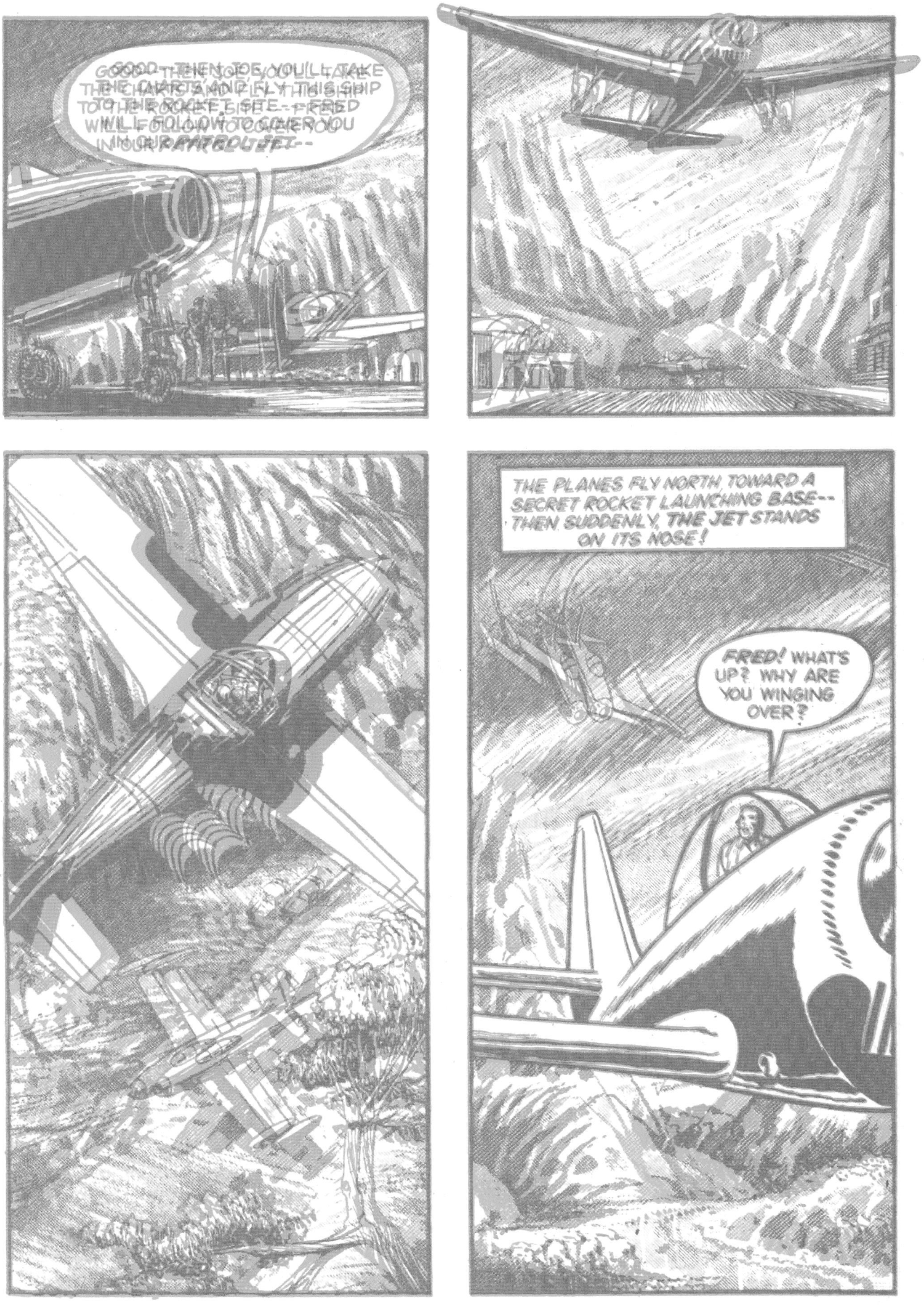
GOOD--THEN JOE, YOU'LL TAKE THE CHARTS AND FLY THIS SHIP TO THE ROCKET SITE--FRED WILL FOLLOW TO COVER YOU IN OUR PATROL JET--
THE PLANES FLY NORTH, TOWARD A SECRET ROCKET LAUNCHING BASE--THEN SUDDENLY, THE JET STANDS ON ITS NOSE!
FRED! WHAT'S UP? WHY ARE YOU WINGING OVER?

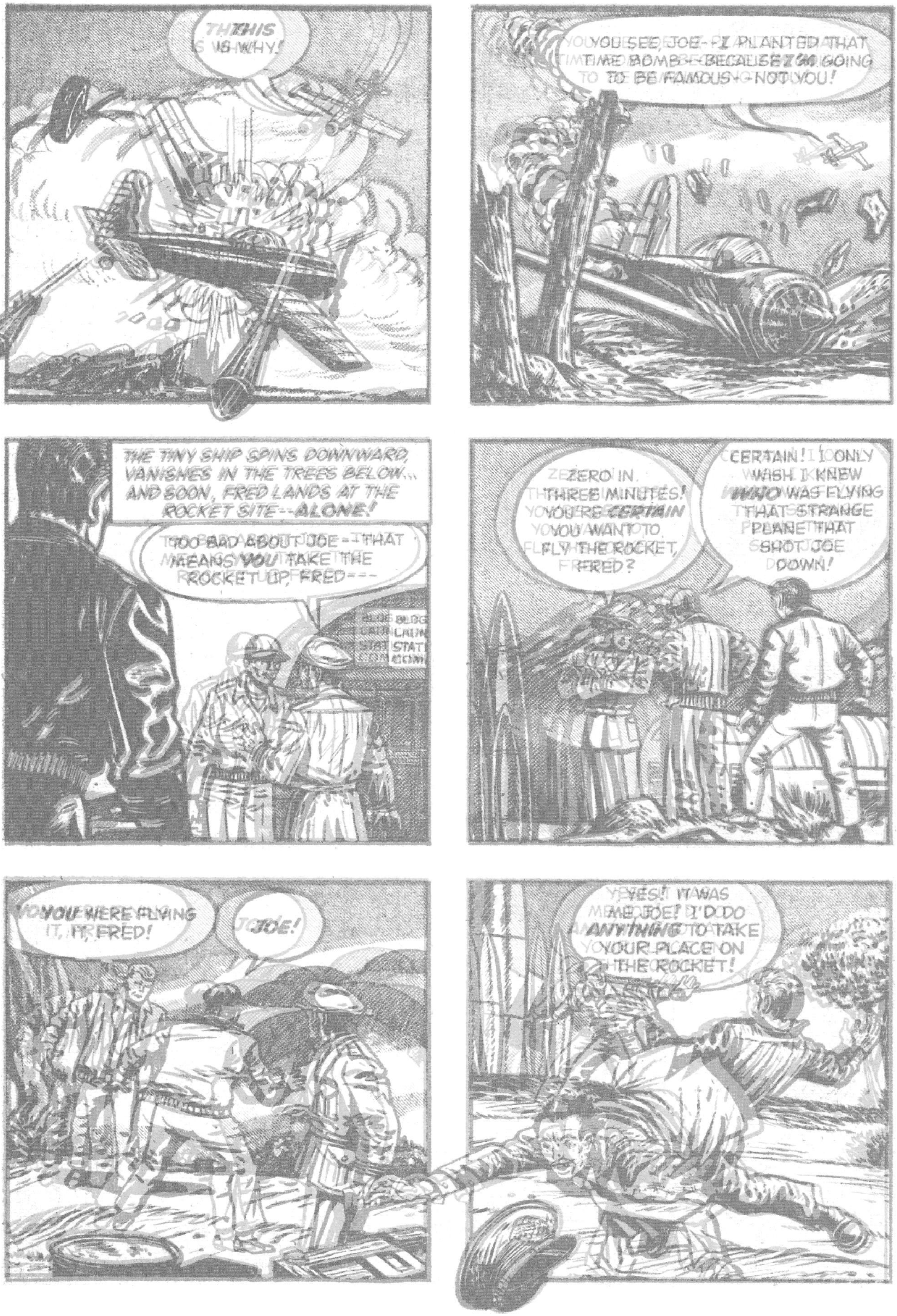

THIS IS WHY!
YOU SEE, JOE--I PLANTED THAT TIME BOMB--BECAUSE I'M GOING TO BE FAMOUS--NOT YOU!
THE TINY SHIP SPINS DOWNWARD, VANISHES IN THE TREES BELOW... AND SOON, FRED LANDS AT THE ROCKET SITE--ALONE!
TOO BAD ABOUT JOE--THAT MEANS YOU TAKE THE ROCKET UP, FRED---
ZERO IN THREE MINUTES! YOU'RE CERTAIN YOU WANT TO FLY THE ROCKET, FRED?
CERTAIN! I ONLY WISH I KNEW WHO WAS FLYING THAT STRANGE PLANE THAT SHOT JOE DOWN!
YOU WERE FLYING IT, FRED!
JOE!
YES! IT WAS ME, JOE! I'D DO ANYTHING TO TAKE YOUR PLACE ON THE ROCKET!

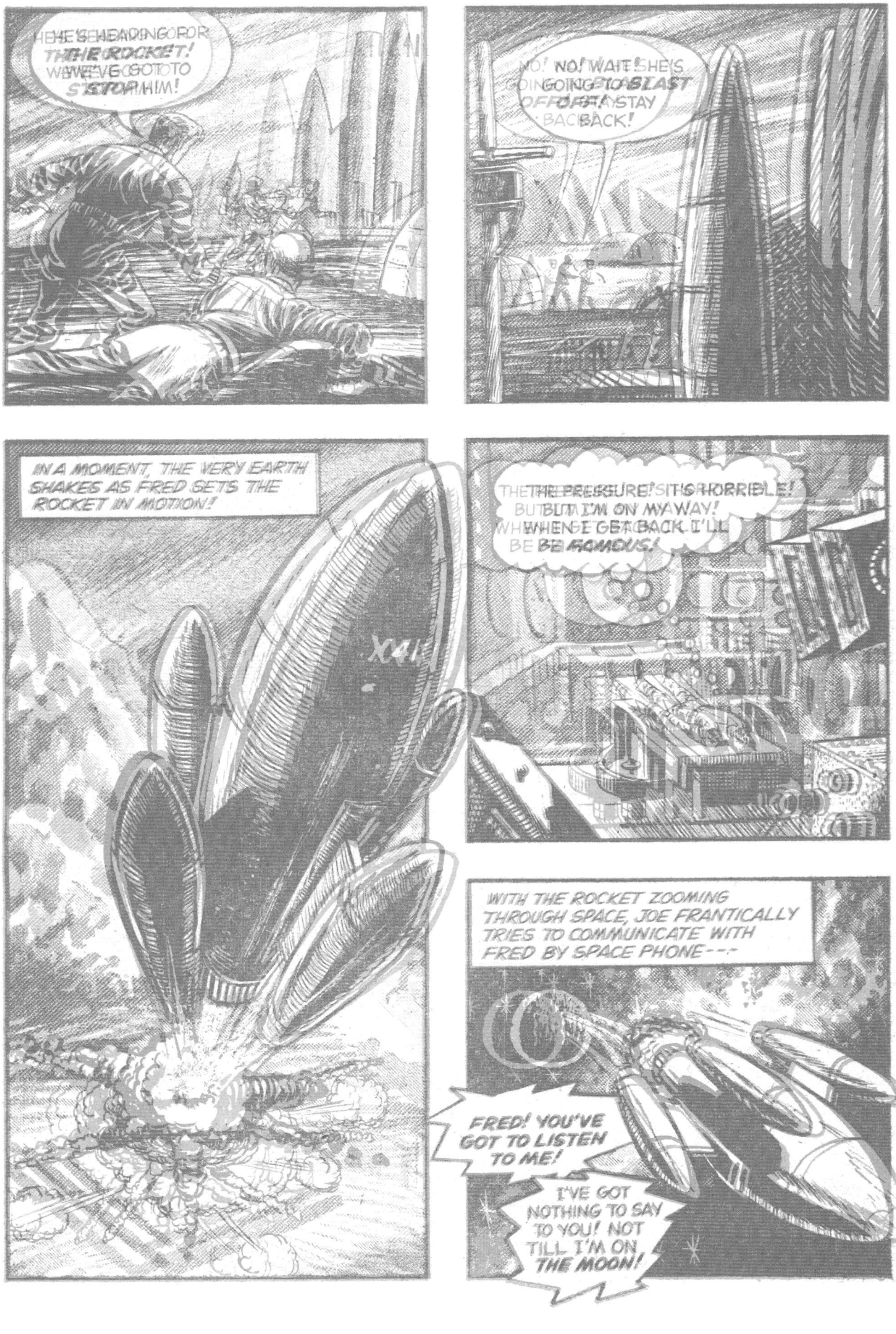
HE'S HEADING FOR THE ROCKET! WE'VE GOT TO STOP HIM!
NO! WAIT! SHE'S GOING TO BLAST OFF! STAY BACK!
IN A MOMENT, THE VERY EARTH SHAKES AS FRED SETS THE ROCKET IN MOTION!
THE PRESSURE! IT'S HORRIBLE! BUT I'M ON MY WAY! WHEN I GET BACK I'LL BE FAMOUS!
WITH THE ROCKET ZOOMING THROUGH SPACE, JOE FRANTICALLY TRIES TO COMMUNICATE WITH FRED BY SPACE PHONE---
FRED! YOU'VE GOT TO LISTEN TO ME!
I'VE GOT NOTHING TO SAY TO YOU! NOT TILL I'M ON THE MOON!

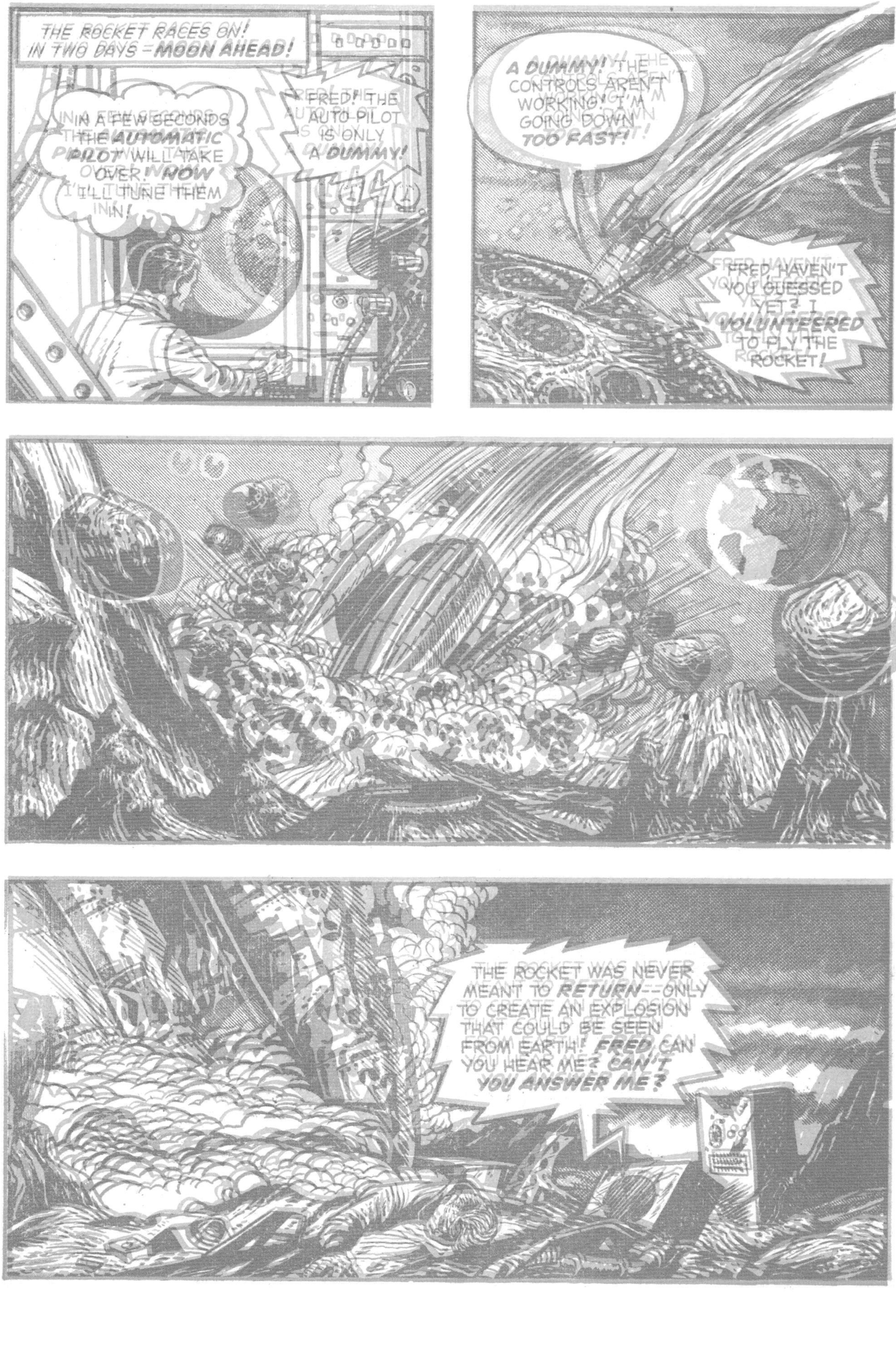
THE ROCKET RACES ON! IN TWO DAYS — MOON AHEAD!
IN A FEW SECONDS THE AUTOMATIC PILOT WILL TAKE OVER! NOW I'LL TUNE THEM IN!
FRED! THE AUTO-PILOT IS ONLY A DUMMY!
A DUMMY! THE CONTROLS AREN'T WORKING! I'M GOING DOWN TOO FAST!
FRED HAVEN'T YOU GUESSED YET? I VOLUNTEERED TO FLY THE ROCKET!
THE ROCKET WAS NEVER MEANT TO RETURN--ONLY TO CREATE AN EXPLOSION THAT COULD BE SEEN FROM EARTH! FRED CAN YOU HEAR ME? CAN'T YOU ANSWER ME?

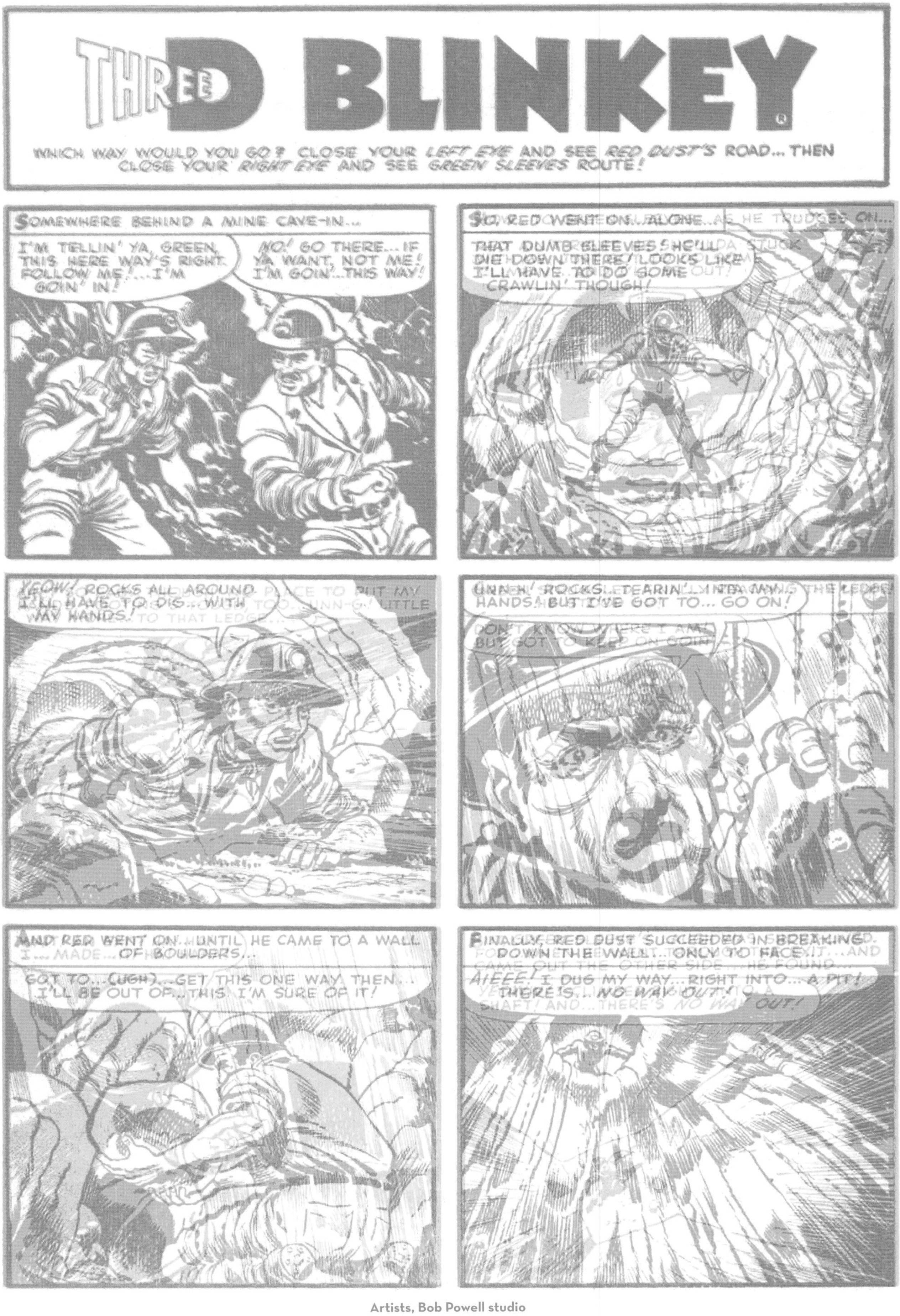
THREE D BLINKEY
WHICH WAY WOULD YOU GO? CLOSE YOUR LEFT EYE AND SEE RED DUST'S ROAD... THEN CLOSE YOUR RIGHT EYE AND SEE GREEN SLEEVES ROUTE!
SOMEWHERE BEHIND A MINE CAVE-IN...
I'M TELLIN' YA, GREEN, THIS HERE WAY'S RIGHT. FOLLOW ME!...I'M GOIN' IN!
NO! GO THERE... IF YA WANT, NOT ME! I'M GOIN'...THIS WAY!
SO, RED WENT ON... ALONE...
THAT DUMB SLEEVES! HE'LL DIE DOWN THERE! LOOKS LIKE I'LL HAVE TO DO SOME CRAWLIN' THOUGH!
YEOW! ROCKS ALL AROUND... I'LL HAVE TO DIG... WITH MY HANDS!
UNNH! ROCKS... TEARIN'... MY HANDS! BUT I'VE GOT TO... GO ON!
AND RED WENT ON... UNTIL HE CAME TO A WALL... OF BOULDERS...
FINALLY, RED DUST SUCCEEDED IN BREAKING DOWN THE WALL... ONLY TO FACE...
AIEEE! I DUG MY WAY... RIGHT INTO... A PIT! THERE IS... NO WAY OUT!

Artists, Bob Powell studio

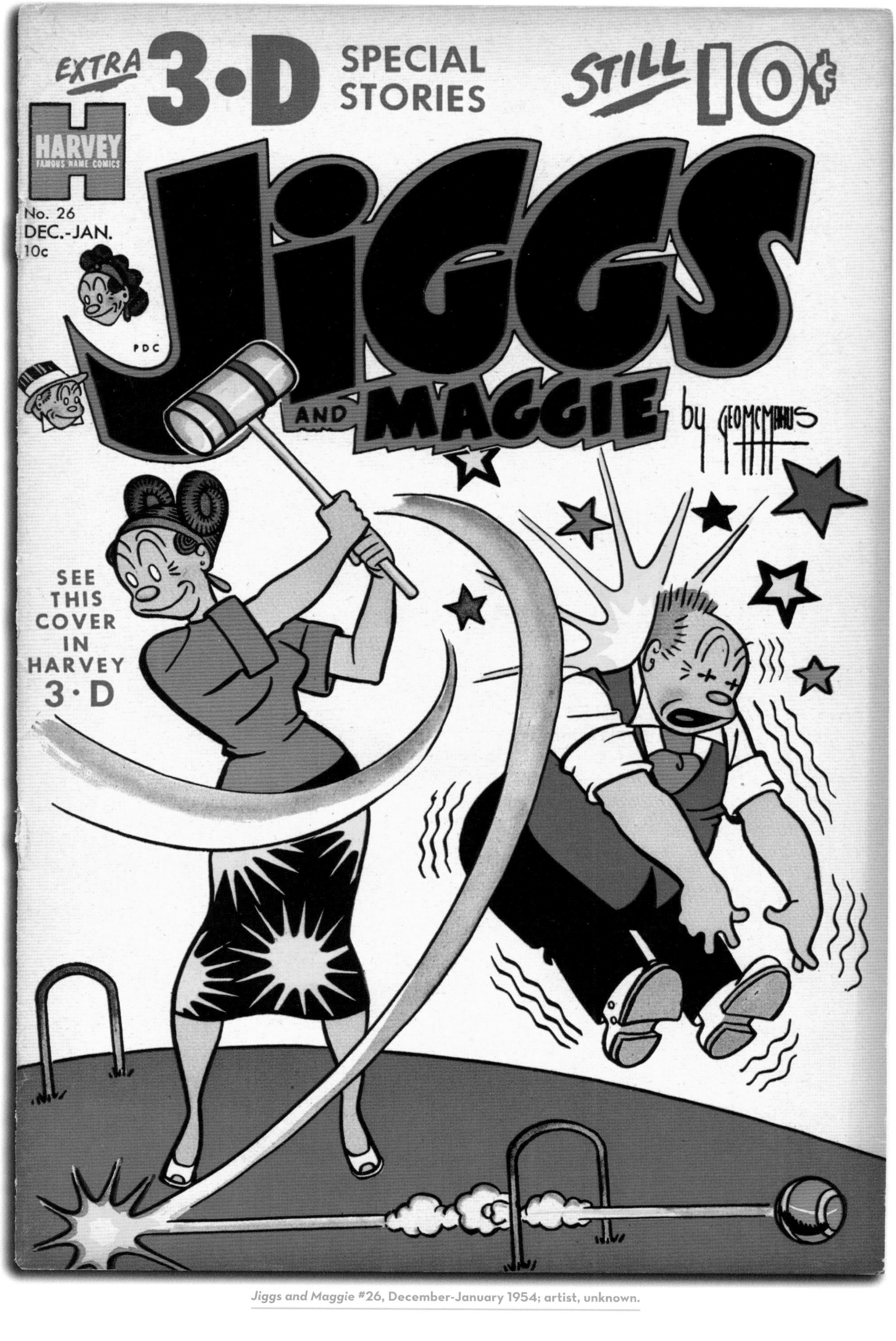
EXTRA 3-D SPECIAL STORIES
STILL 10¢
HARVEY
FAMOUS NAME COMICS
No. 26
DEC.-JAN.
10c
JiGGS AND MAGGIE by GEO McMANUS
SEE THIS COVER IN HARVEY 3-D

Jiggs and Maggie #26, December-January 1954; artist, unknown.

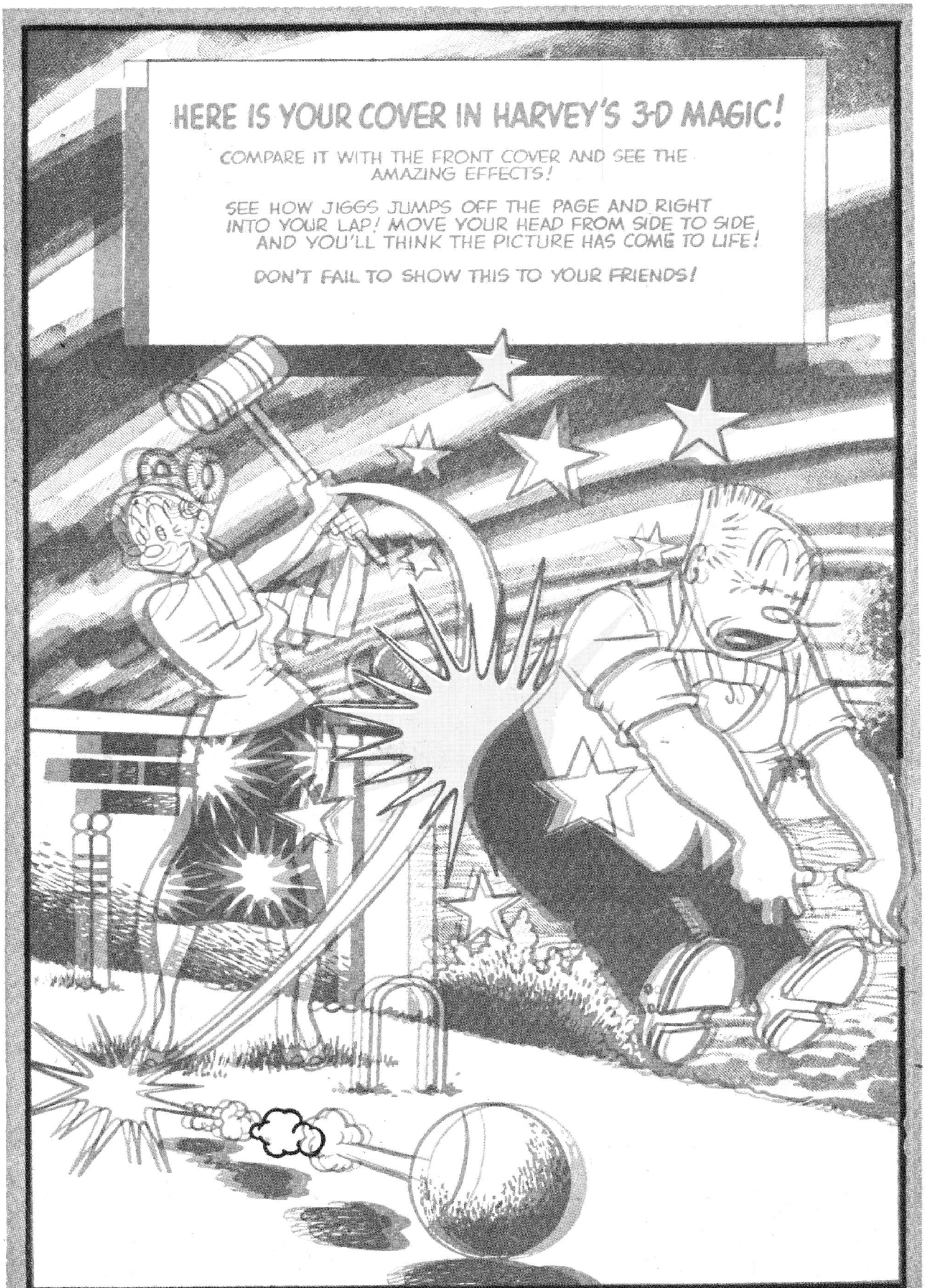
HERE IS YOUR COVER IN HARVEY'S 3-D MAGIC!
COMPARE IT WITH THE FRONT COVER AND SEE THE AMAZING EFFECTS!
SEE HOW JIGGS JUMPS OFF THE PAGE AND RIGHT INTO YOUR LAP! MOVE YOUR HEAD FROM SIDE TO SIDE AND YOU'LL THINK THE PICTURE HAS COME TO LIFE!
DON'T FAIL TO SHOW THIS TO YOUR FRIENDS!

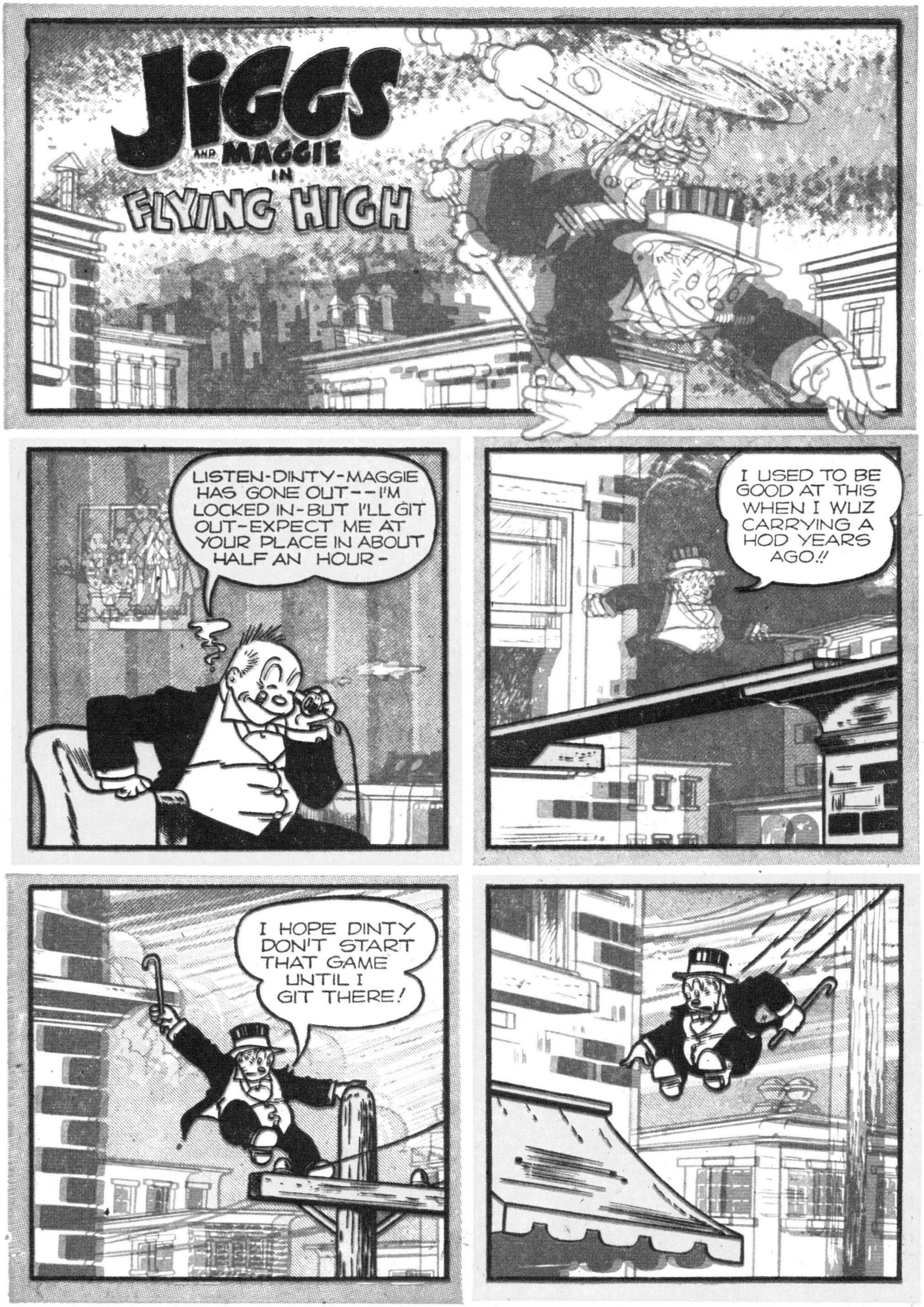
JIGGS AND MAGGIE IN
FLYING HIGH
LISTEN-DINTY-MAGGIE HAS GONE OUT--I'M LOCKED IN-BUT I'LL GIT OUT-EXPECT ME AT YOUR PLACE IN ABOUT HALF AN HOUR-
I USED TO BE GOOD AT THIS WHEN I WUZ CARRYING A HOD YEARS AGO.!!
I HOPE DINTY DON'T START THAT GAME UNTIL I GIT THERE!

Artist unknown

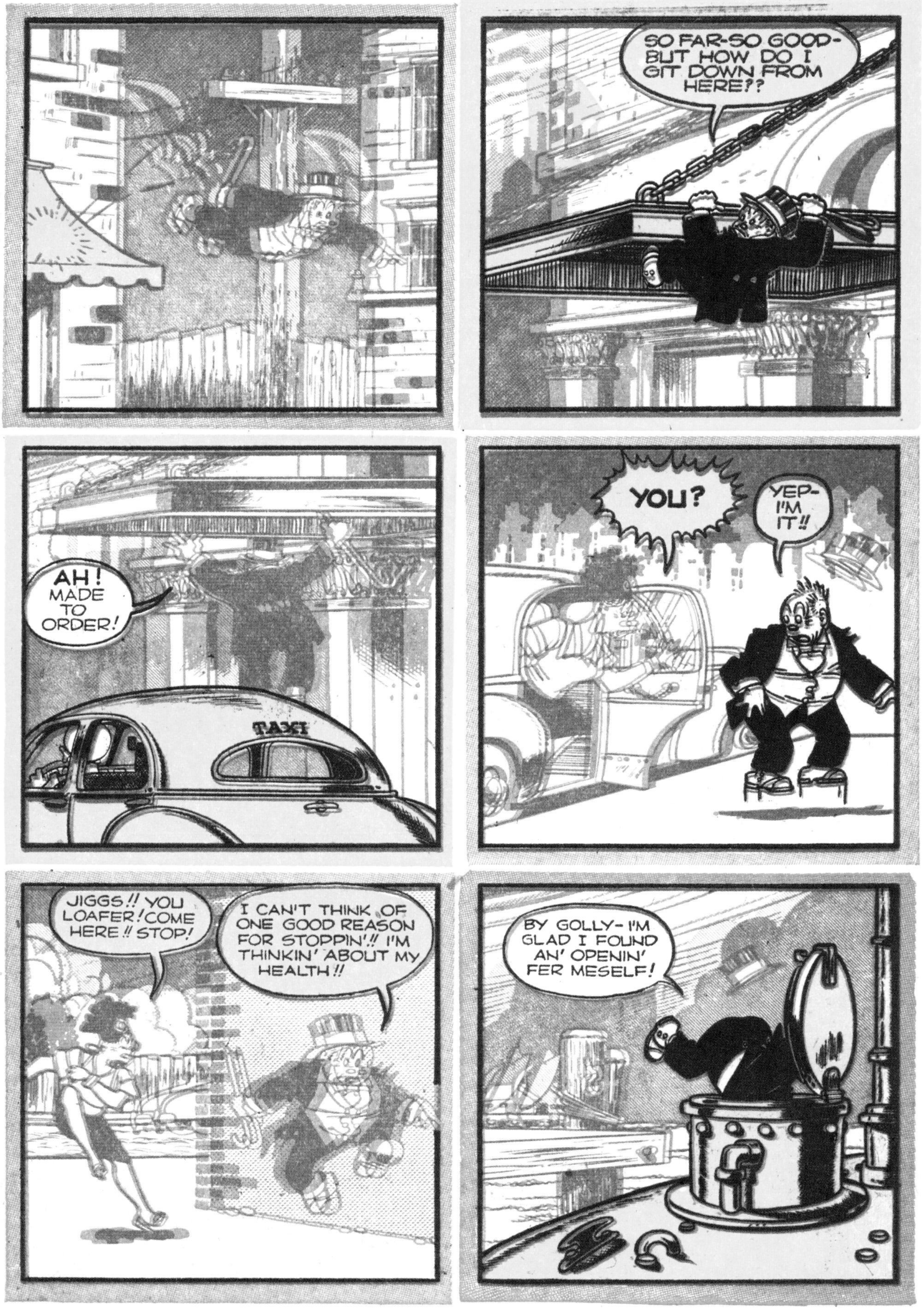
SO FAR-SO GOOD-BUT HOW DO I GIT DOWN FROM HERE??
AH! MADE TO ORDER!
YOU?
YEP-I'M IT!!
JIGGS!! YOU LOAFER! COME HERE!! STOP!
I CAN'T THINK OF ONE GOOD REASON FOR STOPPIN'!! I'M THINKIN' ABOUT MY HEALTH!!
BY GOLLY- I'M GLAD I FOUND AN' OPENIN' FER MESELF!

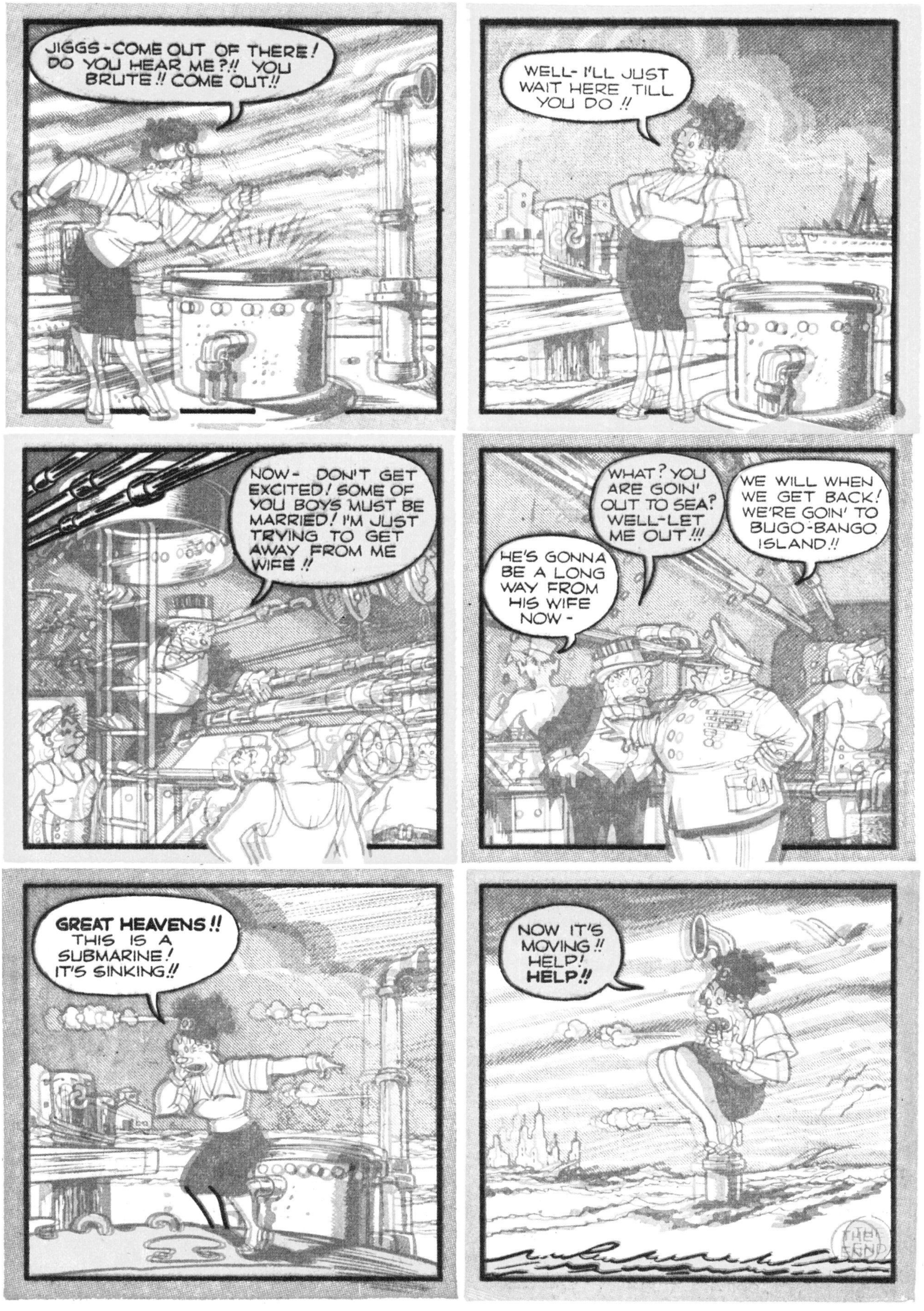
JIGGS-COME OUT OF THERE! DO YOU HEAR ME?!! YOU BRUTE!! COME OUT!!
WELL- I'LL JUST WAIT HERE TILL YOU DO !!
NOW- DON'T GET EXCITED! SOME OF YOU BOYS MUST BE MARRIED! I'M JUST TRYING TO GET AWAY FROM ME WIFE !!
HE'S GONNA BE A LONG WAY FROM HIS WIFE NOW -
WHAT? YOU ARE GOIN' OUT TO SEA? WELL-LET ME OUT!!!
WE WILL WHEN WE GET BACK! WE'RE GOIN' TO BUGO-BANGO ISLAND!!
GREAT HEAVENS!! THIS IS A SUBMARINE! IT'S SINKING!!
NOW IT'S MOVING!! HELP! HELP!!
THE END

Please remove your 3-D glasses to experience the rest of the stories!

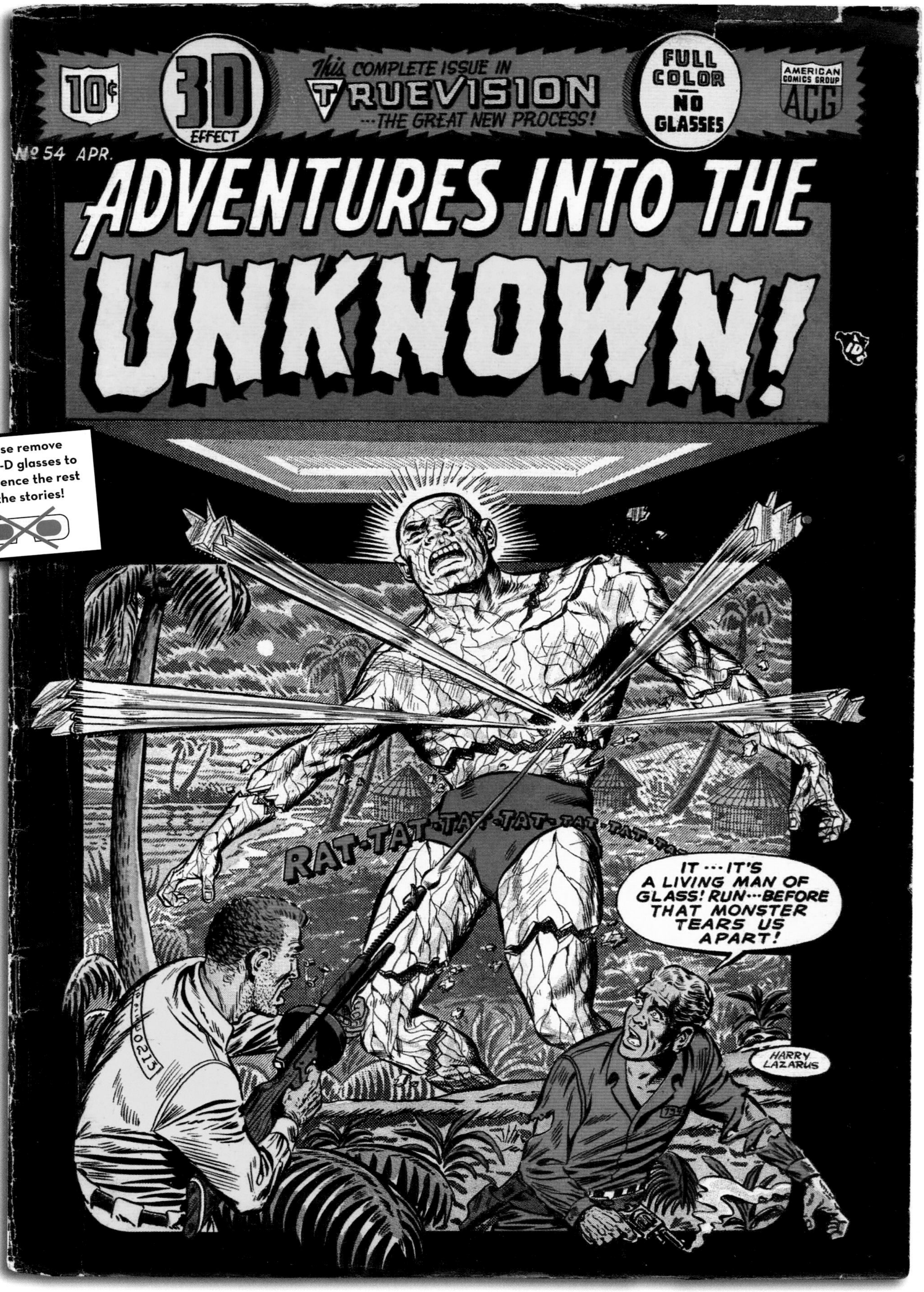
10¢
3D EFFECT
This COMPLETE ISSUE IN TRUEVISION ---THE GREAT NEW PROCESS!
FULL COLOR NO GLASSES
AMERICAN COMICS GROUP ACG
Nº 54 APR.
ADVENTURES INTO THE UNKNOWN!
RAT-TAT-TAT-TAT-TAT-TAT-TAT
IT --- IT'S A LIVING MAN OF GLASS! RUN --- BEFORE THAT MONSTER TEARS US APART!
HARRY LAZARUS

Adventures Into The Unknown #54, April 1954; artist, Harry Lazarus.

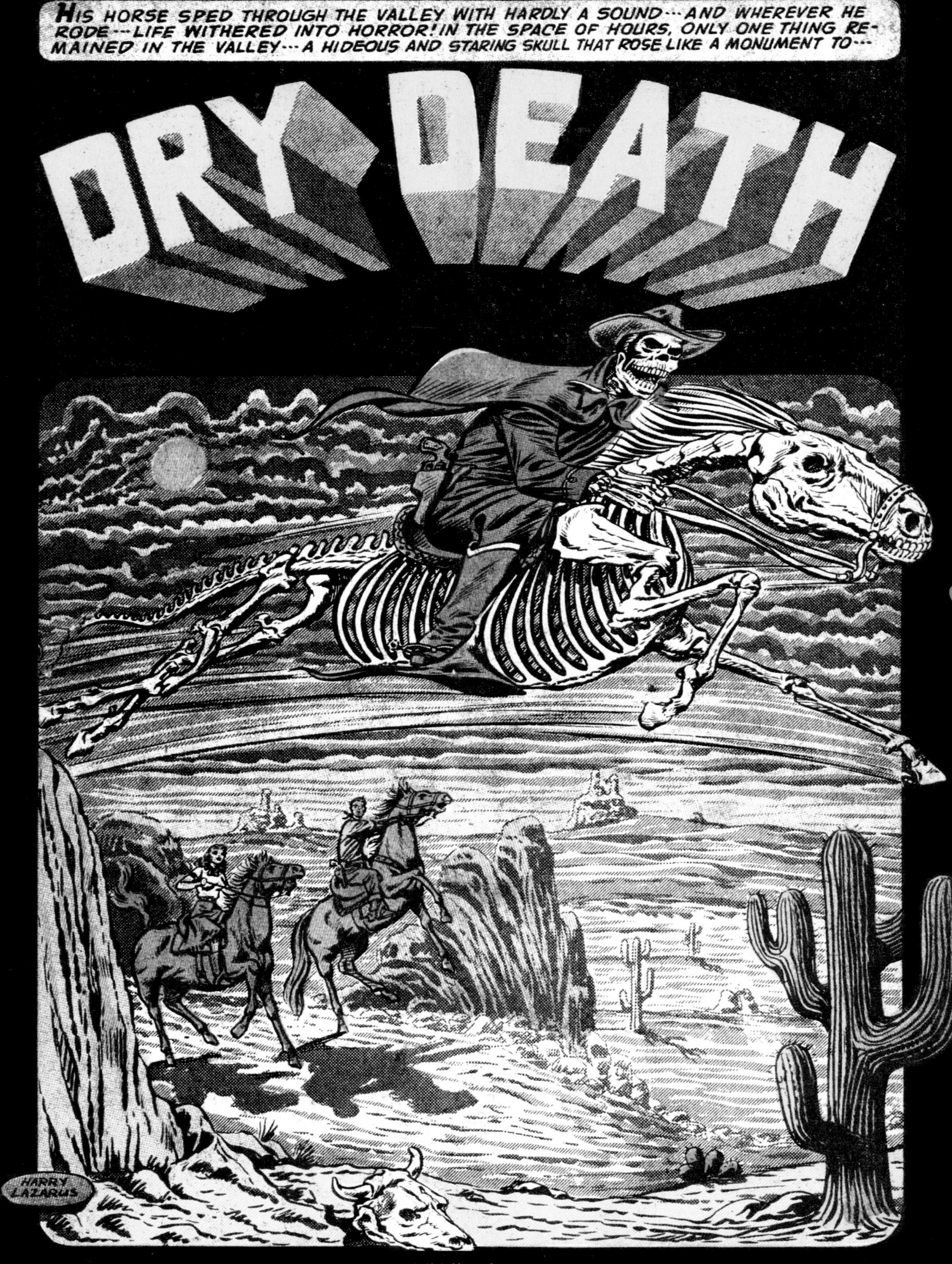
HIS HORSE SPED THROUGH THE VALLEY WITH HARDLY A SOUND... AND WHEREVER HE RODE... LIFE WITHERED INTO HORROR! IN THE SPACE OF HOURS, ONLY ONE THING REMAINED IN THE VALLEY... A HIDEOUS AND STARING SKULL THAT ROSE LIKE A MONUMENT TO...
DRY DEATH
HARRY LAZARUS

Artist, Harry Lazarus

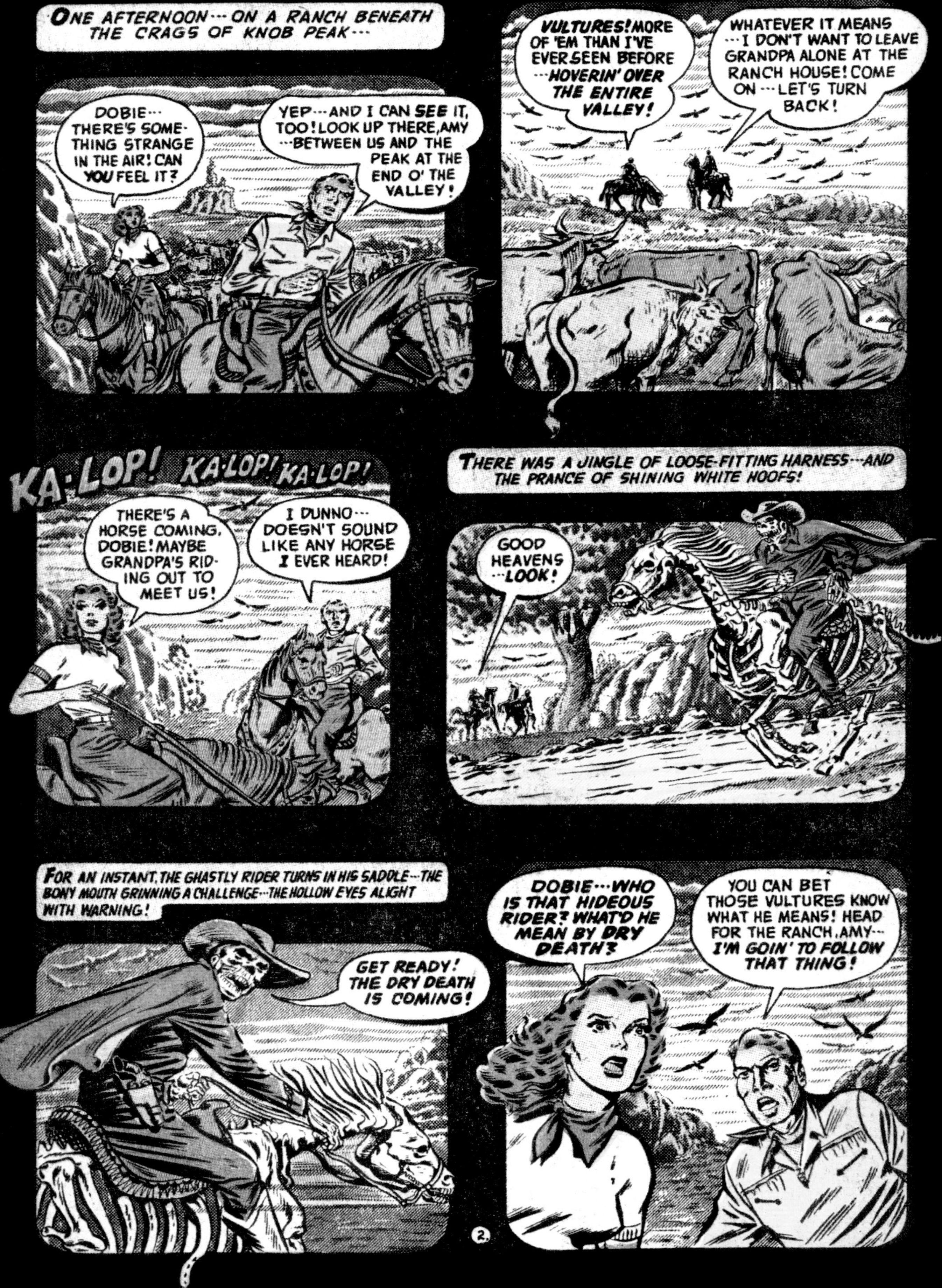

ONE AFTERNOON --- ON A RANCH BENEATH THE CRAGS OF KNOB PEAK ---
DOBIE --- THERE'S SOME-THING STRANGE IN THE AIR! CAN YOU FEEL IT?
YEP --- AND I CAN SEE IT, TOO! LOOK UP THERE, AMY --- BETWEEN US AND THE PEAK AT THE END O' THE VALLEY!
VULTURES! MORE OF 'EM THAN I'VE EVER SEEN BEFORE --- HOVERIN' OVER THE ENTIRE VALLEY!
WHATEVER IT MEANS --- I DON'T WANT TO LEAVE GRANDPA ALONE AT THE RANCH HOUSE! COME ON --- LET'S TURN BACK!
KA-LOP! KA-LOP! KA-LOP!
THERE'S A HORSE COMING, DOBIE! MAYBE GRANDPA'S RID-ING OUT TO MEET US!
I DUNNO --- DOESN'T SOUND LIKE ANY HORSE I EVER HEARD!
THERE WAS A JINGLE OF LOOSE-FITTING HARNESS --- AND THE PRANCE OF SHINING WHITE HOOFS!
GOOD HEAVENS --- LOOK!
FOR AN INSTANT, THE GHASTLY RIDER TURNS IN HIS SADDLE --- THE BONY MOUTH GRINNING A CHALLENGE --- THE HOLLOW EYES ALIGHT WITH WARNING!
GET READY! THE DRY DEATH IS COMING!
DOBIE --- WHO IS THAT HIDEOUS RIDER? WHAT'D HE MEAN BY DRY DEATH?
YOU CAN BET THOSE VULTURES KNOW WHAT HE MEANS! HEAD FOR THE RANCH, AMY --- I'M GOIN' TO FOLLOW THAT THING!
2.

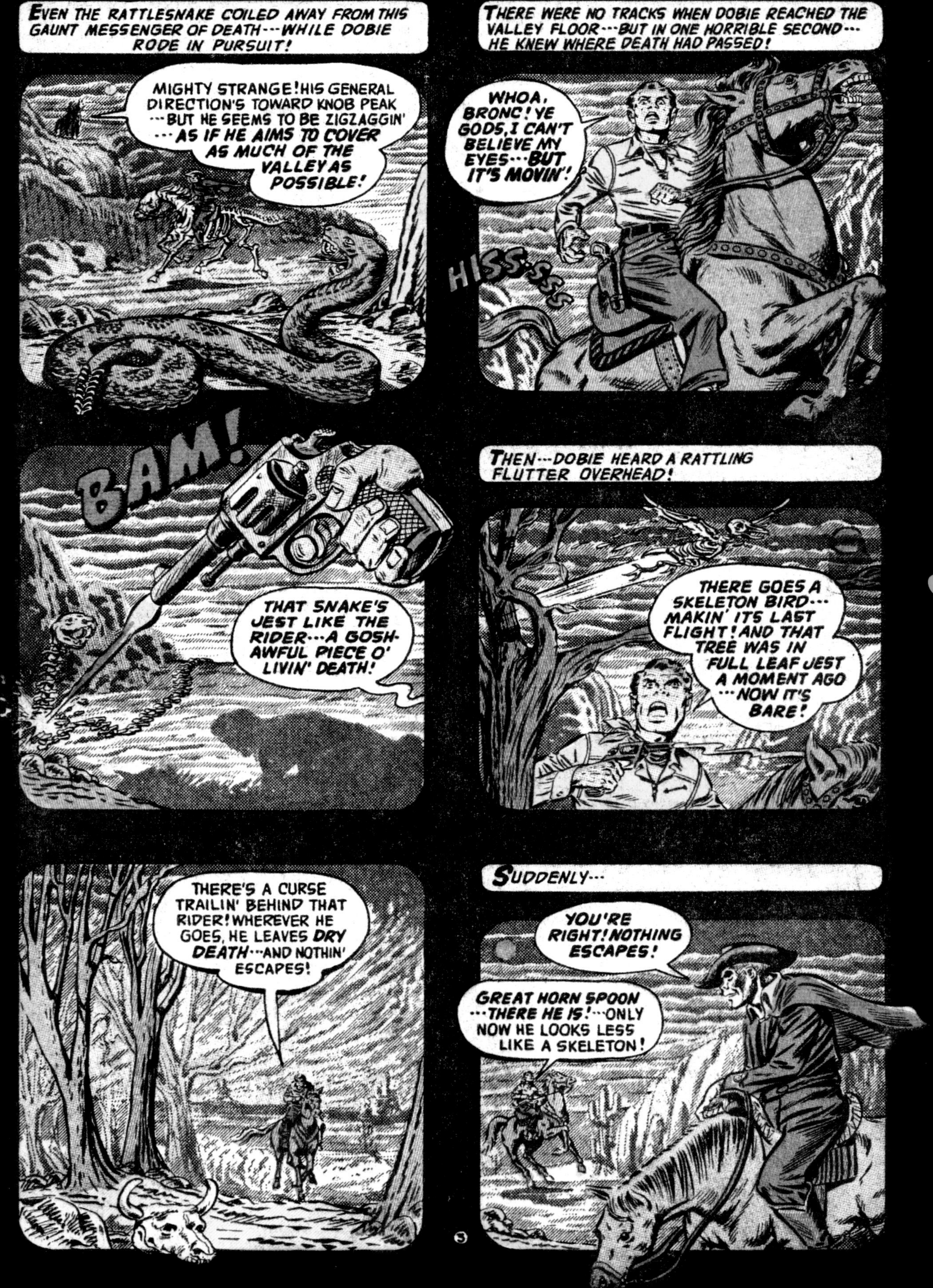

EVEN THE RATTLESNAKE COILED AWAY FROM THIS GAUNT MESSENGER OF DEATH---WHILE DOBIE RODE IN PURSUIT!
MIGHTY STRANGE! HIS GENERAL DIRECTION'S TOWARD KNOB PEAK ---BUT HE SEEMS TO BE ZIGZAGGIN' ---AS IF HE AIMS TO COVER AS MUCH OF THE VALLEY AS POSSIBLE!
THERE WERE NO TRACKS WHEN DOBIE REACHED THE VALLEY FLOOR---BUT IN ONE HORRIBLE SECOND--- HE KNEW WHERE DEATH HAD PASSED!
WHOA, BRONC! YE GODS, I CAN'T BELIEVE MY EYES---BUT IT'S MOVIN'!
HISS-SSS
BAM!
THAT SNAKE'S JEST LIKE THE RIDER---A GOSH-AWFUL PIECE O' LIVIN' DEATH!
THEN---DOBIE HEARD A RATTLING FLUTTER OVERHEAD!
THERE GOES A SKELETON BIRD--- MAKIN' ITS LAST FLIGHT! AND THAT TREE WAS IN FULL LEAF JEST A MOMENT AGO ---NOW IT'S BARE!
THERE'S A CURSE TRAILIN' BEHIND THAT RIDER! WHEREVER HE GOES, HE LEAVES DRY DEATH---AND NOTHIN' ESCAPES!
SUDDENLY---
YOU'RE RIGHT! NOTHING ESCAPES!
GREAT HORN SPOON ---THERE HE IS!---ONLY NOW HE LOOKS LESS LIKE A SKELETON!

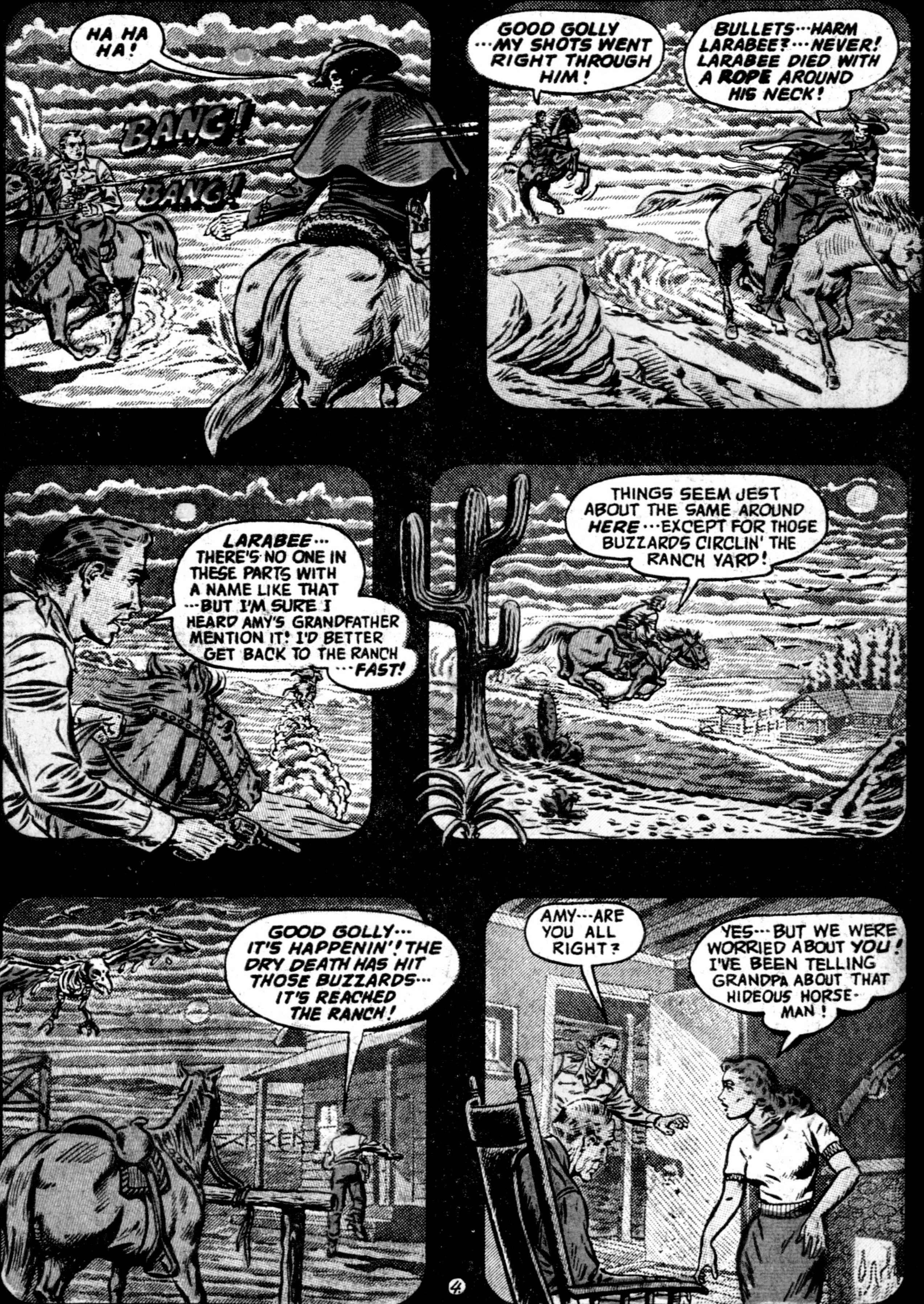
HA HA HA!
BANG!
BANG!
GOOD GOLLY ...MY SHOTS WENT RIGHT THROUGH HIM!
BULLETS...HARM LARABEE?...NEVER! LARABEE DIED WITH A ROPE AROUND HIS NECK!
LARABEE... THERE'S NO ONE IN THESE PARTS WITH A NAME LIKE THAT ...BUT I'M SURE I HEARD AMY'S GRANDFATHER MENTION IT! I'D BETTER GET BACK TO THE RANCH ...FAST!
THINGS SEEM JEST ABOUT THE SAME AROUND HERE...EXCEPT FOR THOSE BUZZARDS CIRCLIN' THE RANCH YARD!
GOOD GOLLY... IT'S HAPPENIN'! THE DRY DEATH HAS HIT THOSE BUZZARDS... IT'S REACHED THE RANCH!
AMY...ARE YOU ALL RIGHT?
YES...BUT WE WERE WORRIED ABOUT YOU! I'VE BEEN TELLING GRANDPA ABOUT THAT HIDEOUS HORSE-MAN!
4

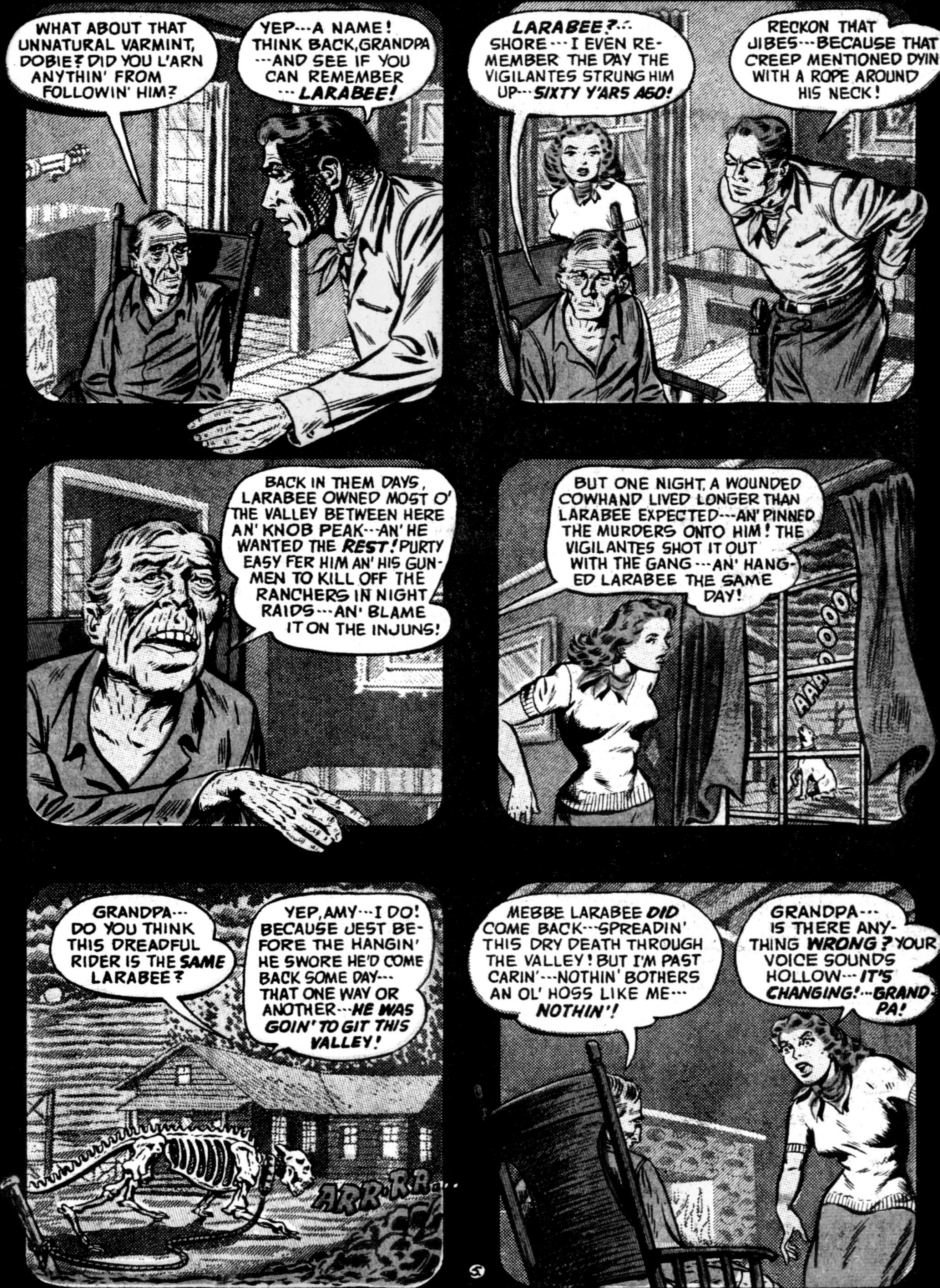
WHAT ABOUT THAT UNNATURAL VARMINT, DOBIE? DID YOU L'ARN ANYTHIN' FROM FOLLOWIN' HIM?
YEP---A NAME! THINK BACK, GRANDPA ---AND SEE IF YOU CAN REMEMBER ---LARABEE!
LARABEE?--- SHORE --- I EVEN REMEMBER THE DAY THE VIGILANTES STRUNG HIM UP--- SIXTY Y'ARS AGO!
RECKON THAT JIBES---BECAUSE THAT CREEP MENTIONED DYIN' WITH A ROPE AROUND HIS NECK!
BACK IN THEM DAYS, LARABEE OWNED MOST O' THE VALLEY BETWEEN HERE AN' KNOB PEAK---AN' HE WANTED THE REST! PURTY EASY FER HIM AN' HIS GUNMEN TO KILL OFF THE RANCHERS IN NIGHT RAIDS---AN' BLAME IT ON THE INJUNS!
BUT ONE NIGHT, A WOUNDED COWHAND LIVED LONGER THAN LARABEE EXPECTED---AN' PINNED THE MURDERS ONTO HIM! THE VIGILANTES SHOT IT OUT WITH THE GANG---AN' HANGED LARABEE THE SAME DAY!
OOOOO
AAA
GRANDPA--- DO YOU THINK THIS DREADFUL RIDER IS THE SAME LARABEE?
YEP, AMY---I DO! BECAUSE JEST BEFORE THE HANGIN' HE SWORE HE'D COME BACK SOME DAY--- THAT ONE WAY OR ANOTHER---HE WAS GOIN' TO GIT THIS VALLEY!
ARR-RR...
MEBBE LARABEE DID COME BACK---SPREADIN' THIS DRY DEATH THROUGH THE VALLEY! BUT I'M PAST CARIN'---NOTHIN' BOTHERS AN OL' HOSS LIKE ME--- NOTHIN'!
GRANDPA--- IS THERE ANYTHING WRONG? YOUR VOICE SOUNDS HOLLOW--- IT'S CHANGING!---GRANDPA!
5

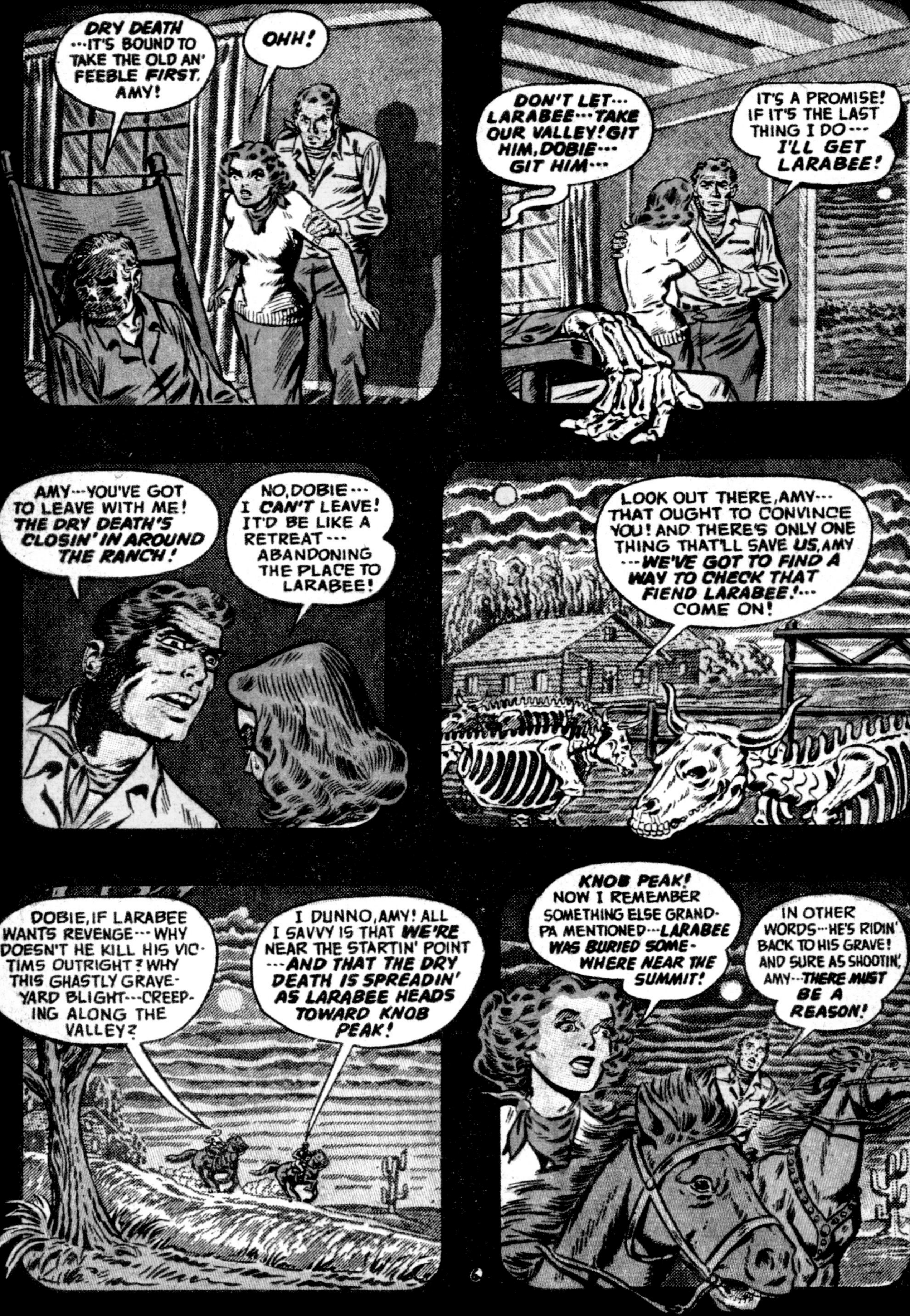
DRY DEATH ...IT'S BOUND TO TAKE THE OLD AN' FEEBLE FIRST, AMY!
OHH!
DON'T LET... LARABEE... TAKE OUR VALLEY! GIT HIM, DOBIE... GIT HIM...
IT'S A PROMISE! IF IT'S THE LAST THING I DO... I'LL GET LARABEE!
AMY... YOU'VE GOT TO LEAVE WITH ME! THE DRY DEATH'S CLOSIN' IN AROUND THE RANCH!
NO, DOBIE... I CAN'T LEAVE! IT'D BE LIKE A RETREAT... ABANDONING THE PLACE TO LARABEE!
LOOK OUT THERE, AMY... THAT OUGHT TO CONVINCE YOU! AND THERE'S ONLY ONE THING THAT'LL SAVE US, AMY ...WE'VE GOT TO FIND A WAY TO CHECK THAT FIEND LARABEE!... COME ON!
DOBIE, IF LARABEE WANTS REVENGE... WHY DOESN'T HE KILL HIS VICTIMS OUTRIGHT? WHY THIS GHASTLY GRAVEYARD BLIGHT... CREEPING ALONG THE VALLEY?
I DUNNO, AMY! ALL I SAVVY IS THAT WE'RE NEAR THE STARTIN' POINT ...AND THAT THE DRY DEATH IS SPREADIN' AS LARABEE HEADS TOWARD KNOB PEAK!
KNOB PEAK! NOW I REMEMBER SOMETHING ELSE GRANDPA MENTIONED... LARABEE WAS BURIED SOMEWHERE NEAR THE SUMMIT!
IN OTHER WORDS... HE'S RIDIN' BACK TO HIS GRAVE! AND SURE AS SHOOTIN', AMY... THERE MUST BE A REASON!

142

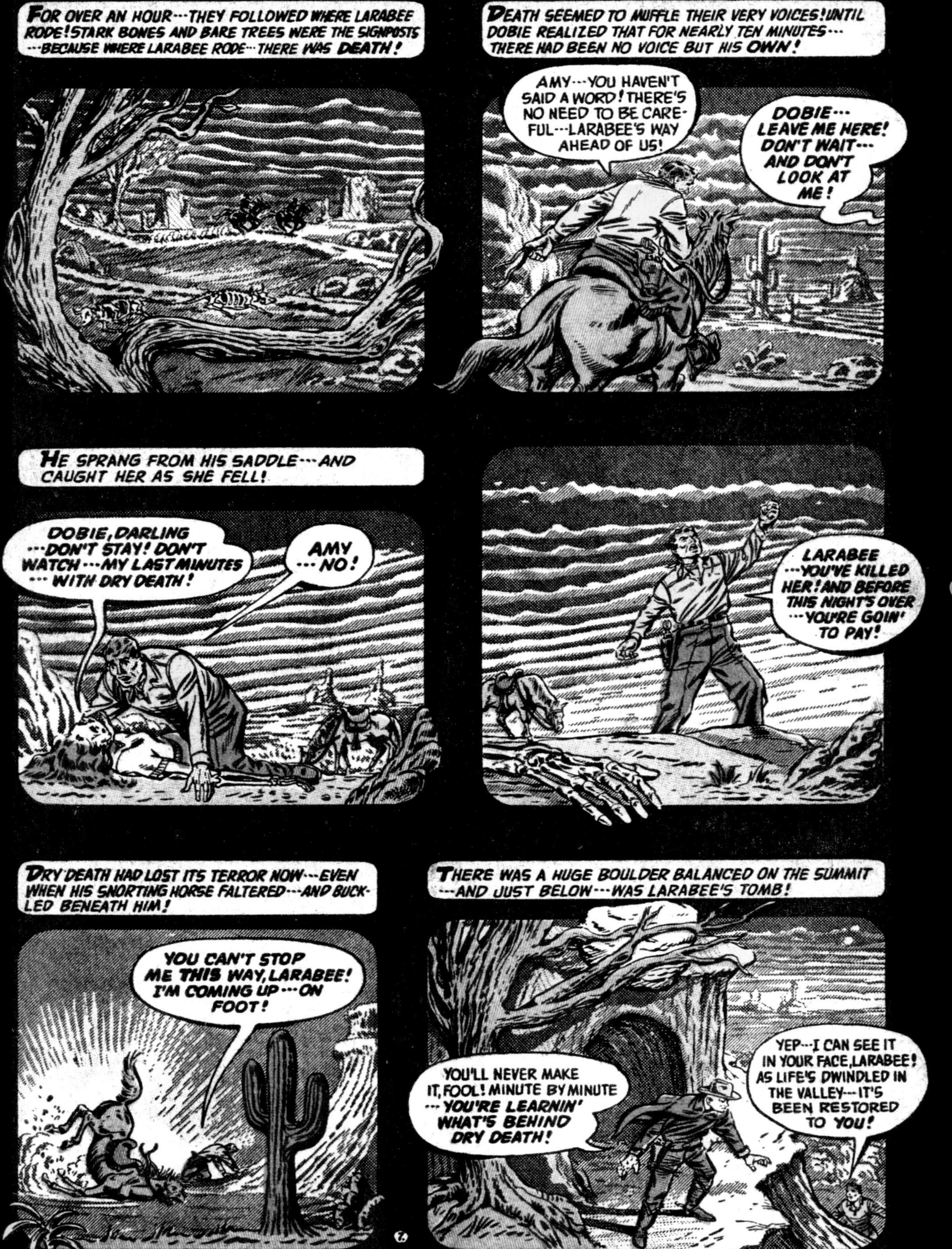
FOR OVER AN HOUR---THEY FOLLOWED WHERE LARABEE RODE! STARK BONES AND BARE TREES WERE THE SIGNPOSTS ---BECAUSE WHERE LARABEE RODE--- THERE WAS DEATH!
DEATH SEEMED TO MUFFLE THEIR VERY VOICES! UNTIL DOBIE REALIZED THAT FOR NEARLY TEN MINUTES--- THERE HAD BEEN NO VOICE BUT HIS OWN!
AMY---YOU HAVEN'T SAID A WORD! THERE'S NO NEED TO BE CAREFUL---LARABEE'S WAY AHEAD OF US!
DOBIE--- LEAVE ME HERE! DON'T WAIT--- AND DON'T LOOK AT ME!
HE SPRANG FROM HIS SADDLE---AND CAUGHT HER AS SHE FELL!
DOBIE, DARLING ---DON'T STAY! DON'T WATCH---MY LAST MINUTES --- WITH DRY DEATH!
AMY ---NO!
LARABEE ---YOU'VE KILLED HER! AND BEFORE THIS NIGHT'S OVER ---YOU'RE GOIN' TO PAY!
DRY DEATH HAD LOST ITS TERROR NOW---EVEN WHEN HIS SNORTING HORSE FALTERED---AND BUCKLED BENEATH HIM!
YOU CAN'T STOP ME THIS WAY, LARABEE! I'M COMING UP---ON FOOT!
THERE WAS A HUGE BOULDER BALANCED ON THE SUMMIT ---AND JUST BELOW---WAS LARABEE'S TOMB!
YOU'LL NEVER MAKE IT, FOOL! MINUTE BY MINUTE --- YOU'RE LEARNIN' WHAT'S BEHIND DRY DEATH!
YEP---I CAN SEE IT IN YOUR FACE, LARABEE! AS LIFE'S DWINDLED IN THE VALLEY---IT'S BEEN RESTORED TO YOU!

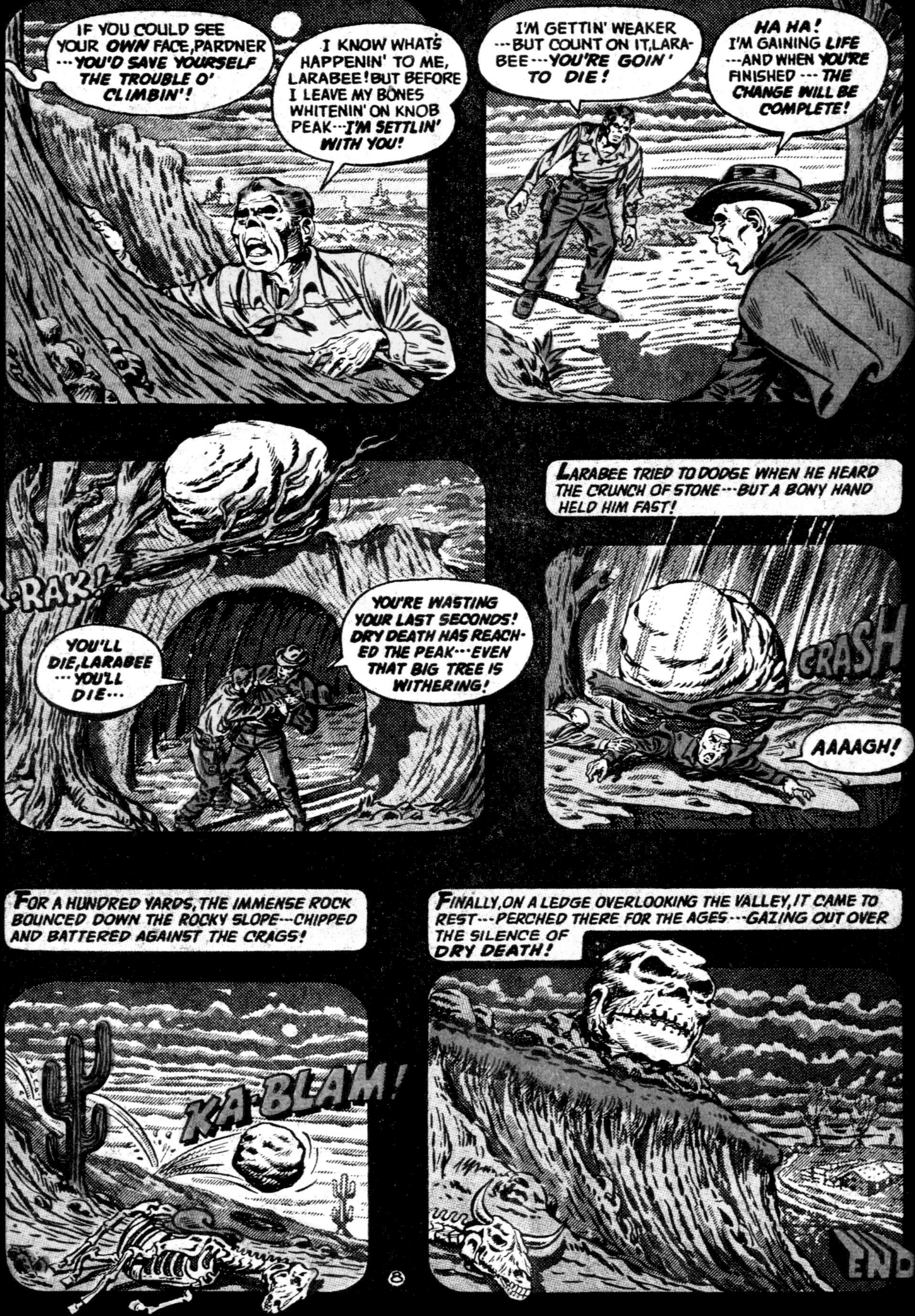
IF YOU COULD SEE YOUR OWN FACE, PARDNER --- YOU'D SAVE YOURSELF THE TROUBLE O' CLIMBIN'!
I KNOW WHAT'S HAPPENIN' TO ME, LARABEE! BUT BEFORE I LEAVE MY BONES WHITENIN' ON KNOB PEAK --- I'M SETTLIN' WITH YOU!
I'M GETTIN' WEAKER --- BUT COUNT ON IT, LARABEE --- YOU'RE GOIN' TO DIE!
HA HA! I'M GAINING LIFE --- AND WHEN YOU'RE FINISHED --- THE CHANGE WILL BE COMPLETE!
CR-RAK!
YOU'LL DIE, LARABEE --- YOU'LL DIE ---
YOU'RE WASTING YOUR LAST SECONDS! DRY DEATH HAS REACHED THE PEAK --- EVEN THAT BIG TREE IS WITHERING!
LARABEE TRIED TO DODGE WHEN HE HEARD THE CRUNCH OF STONE --- BUT A BONY HAND HELD HIM FAST!
CRASH
AAAAGH!
FOR A HUNDRED YARDS, THE IMMENSE ROCK BOUNCED DOWN THE ROCKY SLOPE --- CHIPPED AND BATTERED AGAINST THE CRAGS!
KA-BLAM!
FINALLY, ON A LEDGE OVERLOOKING THE VALLEY, IT CAME TO REST --- PERCHED THERE FOR THE AGES --- GAZING OUT OVER THE SILENCE OF DRY DEATH!
END
8

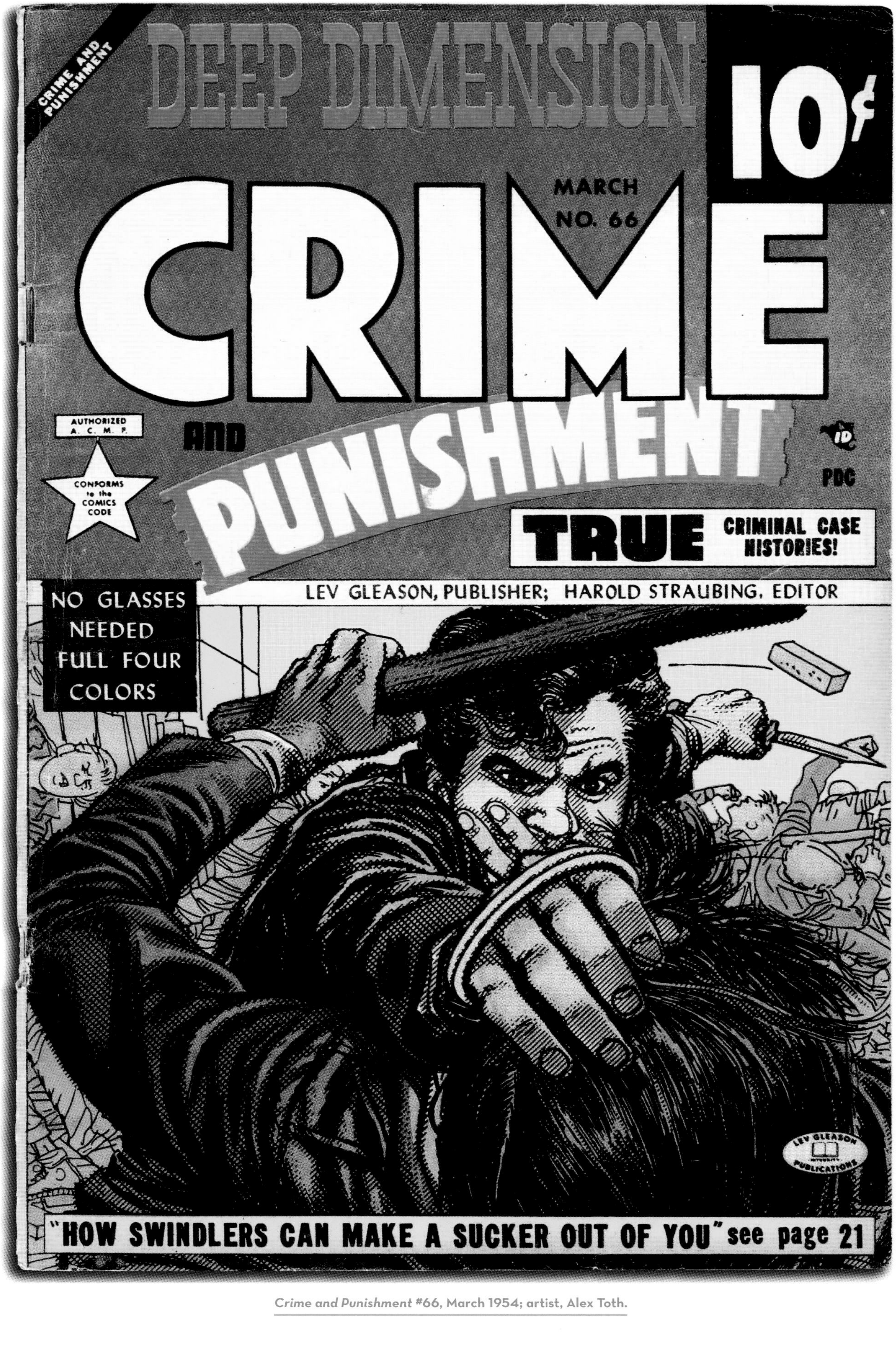
CRIME AND PUNISHMENT
DEEP DIMENSION
10¢
MARCH
NO. 66
CRIME
AND
PUNISHMENT
AUTHORIZED
A. C. M. P.
CONFORMS to the COMICS CODE
PDC
TRUE CRIMINAL CASE HISTORIES!
LEV GLEASON, PUBLISHER; HAROLD STRAUBING, EDITOR
NO GLASSES NEEDED FULL FOUR COLORS
LEV GLEASON PUBLICATIONS
"HOW SWINDLERS CAN MAKE A SUCKER OUT OF YOU" see page 21

Crime and Punishment #66, March 1954; artist, Alex Toth.

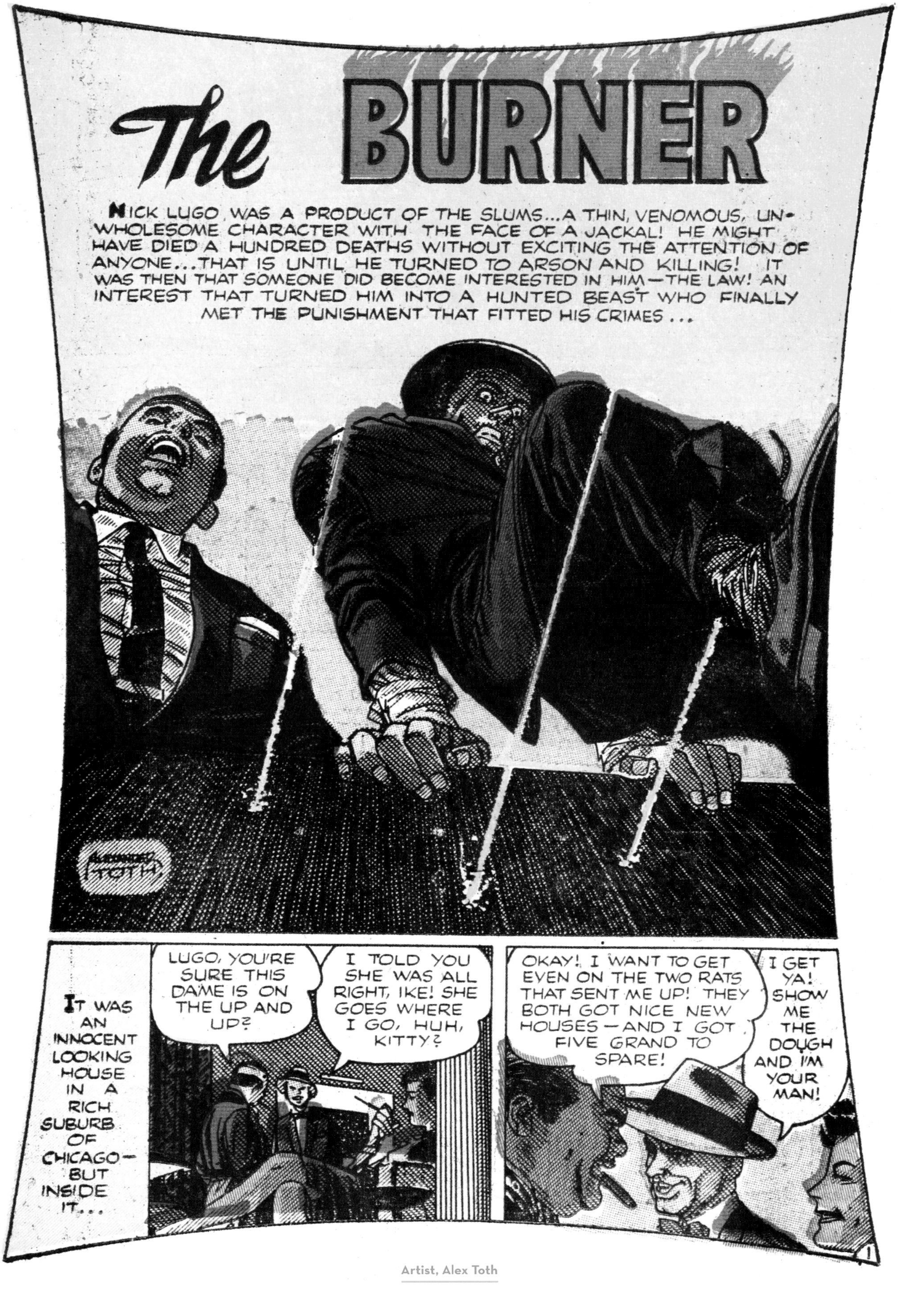

The BURNER
NICK LUGO WAS A PRODUCT OF THE SLUMS...A THIN, VENOMOUS, UNWHOLESOME CHARACTER WITH THE FACE OF A JACKAL! HE MIGHT HAVE DIED A HUNDRED DEATHS WITHOUT EXCITING THE ATTENTION OF ANYONE...THAT IS UNTIL HE TURNED TO ARSON AND KILLING! IT WAS THEN THAT SOMEONE DID BECOME INTERESTED IN HIM—THE LAW! AN INTEREST THAT TURNED HIM INTO A HUNTED BEAST WHO FINALLY MET THE PUNISHMENT THAT FITTED HIS CRIMES...
TOTH
IT WAS AN INNOCENT LOOKING HOUSE IN A RICH SUBURB OF CHICAGO—BUT INSIDE IT...
LUGO, YOU'RE SURE THIS DAME IS ON THE UP AND UP?
I TOLD YOU SHE WAS ALL RIGHT, IKE! SHE GOES WHERE I GO, HUH, KITTY?
OKAY! I WANT TO GET EVEN ON THE TWO RATS THAT SENT ME UP! THEY BOTH GOT NICE NEW HOUSES—AND I GOT FIVE GRAND TO SPARE!
I GET YA! SHOW ME THE DOUGH AND I'M YOUR MAN!
1

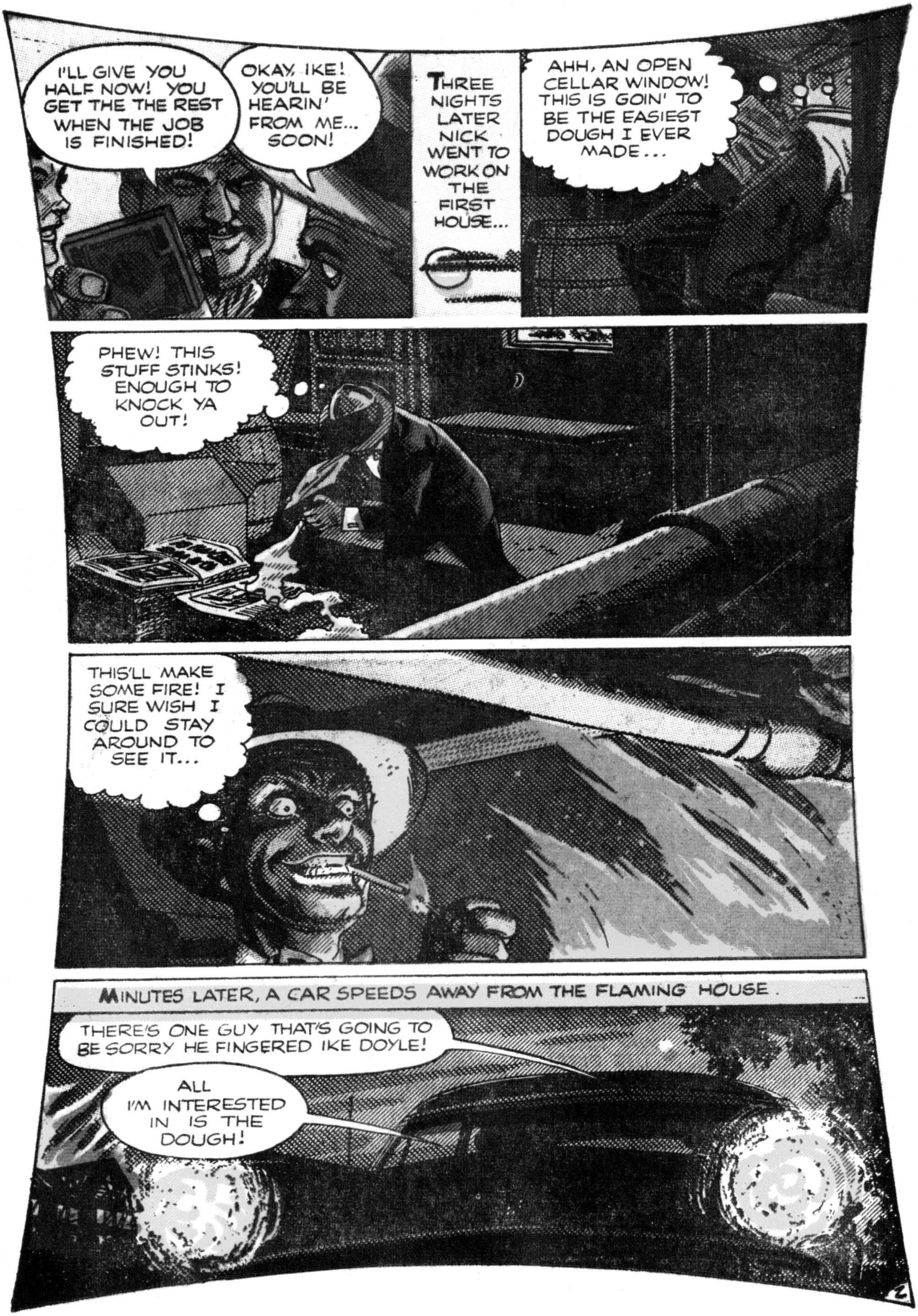
I'LL GIVE YOU HALF NOW! YOU GET THE THE REST WHEN THE JOB IS FINISHED!
OKAY, IKE! YOU'LL BE HEARIN' FROM ME... SOON!
THREE NIGHTS LATER NICK WENT TO WORK ON THE FIRST HOUSE...
AHH, AN OPEN CELLAR WINDOW! THIS IS GOIN' TO BE THE EASIEST DOUGH I EVER MADE...
PHEW! THIS STUFF STINKS! ENOUGH TO KNOCK YA OUT!
THIS'LL MAKE SOME FIRE! I SURE WISH I COULD STAY AROUND TO SEE IT...
MINUTES LATER, A CAR SPEEDS AWAY FROM THE FLAMING HOUSE.
THERE'S ONE GUY THAT'S GOING TO BE SORRY HE FINGERED IKE DOYLE!
ALL I'M INTERESTED IN IS THE DOUGH!
2

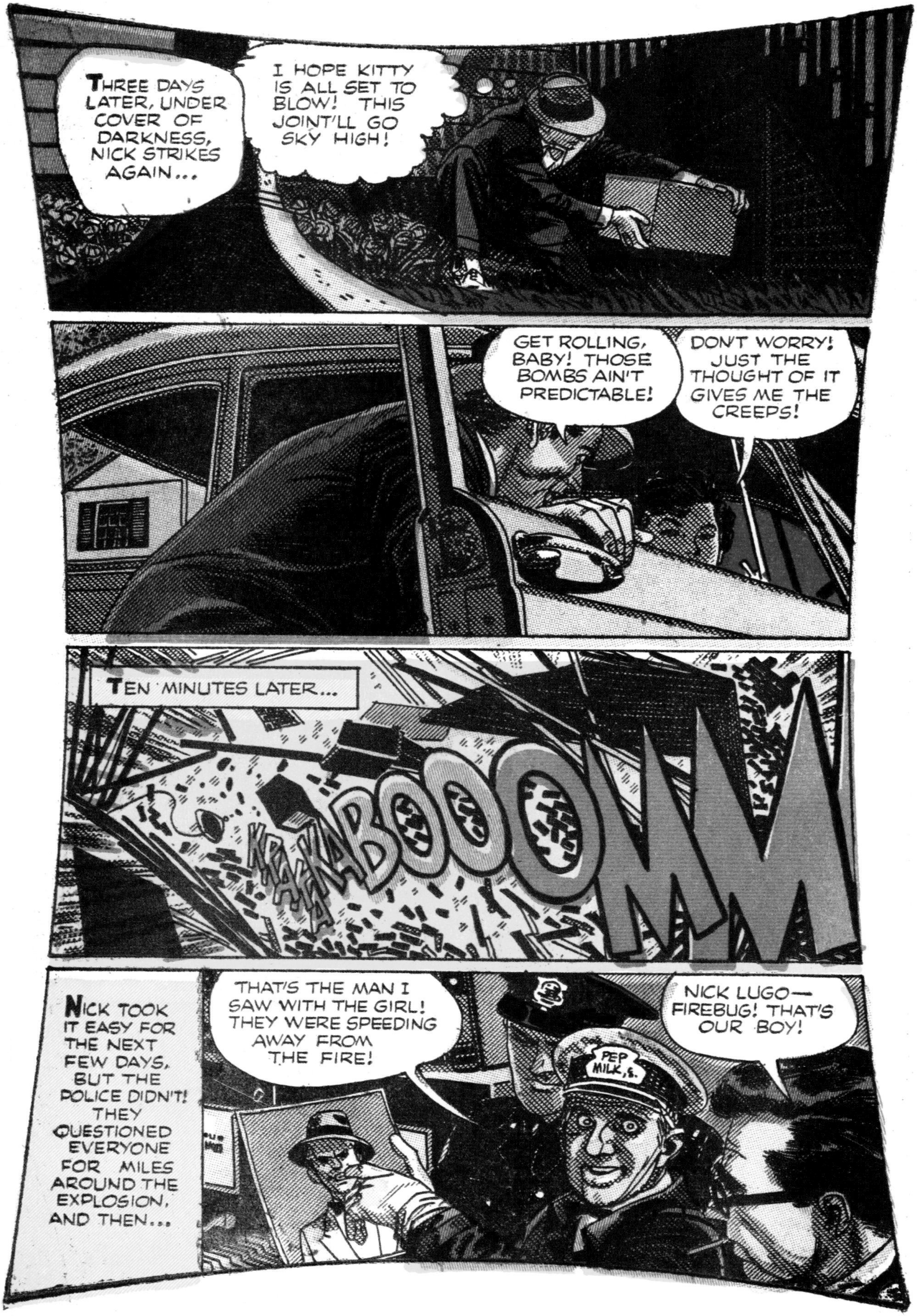
THREE DAYS LATER, UNDER COVER OF DARKNESS, NICK STRIKES AGAIN...
I HOPE KITTY IS ALL SET TO BLOW! THIS JOINT'LL GO SKY HIGH!
GET ROLLING, BABY! THOSE BOMBS AIN'T PREDICTABLE!
DON'T WORRY! JUST THE THOUGHT OF IT GIVES ME THE CREEPS!
TEN MINUTES LATER...
KRAKABOOOOMM
NICK TOOK IT EASY FOR THE NEXT FEW DAYS, BUT THE POLICE DIDN'T! THEY QUESTIONED EVERYONE FOR MILES AROUND THE EXPLOSION, AND THEN...
THAT'S THE MAN I SAW WITH THE GIRL! THEY WERE SPEEDING AWAY FROM THE FIRE!
NICK LUGO— FIREBUG! THAT'S OUR BOY!
PEP MILK

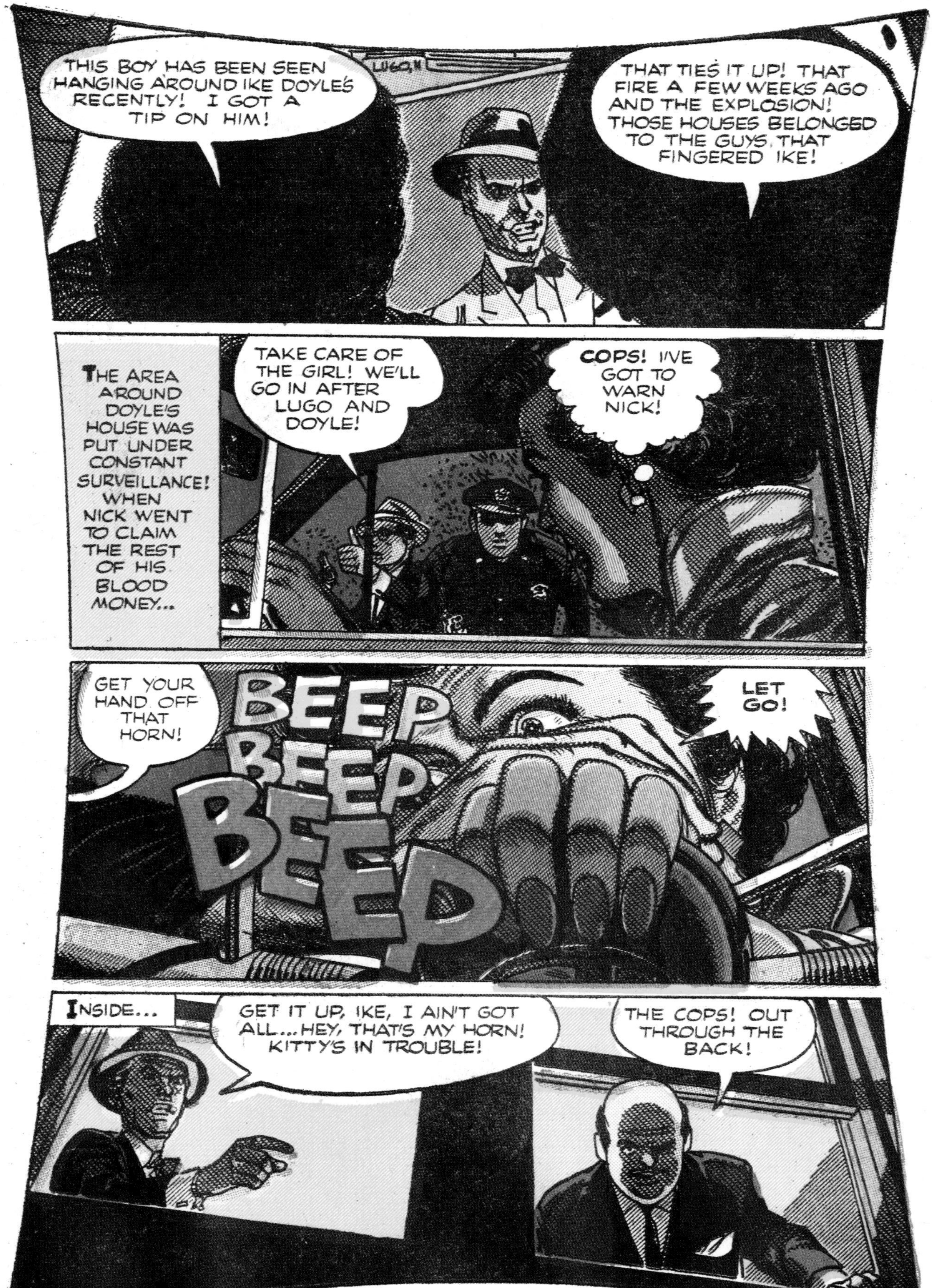
LUGO, N
THIS BOY HAS BEEN SEEN HANGING AROUND IKE DOYLE'S RECENTLY! I GOT A TIP ON HIM!
THAT TIES IT UP! THAT FIRE A FEW WEEKS AGO AND THE EXPLOSION! THOSE HOUSES BELONGED TO THE GUYS THAT FINGERED IKE!
THE AREA AROUND DOYLE'S HOUSE WAS PUT UNDER CONSTANT SURVEILLANCE! WHEN NICK WENT TO CLAIM THE REST OF HIS BLOOD MONEY...
TAKE CARE OF THE GIRL! WE'LL GO IN AFTER LUGO AND DOYLE!
COPS! I'VE GOT TO WARN NICK!
GET YOUR HAND OFF THAT HORN!
BEEP BEEP BEEP
LET GO!
INSIDE...
GET IT UP, IKE, I AIN'T GOT ALL... HEY, THAT'S MY HORN! KITTY'S IN TROUBLE!
THE COPS! OUT THROUGH THE BACK!

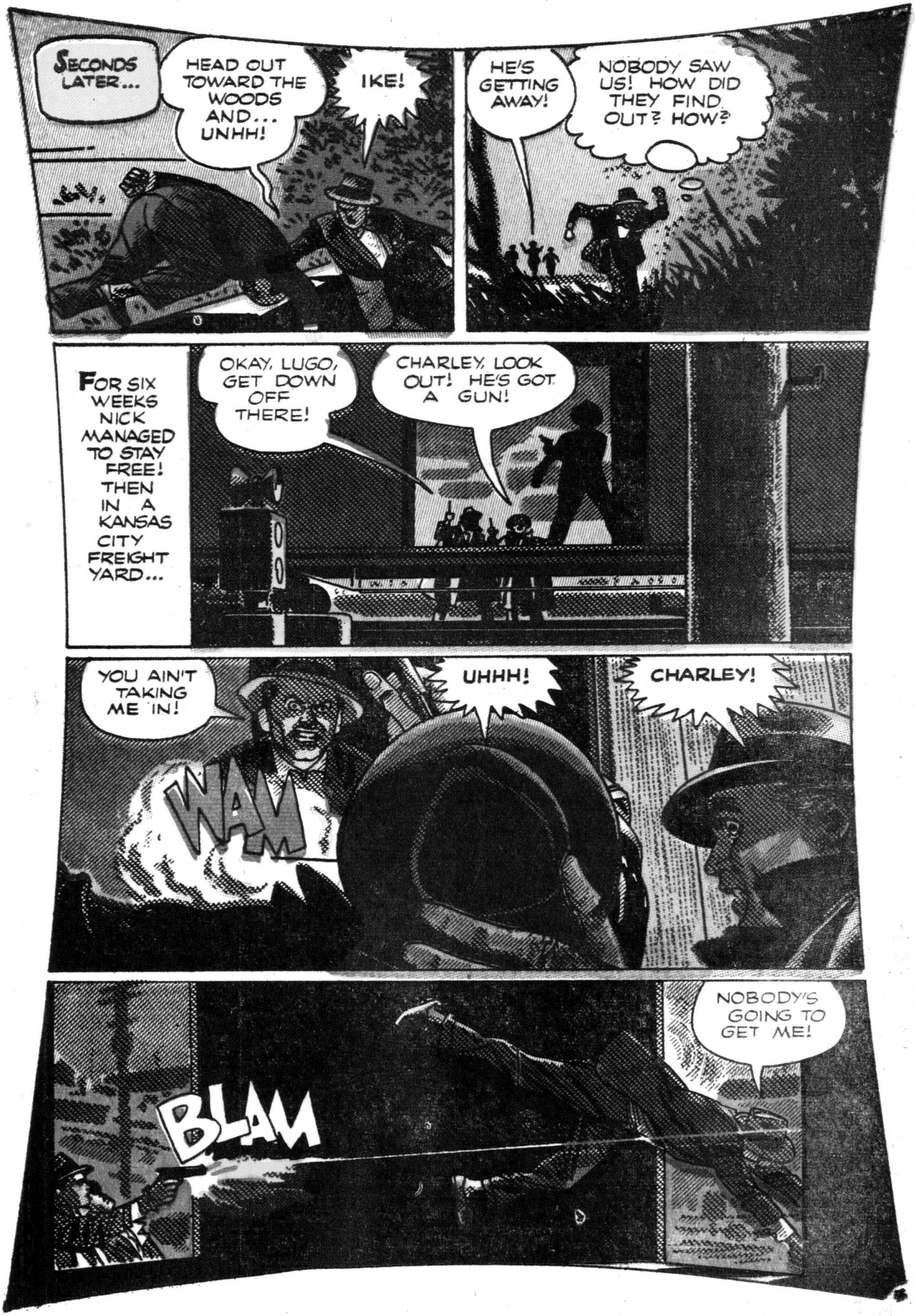
SECONDS LATER...
HEAD OUT TOWARD THE WOODS AND... UNHH!
IKE!
HE'S GETTING AWAY!
NOBODY SAW US! HOW DID THEY FIND OUT? HOW?
FOR SIX WEEKS NICK MANAGED TO STAY FREE! THEN IN A KANSAS CITY FREIGHT YARD...
OKAY, LUGO, GET DOWN OFF THERE!
CHARLEY, LOOK OUT! HE'S GOT A GUN!
YOU AIN'T TAKING ME IN!
UHHH!
CHARLEY!
WAM
NOBODY'S GOING TO GET ME!
BLAM

AHHH!
IN DESPERATION NICK ROLLS OUT OF THE WAY...
OHHHH!
ONLY TO BE ELECTROCUTED BY THE THIRD RAIL ON THE OTHER TRACK! FITTING END TO A BURNER!
ZZZZZZZZZZZZTTTKRAKKKZZZZTTT
The End

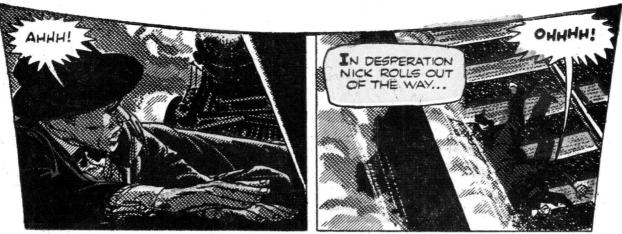

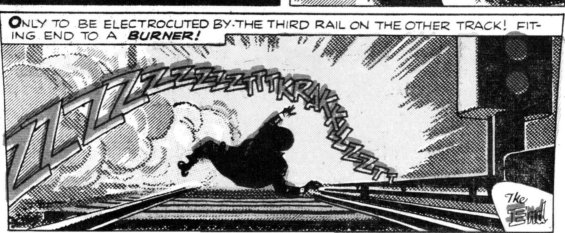

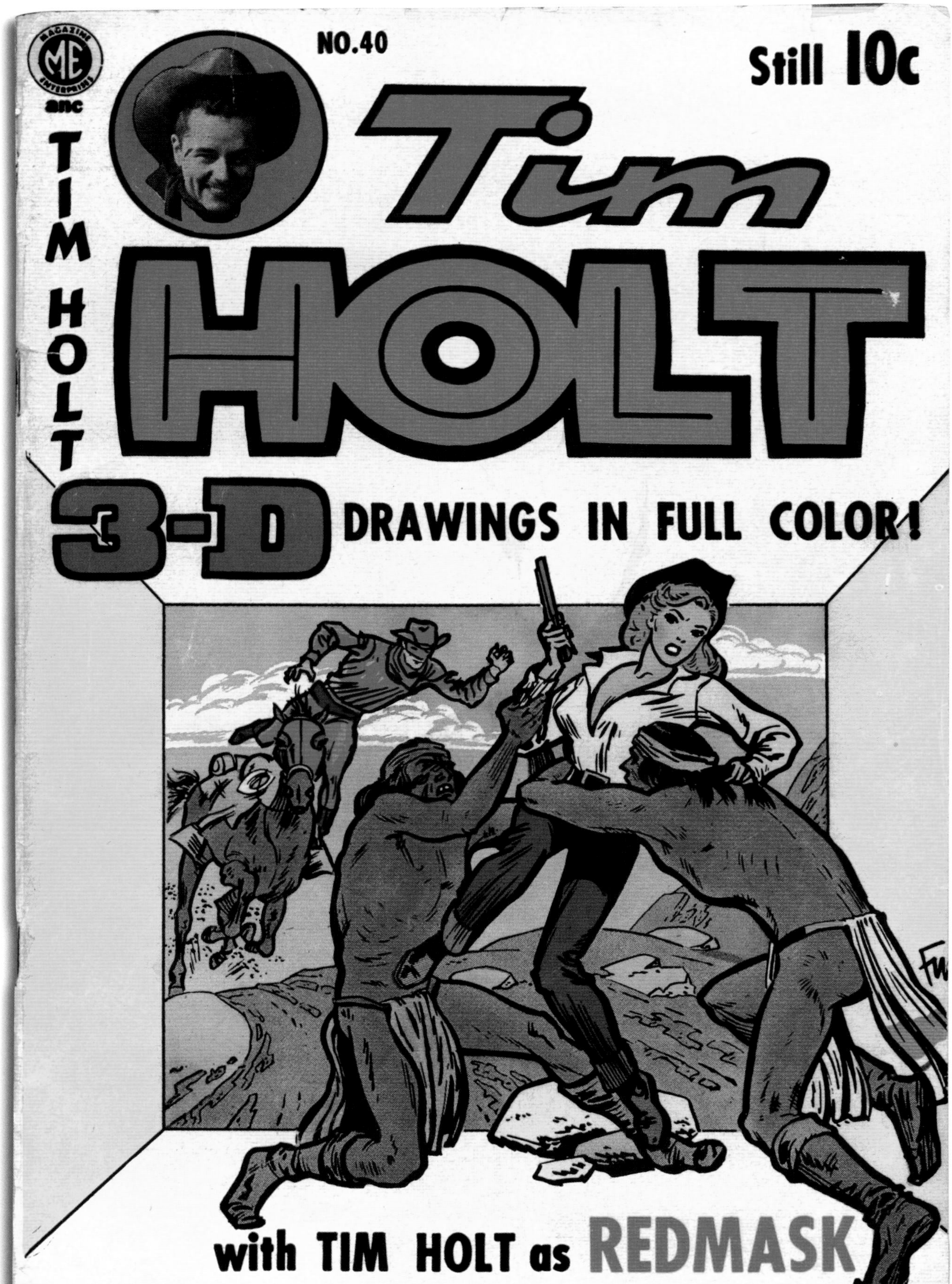
MAGAZINE ME ENTERPRISES
anc
NO.40
Still 10c
Tim HOLT
TIM HOLT
3-D DRAWINGS IN FULL COLOR!
with TIM HOLT as REDMASK

Tim Holt #40, February-March 1954; artist, Frank Bolle.

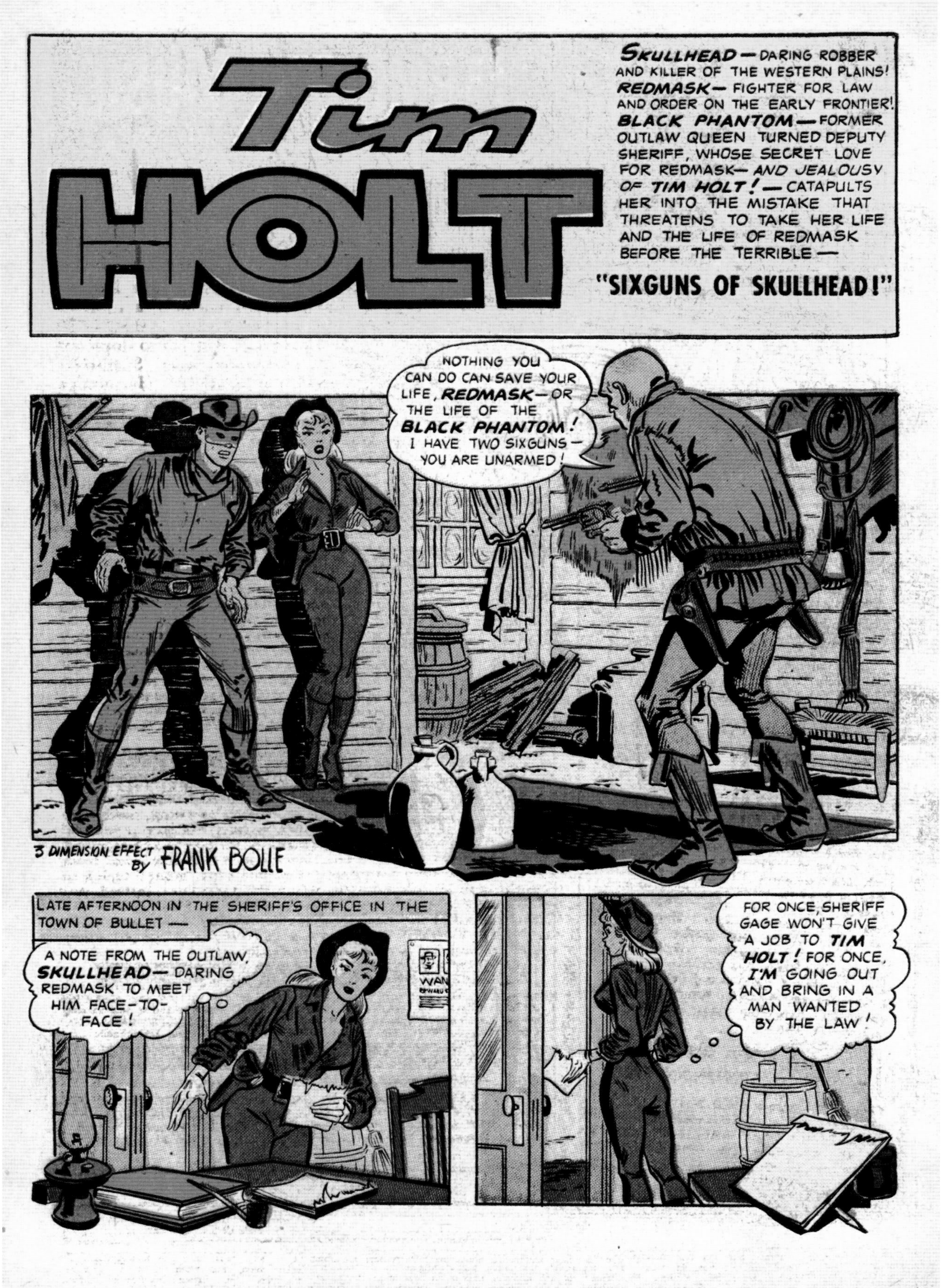
Tim HOLT
SKULLHEAD — DARING ROBBER AND KILLER OF THE WESTERN PLAINS! REDMASK— FIGHTER FOR LAW AND ORDER ON THE EARLY FRONTIER! BLACK PHANTOM — FORMER OUTLAW QUEEN TURNED DEPUTY SHERIFF, WHOSE SECRET LOVE FOR REDMASK— AND JEALOUSY OF TIM HOLT! — CATAPULTS HER INTO THE MISTAKE THAT THREATENS TO TAKE HER LIFE AND THE LIFE OF REDMASK BEFORE THE TERRIBLE —
"SIXGUNS OF SKULLHEAD!"
NOTHING YOU CAN DO CAN SAVE YOUR LIFE, REDMASK — OR THE LIFE OF THE BLACK PHANTOM! I HAVE TWO SIXGUNS — YOU ARE UNARMED!
3 DIMENSION EFFECT BY FRANK BOLLE
LATE AFTERNOON IN THE SHERIFF'S OFFICE IN THE TOWN OF BULLET —
A NOTE FROM THE OUTLAW, SKULLHEAD— DARING REDMASK TO MEET HIM FACE-TO-FACE!
FOR ONCE, SHERIFF GAGE WON'T GIVE A JOB TO TIM HOLT! FOR ONCE, I'M GOING OUT AND BRING IN A MAN WANTED BY THE LAW!

Artist, Frank Bolle

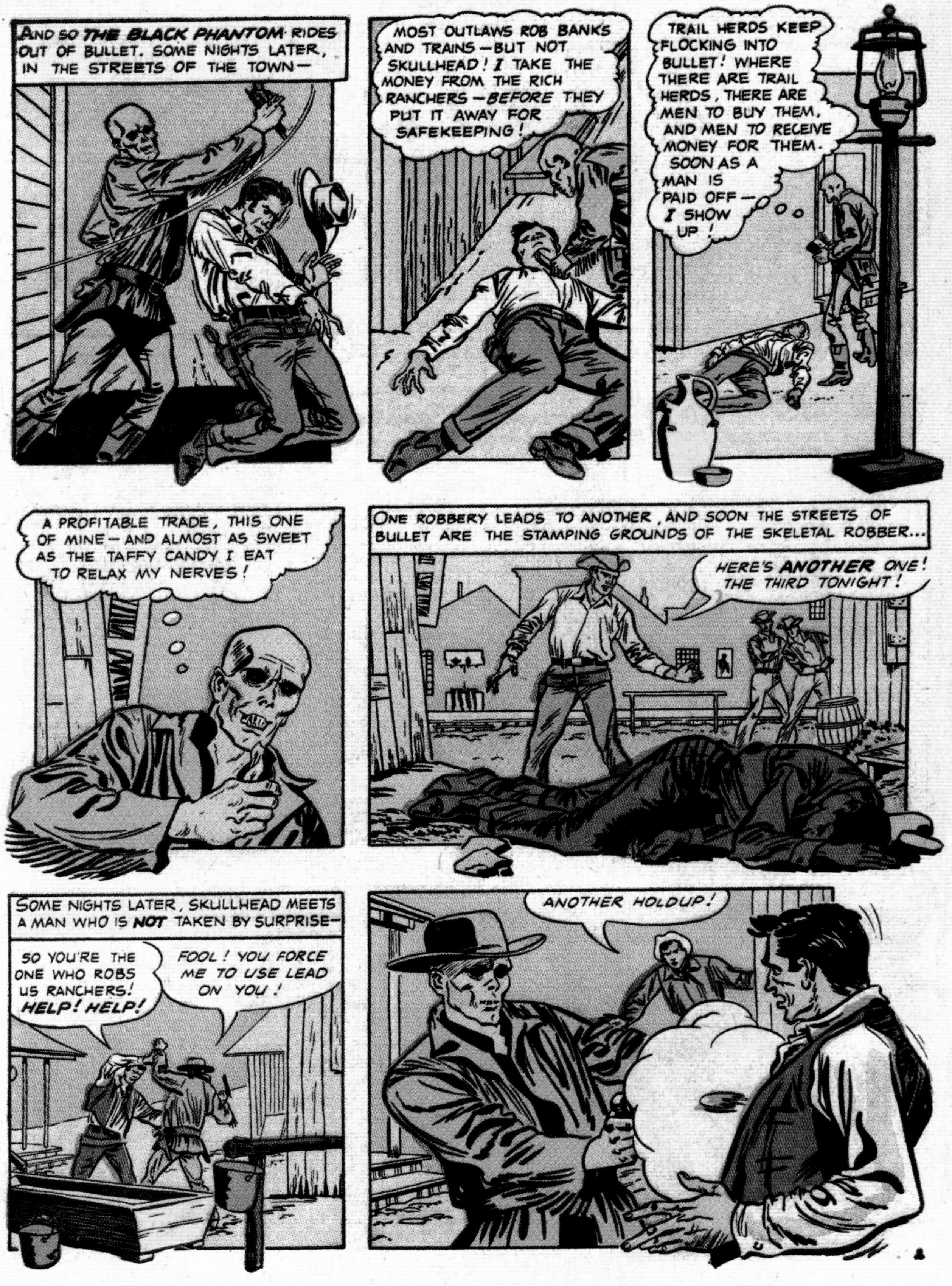
AND SO THE BLACK PHANTOM RIDES OUT OF BULLET. SOME NIGHTS LATER, IN THE STREETS OF THE TOWN—
MOST OUTLAWS ROB BANKS AND TRAINS—BUT NOT SKULLHEAD! I TAKE THE MONEY FROM THE RICH RANCHERS—BEFORE THEY PUT IT AWAY FOR SAFEKEEPING!
TRAIL HERDS KEEP FLOCKING INTO BULLET! WHERE THERE ARE TRAIL HERDS, THERE ARE MEN TO BUY THEM, AND MEN TO RECEIVE MONEY FOR THEM. SOON AS A MAN IS PAID OFF— I SHOW UP!
A PROFITABLE TRADE, THIS ONE OF MINE—AND ALMOST AS SWEET AS THE TAFFY CANDY I EAT TO RELAX MY NERVES!
ONE ROBBERY LEADS TO ANOTHER, AND SOON THE STREETS OF BULLET ARE THE STAMPING GROUNDS OF THE SKELETAL ROBBER...
HERE'S ANOTHER ONE! THE THIRD TONIGHT!
SOME NIGHTS LATER, SKULLHEAD MEETS A MAN WHO IS NOT TAKEN BY SURPRISE—
SO YOU'RE THE ONE WHO ROBS US RANCHERS! HELP! HELP!
FOOL! YOU FORCE ME TO USE LEAD ON YOU!
ANOTHER HOLDUP!

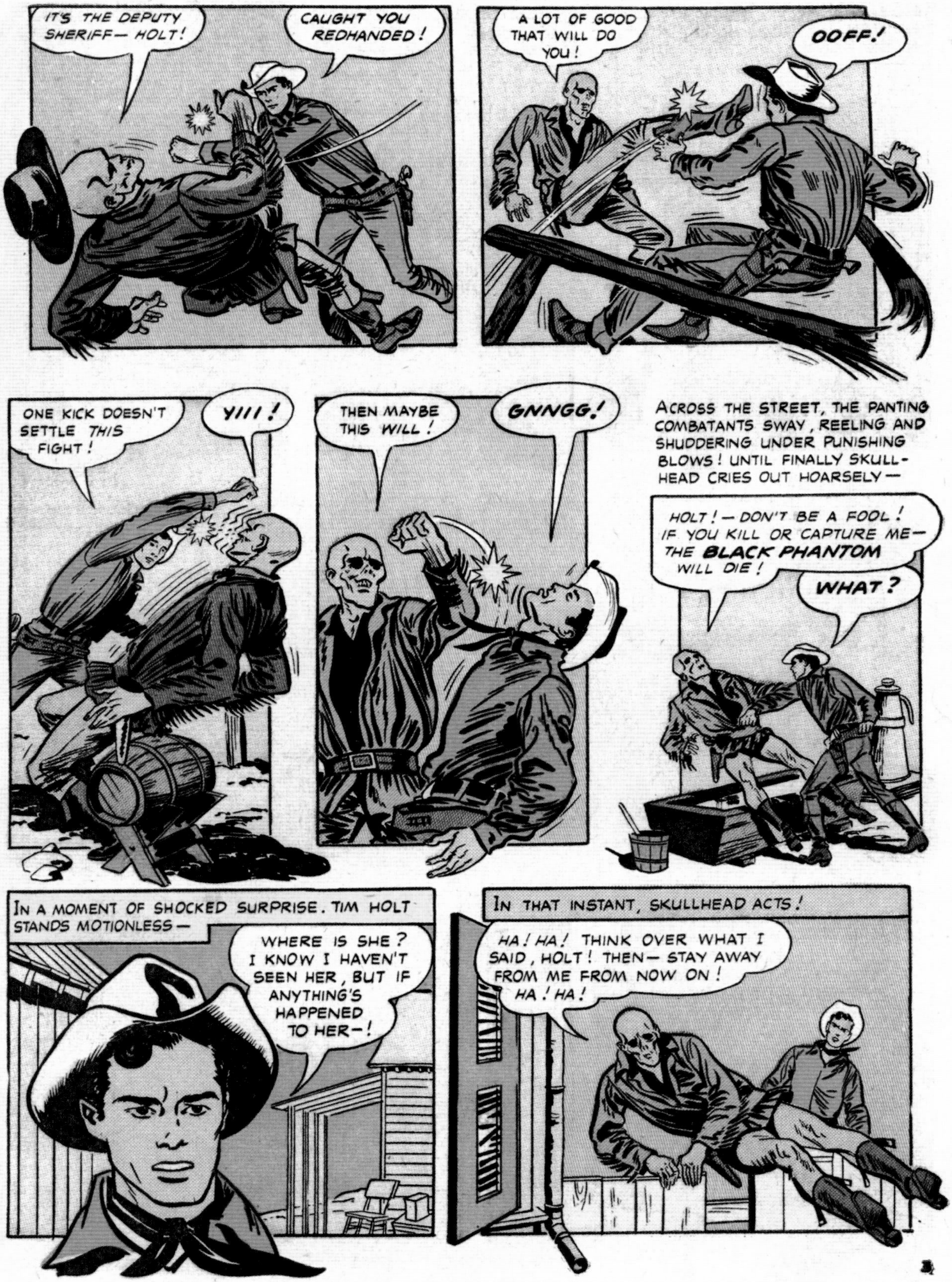

IT'S THE DEPUTY SHERIFF— HOLT!
CAUGHT YOU REDHANDED!
A LOT OF GOOD THAT WILL DO YOU!
OOFF!
ONE KICK DOESN'T SETTLE THIS FIGHT!
YIII!
THEN MAYBE THIS WILL!
GNNGG!
ACROSS THE STREET, THE PANTING COMBATANTS SWAY, REELING AND SHUDDERING UNDER PUNISHING BLOWS! UNTIL FINALLY SKULL-HEAD CRIES OUT HOARSELY—
HOLT! — DON'T BE A FOOL! IF YOU KILL OR CAPTURE ME— THE BLACK PHANTOM WILL DIE!
WHAT?
IN A MOMENT OF SHOCKED SURPRISE. TIM HOLT STANDS MOTIONLESS —
WHERE IS SHE? I KNOW I HAVEN'T SEEN HER, BUT IF ANYTHING'S HAPPENED TO HER—!
IN THAT INSTANT, SKULLHEAD ACTS!
HA! HA! THINK OVER WHAT I SAID, HOLT! THEN— STAY AWAY FROM ME FROM NOW ON! HA! HA!

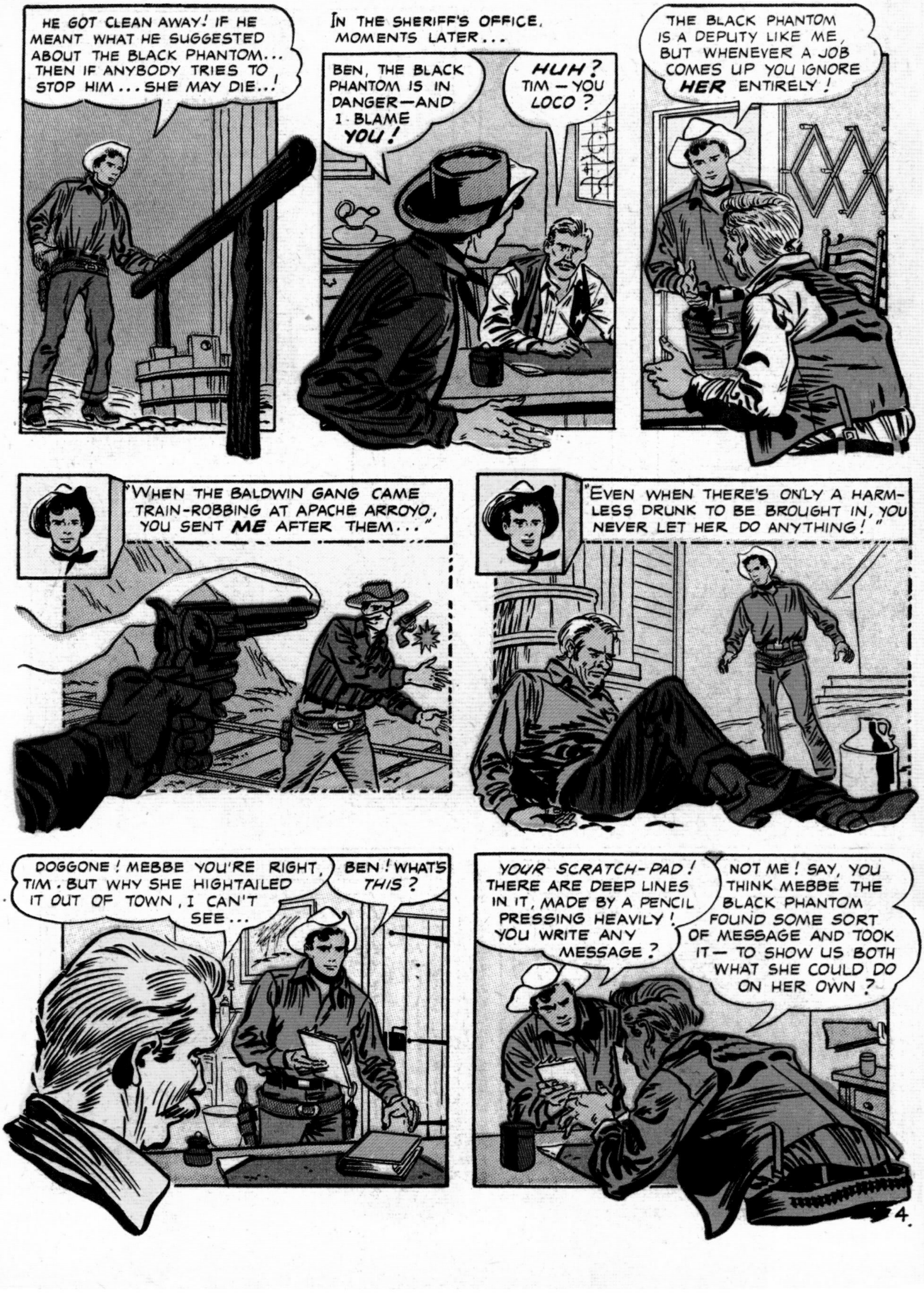
HE GOT CLEAN AWAY! IF HE MEANT WHAT HE SUGGESTED ABOUT THE BLACK PHANTOM... THEN IF ANYBODY TRIES TO STOP HIM... SHE MAY DIE..!
IN THE SHERIFF'S OFFICE, MOMENTS LATER...
BEN, THE BLACK PHANTOM IS IN DANGER—AND I BLAME YOU!
HUH? TIM — YOU LOCO?
THE BLACK PHANTOM IS A DEPUTY LIKE ME, BUT WHENEVER A JOB COMES UP YOU IGNORE HER ENTIRELY!
"WHEN THE BALDWIN GANG CAME TRAIN-ROBBING AT APACHE ARROYO, YOU SENT ME AFTER THEM..."
"EVEN WHEN THERE'S ON'LY A HARMLESS DRUNK TO BE BROUGHT IN, YOU NEVER LET HER DO ANYTHING!"
DOGGONE! MEBBE YOU'RE RIGHT, TIM. BUT WHY SHE HIGHTAILED IT OUT OF TOWN, I CAN'T SEE...
BEN! WHAT'S THIS?
YOUR SCRATCH-PAD! THERE ARE DEEP LINES IN IT, MADE BY A PENCIL PRESSING HEAVILY! YOU WRITE ANY MESSAGE?
NOT ME! SAY, YOU THINK MEBBE THE BLACK PHANTOM FOUND SOME SORT OF MESSAGE AND TOOK IT— TO SHOW US BOTH WHAT SHE COULD DO ON HER OWN?
4.

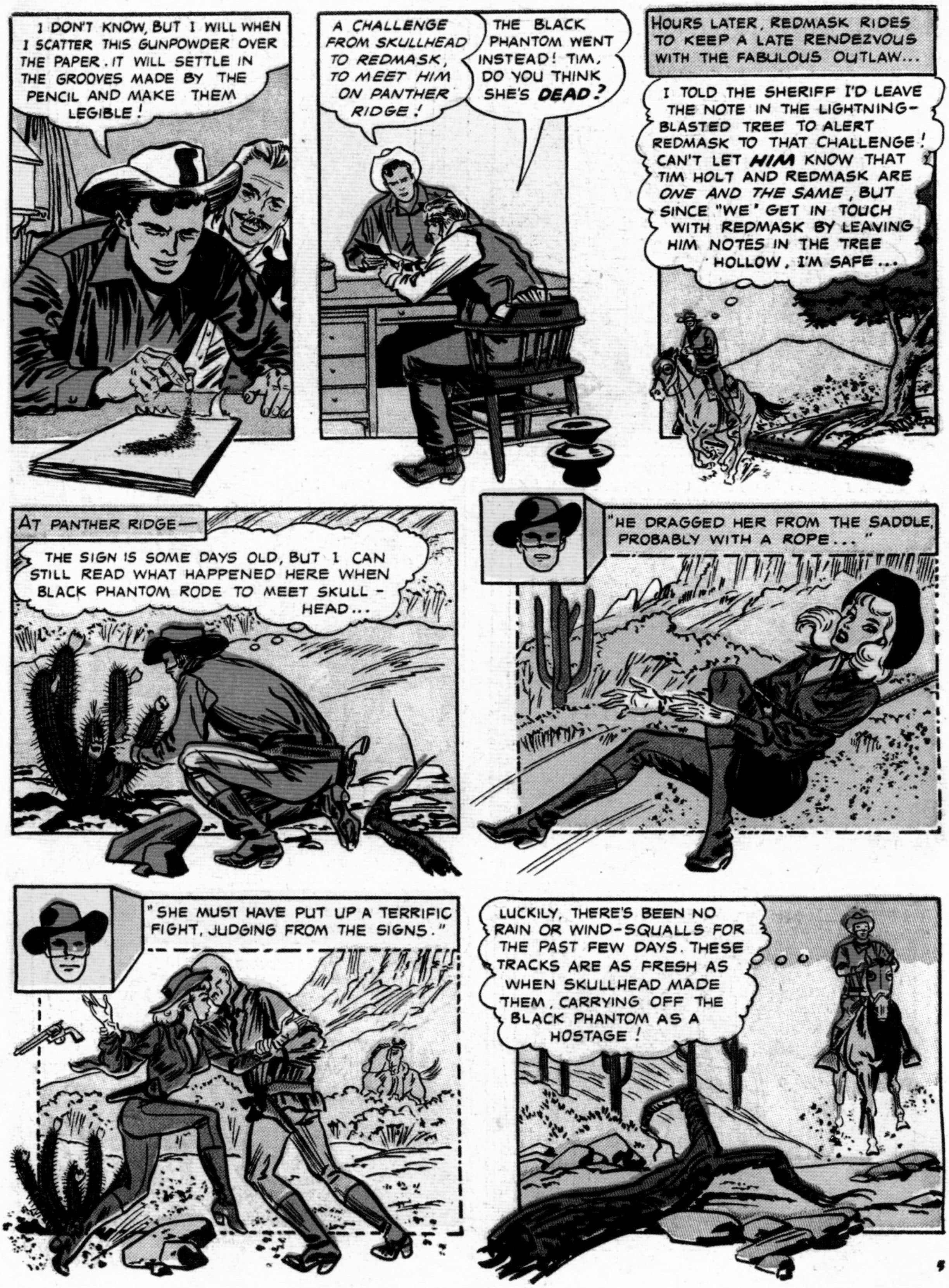
I DON'T KNOW, BUT I WILL WHEN I SCATTER THIS GUNPOWDER OVER THE PAPER. IT WILL SETTLE IN THE GROOVES MADE BY THE PENCIL AND MAKE THEM LEGIBLE!
A CHALLENGE FROM SKULLHEAD TO REDMASK, TO MEET HIM ON PANTHER RIDGE!
THE BLACK PHANTOM WENT INSTEAD! TIM, DO YOU THINK SHE'S DEAD?
HOURS LATER, REDMASK RIDES TO KEEP A LATE RENDEZVOUS WITH THE FABULOUS OUTLAW...
I TOLD THE SHERIFF I'D LEAVE THE NOTE IN THE LIGHTNING-BLASTED TREE TO ALERT REDMASK TO THAT CHALLENGE! CAN'T LET HIM KNOW THAT TIM HOLT AND REDMASK ARE ONE AND THE SAME, BUT SINCE "WE" GET IN TOUCH WITH REDMASK BY LEAVING HIM NOTES IN THE TREE HOLLOW, I'M SAFE...
AT PANTHER RIDGE—
THE SIGN IS SOME DAYS OLD, BUT I CAN STILL READ WHAT HAPPENED HERE WHEN BLACK PHANTOM RODE TO MEET SKULL-HEAD...
"HE DRAGGED HER FROM THE SADDLE, PROBABLY WITH A ROPE..."
"SHE MUST HAVE PUT UP A TERRIFIC FIGHT, JUDGING FROM THE SIGNS."
LUCKILY, THERE'S BEEN NO RAIN OR WIND-SQUALLS FOR THE PAST FEW DAYS. THESE TRACKS ARE AS FRESH AS WHEN SKULLHEAD MADE THEM, CARRYING OFF THE BLACK PHANTOM AS A HOSTAGE!

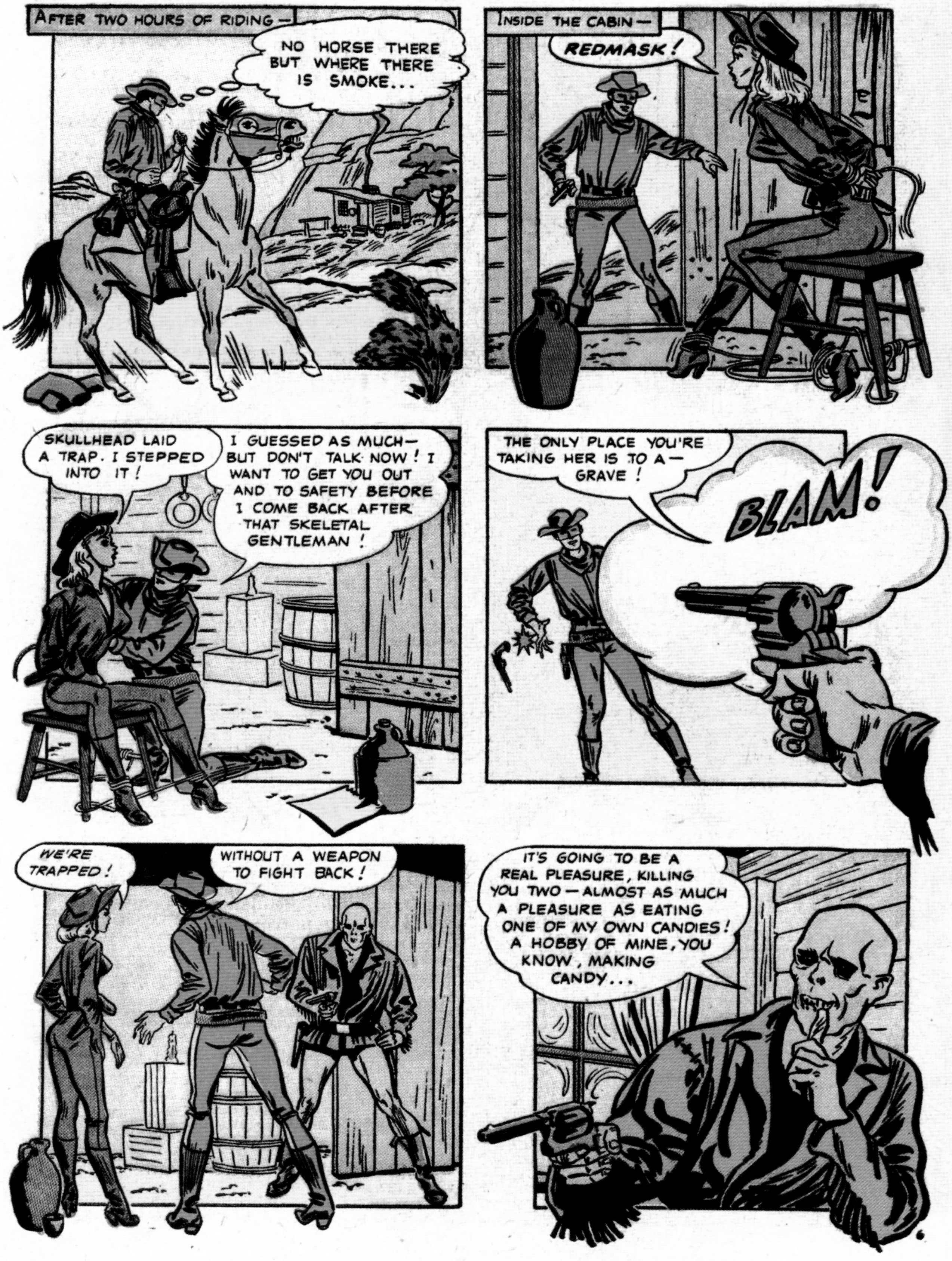

AFTER TWO HOURS OF RIDING—
NO HORSE THERE BUT WHERE THERE IS SMOKE...
INSIDE THE CABIN—
REDMASK!
SKULLHEAD LAID A TRAP. I STEPPED INTO IT!
I GUESSED AS MUCH—BUT DON'T TALK NOW! I WANT TO GET YOU OUT AND TO SAFETY BEFORE I COME BACK AFTER THAT SKELETAL GENTLEMAN!
THE ONLY PLACE YOU'RE TAKING HER IS TO A—GRAVE!
BLAM!
WE'RE TRAPPED!
WITHOUT A WEAPON TO FIGHT BACK!
IT'S GOING TO BE A REAL PLEASURE, KILLING YOU TWO—ALMOST AS MUCH A PLEASURE AS EATING ONE OF MY OWN CANDIES! A HOBBY OF MINE, YOU KNOW, MAKING CANDY...
6

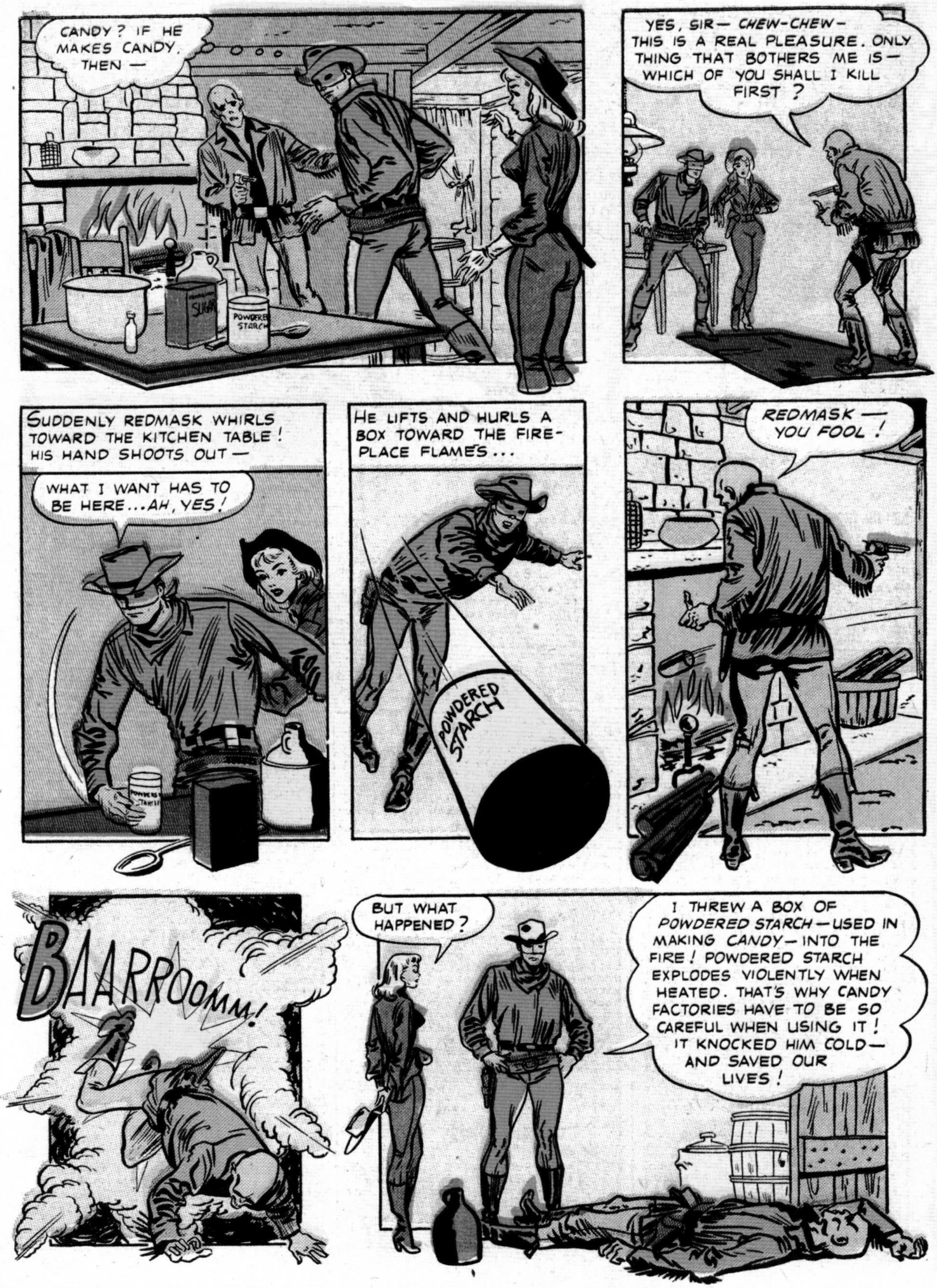

CANDY? IF HE MAKES CANDY, THEN —
YES, SIR— CHEW-CHEW— THIS IS A REAL PLEASURE. ONLY THING THAT BOTHERS ME IS— WHICH OF YOU SHALL I KILL FIRST?
SUDDENLY REDMASK WHIRLS TOWARD THE KITCHEN TABLE! HIS HAND SHOOTS OUT—
WHAT I WANT HAS TO BE HERE...AH, YES!
HE LIFTS AND HURLS A BOX TOWARD THE FIRE-PLACE FLAMES...
POWDERED STARCH
REDMASK — YOU FOOL!
BAARROOMM!
BUT WHAT HAPPENED?
I THREW A BOX OF POWDERED STARCH—USED IN MAKING CANDY—INTO THE FIRE! POWDERED STARCH EXPLODES VIOLENTLY WHEN HEATED. THAT'S WHY CANDY FACTORIES HAVE TO BE SO CAREFUL WHEN USING IT! IT KNOCKED HIM COLD— AND SAVED OUR LIVES!

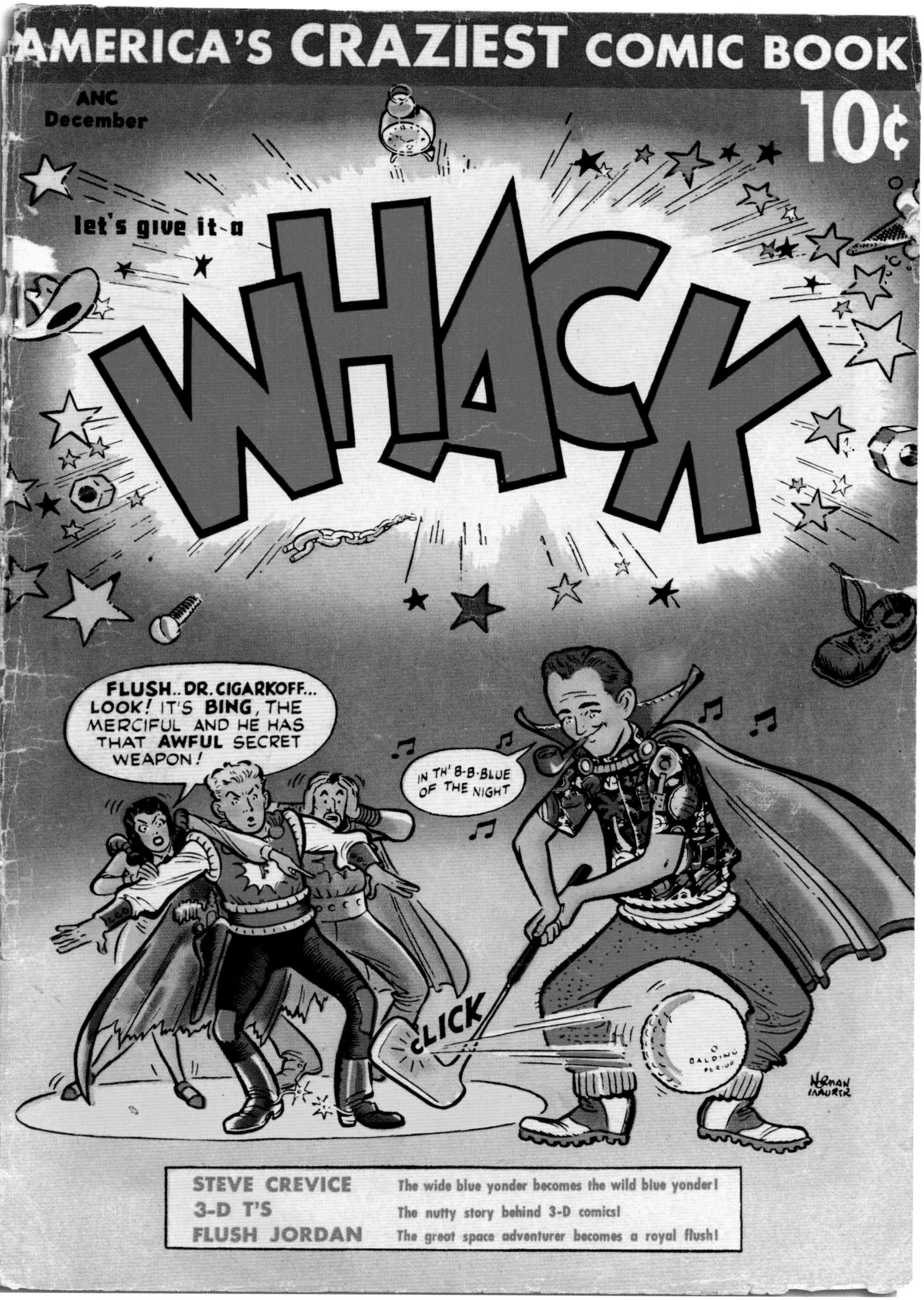
AMERICA'S CRAZIEST COMIC BOOK
ANC
December
10¢
let's give it a
WHACK
FLUSH.. DR. CIGARKOFF... LOOK! IT'S BING, THE MERCIFUL AND HE HAS THAT AWFUL SECRET WEAPON!
IN TH' B-B-BLUE OF THE NIGHT
CLICK
NORMAN MAURER
STEVE CREVICE The wide blue yonder becomes the wild blue yonder!
3-D T'S The nutty story behind 3-D comics!
FLUSH JORDAN The great space adventurer becomes a royal flush!

Whack #2, December 1953; artist, Norman Maurer. *Whack* is back! It's no longer in 3-D, but now satirizing the quickly fading fad.

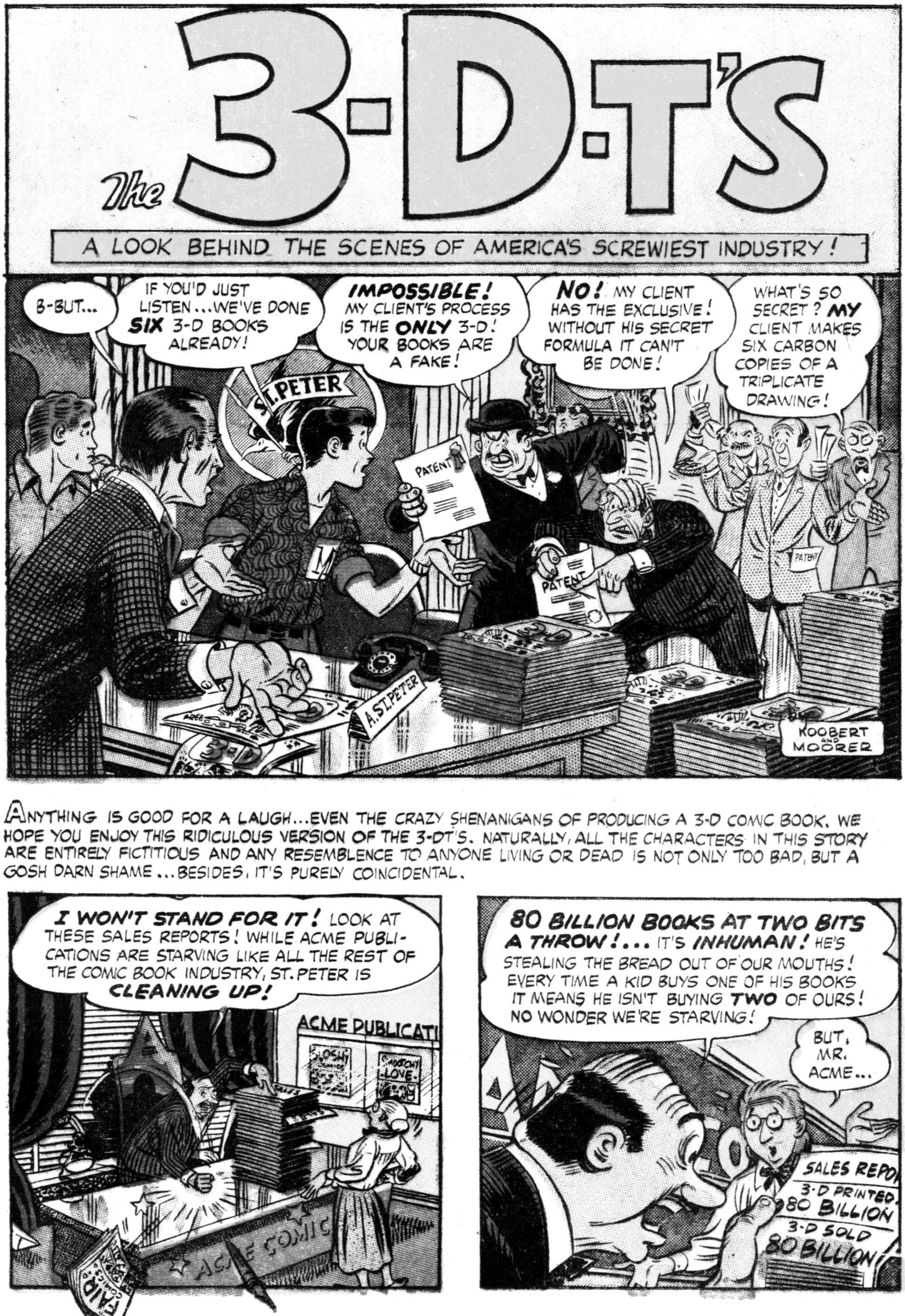
The 3-D-T's
A LOOK BEHIND THE SCENES OF AMERICA'S SCREWIEST INDUSTRY!
B-BUT...
IF YOU'D JUST LISTEN...WE'VE DONE SIX 3-D BOOKS ALREADY!
IMPOSSIBLE! MY CLIENT'S PROCESS IS THE ONLY 3-D! YOUR BOOKS ARE A FAKE!
NO! MY CLIENT HAS THE EXCLUSIVE! WITHOUT HIS SECRET FORMULA IT CAN'T BE DONE!
WHAT'S SO SECRET? MY CLIENT MAKES SIX CARBON COPIES OF A TRIPLICATE DRAWING!
ST. PETER
PATENT
A. ST. PETER
KOOBERT AND MOORER
ANYTHING IS GOOD FOR A LAUGH...EVEN THE CRAZY SHENANIGANS OF PRODUCING A 3-D COMIC BOOK. WE HOPE YOU ENJOY THIS RIDICULOUS VERSION OF THE 3-DT'S. NATURALLY, ALL THE CHARACTERS IN THIS STORY ARE ENTIRELY FICTITIOUS AND ANY RESEMBLENCE TO ANYONE LIVING OR DEAD IS NOT ONLY TOO BAD, BUT A GOSH DARN SHAME...BESIDES, IT'S PURELY COINCIDENTAL.
I WON'T STAND FOR IT! LOOK AT THESE SALES REPORTS! WHILE ACME PUBLICATIONS ARE STARVING LIKE ALL THE REST OF THE COMIC BOOK INDUSTRY, ST. PETER IS CLEANING UP!
ACME PUBLICATI
ACME COMICS
80 BILLION BOOKS AT TWO BITS A THROW!... IT'S INHUMAN! HE'S STEALING THE BREAD OUT OF OUR MOUTHS! EVERY TIME A KID BUYS ONE OF HIS BOOKS IT MEANS HE ISN'T BUYING TWO OF OURS! NO WONDER WE'RE STARVING!
BUT, MR. ACME...
SALES REPO
3-D PRINTED 80 BILLION
3-D SOLD 80 BILLION

Signed as Koobert and Moorer, but of course it's Joe Kubert and Norman Maurer!

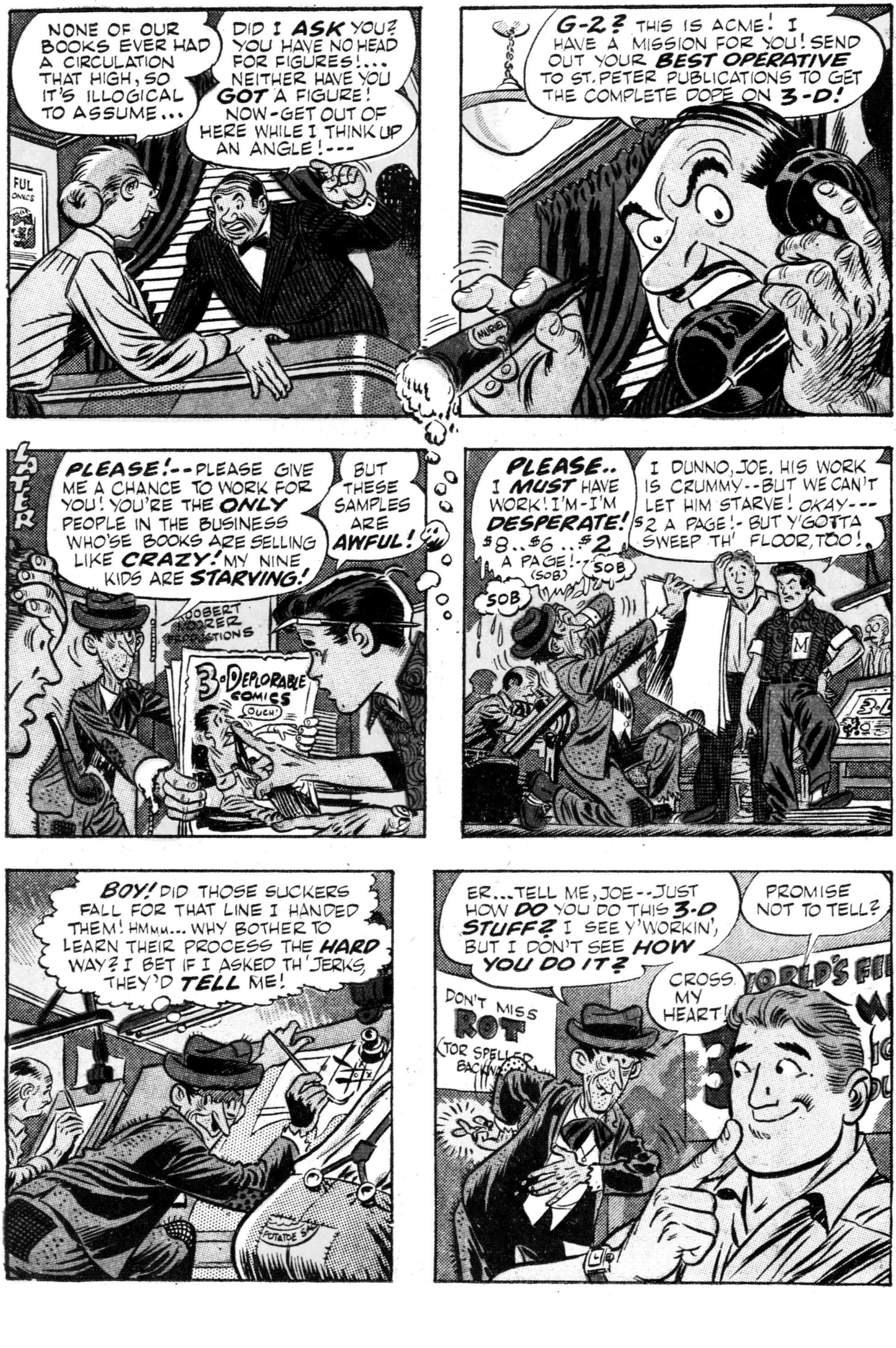

NONE OF OUR BOOKS EVER HAD A CIRCULATION THAT HIGH, SO IT'S ILLOGICAL TO ASSUME...
DID I ASK YOU? YOU HAVE NO HEAD FOR FIGURES!... NEITHER HAVE YOU GOT A FIGURE! NOW-GET OUT OF HERE WHILE I THINK UP AN ANGLE!---
G-2? THIS IS ACME! I HAVE A MISSION FOR YOU! SEND OUT YOUR BEST OPERATIVE TO ST. PETER PUBLICATIONS TO GET THE COMPLETE DOPE ON 3-D!
MURIEL
LATER
PLEASE!--PLEASE GIVE ME A CHANCE TO WORK FOR YOU! YOU'RE THE ONLY PEOPLE IN THE BUSINESS WHO'SE BOOKS ARE SELLING LIKE CRAZY! MY NINE KIDS ARE STARVING!
BUT THESE SAMPLES ARE AWFUL!
3-DEPLORABLE COMICS
OUCH!
PLEASE.. I MUST HAVE WORK! I'M-I'M DESPERATE! $8..$6..$2 A PAGE!--
(SOB)
SOB
SOB
I DUNNO, JOE. HIS WORK IS CRUMMY--BUT WE CAN'T LET HIM STARVE! OKAY--- $2 A PAGE!- BUT Y'GOTTA SWEEP TH' FLOOR, TOO!
M
BOY! DID THOSE SUCKERS FALL FOR THAT LINE I HANDED THEM! HMMM... WHY BOTHER TO LEARN THEIR PROCESS THE HARD WAY? I BET IF I ASKED TH' JERKS, THEY'D TELL ME!
ER...TELL ME, JOE--JUST HOW DO YOU DO THIS 3-D STUFF? I SEE Y'WORKIN', BUT I DON'T SEE HOW YOU DO IT?
PROMISE NOT TO TELL?
CROSS MY HEART!
DON'T MISS ROT

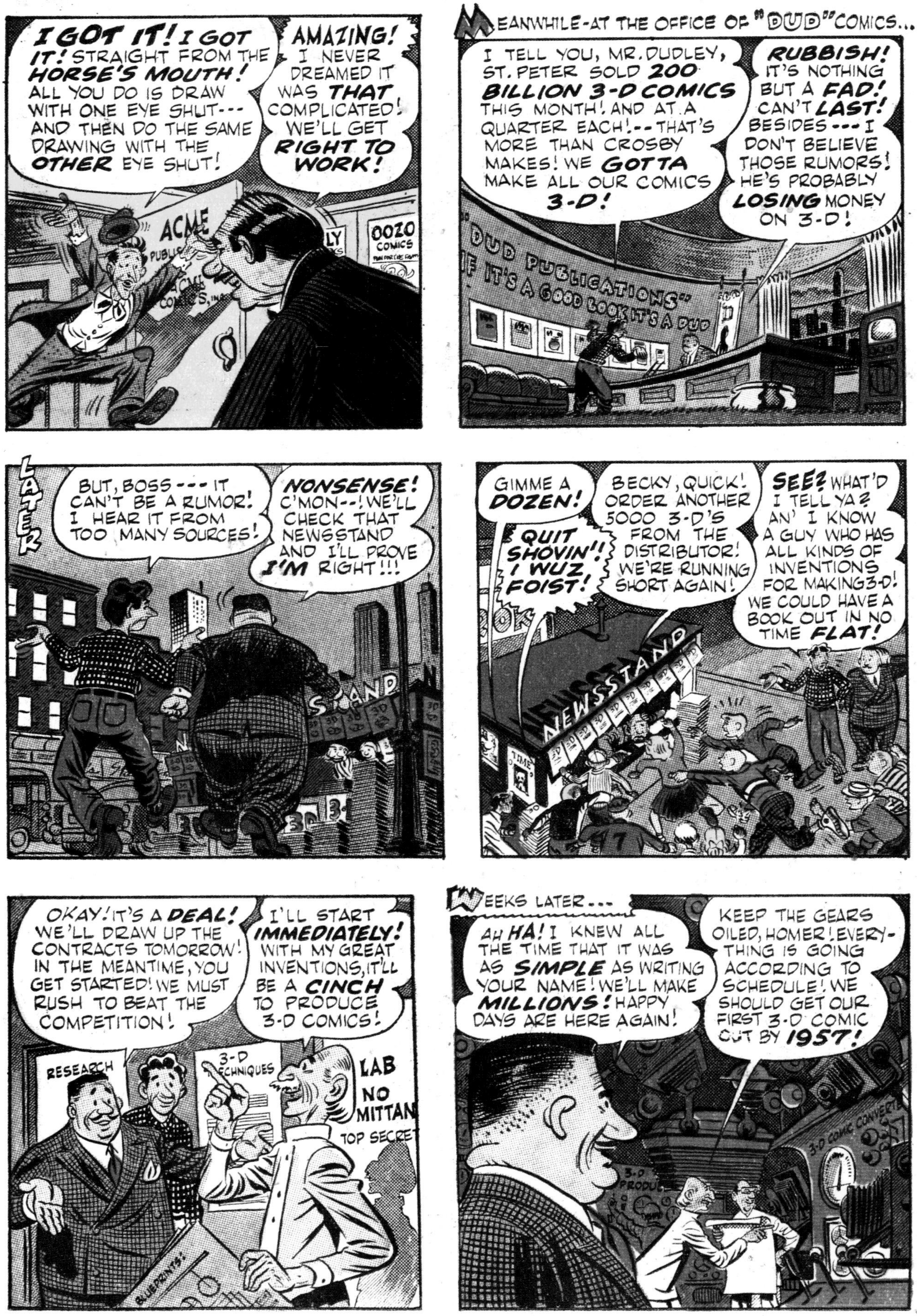
I GOT IT! I GOT IT! STRAIGHT FROM THE HORSE'S MOUTH! ALL YOU DO IS DRAW WITH ONE EYE SHUT--- AND THEN DO THE SAME DRAWING WITH THE OTHER EYE SHUT!
AMAZING! I NEVER DREAMED IT WAS THAT COMPLICATED! WE'LL GET RIGHT TO WORK!
ACME
OOZO COMICS
MEANWHILE-AT THE OFFICE OF "DUD" COMICS...
I TELL YOU, MR. DUDLEY, ST. PETER SOLD 200 BILLION 3-D COMICS THIS MONTH! AND AT A QUARTER EACH!--THAT'S MORE THAN CROSBY MAKES! WE GOTTA MAKE ALL OUR COMICS 3-D!
RUBBISH! IT'S NOTHING BUT A FAD! CAN'T LAST! BESIDES --- I DON'T BELIEVE THOSE RUMORS! HE'S PROBABLY LOSING MONEY ON 3-D!
"DUD PUBLICATIONS" IF IT'S A GOOD BOOK IT'S A DUD
LATER
BUT, BOSS --- IT CAN'T BE A RUMOR! I HEAR IT FROM TOO MANY SOURCES!
NONSENSE! C'MON--! WE'LL CHECK THAT NEWSSTAND AND I'LL PROVE I'M RIGHT!!!
GIMME A DOZEN!
QUIT SHOVIN'! I WUZ FOIST!
BECKY, QUICK! ORDER ANOTHER 5000 3-D'S FROM THE DISTRIBUTOR! WE'RE RUNNING SHORT AGAIN!
SEE? WHAT'D I TELL YA? AN' I KNOW A GUY WHO HAS ALL KINDS OF INVENTIONS FOR MAKING 3-D! WE COULD HAVE A BOOK OUT IN NO TIME FLAT!
NEWSSTAND
OKAY! IT'S A DEAL! WE'LL DRAW UP THE CONTRACTS TOMORROW! IN THE MEANTIME, YOU GET STARTED! WE MUST RUSH TO BEAT THE COMPETITION!
I'LL START IMMEDIATELY! WITH MY GREAT INVENTIONS, IT'LL BE A CINCH TO PRODUCE 3-D COMICS!
RESEARCH
3-D TECHNIQUES
LAB
NO MITTAN
TOP SECRET
BLUEPRINTS!
WEEKS LATER...
AH HA! I KNEW ALL THE TIME THAT IT WAS AS SIMPLE AS WRITING YOUR NAME! WE'LL MAKE MILLIONS! HAPPY DAYS ARE HERE AGAIN!
KEEP THE GEARS OILED, HOMER! EVERY-THING IS GOING ACCORDING TO SCHEDULE! WE SHOULD GET OUR FIRST 3-D COMIC OUT BY 1957!

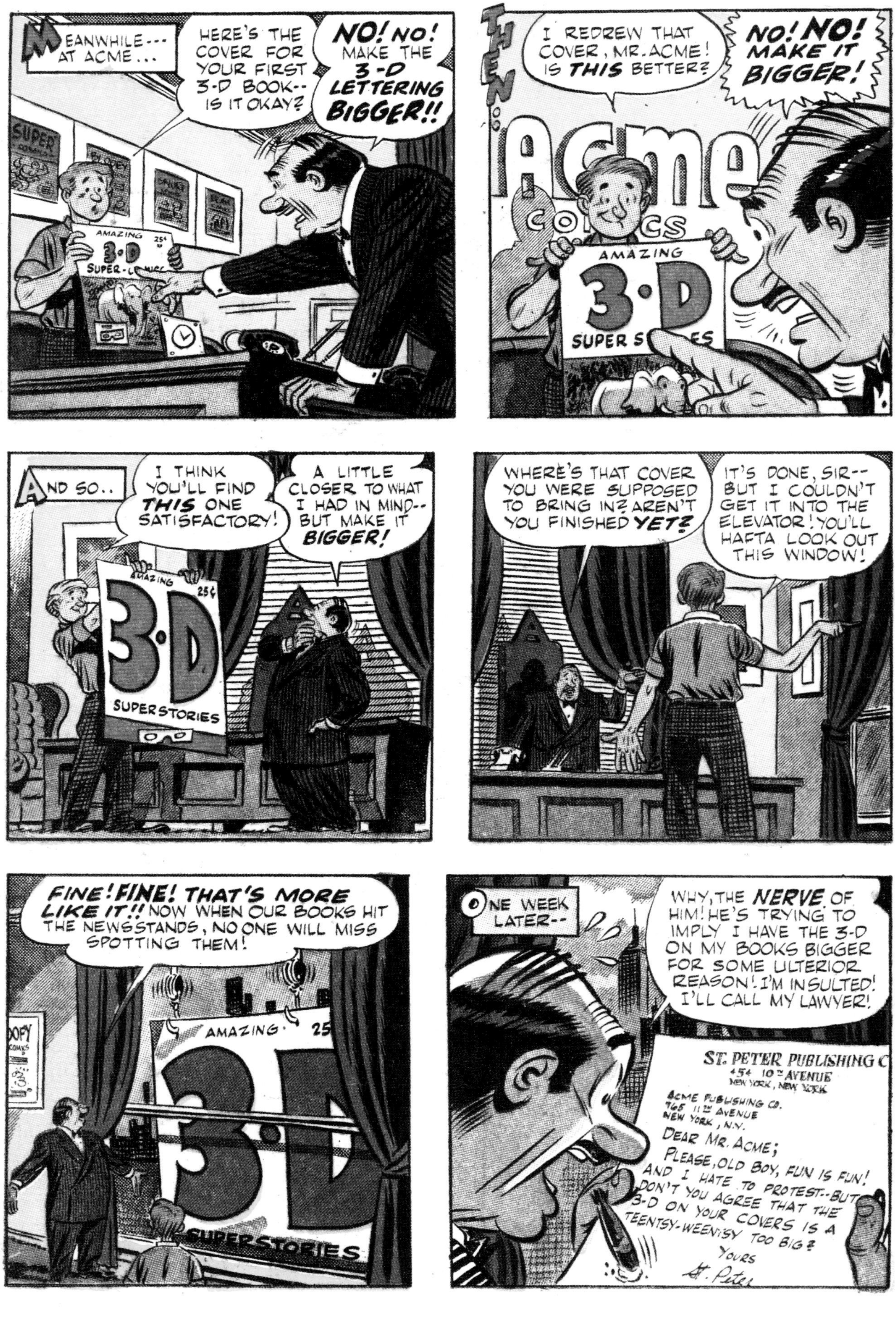
MEANWHILE--- AT ACME...
HERE'S THE COVER FOR YOUR FIRST 3-D BOOK-- IS IT OKAY?
NO! NO! MAKE THE 3-D LETTERING BIGGER!!
AMAZING 3-D 25¢
THEN...
I REDREW THAT COVER, MR. ACME! IS THIS BETTER?
NO! NO! MAKE IT BIGGER!
ACME COMICS
AMAZING 3-D
AND SO..
I THINK YOU'LL FIND THIS ONE SATISFACTORY!
A LITTLE CLOSER TO WHAT I HAD IN MIND-- BUT MAKE IT BIGGER!
AMAZING 25¢ 3-D SUPERSTORIES
WHERE'S THAT COVER YOU WERE SUPPOSED TO BRING IN? AREN'T YOU FINISHED YET?
IT'S DONE, SIR-- BUT I COULDN'T GET IT INTO THE ELEVATOR! YOU'LL HAFTA LOOK OUT THIS WINDOW!
FINE! FINE! THAT'S MORE LIKE IT!! NOW WHEN OUR BOOKS HIT THE NEWSSTANDS, NO ONE WILL MISS SPOTTING THEM!
AMAZING 25 3-D SUPERSTORIES
ONE WEEK LATER--
WHY, THE NERVE OF HIM! HE'S TRYING TO IMPLY I HAVE THE 3-D ON MY BOOKS BIGGER FOR SOME ULTERIOR REASON! I'M INSULTED! I'LL CALL MY LAWYER!
ST. PETER PUBLISHING C
454 10TH AVENUE
NEW YORK, NEW YORK
ACME PUBLISHING CO.
765 11TH AVENUE
NEW YORK, N.Y.
DEAR MR. ACME;
PLEASE, OLD BOY, FUN IS FUN! AND I HATE TO PROTEST--BUT DON'T YOU AGREE THAT THE 3-D ON YOUR COVERS IS A TEENTSY-WEENTSY TOO BIG?
YOURS
St. Peter

164

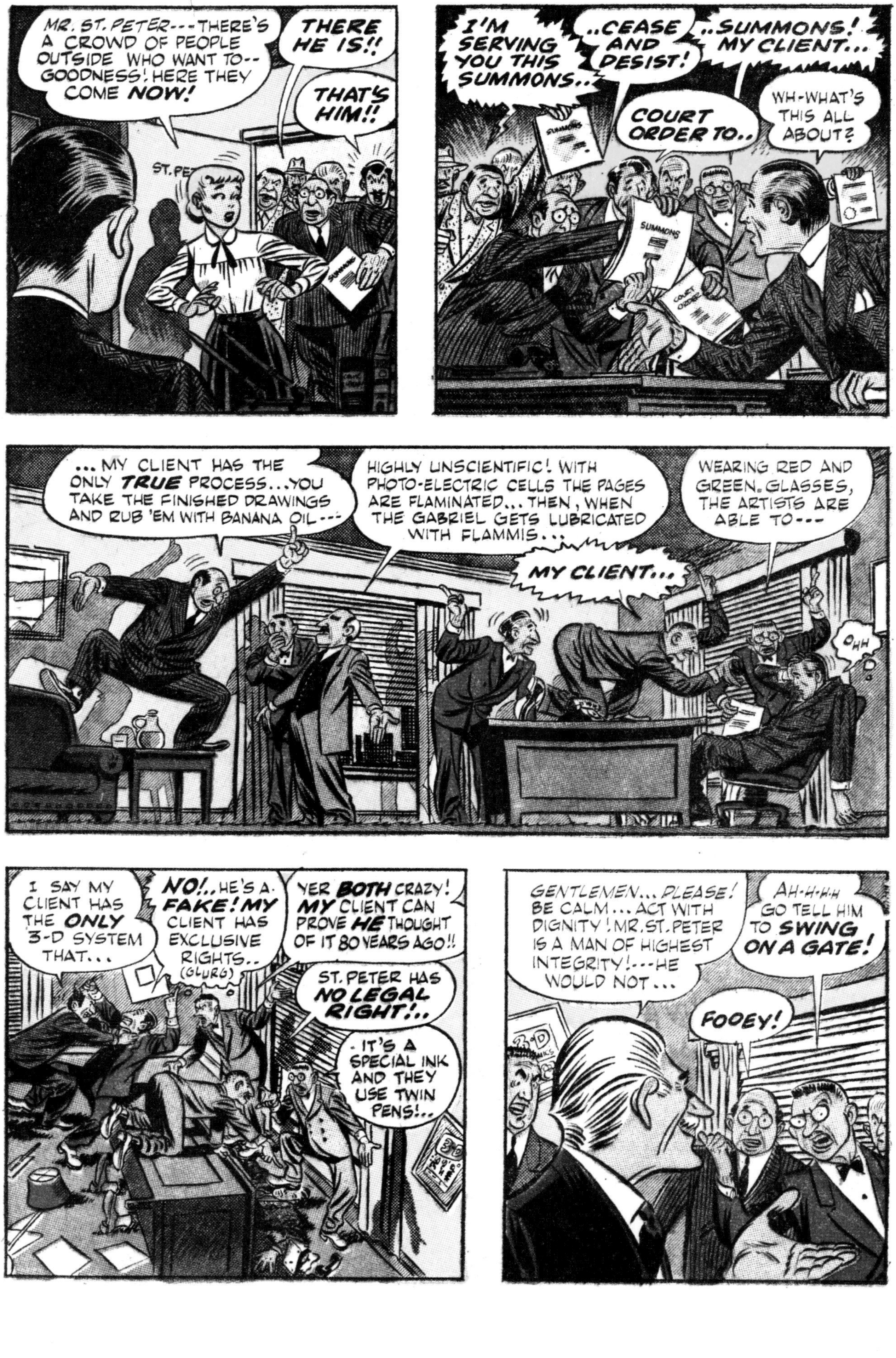

MR. ST. PETER---THERE'S A CROWD OF PEOPLE OUTSIDE WHO WANT TO--GOODNESS! HERE THEY COME NOW!
THERE HE IS!!
THAT'S HIM!!
ST. PE
I'M SERVING YOU THIS SUMMONS..
..CEASE AND DESIST!
..SUMMONS! MY CLIENT...
COURT ORDER TO..
WH-WHAT'S THIS ALL ABOUT?
SUMMONS
...MY CLIENT HAS THE ONLY TRUE PROCESS...YOU TAKE THE FINISHED DRAWINGS AND RUB 'EM WITH BANANA OIL---
HIGHLY UNSCIENTIFIC! WITH PHOTO-ELECTRIC CELLS THE PAGES ARE FLAMINATED... THEN, WHEN THE GABRIEL GETS LUBRICATED WITH FLAMMIS...
WEARING RED AND GREEN GLASSES, THE ARTISTS ARE ABLE TO---
MY CLIENT...
OHH
I SAY MY CLIENT HAS THE ONLY 3-D SYSTEM THAT...
NO!..HE'S A FAKE! MY CLIENT HAS EXCLUSIVE RIGHTS.. (GLURG)
YER BOTH CRAZY! MY CLIENT CAN PROVE HE THOUGHT OF IT 80 YEARS AGO!!
ST. PETER HAS NO LEGAL RIGHT!..
-IT'S A SPECIAL INK AND THEY USE TWIN PENS!..
GENTLEMEN... PLEASE! BE CALM... ACT WITH DIGNITY! MR. ST. PETER IS A MAN OF HIGHEST INTEGRITY!--HE WOULD NOT...
AH-H-H-H GO TELL HIM TO SWING ON A GATE!
FOOEY!

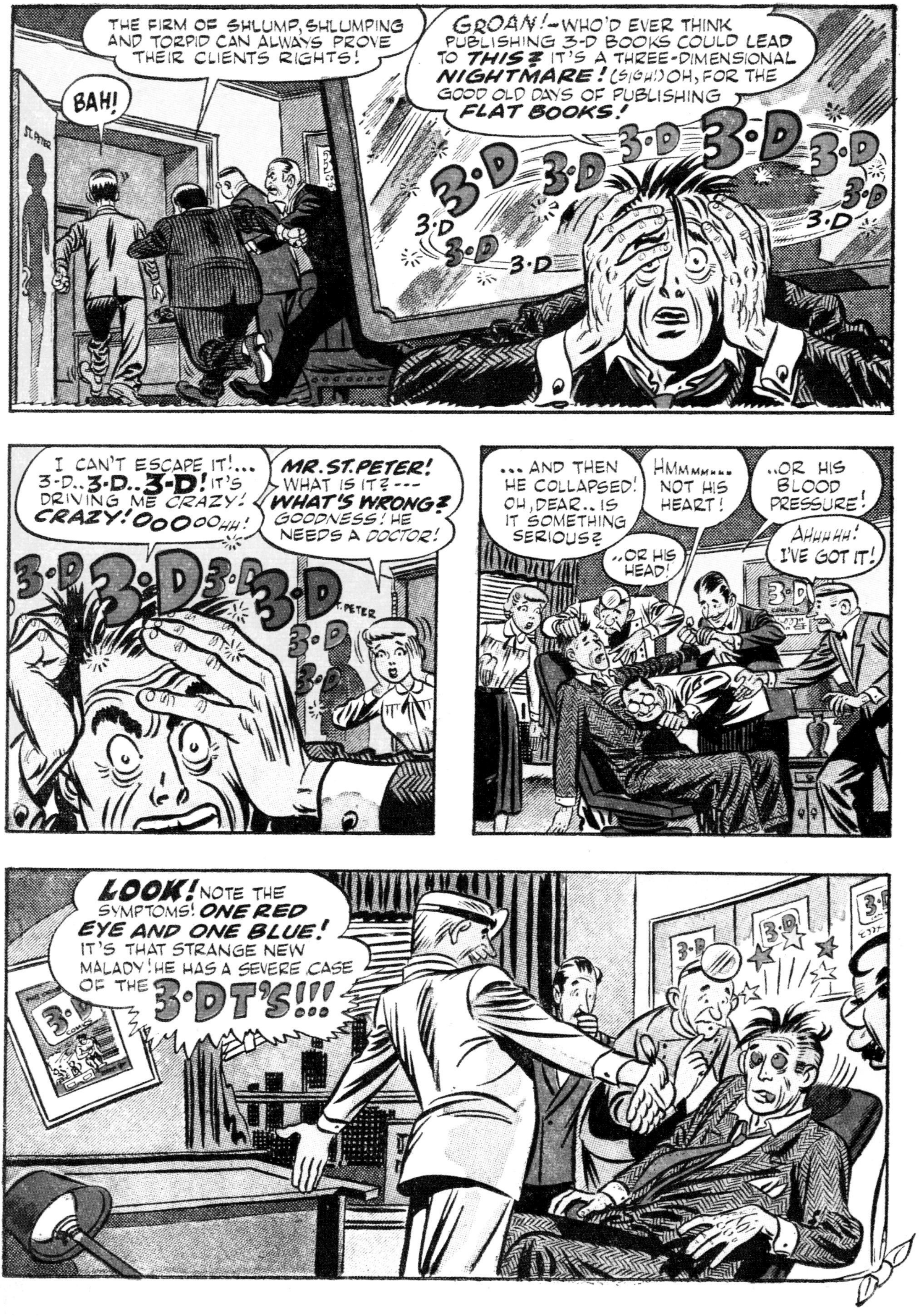
THE FIRM OF SHLUMP, SHLUMPING AND TORPID CAN ALWAYS PROVE THEIR CLIENTS RIGHTS!
BAH!
ST. PETER
GROAN! — WHO'D EVER THINK PUBLISHING 3-D BOOKS COULD LEAD TO THIS? IT'S A THREE-DIMENSIONAL NIGHTMARE! (SIGH!) OH, FOR THE GOOD OLD DAYS OF PUBLISHING FLAT BOOKS!
3-D 3-D 3-D 3-D 3-D 3-D 3-D 3-D 3-D 3-D
I CAN'T ESCAPE IT!... 3-D.. 3-D.. 3-D! IT'S DRIVING ME CRAZY! CRAZY! OOOOOHH!
MR. ST. PETER! WHAT IS IT? --- WHAT'S WRONG? GOODNESS! HE NEEDS A DOCTOR!
3-D 3-D 3-D 3-D 3-D 3-D
... AND THEN HE COLLAPSED! OH, DEAR.. IS IT SOMETHING SERIOUS?
HMMMMM... NOT HIS HEART!
..OR HIS HEAD!
..OR HIS BLOOD PRESSURE!
AHHHHH! I'VE GOT IT!
LOOK! NOTE THE SYMPTOMS! ONE RED EYE AND ONE BLUE! IT'S THAT STRANGE NEW MALADY! HE HAS A SEVERE CASE OF THE 3-DT'S!!!

Did you know that the principle behind 3-D was known in 300 B.C.? Did you know that Leonardo DaVinci, in 1584, made diagrams that helped lead to the development of this great medium?

Yes, the thinking behind 3-D is an old, old story. But today, it is progressing by leaps and bounds.

But how does 3-D work? The principle can be explained very simply. First, understand that it works much the same way as our eyes. Our eyes are separated by a distance of about two and a half inches, and inasmuch as they are in different positions, we see the objects sighted from two different points of view at the same time.

To give you a good example of this, try this simple trick. Hold your finger upwards about a foot away from the bridge of your nose and in line with a window. Stare past the finger and at the window. You will see a double image of the window. However, when you focus your eyes on the window, you should see a double image of the finger. This is the basic idea behind 3-D.

Harvey's "Adventures in 3-D" makes use of a two-color printing process and two-colored viewers. Much the same picture is printed first with red ink and then with a greenish-blue ink. Your left eye, looking through the red viewer that filters out the red lines, will only see the greenish-blue lines on the page. Your right eye, looking through the greenish-blue viewer that filters out the greenish blue lines, will only see the red lines on the page. Then your eyes bring these two images together, and you see true depth and real life . . . as the picture was meant to be! This is technically called an ANA-GLYPH.

Some 3-D movies follow a similar process. The photographers use a camera with two lenses, each lens taking the picture from a different position—just like our eyes. When the picture is projected on a screen, it is blurred—much like our 3-D pages—but the glasses you wear bring the images together as one, and give you the picture in three dimensions.

Now, understanding the basic principles of 3-D and knowing that men have been aware of it for centuries, one wonders why advancement had previously been so slow. Well, it had been popular in the 1850's, but was forgotten when moving pictures and "snapshots" were developed in the early 1900's.

But today, with the many successful movies, the use of 3-D in science and industry, the entrance of 3-D into the advertising field, and now with the new Harvey 3-D comic technique, we can safely say . . . 3-D is here to stay!

Adventures in 3-D #1, November 1953. I concur with the closing sentiments: 3-D is here to stay!

INDEX

Page numbers in italic refer to illustrations.

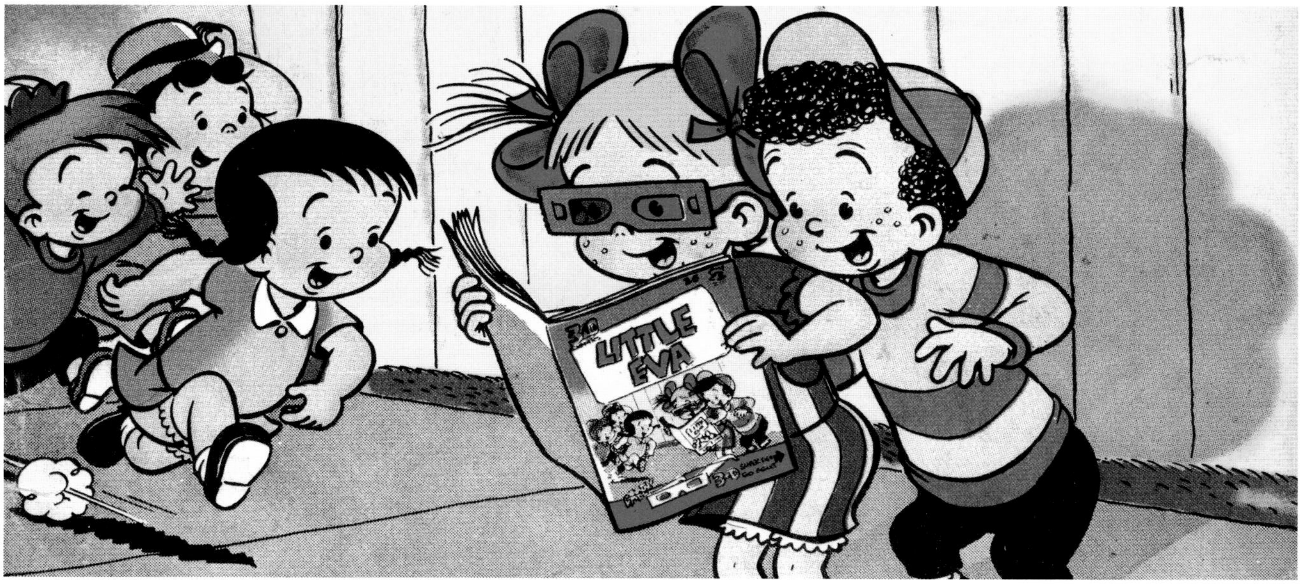

LITTLE EVA

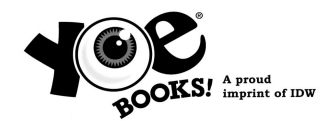

YOE® BOOKS! A proud imprint of IDW

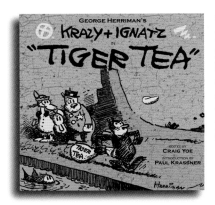

GEORGE HERRIMAN'S
KRAZY + IGNATZ
IN
"TIGER TEA"
TIGER TEA
EDITED BY
CRAIG YOE
INTRODUCTION BY
PAUL KRASSNER

George Herriman's Krazy & Ignatz in "Tiger Tea"

Introduction by **Paul Krassner**

"A highly enjoyable collection!"
—The NY Examiner

ISBN
978-1-60010-645-3

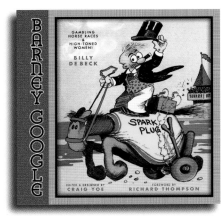

BARNEY GOOGLE
GAMBLING HORSE RACES & HIGH-TONED WOMEN!
BILLY DE BECK
SPARK PLUG
EDITED & DESIGNED BY
CRAIG YOE
FOREWORD BY
RICHARD THOMPSON

Barney Google: Gambling, Horse Races & High-Toned Women

Foreword by **Richard Thompson,** cartoonist of *Cul de Sac*

Fascinating ephemera precedes the rousing first story of Barney Google's race horse, Spark Plug.

ISBN
978-1-60010-670-5

THE CHILLING ARCHIVES OF HORROR
DICK BRIEFER'S
FRANKENSTEIN
CRAIG YOE

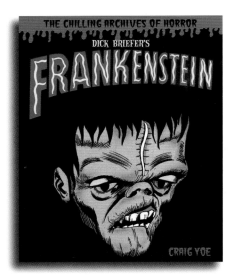

Dick Briefer's Frankenstein

"A definitive collection... Excellent and heavily illustrated introduction. Highly recommended reading and as with all the Yoe collections, a grand entertainment from cover to cover."
—Stephen Bissette
Schulz Library Blog

ISBN
978-1-60010-722-1

THE GOOD GIRL ART LIBRARY
DAN DeCARLO'S
JETTA
NEUTRON HIGH SCHOOL
INTRODUCTION BY
CRAIG YOE
PLUS
37 Master Pin-Up Artists

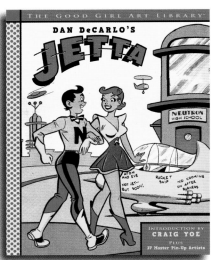

Dan DeCarlo's Jetta

Plus 37 Master Pin-Up Artists

"Beautifully designed hardcover collecting all three issues of Jetta, plus almost 40 pin-ups of the character from a wide variety of artists"
—J. Caleb Mozzocco
Newsarama.com

ISBN
978-1-60010-646-0

THE
ART
OF
Ditko
CRAIG YOE
Introduction by STAN LEE

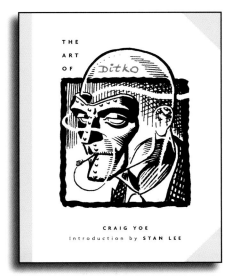

The Art of Ditko

Introduction by **Stan Lee**

"Craig's book revealed to me a genius I had ignored my entire life!"
—Mark Frauenfelder
BoingBoing.net

"The soul of Ditko's art appears most nakedly... A mountain of graphic genius... A fine connoisseur of comic art history, Yoe selects the best of a vintage crop."
—Bob Duggan
BigThink.com

ISBN
978-160010-542-5

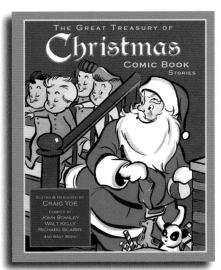

THE GREAT TREASURY OF
Christmas
COMIC BOOK
STORIES
EDITED & DESIGNED BY
CRAIG YOE
COMICS BY
JOHN STANLEY
WALT KELLY
RICHARD SCARRY
AND MANY MORE!

The Great Treasury of Christmas Comic Book Stories

"Beautifully designed, lovingly restored comics in a bright Christmas package. Buy two—one for you and one to give as a gift. It's perfect for anyone—comic book fans, animation buffs, and/or everyone who enjoys the fantasies of the holiday season. Fun!"
—Jerry Beck
CartoonBrew.com

ISBN
978-1-60010-773-3

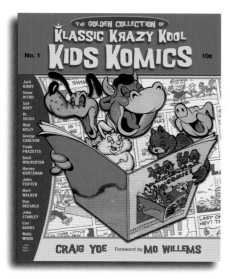

THE GOLDEN COLLECTION OF
KLASSIC KRAZY KOOL
KIDS KOMICS
No. 1
10¢
CRAIG YOE
Foreword by MO WILLEMS

The Golden Collection of Klassic Krazy Kool Kids Komics

Introduction by
Mo Willems

"The most beautifully done comics retrospective book I have seen since forever."
—Mykal Banta
BigBlogComics.com

ISBN
978-1-60010-520-3

FELIX the CAT
THE GREAT COMIC BOOK TAILS
Edited & Designed by
CRAIG YOE
Introduction by
DON ORIOLO

Felix The Cat: The Great Comic Book Tails

Introduction by
Don Oriolo

"A beautiful love letter to the comic book legacy of Otto Messmer/Joe Oriolo's Felix The Cat... An art book that is unto itself a thing of art... Another must-have!"
—Jerry Beck
CartoonBrew.com

ISBN
978-1-60010-705-4

BARKS' BEAR BOOK
CARL BARKS OF DONALD DUCK TAKES ON BARNEY BEAR!
EDITED + DESIGNED BY
CRAIG YOE
COVER + INTRODUCTION BY
JEFF SMITH

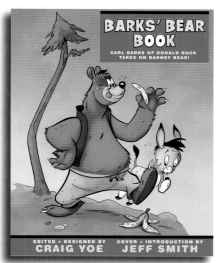

Barks' Bear Book

Cover and introduction by
Jeff Smith

Carl Barks of Donald Duck takes on Barney Bear!

ISBN
978-1-60010-929-4

HEY HUMBUGS! DON'T PANIC! IT'S MADDER, IT'S CRAZIER, IT'S SICKER, IT TRUMPS THEM ALL! YOU'LL CRACK UP WITH THIS LAMPOONING:
The Best of
Archie's
MAD HOUSE
CRAIG YOE

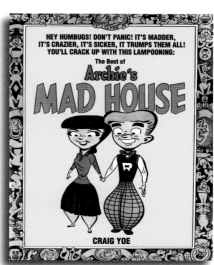

The Best of Archie's Mad House

Hey, humbugs! Don't panic! It's madder, it's crazier, it's sicker, and it trumps them all! You'll crack up with this lampooning!

Art by **Dan DeCarlo, Harry Lucey, Wally Wood,** and more!

ISBN
978-1-60010-790-0

The Complete
MILT GROSS
Comic Books and Life Story
10¢
OOPS! MISSED!!
Craig Yoe
FOLD-INtroduction Al Jaffee

The Complete Milt Gross Comic Books and Life Story

FOLD-INtroduction by
Al Jaffee of *Mad* magazine.

"Craig Yoe's massive new tome reprinting the comic book art of Milt Gross is an absolute must-have by everyone reading this blog. Buy it now!"
—Jerry Beck
CartoonBrew.com

"Lots of awesome Milt Gross art!"
—Heidi MacDonald
ComicsBeat.com

ISBN
978-1-60010-546-3

Popeye
THE GREAT COMIC BOOK TALES BY
BUD SAGENDORF
Edited & Designed by
CRAIG YOE
Introduction by
JERRY BECK

Popeye: The Great Comic Book Tales by Bud Sagendorf

Introduction by
Jerry Beck.

"Absolutely prime Sagendorf Popeye, every one the cream of those great Dell comics! In the same rarefied genius status as Carl barks and John Stanley!"
—Mykal Banta
BigBlogComics.com

ISBN
978-1-60010-747-4

Vice magazine has called Craig Yoe the "Indiana Jones of comics historians." *Publishers Weekly* says he's the "archivist of the ridiculous and sublime" and calls his work "brilliant." *The Onion* calls him "the celebrated designer," *The Library Journal*, "a comics guru." *BoingBoing* hails him "a fine cartoonist and a comic book historian of the first water." Yoe was Creative Director/Vice President/General Manager of Jim Henson's Muppets, and a Creative Director at Nickelodeon and Disney. Craig has won an Eisner Award and the Gold Medal from the Society of Illustrators.
Yoe Books are produced with cartoonist and designer Clizia Gussoni, author of the bestselling title, *The Awesome Book of Sharks.*

▶ BACK ENDPAPERS A 3-Dorama depicting the attack on Pearl Harbor, President Franklin D. Roosevelt, and the proclamation of war. From *True 3-D* #2, February 1954; artist, attributed to Howard Nostrand.

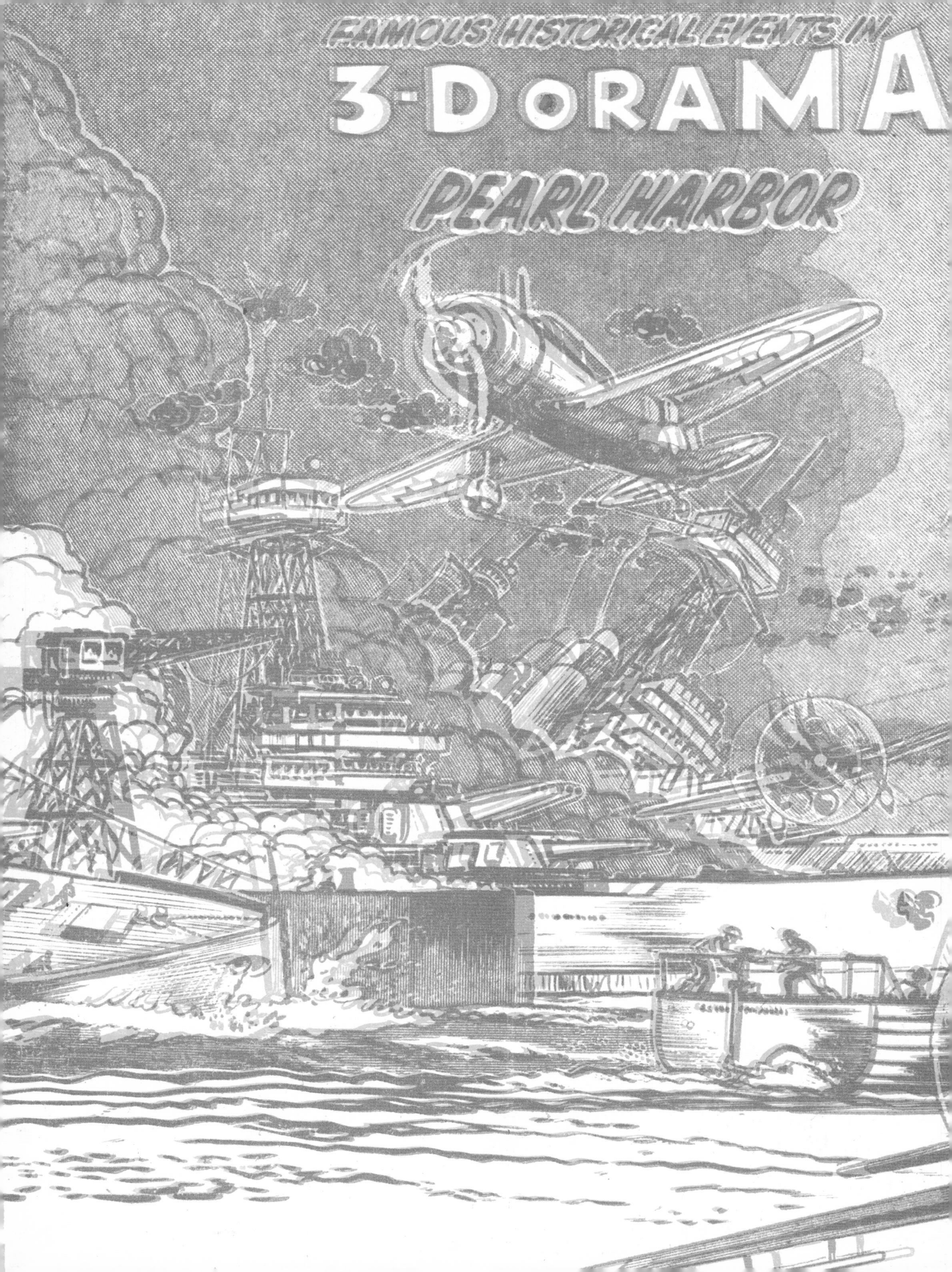
FAMOUS HISTORICAL EVENTS IN
3-D oRAMA
PEARL HARBOR